ZHOU ENLAI

By the same author

A Quarter of Mankind
Asia Awakes
East Meets West: Singapore
The Long March 1935
The Future Role of Singapore
The Neutralisation of Southeast Asia
Mao Tse-tung in the Scales of History (editor)
Mao the People's Emperor
The Great Wall (co-author)
When Tigers Fight: The Sino-Japanese War 1937–1945

ZHOU ENLAI
A Biography

DICK WILSON

Viking

VIKING
Viking Penguin Inc.,
40 West 23rd Street,
New York, New York 10010, U.S.A.

First American Edition

Published in 1984

Originally published in Great Britain under the title
Chou: The Story of Zhou Enlai 1898–1976.

LIBRARY OF CONGRESS CATALOGING IN PUBLICATION DATA
Wilson, Dick, 1928–
Zhou Enlai.
Bibliography: p.
Includes index.
1. Chou, En-lai, 1898–1976.   2. Prime ministers—
China—Biography.   I. Title.
DS778.C593W54   1984   951.05′092′4 [B]   83-47928
ISBN 0-670-22011-6

Printed in the United States of America
Set in Ehrhardt and Electra

To
Ben and Emma

Contents

Illustrations 9

A Note on Names 11

Zhou Family Tree 13

Map: Zhou Enlai's China 14

Preface 15

1 The Much Adopted 1898–1913 19

2 Slinging Satchels in Tianjin 1913–17 28

3 Treading the Sea 1917–19 37

4 In Prison 1919–20 45

5 Commitment in France 1920–24 54

6 Revolutionary Marriages 1924–25 71

7 Capture in Shanghai 1925–27 80

8 The Nanchang Test 1927 88

9 Regaining Russian Confidence 1928–30 99

10 A Magician Trumped 1931–34 107

11 On the Long March 1934–36 120

12 The Tiger Trapped 1936–40 134

13 Metamorphosis of a Pig 1940–43 153

14 The World Is Ours 1943–49 162

15 A Pair of Blue Pyjamas 1949–52 179

16 Geneva and Bandung 1953–55 192

17 The Hundred Flowers 1956–58 206

18 Cleaning Up the Mess 1959–61 219

CONTENTS

19   The Great Safari   1962–65   228
20   Cultural Revolution   1966–67   238
21   Detained by Red Guards   1967–68   258
22   Disciple in the White House   1969–76   270

Epilogue   291
A Summing-up   294
Acknowledgements   303
Glossary of Personal Names   304
Glossary of Placenames   306
A Note on Sources   307
Notes   310
Index   337

Illustrations

Zhou Enlai on leaving Nankai

Members of the Awakening Society, Tianjin, at its founding in 1919

The French branch of the Chinese Communist Youth League, Paris, 1924

Zhou as head of the political department of the Huangpu Military Academy, 1924–26

Zhou Enlai on the Long March, 1935

Zhou returns to Yan'an after negotiating on the Xi'an incident, 1936

Zhou Enlai, Mao Zedong and Zhu De, Yan'an, 1939

Zhou with Chen Yi and Ye Ting, 1939

Zhou and his wife, Deng Yingchao, in Chongqing, 1940

Zhou leads the Chinese Communist delegation in Nanjing to negotiate with the Guomindang, 1946

Zhou Enlai and Mao Zedong take up residence in Zhongnanhai, 1949

Chairman Mao and Premier Zhou at an army athletics competition, 1952

Premier Zhou in his office in Beijing

Zhou enjoying the traditional Dai water-splashing festival, Yunnan, 1961

Zhou, suffering from cancer, in 1973

Grieving Chinese file past Zhou's body, January 1976

Photographs reproduced by kind permission of the Xinhua News Agency

A Note on Names

Chou En-lai is how tens of millions of English-speaking readers came to know the late Premier of China. The suggestion of that slightly absurd French endearment '*mon petit chou*' – 'my little cabbage' – may have helped, however unconsciously, to make the man likeable, and to encourage Anglo-Saxons to be receptive to his good qualities.

But he did not spell his name Chou. Nor, for that matter, did he spell it Tcheou as the French used to, Zhou as the Russians do, or Tschou as the Germans did (though he did for a time, in English-language letters, sign himself as 'Chow').* All these are arbitrary attempts to present in a European script the equivalent sound to a Beijing (or Peking) Chinese pronouncing the characters of his name 周恩來.

The Chinese did not at first concern themselves with the various barbarian ways of romanizing their ideographic characters. But now they have decided which system they will use, and it is not the Wade-Giles system to which the Anglo-Saxon world has grown accustomed, but rather the pinyin system. To avoid confusion, most Western universities, publishers and media have followed suit. So this book uses pinyin and Chou becomes Zhou. (The Chinese custom of putting the family name – Zhou – first and the individual's given name – Enlai – second is also followed here.)

Whatever the spelling the name is actually the same. It should always be pronounced 'Joe'. In losing his gently curving C for that rough jagged Z, the man may appear less sympathetic. If this suggests that behind his conventional image of bland reasonableness there lurks a tough personality, scarred by the wounds of childhood, who played his full part in underground

---

* See, for example, his letter to John Paton Davies Jr in the latter's *Dragon by the Tail* (Robson, London, 1974), p. 386.

11

revolt, civil war and forced social change on the Soviet scale, then that is no bad thing.

For fainthearts who miss their soft Cs, however, exceptions have been made for four names so familiar to English-language readers in their Wade-Giles form and so different in pinyin that pedantry would constitute an imposition: Sun Yat-sen, Chiang Kai-shek and his son Chiang Ching-kuo, and the city of Canton (instead of the less recognizable pinyin Sun Zhongshan, Jiang Jieshi, Jiang Jingguo and Guangzhou). And in any case the glossary on page 304 gives the old-fashioned Wade-Giles equivalents of most of the pinyin names used in the text.

Zhou Family Tree

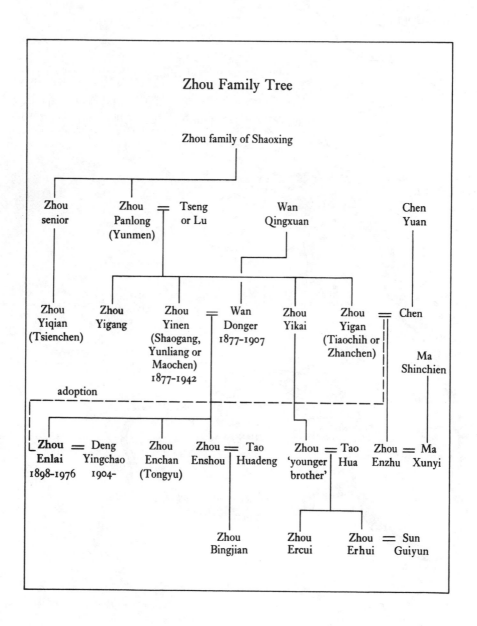

Zhou family of Shaoxing

Zhou senior

Zhou Panlong (Yunmen) = Tseng or Lu

Wan Qingxuan

Chen Yuan

Zhou Yiqian (Tsienchen)

Zhou Yigang

Zhou Yinen (Shaogang, Yunliang or Maochen) 1877-1942 = Wan Donger 1877-1907

Zhou Yikai

Zhou Yigan (Tiaochih or Zhanchen) = Chen

Ma Shinchien

adoption

Zhou Enlai 1898-1976 = Deng Yingchao 1904-

Zhou Enchan (Tongyu)

Zhou Enshou = Tao Huadeng

Zhou 'younger brother' = Tao Hua

Zhou Enzhu = Ma Xunyi

Zhou Bingjian

Zhou Ercui

Zhou Erhui = Sun Guiyun

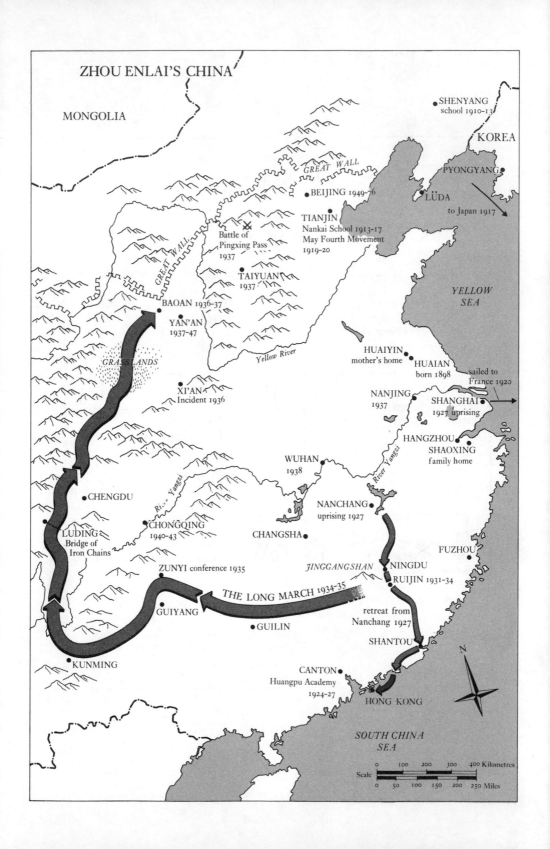

ZHOU ENLAI'S CHINA

MONGOLIA

SHENYANG
school 1910–13

KOREA

GREAT WALL

PYONGYANG

BEIJING 1949–76

LÜDA
to Japan 1917

Battle of
Pingxing Pass
1937

TIANJIN
Nankai School 1913–17
May Fourth Movement
1919–20

GREAT WALL

TAIYUAN
1937

YELLOW
SEA

BAOAN 1936–37

YAN'AN
1937–47

Yellow River

HUAIYIN
mother's home

HUAIAN
born 1898

sailed to
France 1920

GRASSLANDS

XI'AN
Incident 1936

NANJING
1937

SHANGHAI
1927 uprising

HANGZHOU

SHAOXING
family home

WUHAN
1938

CHENGDU

River Yangzi

LUDING
Bridge of
Iron Chains

CHONGQING
1940–43

NANCHANG
uprising 1927

CHANGSHA

FUZHOU

ZUNYI conference 1935

JINGGANGSHAN

NINGDU

RUIJIN 1931–34

THE LONG MARCH 1934–35

GUIYANG

retreat from
Nanchang 1927

GUILIN

SHANTOU

KUNMING

CANTON
Huangpu Academy
1924–27

N

HONG KONG

SOUTH CHINA
SEA

Scale

0   100   200   300   400 Kilometres

0   50   100   150   200 250 Miles

Preface

'Oh my goodness! You have been waiting here! The press conference was changed, you know. We held it in the secretariat building. But you were not informed. I am sorry, very sorry. I am sure that the Prime Minister will make it up to you by giving you an exclusive interview. . . .'

The Nepalese protocol official in his tall white hat and baggy white breeches ushered me towards a huge knot of people who had just arrived at the Rana Palace. Gradually they opened, to reveal in the centre a surprisingly small and frail-looking figure – the Prime Minister of the People's Republic of China, Zhou Enlai.

It was a curious situation. In the original schedule, Zhou, on this 1960 visit to Nepal, should have met the world press at his residence, this old Rana Palace some three miles out of the centre of Kathmandu, capital of the Kingdom of Nepal. The Chinese visitors were only one of my reasons for being in Nepal, and on their last day I had other business to do for my magazine, so I had missed the announcement of a change of venue for the press conference.

At the appointed hour of midnight I had gone alone to the Rana Palace, therefore, for the press conference, to find the place empty and deserted, save for two armed but sleeping Gurkha sentries. Stepping gingerly across them, I could see nothing in the barn-like hall which took up the whole of the ground floor, only a generous scattering of cigar butts and chicken bones on the wall-to-wall carpet. No Chinese visitors, no Nepalese officials.

And now I was face to face with the sixty-two-year-old Chinese Premier, who accepted the suggestion of a compensatory press interview with grace and seeming interest, although it was through the Nepalese fault and not his that I had missed the conference. It was long past midnight, and the Chinese party, which had been on the move for several weeks, was due to fly out at

15

dawn next morning. Everybody was tired, yet the dozens of officials in Zhou's party, including the Foreign Minister, Chen Yi, stood about waiting for this unscheduled meeting to finish before they could go to bed and prepare for their journey. Some of them stared at me with ill-concealed irritation.

But not Zhou. He held my eyes for the best part of forty minutes, during which he exuded courtesy and patience. I felt a little embarrassed, and limited myself to some general questions about how China's relations with the countries of the region had been improved by Zhou's visits, expecting a perfunctory reply. But Zhou proceeded to give extremely detailed answers, separate ones for each country that had been visited. This went on altogether for about half an hour, including the time taken by his interpreter. Actually, as I subsequently found out, what he said was virtually the same as had transpired at the press conference, so my exclusive interview was not of great value.

If only Zhou had been there, I would have accepted his invitation to ask more questions, but with Chen Yi shifting his considerable weight moodily from one leg to the other, and the more junior Chinese looking askance, I decided to call it a day. Zhou was not finished, however. He went on talking as if there were all the time in the world. Had I been to China? he asked me. Did I know that Viscount Montgomery was going to visit China? Would I like to go too?

My heart suddenly raced. I had been trying without success to get into China for a year and a half.

'Welcome you,' said the Premier, suddenly lapsing into schoolboy English and throwing up his hands in an accepting gesture.

The Chinese officials looked at one another as if to say, 'At last!' and I stumped out into the cold Himalayan night air. It had been like a dream.

Zhou was good at making things seem dream-like, but not quite so good at making the dreams come true. I wrote to him many times afterwards, but never heard any more about the invitation. It was some years later, after Montgomery had been and gone, that I made my first visit to China. But that first impression which Zhou made on me remains vivid. He gave his complete and undivided attention to meeting my needs, totally without arrogance or any air of superiority. His behaviour was almost humble, but for the aura of political power which emanated so strongly from him, reflected by the deferential attitudes of his aides.

At that particular time a fair number of Chinese were starving, the Russians were about to withdraw their economic aid, implacable antagonism had developed between the two figures senior to Zhou in the Chinese hierarchy, China felt surrounded by hostile American power and Nehru would not compromise on the Sino-Indian border dispute. Yet for those forty minutes, at the very end of a long working day, itself near the end of a long succession of working days on the wing, away from the comforts of home, Zhou made it seem as if nothing else was on his mind but my questions, irrespective of how often they had been put before by other newsmen.

In a lifetime of reporting, that kind of feeling has occasionally been conveyed to me by such powerful leaders as Kennedy or Nehru, but never with such intensity. The same impression was made by Zhou on almost everyone he met. [He personified the old-world Chinese virtues of gentleness, politeness and humility, yet put them to work for a political ideology that invoked violence and destruction as a necessary part of its programme. And that is what puzzled everyone about this urbane Premier.] He spoke so softly, moved so meekly, and yet some of the things he said and did in order to give his country a swift passage from feudalism to modernity in one lifetime were cruel, militant, unforgiving. The man who breathed such sweet reasonableness at the Geneva Conference of 1954 or the Bandung Conference of 1955, was also the man who ordered the execution of innocent members of a traitor's family, in order to deter others, and who approved the slaughter of millions of landlords and rural gentry in the first wave of the Communist revolution in the 1950s.

Zhou projected himself differently to different civilizations. Continental Europeans were uniformly impressed by his gifts and intelligence. The headline in *Le Monde*, '*Un Révolutionnaire Gentleman*', summed up the superficial impression. Henry Kissinger, who found Zhou 'one of the two or three most impressive men' he had ever met, called him 'urbane, infinitely patient, extraordinarily intelligent, subtle.' Dag Hammarskjöld pronounced Zhou 'the most superior brain I have so far met in the field of foreign politics.' For Etienne Manac'h of the French Foreign Ministry, the Chinese Premier was '*un homme complet*'.

The Anglo-Saxons yielded up their hearts slightly differently, but gave them all the same. Theodore White, like Kissinger, found Zhou one of the three great men whom he had met 'in whose presence I had near total suspension of disbelief.' Zhou, he said, 'could act with an absolute daring, with the delicacy of a cat pouncing on a mouse. . . . Yet he was capable of warm kindness, irrepressible humanity and silken courtesy. . . . He won my affection completely.' But later, White changed his mind as he identified Zhou with the excesses of the Communist administration after 1949. And so there emerged the other view, of Zhou as 'perhaps the best Communist of them all', as 'a much more resilient revolutionary, and a more dangerous long-term enemy to capitalism than the Chairman himself,' in Dennis Bloodworth's words.

How did such a man first acquire his drive to reform and democratize his motherland? That is the first big question about Zhou Enlai. How he came to choose Marxism as the best vehicle for that transformation is the second.

17

Why, for over half a century of leadership in the Chinese Communist Party, he consistently helped others up to the very top while refusing the crown himself is the third question. And why he went on backing his old rival, Mao Zedong, after all the latter's wild and damaging escapades – the Great Leap Forward in 1958, and the Cultural Revolution in 1965 – constitutes the fourth enigma.

Compared with Mao and other Chinese Communist leaders, Zhou was more open, confided in more people, had a wider sense of world history, travelled more and received more visitors. But the real Zhou underneath the smiling bureaucrat and winning diplomat requires much excavating.

As I left the Rana Palace that April night in Kathmandu I glowed with the good feeling that Zhou Enlai had projected towards me. I admired his glamour and his skill. But afterwards I began to wonder about the personality and private feelings behind all his artifice, dexterity and flair. That curiosity has led, twenty years later, to this portrayal of the man and his life's work.

1

The Much Adopted
1898–1913

The elegant upper-class house in Huaian was an unlikely starting place for a man destined to be Secretary-General of the world's largest Communist Party. But the rundown gentry of the Zhou clan, struggling to sustain their mandarin class pretensions in that pleasant market town near China's eastern seaboard, would not have been at all surprised to learn that the boy born to them on 5 March 1898 would go on to become China's most famous Prime Minister. They would have felt thoroughly vindicated.

If you go today to Huaian in Jiangsu province, you are taken along a white-walled alley to that same old house bearing the new legend, 'Premier Zhou Enlai used to live here'. It is not a grand house, only single-storeyed, but the brick walls are thick, the wooden pillars supporting the eaves are ornately carved, and the conventional grey Chinese tiles sweep the eye up to the sky.

Inside you are shown the room where Zhou came into the world, his grandfather's parlour, his parents' room – and, within the courtyard, a little vegetable plot and an antique well. It is old-fashioned, an island of calm in the bustle of a country now in the process of modernization. By provincial standards it suggests a certain good taste.

The town is set on the Grand Canal, that remarkable artefact of earlier emperors linking China's two great rivers, the Yangzi and the Yellow, via the marshes, lakes and waterways which give central Jiangsu the look of a Chinese Holland. This is the setting for Zhou Enlai's home town, made rich by the abundant ricefields of the Yangzi valley.

Entering his date of birth on a university entrance form, Zhou Enlai wrote that it had been in 'the thirteenth year before the Republic' – that republic for which intelligent Chinese yearned and which Zhou did his part to consolidate. Born as the old century was dying, Zhou overlapped in his boyhood the final years of the anachronistic Manchu emperor, last in the celestial series to rule China.

His family elders were cultivated gentlemen overtaken by bad times, and his country advertised to what indignities a proud and civilized land could descend under incompetent government and imperialist pressure from across the seas. The European powers were humiliating China, taking her territory and forcing her to accept their trade on outrageous terms. Effete imperial rulers could do nothing about it.

Zhou's father, Yinen (1877–1942), typified the irresponsible mood of the times. A delightful if ineffectual gentleman, disgruntled by the crumbling mandarin system that had served China for too long, he never won the post of county magistrate to which his education called him. He was only twenty-one when his famous son was born. The child was named Enlai, meaning 'advent of grace', in homage to the father's expected success. But Yinen waited in vain, reaching only a less important rank in a provincial government treasury. When Zhou Enlai was Prime Minister, many decades later, he used to reminisce rather severely about his father, 'a magistrate whose monthly income constituted less than 30 *yuan*' – say US $30 in those days.* Zhou conceded that his father must have been corrupt. 'If it were not corruption, where could he have got the money for his long robes and his house?'

This father was gentle and retiring, overshadowed by more successful brothers. He escaped the pressures of life to enjoy his tiny sinecure as best he could, improving the day with rice wine and a book of odes. In the yellowing photograph on the wall at Huaian he lolls with genial indiscipline in an old-fashioned balloon-sleeved jacket, rough in features but exuding tranquil savoir-faire.

If his father had been 'successful', Zhou might have acquired a thoroughly elite class viewpoint. As it was, living in what he afterwards described as a 'bankrupt mandarin family' – or among, in the phrase of one of his Chinese biographers, 'fallen feudal bureaucrats' – he came to know what poverty meant, and his sense of injustice was heightened. In the Chinese cycle of beasts, Zhou was born in the Year of the Dog, and an astrologer would therefore have marked him as a potential champion of justice – discreet, charismatic, but also emotionally cold, a fault-finder, selfish and stubborn.

Zhou Enlai's mother was Wan Donger (1877–1907), an accomplished girl from a distinguished local family, skilled in the traditional Chinese female arts of music, painting and chess. Her photograph in the family house shows intense, fine good looks and an almost palpable intelligence, which was not developed by education. By mischance, her own father died on the day after

* For the larger part of Zhou's lifetime the Chinese dollar was approximately equal to the American dollar.

she gave birth to Zhou Enlai, and her sorrow may have provoked her to lose interest in the boy.

Zhou was to find comfort instead from his father's side of the family tree, notably from a trio of remarkable uncles. The legendary Zhou Panlong, Zhou's grandfather, had a career of distinguished public office, which had brought him to Huaian sometime in the 1870s, accompanied by his brother. In Huaian, Panlong had married into the local Tseng family and raised his four sons. Later he retired to his native town of Shaoxing, famous for its rice wine, scholarship and libraries, some 300 miles south of Huaian in Zhejiang province. He took the four boys with him, but after a while they returned to Huaian to join the Tsengs, because, according to one story, their mother died, their father married again, and they could not bear to be ruled by a young stepmother. The Tsengs were rich and could look after the four boys adequately.

Following the Chinese convention of taking one's father's original home as one's native place, Zhou Enlai used to claim that, although he had been born in Huaian, 'my home is Shaoxing'. It was said that he and his brothers and cousins used to go back to grandfather Panlong's ancestral home in Shaoxing every year to pay their respects to the ancestral tablets and visit the famous Hundred Year Hall where five generations of Zhous had once lived together.

If Zhou Enlai was indeed so attentive to the Shaoxing tablets, it probably reflected his debt, from the very beginning, to his three uncles – with whom the family usually associated two cousins of the same generation, children of grandfather Panlong's brother, to make five 'uncles' in all. They were a distinguished group. Three of them held the degree of *juren*, the government's secondary literary examination. One became a senior magistrate and landowner, another a businessman, a third a trained police officer, and a fourth secretary to the inspector-general of three provinces.

Zhou's infancy was not the uneventful idyll of the typical upper-class Chinese child. While still a babe in arms of four months, Zhou, the first to be born to the four migrant brothers, was given to his Uncle Yigan, who was mortally ill and about to die childless. The adoption did not mean moving house, since many of the uncles lived together with Zhou's parents in the same compound. This remarkable demonstration of the collective spirit of the large family of Zhous is usually explained by Zhou's natural father's wish to assure his flagging brother that his line would continue in the family tablets through male posterity, so important in the Chinese tradition. Another motive put recently to visitors to Huaian was to cure the uncle's illness. If so, the gesture was unsuccessful.

A Chinese writer has commented how the episode shows that 'Chinese tradition has a way of relieving ineffective parents of their charges'. One cannot help suspecting that the natural father's irresponsibility, together with the natural mother's grief over her own father's death, may have rendered them jointly incapable of looking after the child. And that would mean that from the very earliest age Zhou was made to experience rejection, all the more painful because his natural parents proceeded to produce two later sons whom they retained in their own family. Certainly Zhou's later attitude towards his natural father was consistently bitter and angry.

According to one account, misfortune pursued the infant Zhou with the death of his adoptive father soon after the adoption, leaving him, scarcely a year old, doubly fatherless. He was left to be brought up by the widow, his imperious, highly intelligent and socially aware adoptive mother from the Chen family of Huaian, the most remarkable woman in the entire clan. Zhou was so deeply influenced by this woman that in later life he referred to her simply as 'mother', the same appellation as he used for his natural mother. He thus recognized, to the confusion of biographers, two mothers. To add to the confusion, this adoptive mother gave birth soon after the uncle's death to a baby boy, Zhou Enzhu.

Adoptive mother Chen was little educated, because, it was said, of her fierce temper, which made her impossible to teach. She never learned to read, her skills being limited to the usual feminine ones of running the house, cooking and embroidery. But she asserted her authority with great force, and lectured the children frequently on discipline. When she stood up, nobody else, not even Zhou, risked remaining seated. When she was angry, nobody dared to speak – unless it was Zhou, who might with a soothing smile offer some discreet suggestion or try to calm her down. She showed a certain favouritism to Zhou as he was better behaved and more intelligent than Enzhu, her own child. She had a quick mind and could hold her own in arguments with the local Buddhist priests, for example.

One of her delights was story-telling, especially classical tales of rebellion against authority. At her feet Zhou drank in the same influences, possibly legitimizing his dreams of mutiny against family authority. His colleagues in later life were amazed by the extent of his knowledge of these stories, and the excitement they could still kindle in him. 'I feel grateful for my mother's guidance,' he remarked. 'Without her care I would not have been able to cultivate any interest in academic pursuits.'

One of the remarkable acts of this woman was to hire one of the 'red-haired people', a Western missionary, to teach her two children at home. Zhou thus had an unusually early encounter with the Western personality and eagerly imbibed the English language and 'new learning'. Chen's nonconformism, ignoring criticism from her neighbours and friends, went quite against the mood of the times. The anti-foreign Boxer movement had been founded in the year of Zhou's birth, when European imperialists were at the height of their hunger for more pieces of Chinese territory. To take a

22

Westerner into one's house in those days showed great independence of mind.

Yet another woman who played a formative role in the development of Zhou's character was the family wet nurse, who was very fond of him and used to tell him about the hard life of the peasants in the world beyond the Zhou family compound gate. She retailed old stories about the Taiping rebels of fifty years earlier punishing corrupt officials and distributing money to the poor.

When Zhou was six years old, his natural mother made something of a comeback. She and her brother won a lottery prize of $10,000 between them, enough to enable them to try to re-establish their dilapidated family home at Huaiyin (now called Qingjiang), some ten miles farther up the Grand Canal. A curious menage accompanied her there, which included her husband (Zhou's natural father), Zhou Enlai, his two younger brothers (Enchan and Enshou), who had been kept in the Yinen family, and Zhou's adoptive mother, presumably with his adoptive brother Enzhu. The coming together in this venture of his three surviving 'parents' shows how too much should not be made of the earlier separations. Zhou had remained in the same family compound throughout, although his most intimate relationships were switched from one sub-unit of that community to another.

In Huaiyin Zhou had the run of the large library left by his maternal grandfather. During his three years there he developed a taste for Tang poetry (he later surprised his friends with his sharp memory for classical verse).

That was the brighter side of his life there. But the misfortune was that his natural mother's lottery money was soon spent, her health slipped with her fortune, and this part of China was now devastated by famine and economic depression. Zhou, now nine years old, had to haunt the pawnshop, visit neighbours to beg for loans, and carry medicine back from the chemist's to help his ailing mother. But she was past saving, and died in 1907.

Just as he had 'lost' two fathers before he was even a year old, Zhou Enlai now lost two mothers when he was barely ten. His adoptive mother quickly followed his natural mother to the grave. He had inherited so much from each of them, biologically from the first and culturally from the second, but he was always clear about his own ranking of them. 'My aunt,' he later explained, 'became my real mother when I was a baby. I did not leave her for even one day until I was ten years old – when she and my natural mother both died.'

This was surely the worst moment in Zhou's life, before he was yet out of childhood. He and his diminished kinsmen returned sadly to their original home at Huaian, poorer than ever. Only the faithful old wet nurse remained to look after Zhou, his father and younger brothers. He resumed his errands to the pawnshop, and was put in charge of growing vegetables in the yard to feed everyone.

But the advantage of the Chinese family system is the number of avenues it can open for an aspiring youngster. The other uncles now began to take an interest in Zhou. One of them is said to have talked to the boy during a visit to Huaian and invited him to the north. According to another report, Zhou wrote to two uncles on his own initiative, and this sounds more like the man whose sister-in-law later remembered as one who 'talked and manoeuvred and always had his way'.

At the age of twelve, in the spring of 1910, Zhou left his green-leaved homeland for the dry far north, the part of China on which Japan cast greedy eyes, Manchuria. Of the two uncles who were then working in Shenyang (then called Mukden), the Manchurian capital, Zhou first stayed with the enlightened Yiqian, who worked in a tax office, and delighted in demonstrating to his nephew precisely how the country was falling apart, and what changes were needed to restore authority and efficiency. Zhou began to read the books and pamphlets of the reformers, such as Liang Qichao, whose ideas the imperial court had tried to suppress.

'In my younger days I wore a pigtail, and my head was so full of the old, old stuff that there was no room even for capitalism – which got in there later. And it was a long time before I found Marxism–Leninism.'

For a few months Zhou joined a nearby classical primary school. But his other uncle, Yigang, who was childless, soon came to collect him and enrol him at the much superior Dongguan primary school near the eastern gate of the old city of Shenyang. As a school sponsored by missionaries, this was more progressive than others. Zhou came top of his class in both calligraphy and English during his three years there. One of his essays was designated a model for the entire district: another was published in a book and exhibited.

He dealt with the school bullies by a tactic which he used time and again in his subsequent political career: making friends with the other boys who were picked on, and organizing them to present a joint front against the bullies. Yet a schoolfriend described him as 'shy', especially when asked to read aloud.

Unlike the other boys, he seemed to know exactly what he wanted to study, and why. He read widely at home in history and politics. Once the headmaster asked them all why they were studying, and got the usual answers – 'to get rich' or 'to get a good job'. Only Zhou, it was said, replied: 'So that China can rise up.'

The teenage and adolescent Zhou now left the world of women and began his lifelong encounter with the world of ideas, surrounded by quite new elder male figures – his formerly distant uncles at home and his new teachers at school. Gao Erwu, the history and geography master, introduced him to a radical new journal, full of exciting political notions and expressions of heady nationalism. Zhou came to learn about Darwin, Mill, Rousseau and the concept of human rights under constitutional guarantee. Through the writing of Kang Youwei he pursued the utopian visions of free love, common property and idealistic communism that were finding enthusiasts among the Chinese of his generation, including another thoughtful teenager in Hunan province called Mao Zedong.

The targets of the young reformers, including Zhou, were the government's unaccountability to popular wishes, the arbitrary way in which China was being administered, the refusal of those in power to consider even basic social and political reforms of the kind which had been taken for granted in Europe for centuries, the depressed status of women, the painful and degrading custom of female footbinding* and the very tight restriction on intellectual activity and education.

Zhou's mathematics teacher helped to point him in a revolutionary direction by showing him the famous *New People's Journal* in which Liang Qichao was writing with eloquent passion about contemporary injustices. These two schoolteachers showed Zhou Enlai where to channel his emotional energy and indignation. They talked of the martyrdoms of earlier Chinese reformers in a manner which made Zhou and his schoolmates weep with anger.

An opportunity to put some of these ideas into practice came in Zhou's first year at the Dongguan School. In 1911 revolutionaries finally toppled the Manchu dynasty and replaced it with China's first republic. When the revolutionary waves washed up to the gates of Shenyang, the history teacher Gao cut off his queue, or pigtail, flouting the ridiculous old imperial regulation that every man must wear one. Zhou also cut his little queue and joined those Chinese who liberated themselves from this alien Manchu custom. He was soon disillusioned, however, by the way in which the revolutionaries split into cliques and factions, each pursuing their own interest.

The only political group which showed any promise was that, including Sun Yat-sen,which in 1912 founded the Guomindang, or Nationalist Party, on a platform of making the republic parliamentary. Zhou was later to spend some of his politically formative years within its ranks.

Coming from country where fish and rice could almost always be seen on either hand, and where the landscape was a milky green all the year round, Zhou found the north of China bleak and strange. The other schoolchildren were taller and better built: they called him 'Little Southerner', which can

---

* Women's feet were thought prettier for being small, and fashion was carried to the length of deforming them in infancy so that women could barely walk. 'My mother,' Zhou later confirmed, 'had her feet bound.'

also mean 'Little Fierce One'. They ate *gaoliang* (a kind of millet) and wheat instead of the husked rice which he was used to. 'I came to Shenyang in 1910,' he later reminisced, 'and lived there three years. When I came I wore a pigtail. That my health is as good as it is now is thanks to Shenyang's husked *gaoliang* and to the strong wind that presses on the yellow earth.'

'There were advantages to being in Manchuria,' Zhou recollected. 'When I was at school, winter or summer, we had to do physical exercises outdoors, tempering a weak body to become a strong one. Another benefit was that we ate *gaoliang*, and this changed my living habits. My bones grew bigger and I tempered my stomach, so that later my body was able to survive the war years and the great work load.'

One admirer of Zhou's personality attributes it to a 'poised blend of that flexibility unique to the southerners in China with the intrepidity of the north.' Perhaps he did in a way get the best of both these Chinese worlds, emerging the better able to understand – and dare to command – that vast and varied country.

In 1911 a friend took him to see the site of one of the battles of the Japan–Russia war which had been fought only six years earlier. His friend's grandfather talked indignantly of the fighting between two foreign powers on Chinese soil, of the Chinese who were killed and made to suffer from the intrusion. Zhou, it is said, vowed secretly on the spot to revenge this calamity. At the age of thirteen he was already a patriot.

He graduated from his Shenyang school in 1913, at the age of fifteen, amid a flurry of flowery farewells. To one friend Zhou penned the stirring words: 'Keep this in mind everywhere: when China soars over the world I would like us to meet again.' This particular schoolboy was lucky enough to survive the ensuing forty years and he took the tattered note to Beijing to show to Prime Minister Zhou as proof of his perspicacity. As a middle-aged office-holder, Zhou re-read his juvenile if high-minded note. Probably he did not feel entirely comfortable with the reminder of his chauvinistic brashness of 1913, and it is recorded that he quickly hid the note where no one was ever able to find it.

In the 1960s, in a rare public reference to his family, Premier Zhou Enlai explained why he had not gone back to visit his home town for half a century. Although Zhou had 'donated my family house to the government', his mother had once inconveniently 'pointed out a particular place where I was supposed to have been born. As a matter of fact, she did not really know.' (He meant, presumably, his adoptive mother.) 'The Jiangsu Provincial Committee insisted on keeping one room for memorial purposes. . . . What advantage can possibly be served by introducing such a feudalistic idea? Isn't it a bad thing? There are also involved some ancestral graves, which are utterly unreasonable matters.' As a Communist leader, Zhou wanted to fade inconspicuously from the Huaian scene, but there came to be vested interests in the memory of the local hero.

His childhood was one of unusual mobility – physical movement among different towns in China's soft fecund centre and icy north, as well as emotional transfer, from his first parents while still a baby to join adoptive parents, then caught up again at six by his first parents, then grieving as a ten-year-old at the funerals of both his mothers, but bouncing resiliently into the households of uncles more than 500 miles away. The way in which he spoke of his family as bankrupt and spendthrift, and his ungenerous behaviour in middle age to his elderly father, suggest a bitterness that could never have lain far below the surface. With his natural father irresponsibly uncaring, his adoptive father dying before he knew him and his successive uncles only partial substitutes, Zhou never found a satisfactory father figure, a model of adult male behaviour to emulate.

Zhou was to make these experiences a training ground for revolution. His parents' generation lived in perpetual regret for the vanishing past, for ever uncertain about the approaching future. How could they prepare their children for a quicksilver world which they no longer comprehended? The anger which Zhou carried over from his childhood was bottled up to fuel an adult obsession with reforming society, if necessary by force.

2
Slinging Satchels in Tianjin
1913–17

At the age of fifteen Zhou asserted himself against his leaderless family by beginning to take charge of his own education. In the absence of any parents, and with his uncles divided and scattered, he was able from Shenyang to insist on his own choice of secondary school in 1913. His first preference was the Qinghua School in Beijing (predecessor of the present university there, set up with American support to train Chinese students for entry to colleges in the United States). It is worth imagining what Zhou's – and China's – history might have been, had he gone to Harvard or Berkeley instead of to Europe: the People's Republic might never have been formed. But Zhou failed the English oral examination. This was not to his discredit, because the school imposed a geographical criterion in order to get an equitable spread of candidates, and the competition from the Yangzi delta area of motivated bourgeois was doubly intense. It is said that Zhou's family was not disappointed at the result, but he himself felt it keenly. He knew that his ambitions would not be served by a conventional school.

Zhou's second choice was the Nankai School in Tianjin. This was also American-endorsed, with a reputation for nonconformism which aroused his uncles' and father's alarm. But having passed the entrance examination, Zhou enrolled in defiance of his elders.

Tianjin, an old industrial city and commercial port, was full of object lessons for China's future integrity, including a large foreign population in districts beyond Chinese jurisdiction, called 'concessions', as well as a cruel warlord regime. Nankai was to prove an appropriate forcing ground for Zhou's instincts and ideas. His experience of decaying feudal life with his family had conditioned him for radicalism. Those feelings were now given organization.

At the end of the summer of 1913, Zhou travelled to Tianjin to stay in the house of his fourth aunt (Chinese families like Zhou's usually had a

28

representative in every place of importance) and enrol at the Nankai School. The man who had taught him literature in his younger days celebrated the event with five poems 'dedicated to Zhou Enlai on his return to the south'.

Nankai was liberal, even democratic in its treatment of students and their ideas, and yet academic standards were excellent and the examinations tough. The principal believed in encouraging students to develop themselves according to their own lights. He sympathized with Zhou's desire to be independent. Until now Zhou had relied on his uncle in Shenyang for financial support, but the latter's income had dried up, and the school fees were high. In Tianjin Zhou had to work in his spare time, copying and cutting out stencils for the school, in order to earn some money.

One fellow-student recalled how Zhou had only one blue cotton jacket which he washed every Sunday, leaving it to dry overnight and wearing it to school again the following week.

According to the results of his entrance examination, Zhou was entitled to enter Class V. But because of his good background and the impression he made, the school allowed him to go straight into Class IV. When he first walked in, the only free seat was next to a very tall student called Wu Dager, with whom he had to share a desk. The students of Nankai, like those in other Chinese schools, used to form small groups according to the district from which they came. Wu, a champion wrestler, was the leader of the Manchurian group, bigger and noisier than the others. This is how he told the story afterwards:

When the class had finished, Zhou introduced himself to his neighbour.

'Hey, Wu, where did you find such a nice-looking boy?' said one of the other Manchurians.

'And pretty fancy socks, too,' another added.

Zhou was indeed wearing red and blue socks, which the Manchurians evidently found amusing, if not effeminate, especially on such a short, fair-skinned, fine-featured boy who blushed. Wu showed his new neighbour round. For the next few days the Manchurians teased Zhou about his colourful socks, as well as his neat shirt. But then they made the mistake of teasing him when he was on his way to class with Wu at his side, and his new protector turned to rebuke them – after which there were no more such jokes. But Zhou was still bullied in the dormitories. 'They taunted his daintiness,' a contemporary remembers.

Zhou was to form a strong friendship with Wu, and together they recruited a gang of six blood brothers. Another companion was one of the best students at the school, Ma Jun, a Moslem who was later to work closely with Zhou as an early Communist Party member in Tianjin.

The central figure in Zhou's progress through Nankai School was not, however, any of the students but the principal, Dr Zhang Boling. This outstanding modern educator took an interest in Zhou almost from the beginning. He recognized the boy's talent after seeing him repeatedly finish in under one hour what was meant to be a two-hour composition. A mutual affection and respect grew between them which ignored the lines of politics, since Zhang – a Christian – never became a Communist. After a childhood littered with unsatisfactory father figures, Zhou seized upon this headmaster as a steady source of authority and guidance, so much so that on first leaving school he named schoolmastering as his chosen career.

In his first year at Nankai School, Zhou wrote an essay urging students to accept responsibility for China's future by working as hard as possible for it – a blend of puritanical and patriotic fervour that was to remain his hallmark. He joined the Chinese Language Society and took part in debates with other schools. To achieve all his successes, he used to work late into the night after the other students had gone to sleep.

All this eased his financial problems, because one of his teachers recommended that in view of his inadequate home finances and his excellent work at school, he be excused from paying fees; in his second year, he became the only non-paying student in the entire school. The tuition fee at that time was $36 a year, with boarding at $24 and another $4 or $5 a month for food. Zhou's life style was therefore austere. 'During my last two years at Nankai Middle School I received no help from my family. I lived on a scholarship which I won as best student in my class.'

One of Zhang Boling's novel enthusiasms as headmaster was drama, and he soon had Zhou involved in the school's stage productions. What was unusual was that the plays, often improvised by the schoolboy actors, were intended not just to entertain but to educate. They were designed to make audiences see the point of democracy, of scientific thought, of liberating women from their old status and shattering superstition.

Among the feudal customs which they were trying to – but could not yet – break was one dictating that women should not appear together with men on the stage. As in Shakespeare's England, boys had to volunteer for the female roles. With his good looks, his shrill voice and his immense charm and self-possession, Zhou was an obvious candidate for these parts. And having volunteered once, it became a habit: he always took the women's lead, playing Nora in *A Doll's House*, as well as more homespun parts in *A Dollar Coin*, *A Moment's Mistake* and *The New Village Head*.

Zhou won high praise for his acting, and boasted that when *A Dollar Coin* was 'transferred' from Nankai to Beijing in 1915, it caused quite a sensation. He even got fan mail for his female roles. He was so handsome that he could have become a cinema idol, had his acting skills and interest tempted him in that direction.

His own family apparently thought it degrading for their boy to stoop to female impersonation, perhaps because they looked down upon the acting profession. Actors were, after all, disqualified from taking the examinations for the civil service – the gateway to social distinction.

Among his friends, one at least felt that Zhou was 'effeminate', even perverted. 'He had too many women's airs about him. He liked to dress up and go on stage. That kind of person makes me feel sick. . . .'

An American scholar has indeed speculated that unresolved oedipal conflicts in Zhou's childhood may have been responsible for the 'strong implication of latent homosexuality' in his stage appearances. But there seems no need to read anything more into his success with female roles than his innate enjoyment of play-acting, his never-failing adaptability and his stunning charm.

He used these stage techniques to enormous effect in later life as a public speaker. 'His art of presenting arguments is beautiful,' a colleague observed, 'including the calculated effects of his stammering and incoherence at times – and he convinces everyone. He is the greatest actor I have ever seen. He'd laugh one moment and cry the next, and make all his audience laugh and cry with him. But it's all acting!'

Zhou went to see his old school put on a play with mixed actors some thirty years later and whispered to his old headmaster, Dr Zhang: 'Teacher, the times have really changed. Now boy and girl students can freely join the same cast in a play. I remember how we had to stage them without girls at Nankai.'

To which the teacher responded by looking his former pupil up and down and pronouncing with a grin: 'You know, you could still put on make-up and get up there to do it. I bet you'd be better than that girl on the stage now.'

When Zhou became Premier of China he was able to indulge his love of dressing up in another legitimate way, by putting on local costume when visiting national minorities or neighbouring countries, and there are several pictures of him wearing the sarong or lunghi. There is also a snap of him trying on a resplendent Pakistani headdress, with a mischievous look and eloquent gesture that could have won him many a movie part.

At the beginning of 1914, Zhou, with two friends, founded a new society for extracurricular studies called the Respect Work and Enjoy Company Society. The idea was to make up for deficiencies in the curriculum by exchanging books and organizing lectures and seminars, sociably encouraging people to make friends – something about which Zhou, himself, was still surprisingly shy. Under the aegis of this society Zhou helped students weaker or more shy than himself, and thus bolstered his own social confidence.

The society put out a six-monthly journal called *Respect Work*, of which six issues were eventually published. Zhou wrote prolifically in them under the bylines 'Enlai', 'Xiang Yu' (his familiar name from childhood), and 'Fei-fei' (meaning to fly). The later issues of the magazine, which Zhou edited, carried a special column under the heading 'Fei-fei's Flowing Ink', in which he advanced progressive ideas for attacking the ideology of Confucius and Mencius, the two spiritual pillars of China's corrupt feudal society. And here, in 1914, he began his modest career as a published poet.

NOTES ON A SPRING DAY

At the lookout on the edge of town
Stifling fumes reek and swirl.
Deer are hunted in our heartland;
Another Polang's close at heel.

Cherry blossoms flood the path with pink,
Green willows shade the bank.
Again the twittering of swallows:
Another year of parting and of longing.

The classical allusions are so thick that only a literary Chinese would understand these two verses. A chase of deer always evokes war for dynastic or personal supremacy, and Polang is the place where a patriot of eighteen centuries ago tried to assassinate an alien emperor. Zhou's poem was a metaphorical shaking of the fist against feudal warlord governments and the dictatorship of Yuan Shikai, the ambitious general who had taken charge of the republican revolution and now ruled as President in Beijing.

During all this intellectual effort and desk work, Zhou did not neglect his body. He used to go running early every morning, and after classes would do some kind of sport. It is recorded that he once came third in the high jump, was captain of his class basketball team and represented the class at volleyball – but never qualified for the five-mile run.

He continued to win essay competitions, including, in his third year, one for the whole school in which he competed with his seniors, coming top out of 800 pupils. What impressed the teachers was that he always wrote his final text at the first effort, never bothering with preliminary drafts.

Meanwhile he was reading outside the classroom more and more revolutionary tracts and radical opinion. He enjoyed a radical Shanghai newspaper and the rather democratic *Da Gong Bao* of Tianjin. He was already familiar with the works of Montesquieu and was reading several English authors.

All this was in the evenings and at weekends, and since there were no lending libraries in those days he had to buy the books he needed with money saved on food and clothes. He once saw a copy of Sima Qian's *History* in a bookshop, and promptly bought it with his next meal money. On returning to the student hostel, he could not put it down, and described some of the stories in it to other students, getting them interested too.

Another account shows him reading much Chinese history, as well as Adam Smith. He patronized the Beijing periodical *New Youth* from its first issue in 1915. He began to write essays on the new learning, democracy and science for student newspapers, and demanded educational reform.

He and his friends were constantly talking about the major events in China, sniffing the scent of revolution. Zhou used to make passionate speeches on these occasions. When President Yuan Shikai had to accept the nakedly aggressive Twenty-One Demands advanced by a militarily stronger Japan in 1915, Zhou made a speech in the local park forcefully protesting against China's national humiliation. Again, when Yuan proclaimed himself emperor the following year, he won an angry diatribe from Zhou.

As the only serious modern opponent of the old-fashioned forces still rampant in China, Dr Sun Yat-sen (Sun Zhongshan) provided a focus for the younger generation's anger against the regime. And Zhou, like thousands of others, fell under the influence of Dr Sun's Guomindang or Nationalist Party.

To master the art of speech-making, Zhou practised in the society he had formed and was later made head of the Nankai School debating team which competed successfully against other Tianjin schools.

In May 1916 Zhou again represented his class in an essay competition, writing a blistering attack on the reactionary warlord government, taking examples from Chinese and foreign history and arguing with force and vigour from a materialist standpoint, ending with the phrase: 'You can fool some of the people some of the time, but not all of the people all of the time.' His essay won the prize and the judges wrote on his certificate: 'Able to digest what he reads and studies, understand it and grasp its essence.'

During that year, overcoming his earlier antipathy to natural sciences, Zhou won the best marks in chemistry, and was ranked among the highest in algebra and mathematics. His writing of Chinese characters was judged 'again the most worthy'.

Now came a poem showing a rare personal warmth over parting from a very good friend, Zhang Pengxian, who had been in Zhou's class and was one of the co-founders of the Respect Work and Enjoy Company Society. When Zhang left Nankai School in 1916 to travel to Japan, by way of his home in the far north, Zhou penned these verses of regret:

SAYING GOODBYE TO BROTHER PENGXIAN

I
Our chance encounter brought to light
A predetermined affinity –
No accident that in Tianjin
We two slung satchels together.

33

Your bold eloquence stunned us
Like Wang Meng's lice-catching.*
Now over crabs and wine we chew
Nostalgic memories of lost days.

Constant in trials and trouble
We'll fight to the end for our ideals.
We, the first to struggle for our cause,
Dare not shirk our duty.

But promise me that one day,
When we've done, we'll retire together
To the country. I'll buy an acre
Next to yours to be your neighbour.

II

Now songs of parting drift from the south beach:
The east wind nudges travellers abroad.
Before you know it, you'll be miles away.
It all seems like a dream, consuming souls.

In the sky, stars and clouds part noisily each second:
Here on earth we cannot rule out human partings.
What endures is the pleasure of the past
Recalled in classic poets' images.

III

Of all our band of volunteers in the race,
You are the paragon, first to start.
I am too clumsy even to get off the blocks,
But your feet surely find the faster track.

While flocks of crows roost under foliage,
The single stork must scour the sky alone.
All the same, a deep sadness shakes
The breasts of friends who have to part as we.

Revolutionary ideology here takes second place to personal friendship. True, the cause for which they both fight is mentioned, and so are their responsibilities. But how human is Zhou's plea that, duty done, the two should find themselves some rural backwater to share.

Zhou also seems to recognize his own failings, by admiring his friend's alacrity in contrast to his own clumsiness. We infer that Zhou sees himself as among the 'broods of crows' which roost under the leaves while the

* Wang Meng, a famous poor scholar in Chinese history, used to discourse with high officials on state affairs while uninhibitedly catching the lice on his coat.

envied 'lone stork' goes scouring the skies. It is all too likely that, in spite of the superficial successes in examinations and competitions, and the praise he won from his teachers, Zhou at eighteen still felt ineffectual in the adult world, a thinker rather than a man of action, lacking the courage to strike out and catch the imagination of others.

In September 1916 Yuan Shikai died and the warlords conferred to divide China among themselves. One of Zhou's favourite teachers at Nankai wrote a poem of lament about the life of the nation being cut short by the hands of a few. Zhou replied with a short political comment of his own.

> The whirlwind pounds
> Our heartsick land.
> The nation sinks
> And no one minds.
> Compounding heartbreak,
> Autumn is back:
> Its horrid insect chorus
> Blasts our ears.

In the 1917 report on graduating students, Zhou was cited as top of the whole school in the literature and arts examination, excelling even in science, good at mathematics and often forming his own ideas outside of classes. Even his calligraphy gained a mention. He graduated on 26 June 1917, with an average mark of 89.72 per cent.

Zhou's four years at Nankai School had been happy, exciting and purposeful. But the government went from bad to worse after the demise of the Manchu dynasty, chaos spread over China and foreign threats abounded. Zhou took every opportunity to extend his understanding of the causes of these events, utilizing where necessary the new and unfamiliar methodology of Western theorists. His knack for hanging a political or social commentary on some local or immediate event was first developed at Nankai. He discoursed to his fellow students and others on the need for China to industrialize, unify, win back the alienated patriotism of its populace and modernize social relationships even to the point of allowing free marriage, without the permission of parents.

Despite his brilliant record at school and his high marks on graduation, Zhou was not himself a scholar in the true Chinese sense. Edgar Snow was to describe him later as 'scholar turned insurrectionist', but many compatriots called him a semi-intellectual. Despite his love of argument, his attitude to ideas was utilitarian, seeing them as engines of action for social amelioration. His four years at Nankai constituted his last sustained exposure to academic discipline and he exploited them to the full, trouncing others who were later to become the scholars. But he himself was an implementer rather than an originator of ideas. Nankai helped him to define what actions he should take, and for that reason, and because of the many friendships which he formed and which lasted for years afterwards, Zhou himself always looked back on the Nankai School with the kind of nostalgia he exhibited in his poem to 'Brother Pengxian' leaving for Japan.

More than thirty years later, Zhou came back to address the Nankai staff and students. As befitted the prime minister of a new Communist government speaking to a middle-class institution, his remarks about 'my alma mater' were grudging: 'To be sure, what we received was a capitalist education. But I acquired some knowledge and practised a capability for organization.' On another occasion Premier Zhou stated his debt a little more graciously. 'I still thank Nankai School for that enlightening basic education that enabled me to pursue knowledge further.' The mature Zhou could hardly be fulsome about Nankai with its bourgeois and American connections. Nevertheless he advertised in the 1920s and 1930s his great loyalty to many of his fellow-students and teachers. Three years after graduating, he met other Nankai alumni in France and promised to occupy his retirement with writing their biographies. At many difficult moments in the Communist Revolution, even when the Chinese comrades were forced to go underground, Zhou never failed to telephone the principal whom he so respected, Zhang Boling, whenever he was in the same city. Similarly, he had a classmate who became stationmaster in a railway town to the northeast whom he used to telephone, despite the dangers of discovery, whenever he was in transit.

The ideological gulf between Zhou and Dr Zhang widened over the years, yet Zhou continued to adore this teacher to whom he owed so much. After 1949, in the new People's Republic, he offered Zhang a high post in the national education bureaucracy. But Zhang's integrity was no less than his pupil's. He refused. It must have been one of the most painful crosses for Zhou to bear in his later years that his revered old principal fell foul of minor Communist officials and eventually died from their harassment.

What is obscure about his teenage years at Nankai is Zhou's emotional life. A story circulated that he fell in love with a beautiful classmate from Manchuria and became secretly betrothed to her, but the tale remains unconfirmed. It is hard to believe that a young man of Zhou's energy, emotion and good looks could have avoided friendships with women in spite of the time consumed by his studies, sport and political activities. We must assume that Zhou was, as his classmates insist, too shy for romantic attachments in his secondary schooldays, or else that he was most discreet. He was, above all, a man of discretion. His unstable childhood may well have made him not only weak in relating to others – but also, once related, good at dissembling.

3

Treading the Sea
1917–19

Those teenage blood brothers to whom Zhou had sworn eternal fidelity during his years at Nankai School were now to be his saviours. Thwarted in his earlier longing to enter an American campus, Zhou at nineteen now aimed at a university in the halfway house, Japan – the only part of the region of traditional Chinese influence which had gone all out for Western-style industrialization and modernization. Repressed and frustrated at home, young Chinese patronized Japan as a hotbed of change and reform, where up-to-date natural and social sciences were taught.

As usual, Zhou had no means, but his old friend Wu, the tall Manchurian who had taken him under his wing at school, came to the rescue. Now married and studying on a Chinese government scholarship in Japan, the warmly affectionate Wu persuaded three other blood brothers also studying in Japan, and one other student, to join him in pledging $10 each a month – about a fifth of their respective scholarship incomes – for Zhou's keep.

Zhou wrote a poem of resolution for his departure.

> Song of the Grand River* sung,
> I head resolute for the East.
> In vain I've searched all schools
> For clues to a better world.
> By ten years' driving study
> I'll make my breakthrough,
> Or else die a hero
> Who dared to tread the sea.†

* A Sung-dynasty poet had written that 'the Grand River flows east, sweeping away heroes through the ages'.
† A local hero had resisted Chin aggression by saying he would rather tread the Eastern Sea than submit.

Zhou here pledges to fight imperialism throughout his life. Ironically, he was on his way to learn modernity from a country that had already humbled China more arrogantly than the Europeans, and was soon to go even farther by invading China outright. Zhou took his poetic undertaking seriously, copying this poem out eighteen months later as a memento for his friends in Japan and 'a reminder for myself'.

Zhou probably travelled northwards, via his former haunts in Shenyang, through Korea, reaching Japan in September 1917. He was met at Kobe port by his old friend Wu, and quickly went on to Tokyo to enrol initially at the East Asian Preparatory High School in the Kanda district where he could learn Japanese and prepare for the teacher training college entrance examinations – for he was set on becoming a teacher. There were about 350 students, all Chinese. Completion of this preparatory course would have entitled Zhou to a Chinese government grant, but he never finished it and therefore could not enrol formally in a Japanese university, although he apparently attended some courses at Waseda and perhaps other universities informally. He may also have registered at the Japan–French Law School (forerunner of Hosei University), since he said much later that he had spent a year there.

In spite of his success in getting friends to help him financially, Zhou's life in Japan was austere. Accommodation was a problem. The 4000 Chinese students in Japan already filled the hostels intended for them. But Zhou was helped by a Japanese woman who played godmother to many Chinese students, helping with their problems, taking in their washing and even advising on their romances. Through this kind soul he found lodging with two other Chinese students on the upper floor of the house of a Japanese carpenter, near the Yamabukikan cinema in Ushigome, close to his school.

Zhou was deeply affected by the beauty of the Japanese countryside, especially Mount Fuji and the Chinese-style temples. But what put iron into his soul was the hardship which the Japanese workers had to endure under what he saw as feudalistic capitalism.

Unfortunately he arrived in Japan at a moment when attitudes towards China had become contemptuous and insolent. The Japanese government was now the strongest and best armed in Asia. It had taken advantage of the First World War to impose the quite unjustified Twenty-One Demands on a weak and divided China, and then intervened extensively in Chinese affairs and on Chinese soil. The Japanese regarded China as an old-fashioned weakling incapable of true independence and therefore as legitimate plunder. Like his compatriots in the small Chinese community in Tokyo, Zhou fiercely resented Japanese militarism and the merciless bullying of his homeland and his race. So unbearable did the atmosphere become that he decided very early in his stay that his search for modernity in Japan was

38

fundamentally obstructed by this chauvinistic mood. Similarly bitter and frustrated, many other Chinese students, including all but one of Zhou's financial supporters, packed their bags and sailed for home again without completing their studies.

Zhou himself was tempted to give up, too. He had come to Japan just when its efforts to achieve economic development and gain the West's diplomatic recognition as an equal were beginning to bear fruit. Japan had won the support of the Western allies during the First World War as an equal partner, and Japanese patriots were now understandably elated by their sense that finally Japan's parity with Europe and America was being recognized. But the immediate object of their ambitions could only be China, Japan's rival in the Far East. The young Chinese who remained in Japan to carry on with their studies were regarded by some of their compatriots as cowardly, selfish egoists who were not prepared to go home to help save their country.

Stung by Japanese hostility, the Chinese students formed a New China Learned Society, which met to discuss Japanese imperialism, Chinese feudalism and ways of saving China from both. Zhou joined and wrote propaganda leaflets for it. In May 1918 the Chinese students met secretly in a Chinese restaurant in Kanda to protest against Japan's demand that the Chinese government send troops to Siberia. The meeting was broken up by the police, and the 'return home' movement among the Chinese gained strength. Still, there were minor successes. When the local chief of police used humiliating language about China in a speech, the Chinese students read out a protest drafted by Zhou, and the police chief apologized. Zhou, one of the three organizers of the meeting, himself made speeches against Japanese militarism and Chinese warlordism.

At this low point for Chinese intellectuals the 1917 October Revolution in Russia was welcomed by radical socialists throughout Asia as a deliverance. Zhou shared the general excitement, and read eagerly in Japanese magazines and newspapers about Lenin and his comrades.

As one of his colleagues has remarked, Zhou seldom went to classes, spending his time instead in political meetings and at the editorial office of a nearby revolutionary magazine.

Hardship now caught up with Zhou. Wu was still sending some money from Kyoto, where he was now studying, but Zhou had to tighten his belt. He gave up meat, stopped trying to be accredited as a regular student, and spent all his time reading and helping the other Chinese students organize meetings.

When the autumn of 1918 came on Zhou began to feel the cold. Wu invited him to come and stay with him. With two government stipends and a clever wife, Wu was able to live, by student standards, quite comfortably. 'You stay with us,' he wrote, 'and we will take our time talking about your going to

Kyoto University. The Social Science Faculty at Kyoto . . . is very strong, and you may just like it there. . . . I have asked you several times already, but each time you said you did not want to live off a friend. However, even if you don't consider our Nankai friendship, we are all foreigners in a strange country now. Shouldn't we help each other?' The other arguments Zhou had steeled himself to resist, but the last one moved him. He packed his suitcase, took the train and, at Kyoto station, walked tearfully into the open arms of his old schoolfriend.

Wu and his wife shared a rented house with two other Chinese students, whom Zhou now joined. He made it his task to get up early in the morning, clear away the *futon*, or Japanese mattress, from the floor, and sweep the rooms. Sometimes when the Wus were late coming home, Zhou would cook the evening meal for them. Occasionally Wu would bring home a bottle of wine and they would all enjoy Zhou's cooking together. As with stage acting, Zhou did not mind doing what his fellows would call 'women's work'. Wu would report on the lectures he had listened to and Zhou on the books he had read.

Here, as in Tokyo, Zhou did not actually enter the university. He filled out an application to take courses in politics and economics, giving his address still as Kanda in Tokyo, but whether the form was actually presented or not is unsure.

But Zhou did benefit from the ideas of the pioneer Marxist, Dr Kawakami Hajime, Professor of Economics at Kyoto Imperial University, for in 1919 he became an ardent reader of his fortnightly magazine *Social Problems Research*. This represents the first genuine impact of socialist ideology on Zhou. It is all the more surprising that he never met this scholar. He asked Wu to introduce him, but Wu would not do so. Perhaps he feared that ideological differences between him and his old Nankai friend might widen. Wu had already regretted lending Zhou his copy of *Das Kapital*. He was looking for a Bismarckian leadership for China, authoritative statesmen who could give the country a strong lead towards modernity, whereas Zhou believed that only an ideological remoulding of China's mind would bring about the necessary changes. A strong man of 'iron and blood' could not alter China without a revolution carried out by ordinary people.

Wu's wife often had to intervene in the arguments between the two old friends. On one famous occasion, arguing after dinner about how to save China, Zhou kept filling his cup from the wine bottle, forgetting his manners in the heat of the contest. 'You cannot salvage the situation,' he declared, 'with strong leadership alone. You have to have strong followers to support the leadership. You have to start with a thorough re-education of the younger generation – and the older generation, if that is possible – of the students, the workers and even the peasants. You have to have them all with you before you can push a revolution to successful conclusion. And without a revolution China cannot be saved!'

At which point Wu leaned across to snatch the wine bottle away from his friend and dashed it to the floor. 'You are not going to save China if you hang on to that stuff!' he shouted.

Even his wife put in a word of warning: 'Enlai,' she said, 'you must take care of yourself and not drink too much. Before you came here, Wu was very worried about your staying alone in Tokyo. He said that even at Nankai you were already too fond of wine.'

According to Wu, Zhou's reaction was merely to turn quietly to look for a broom to brush up the mess. The next day he brought a bunch of flowers for his hostess, in spite of being virtually penniless. 'How can you get really angry with a man like that?' Wu later commented. On another occasion when Wu snatched the bottle away from a drunken Zhou, the younger man rushed to his bedroom and bolted himself in. Wu felt that Zhou suffered from having no other friends, his Japanese not being good enough for him to go out much, and attributed his behaviour to simple loneliness.

By the spring of 1919 Zhou was ready to return to China and enlist in the civil struggle that was beginning in his motherland. His feelings were poured into four remarkable poems set in two of Kyoto's famous parks at the beginning of the festive season of the first blossoming of the cherry trees. They were written in free verse instead of the classical phrases that Zhou had used in his earlier poetry. Never before had he expressed his feelings so openly, and never again was he to write so revealingly. The theme was the ray of light which Marxism appeared to bring to this new world that lay at his feet, and how happy it made him to have discovered it. This is the 'beam of sunlight' which breaks through the clouds in the first poem.

ARASHIYAMA IN THE RAIN

My second visit
To Arashiyama in the rain.
Green pines line the banks
With cherries in between.
At the end of the path a hill,
And a stream of jade green twists
Among the rocks, glistening, reflecting.
The drizzle rustles in deepening mist.
Suddenly a sunbeam stabs the clouds,
The more enchanting for its unexpectedness.
Numberless truths
Lodge in the world's complexity.
The more I search, the more confused.

Then in the haze
I see a spark, bright and clear,
So much more beautiful for its suddenness.

ARASHIYAMA AFTER THE RAIN

The rain has gone,
The hill still dark with cloud:
Dusk nears.
A sombre backcloth of green hues
Bears up the cherry blossoms like a halo –
Soft, pink, delicately sweet.
They intoxicate me!

How ravishing is artless nature,
Free from human tie –
Unlike the plaster gauds of priests,
Old rules of feudal conduct, or
Ethic of outdated art and essay.
While nature's free, man loiters
In a prison where sacred pedants
Teach mindless homage to the past.

I climb higher
And stare into the distance,
Where hills melt in grey.
White clouds, partly obscured,
Narrow to a stripe.
A few electric lights glare from the dark and shapeless city.
Just for a second the island people seem to cry from their hearts:
'Statesmen, warlords, party bosses, capitalists –
From all this, how will you ever survive?'

MARUYAMA PARK

Cherries in bloom all over the park
Make brilliant glow.
Lights shine out on every side
While the crowds clamour.
A woman stands by herself at a pond
Under a poplar and weeping willow.
Which is more beautiful,
Cherry or willow?
Forlorn, she makes no sound,
And no one speaks to her.

Would Zhou have liked to talk to this mysterious lady? If so, what inhibition held him back? 'Maruyama Park', of all his poems, shows a vein of pure romanticism.

These three poems were all written on 5 April. The fourth is dated four days later:

FOURTH VISIT TO MARUYAMA PARK

My fourth time here.
Up hill and down vale
A rioting flood of fallen petals!
Only leaves left on the branches
Under the sober pines.
We cannot any longer find
That cherry blossom,
'Soft, pink, delicately sweet'.

The lights go out,
The people leave.
Nine days in Kyoto
Were a feast of bittersweet.
Bloom and decay,
Triumph and defeat,
Are the iron laws of man.
Has there ever been
Perennial flower? Eternal spring?
Natural beauty with a free mind to enjoy it?

What is striking at this distance is the acknowledgement of a certain accidental quality in his attraction to Marxism, 'a chance glimpse of a spark in the haze'. But the substance of the poems is about reactionary Japanese politics, about the contrast between the cleanness of nature and the squalor of human institutions. 'Bloom and decay' is the law of nature; in Zhou's vision it is Marxism that blooms while feudalism decays.

The immediate cause of Zhou's wanting to go home was the outburst of demonstrations in Beijing and by Chinese students in Tokyo against the shabby treatment of China at the Treaty of Versailles negotiations in 1919. This was the famous May Fourth Movement, which symbolized China's patriotic fervour against old-fashioned great-power diplomacy. Ma Jun, Zhou's other good friend from Nankai School, who had just graduated, two years after Zhou, wrote to his older friend in Japan to ask: 'If even our country is about to disappear, what is the use of studying?'

This question aroused heated discussion in the Wu household. Wu himself decided to stay, but to speed up his course of study. Zhou would hear

43

of nothing but going home at once. Against all the efforts by Wu and his wife to make Zhou complete his studies in Japan, the May Fourth Movement called him. Mrs Wu had to go into the centre of town to sell a valuable ring to pay for Zhou's ticket, and that very afternoon she put her impetuous lodger on the train to Tokyo, thence to China.

This sojourn in the only Asian country then undertaking serious modernization was surprisingly barren for Zhou Enlai. In 1971 he confessed to Japanese visitors that: 'Although I was given the unique opportunity of going to Japan, I didn't study anything at all. The Japanese language gave me a lot of trouble. I taught myself Japanese by reading newspapers, relying on my knowledge of Chinese characters. But in the end I wasn't able to master it. My reading ability may be fair, but my command of the spoken language is very poor. Even now I cannot understand Japanese.' The only Japanese word he could produce for the politician Takasaki Tatsunosuke in 1955 was *konnichiwa* – 'good afternoon'.

On another occasion, Zhou told a Japanese delegation that although he had been in Japan for almost two years, 'I have few recollections of the country. . . . The thing I do remember is that Japanese bean curd is tastier than Chinese.'

Wu was, in his own recollection, 'unreservedly awed' by Japan, its modernity, its maturity, its work ethic, its patriotism – and his lodger had the same reactions. But there is no evidence that Zhou ever held up Japan, for himself or for other Chinese, as a model or example of what could be done to modernize an old-fashioned society. So, after eighteen months in Japan, Zhou left in May 1919 with no formal university experience and very little else to show. His books had to be sold to help raise $30 for his passage home. All he could take with him was the memory of the books he had read and his crucial encounter with socialist theory in the pages of Dr Kawakami's journal.

4

In Prison
1919–20

The May Fourth Movement dominated Chinese politics for years. Thousands of students demonstrating against the government and the big powers in Beijing were routed by soldiers and policemen, and the treatment they received sparked off even stronger protests all over China, bringing students together almost for the first time in an organized way to press for political reforms.

One of the leading figures in the protest movement in Tianjin was a young girl named Deng Yingchao, then only fifteen. Another was the brilliant Moslem, Ma Jun. Ma and his other old Nankai friends were delighted when Zhou, now twenty-one, reappeared in his old haunts in Tianjin in the spring of 1919. At a huge teaparty he talked about his experiences in Japan. While Ma briefed him on what the students were doing, he learned that his former headmaster, Dr Zhang Boling, had become president of the new Nankai University. The friendship between Zhou and Zhang was now rather unusual, because Zhang was a leader of the Chinese YMCA and sought to steer his students away from the politics of the street in order to become efficient servants of the democratic state that would, he hoped, soon come to China, while the revolutionary Zhou was rejecting such gradualism. Yet their mutual regard persisted.

Years afterwards Zhou insisted that 'Nankai University did not take me as her student: my name is not included in the list of alumni.' Yet he is recorded as entering the university on 25 September 1919, and his name is included in lists of entrants that have recently come to light. What is certain is that, as usual, he did precious little academic work during his year in Tianjin, treating the university as a mere *pied-à-terre*.

The old problem of finance had to be tackled. His family – 'that spendthrift lot' – could not afford to pay his way through college. Dr Zhang came to the

45

rescue by giving him a job as a secretary, and Zhou afterwards explained how 'at Nankai University I became editor of the student union paper, which helped cover some expenses.' From these two sources he was able to keep body and soul together for a year.

The daily student newspaper had, remarkably, an English slogan at the masthead: 'Democracy: of the people, for the people and by the people.' Zhou quickly persuaded the editorial board to change the language of the body of the paper from classical to modern vernacular Chinese, and they elected him editor-in-chief on the spot. The paper's circulation was 20,000 copies a day, which was quite a responsibility. Zhou spent much time at the printing press on Rong An Street learning about the technical processes – and also indoctrinated the workers about revolution. He saved money by reading proofs himself, sometimes into the night. But the greater part of his time went into writing, for he composed most of the newspaper himself, under various pseudonyms so that the extent of his authorship would not be obvious.

At this stage his ideas were not yet communist, although they were loosely socialist and utopian. He was particularly acerbic against Confucius, Mencius and the warlords, but his editorials also savaged the textile magnates of Lancashire and Osaka, the exploitation of cheap Chinese labour for foreign capital, the useless old family system in China and the impoverished life of workers. In Western terms his orientation most nearly approximated to that of Tolstoy.

When a Beijing University student wrote an article under the pen-name 'Lenin II' welcoming the Russian October Revolution, Zhou – perhaps a little influenced by Dr Zhang Boling – was sceptical. All the same, the Soviet example could not be entirely ignored. Zhou took a group of students to the French Concession to call on Sergei Polevoy, a Russian teacher at Beijing University who also worked for the Comintern. This was his first personal encounter with international communism.

As Deng Yingchao afterwards recalled, the students in that group (of whom 'I was the youngest') would discuss 'socialism, anarchism, Chartism, etc. No one had precise beliefs, or understood communism. We had just heard that the most ideal society was that in which each gave according to his ability and received according to his needs.'

Lodging on Hebei Third Avenue, in the southern part of Tianjin city, Zhou developed a regular routine. He would breakfast off soya-bean milk and doughnuts from a roadside stall, then stop at the public lavatory, where he would begin to plan the daily editorial.

A fellow-worker has recalled how he came to respect Zhou. 'In the Students' Association at that time there were people who wanted to be in the limelight. Zhou wasn't like that. He didn't take part in power struggles. He treated everyone equally, with warmth and kindness. He was good at dealing with things immediately, reading articles given to him at once, instead of putting them to one side.' That is exactly what they thought of him in the People's Republic thirty years later.

In a celebrated editorial of 21 July 1919, Zhou was uncompromising on the need to transform society and spread new ideas, striding head on against the prevailing mood of pessimism. In August the new theme was Japan's shameless use of the Versailles Conference to take advantage of China by annexing parts of Shandong Province. The pro-Japanese Shandong warlord stepped up his oppression of students, disbanding their organizations and killing some leaders of a patriotic society. 'Oh compatriots!' Zhou wrote on 6 August. 'The forces of darkness are for ever increasing. . . . What must we do to defend against them? There must be preparation, there must be method, there must be sacrifice.' He busily organized special meetings of the Tianjin student group to protest and to coordinate with those in other cities. They streamlined their own organization to be better prepared, and sent representatives to Beijing to join in the national protest. When these young people were arrested, Zhou reassured their comrades still at home: 'This is an opportunity to continue to increase the patriotic movement. It's no use getting anxious and nervous, things went according to plan. If only they can stand the test of being arrested, then what does it matter? But our duty now is to rescue them.' In the student newspaper he wrote: 'We must all rise in a mass and fight! We must rescue the arrested representatives!'

Within the next forty-eight hours hundreds of Tianjin students went to Beijing to protest outside the office of the President of China. For three days they waited round the clock, and then military police began to hit them with rifle butts and arrested their leader. At last Zhou went himself with other student leaders to Beijing and organized thousands more students to surround the police offices both there and in Tianjin. At the end of August the government gave in and released the jailed students. Early in September Zhou and the others led a triumphant journey back to Tianjin – and began to plot their next steps against the government.

Zhou wanted to merge the separate patriotic organizations of the men and women students, something considered so modern as to be slightly risqué in the China of that time. After four days of delicate negotiation a new joint organization held its first meeting on 6 September.

'All of us here today,' Zhou declared, 'have been roused by the new trend of thought of the twentieth century, and have become aware that the fundamental solution for Chinese society is to uproot and transform all those things which are incompatible with modern evolution: militarism, the capitalist class, powerful cliques, bureaucrats, sexual discrimination, the feudal grading of human relationships. . . .' Specifically he suggested that they put out a vernacular magazine called *Awakening*, with an 'Awakening Society' to supervise it. This new body, which followed a few days later, was the counterpart of societies with similar aims in other cities, including Mao Zedong's New People's Study Society in Changsha. Its members were all radicals, though they did not all become Communists. Some went on into anarchism, others joined the Guomindang.

When Zhou, with trembling voice, asked the ladies to introduce themselves at that inaugural mixed meeting, one of those who came forward was the capable and comely Deng Yingchao, then at the First Girls' Normal School in Tianjin. Courageous in both thought and action, she was a leading light in the Tianjin Girl Students' Patriotic Association. Her essay on the May Fourth Movement became a classic, and she was just as persistent in organizing lectures and meetings and generally raising the level of political consciousness as Zhou and his men friends. Yet, in Zhou's own proud words, 'she was only fifteen'.

But the path of true love did not run smoothly. One of the most sought-after girls in Tianjin when Zhou returned from Japan was the extremely good-looking daughter of a wealthy merchant, who attended the Nankai Girls' Junior High School. Zhou had known her earlier, and she had no difficulty in attracting his attention on his return. But her father would not hear of her keeping company with a moneyless revolutionary, and made her break off the relationship. She was packed off abroad to recover.

Zhou may have been affected by this episode more than he chose to admit. One of his Chinese biographers comments that 'first love left . . . a bitter taste' – but Zhou was so absorbed in the revolutionary movement that 'private love affairs did not come as a great shock'.

A few days after the start of the Awakening Society in Tianjin, Zhou invited the pioneer Marxist Li Dazhao to come from Beijing to talk to the members. By now he was beginning to succumb to the Marxist message. During this year in Tianjin, he recollected afterwards, 'I read translations of the *Communist Manifesto*, Kautsky's *Class Struggle* and *The October Revolution*' – all published by the revolutionary journal *New Youth* edited by Chen Duxiu, whom he also met.

There was little time for studies. Japanese actions continued to provoke the students. The new police chief appointed in Tianjin was a bully with whom Zhou was to cross swords in a spectacular manner. The students used the pretext of the anniversary of the Republic on 10 October, the famous 'Double Tenth', to hold meetings and demonstrations, and the Nankai sports ground, where the Tianjin students had planned to meet, was surrounded by police. Deng Yingchao led the girl students on a charge, shouting 'Police should also be patriotic' and 'You shouldn't hit patriotic students.' They knocked off the policemen's helmets with sticks, leaving them demoralized, and finally broke through the encirclement and surrounded the police station.

Meanwhile the government banned Zhou's newspaper and the police raided its offices. He himself had a narrow escape from imprisonment – and possibly even worse – probably with the help of the Nankai Registrar, Kang Nairu, who hid him in his house. The house of Deng Yingchao's mother lay in the French Concession, beyond the jurisdiction of the Chinese police, and she allowed the student leaders to use it for meetings to discuss their strike strategy.

The government succeeded in shutting down the paper on 22 September, but Zhou was able to bring it out again, printed by the students themselves with the help of the workers, and it was on the streets two weeks later. He escaped imprisonment, but his friend Ma Jun was taken by the police. For days Zhou went round Tianjin and Beijing mobilizing influential people to intervene for Ma's release. Incensed by police brutality against his younger fellow-student, Zhou wrote less about peaceful persuasion and more about the need to get rid of China's bandit policemen and soldiers, and an angrier tone crept into his writing.

At the end of 1919 he wrote a revealing short poem called 'Convenience of the Dead'.

> Whew! Brrr! The northwest wind!
> Winter is here.
> Going out, I hail a rickshaw.
> The rickshawman's padded cotton coat
> Is just like mine.
> Even with my coat on, I still feel the chill.
> But he regrets the added burden of wearing his,
> So takes it off and puts it on my feet.
> I thank him for his thoughtfulness,
> He thanks me for helping him out, too.
> Coexistence with reciprocal gain?
> No, the sweating of the living,
> The convenience of the dead!

The encounter with the rickshawman and the two overcoats prompts a bitter denunciation of the old order and old exploitation, and it has discernible Marxist overtones.

The poem was published in the first issue of *Awakening* on 20 January 1920. All the contributors were allocated pseudonyms, drawn by lot. Deng Yingchao drew the first lot and wrote under the name 'Yi Hao', meaning number one; Zhou's was 'Wu Hao', because he drew fifth. Zhou clung to his alias for years afterwards.

A group photograph of the society shows Deng sitting pertly at the front – coolly authoritative – while Zhou stands at the end of the second row, caught untidily in a turning, slightly stooping posture.

Zhou's taste of prison was at hand. Traders profiteering from Japanese goods beat up the people boycotting them, and in January 1920 the students protested – a demonstration which the authorities used as an excuse for extensive arrests. The Tianjin students decided to retaliate with a mass rally on 29 January to petition the provincial governor to support the boycott and this was personally led by Zhou and two women students. Deng Yingchao stayed behind to help guard the student headquarters.

A cold north wind blew dry snow into their faces as they waited to set off. Zhou in a thin jacket, his long hair blowing, jumped up on some steps to remind them of their agreed demands.

When they arrived at the governor's compound the gate was open, but the door to his office was tightly closed. 'We are representatives of Tianjin students,' Zhou told an official who came out of a side door to see what they wanted. 'We wish to see the governor to state our patriotic views.'

The official withdrew, followed by the reproachful stares of thousands of angry eyes behind Zhou, their leader. Some twenty minutes later he came out to say that the student representatives would be received but all the others would have to go back outside the gate. They refused to retreat, and there was an impasse.

Suddenly Zhou noticed that the bottom part of the main door had an independent section which the soldiers had forgotten to close. It would just be possible to clamber over the threshold and get in through the gap. 'The only way to break the deadlock and start the fight,' Zhou told his comrades, 'is through the gap over the threshold.'

One of the others protested that it might be dangerous, but Zhou retorted: 'Nothing ventured, nothing gained.'

He crawled through with three comrades, two of them women, and scuffled with the military police inside. Put into an outhouse to await the governor's decision, the resourceful Zhou found a ladder to climb so that he could shout at the other students over the top of the wall: 'If we are not out in an hour, that means defeat, so everyone must think of another way to try again and not give in.'

Soon the soldiers and police were out among the students, drawing their batons to settle the matter in the traditional way. It was a blood bath, conducted while Zhou and his three companions inside were untouched. The police decided to hold the four student leaders indefinitely without interrogation, and separated from each other. But Zhou found a way of communicating in the toilet, and they agreed to start a hunger strike at the beginning of April.

This helped the other students and their families outside to publicize the incident and the arrests. Protests soon flowed in from the press and various public bodies. Deng Yingchao led another batch of students to the police, offering themselves as replacements for the hunger strikers.

The authorities were thus badgered into bringing Zhou to trial, in the course of which he was at last mixed with other prisoners; he seized the opportunity to indoctrinate them with radical ideas. He and the other three students gave impromptu lectures on economics, law, Marxism and even psychology. They encouraged the prisoners to write, and Zhou later edited a collection of their works called *Days at the Criminal Court*. Throughout he kept a diary under the title 'Detention by the Police'.

The first anniversary of the May Fourth Movement was celebrated by a cultural evening, using three doors cobbled together to serve as a stage, quilts for curtains and human voices as orchestral instruments. Zhou produced several plays, and acted in them as well, about landlord repression and French imperialism – and when he did the last act of the Nankai School play *A Dollar Coin*, it brought tears to the eyes of the guards and wrung promises from them to be patriotic in the future.

When the final hearing of the trial opened in August, Zhou sat in the dock razor thin after thirteen weeks behind bars, watched by hundreds of his friends and other students. Asked if he had not entered the provincial government office illegally, Zhou smiled and inquired whether it was a crime to be patriotic, to boycott Japanese goods, to protect the national interest, to petition the provincial government office, to ask to see the governor? On the other hand, was it lawful for police to beat students with rifle butts and spill their blood, or to keep members of the public for many months without trial? And more in this vein of dead pan sarcasm.

'Are you interrogating me,' the angry officer retorted, 'or am I interrogating you?'

The judge's verdict was to acquit the students on most charges, but he gave them small sentences for technical breaches of the law, which they had already in fact served, so face was saved all round. Zhou's wellwishers regarded it as a triumph, and sped him away with banners and flowers.

Zhou was touched by what Deng Yingchao had done to help him during his imprisonment. He also found an unexpected welcome from two new admirers, his defence lawyer in the trial and one of the founders of Nankai School. Each of these men, impressed by Zhou's conduct and qualities, offered him his daughter's hand in marriage. When he declined, they still put up $500 each to finance his further study abroad, for while Zhou spurned romantic attachments, he was actively considering the idea of going to France. The work-study programmes to send young Chinese to Europe had been one of the main preoccupations of the Awakening Society and its counterparts in other provinces, and in a prison poem of 8 June 1920, Zhou had revealed how much the prospect excited him.

This was a farewell to Li Yuru, a girl student and friend of Deng Yingchao, who had come to see Zhou in prison before sailing for France under the work-study programme. In a covering note Zhou explained to the girl: 'Sorry I can't see you off. Let me send you a poem instead! I started composing it at 4.30 p.m. and actually succeeded finishing it by 6.30. In quality, this piece should rank middle-upper in my poetic works.' After recalling the girl's earlier ambitions, Zhou notes:

> From here you'll sail
> Through the East Sea, South Sea,
> Red and Mediterranean Sea,
> Whose waves and waters,
> Tumbling and breaking across the globe,
> Will bring you to the shores of France,
> Cradle of liberty. . . .

> In Nanjing, of course,
> You'll see Shudi*. . . .
> I can imagine for you two
> A painful parting.

> But aren't we in one world?
> Don't talk of parting!
> The fires of love burn endlessly:
> 'You can break the lotus root but not its fibres.'
> In August Shudi's feet
> Will walk the New World.
> The Atlantic breakers
> Will carry your letters of love.
> Like two telegraph poles
> On opposite shores,
> You'll kiss through the void.

> And then, my friend, in September,
> At the docks of Marseilles
> Or in a Paris suburb,
> You and I may meet once more. . . .

Zhou was foreshadowing his own momentous journey a few weeks later, 'through the East Sea, South Sea, Red and Mediterranean Sea . . .' which in turn would carry him 'to the shores of France, cradle of Liberty.' He had

---

* Li's fiancé, Zhou's classmate at Nankai, who went to the United States to study.

specific advice, however, for his femine co-reformer, to 'sweat away . . . and aim for the best marks. Temper your talents, but stay innocent.' The modernist still held old-fashioned ideas about sexual virtue!

At the annual meeting of the Awakening Society in the autumn of 1920, Zhou suggested that Li Dazhao direct a joint conference of Beijing and Tianjin organizations. 'Everyone knows,' he said, 'that the road to saving our nation is, from now on, simply to immerse ourselves in the working people, rely on the working class, and get the organizations and unions, big and small, that have sprung up all over the country after the May Fourth Movement, to adopt common activities. Only then will we be able to rescue China.' That was his last political action before taking ship to France along with various fellow-members of the Awakening Society.

'You have to go out and look for joy,' Li Yuru had written. 'Sitting under a tree and waiting for it won't get you anywhere.' Zhou was certainly not sitting under a tree and waiting. He could hardly restrain his impatience to 'drink Western ink', as the Chinese scholars put it.

5

Commitment in France
1920–24

Patriotic young Chinese with a thirst for modernity were now seizing every opportunity to go to Europe, especially to France. France was regarded as the most liberal and sophisticated of the European countries and the franc happened to be weak. More than 1600 Chinese students went to France in 1919–20, including many who were to become leaders of the Chinese Communist Party – Deng Xiaoping, Li Fuchun, Li Lisan and Chen Yi among them.

Zhou was no less eager than the others, and if he had not been in prison he might have gone in one of the earlier waves. France was the doyen of European revolution as well as being near to Russia, and would provide a place from which he could study and understand not only the European labour movement but also the Soviet revolution.

So he found himself on 7 November 1920, a shy, stuttering student, boarding the Messageries Maritimes ship *Porthos*, sailing from Shanghai to Marseilles. He was twenty-two. As he watched his homeland recede into the distance, among the last things to disappear from view were the prominent British, American, French and other flags flying on top of the buildings owned by Western businesses and on foreign ships in Shanghai waters – a vivid reminder of how much China had come under foreign control. A fellow-passenger recalled that the students talked eagerly during the voyage about their ambitions – how one 'wanted to go to England to study building construction. I wanted to study mining. But Zhou Enlai said he wanted to change Chinese society.'

The ship stopped overnight at Hong Kong, stayed for three days at Saigon, and then called briefly at Singapore and Colombo before clearing the Suez Canal and docking at Marseilles on 13 December. At each place Zhou, with his new friends, found further evidence of imperialism. From Saigon he wrote home that the local Chinese greeted them so warmly with waving flags that they might have been blood relatives. In Colombo, he noticed how workers had to take their rest by the roadside as best they could while flies and mosquitoes gathered in swarms on their food – all in contrast with the tall buildings and great mansions belonging to wealthy foreigners. 'Many of the places we passed through,' recalled a fellow-student, 'were English or French colonies.' He and Zhou and a third student 'all felt that as soon as they left China, Chinese were looked down on, that their international status was very low, and we felt greatly indignant.' Zhou reminded them of the historical background for this, going back to the Opium War of the 1840s, and concluding, 'everyone is responsible for the fate of his country, one cannot sit by and watch.'

After five weeks at sea, Zhou took the train from Marseilles to Paris. Here he was directed to the school at Château Thierry for a language course. He told his colleagues afterwards that he had French lessons with a private tutor for a year, but he behaved just as he had in Japan, never enrolling at a university like the others. One book which he read closely in his early months in Paris was Beer's *Life and Teachings of Karl Marx*, in English. He filled its margins with notes. A Chinese, reading in France the work of a German translated into English – this was indeed the exciting postwar world.

Although he found lodging in a southern suburb of Paris, at Billancourt, Zhou felt restless, perhaps cut off because he knew little or no French. Within a few days he went to see what it was like in England. Before leaving Tianjin, he had arranged, possibly through the Belgian Father Vincent Lebbe, to act as a correspondent for a Catholic paper, the *Yishi Gao*, and his first dispatch, dated 1 February, offers a clue to his interests in London. What excited him was the labour situation.

As a result of the changes brought about by the First World War, the European labour movement was strengthened, and labour questions were having a big impact on politics. Some European workers wanted to adopt the Soviet system without delay, others preferred a more gradual approach. 'I cannot be outside this debate,' Zhou explained. The strike of the highly organized British coalminers, for instance, was relevant, Zhou wrote, 'to my country,' where strikes were usually for just a few more coppers, and where people were treated like machines, unaware that other parts of society were actually ready to help the 'stupid masses'. Workers in England were getting about thirty times the wages of their Chinese counterparts.

There is no record of what Zhou did in London, although he may have spent time with Li Fujing, a Nankai classmate and fellow-actor on the school stage, whom Zhou rather hero-worshipped. They had sailed together on the *Porthos*, and Li was expecting to study building construction in England. Zhou sent a postcard to friends dated 30 January 1921, bearing the address

36 Bernard Street, off Russell Square, in the university area of Bloomsbury, but otherwise his tracks were well covered.

Back in Paris Zhou led a characteristically austere life. He had bought a wooden mushroom with him from China to mend his own socks. He travelled with a small stove so that he could heat water at mealtimes and soak bread in it, to eat with cabbage or other vegetables. When, decades later, a Chinese Communist embassy was established in Paris, Zhou took the trouble to settle 'a bill for the hundred cups of coffee which he had drunk on credit' at the Café Aurore, while another coffee account in the Latin Quarter was settled with 300 Chinese cigarettes. He was said to lodge sometimes in the Rue du Sommerard.

The delicate problem of Zhou's personal finance was worsened by the bankruptcy of the Sino-French Educational Association, which supposedly looked after all the Chinese students, but Zhou had the donations of rich Chinese individuals to support him. 'Many old and patriotic gentlemen,' Zhou conceded, 'privately helped us students, and with no personal political aims.' One who helped Zhou was Yan Fansun, a founder of Nankai University. 'Later on,' Zhou explained, 'when friends remarked that I had used Yan Fansun's money to become a Communist, Yan quoted a Chinese proverb, "Every intelligent man has his own purposes!" ' And there may have been other sources. After Zhou had been in France for about a year, an old schoolfriend called on him. He admired Zhou's good clothes and decent room. Zhou explained that he was getting money both from China and from newspaper publishers in Tianjin and Shanghai, but his friend surmised that he might also be financed by the Comintern.

The story used to go in Paris in those days that you could always get a few francs a month to read *L'Humanité* if you were a Chinese student. One of Zhou's colleagues believed that he might ultimately have been drawing 2500 francs monthly from the Comintern, another 800 francs from the Belgian Catholics and a further 300 francs from Renault. This all sounds much too much, although Zhou may towards the end have been handling some organizational funds not for his personal use, and undoubtedly he would have liked to convey the impression to the other students that he was a proficient fund raiser.

The Catholic newspaper *Yishi Gao* was especially interested in issues of social welfare. Zhou had a general brief to cover the politics and economics of Europe, as well as the workers' movements and national liberation struggles – not to mention the affairs of the work-study students. A series of dispatches published initially under his own name (though he quickly shortened his signature to Enlai, then briefly toyed with his old childhood pseudonym, Xiang Yu, which can be translated as 'floating over the world', before returning to Enlai again – except for a last dispatch from London in early

1922 which he signed Zhou Xiang) appeared weekly for just over a year, from February 1921 to March 1922. They covered the Allied attitude towards Germany and the German war indemnity, European diplomacy towards Russia, the Middle East, Greece, Anglo-French differences, the Silesian question, the Washington Conference and the position of Japan, the Russian drought, and always the position of labour, the progress of various major strikes and the difficulties of the Chinese students in France. They were lively and blunt. Lloyd George's speeches at the Empire Conference, for example, are described as tedious and too long, and coming from a 'cunning' and very determined man.

Although Zhou was veering strongly towards Marxism, he still betrayed many bourgeois attitudes of mind. He once put on his (or a friend's) best clothes and sailed out to have his photograph taken in them. The photographer added colour, which had not been requested, but Zhou liked the result and had the photograph copied onto personal postcards which he immediately sent to friends all over the world. One of them went to Wu, his old mentor in Kyoto. 'Paris beautiful – and so are the women!' he wrote on the back. 'Many friends, many sights. Would you like to come?' Eventually he realized that it was not politic for a revolutionary to distribute his photograph so widely.

Almost all the writers, Chinese and other, who have described Zhou's early life mention that he briefly worked at the Renault motorcar factory outside Paris. Considerable detail buttresses these stories. One has it that he worked a thirteen-hour day there with Li Lisan, another famous Chinese Communist leader, as a common labourer carrying heavy iron bars and making iron moulds for casting. According to this account Li was better at it than the bourgeois Zhou, who left after only three weeks saying, 'This is not a life for human beings.' Deng Xiaoping is cited as a co-worker. Yet when a Paris-based journalist told Zhou years later that the Renault management claimed to have a contemporary memorandum about him, describing him as a dangerous agitator, Zhou protested that he had never worked there at all, and that it must have been somebody else with a similar name. And a French comrade recollected that Zhou 'just laughed out loud' when told later that the French newspapers had written about Zhou's 'creating a furore' at the Renault factory.

It sounds very much as if Renault was on Zhou's list of well-known factories to visit in the course of his inquiries about labour conditions, which might well have been considered provocative by some managers, but that he did not actually work there regularly. He stayed briefly at St Chamond, near Lyons, a steel town with many Chinese workers. Fifty years afterwards one of his landladies still remembered how he used to send her flowers every Christmas, and another French provincial recalls playing tennis with him.

Zhou told President Nixon in 1972 that he had worked for 'some months' in a coal mine in Lille.

Zhou spent some time with the Hunanese students in France, many of them organized by Mao Zedong, especially the brother and sister Cai Hesen and Cai Chang. It was not long before they went sightseeing together, climbing, for example, to the top of Notre Dame, and he wrote a letter about this to Deng Yingchao. After ascending 'hundreds of stone steps' they finally reached the top, out of breath. 'Weird creatures, rather like the evil spirits of Chinese mythology, were crouching there. We gazed at Paris darkening in the dusk. It was a magnificent sight. The water of the River Seine flowed pale blue and the distant Fontainebleau wood was beautifully illuminated by the rays of the setting sun. We shouted *"très bien!"* in French.'

But Cai introduced a graver note. 'Enlai,' he said, the view 'is certainly magnificent.' But they should not be intoxicated. The eyes of a revolutionary should see the underlying pathos of human life. 'Look, even France is pervaded by the oppression of the powerful, exploitation by the capitalist class and the righteous struggle of the working class against it. Even here, although things are not as terrible as in our own China' (a rare Chinese admission of French progressiveness) 'class conflict and exploitation are rife. If we want to create a revolution in our own country, I think we should first organize a revolutionary cell here in France and fight hand in hand with the working class of this country.'

Zhou was duly impressed. He added, for Deng's benefit, 'I haven't made a single female friend since I came to France and I have no intention of having one in the future. Instead, I think that the most fruitful thing for me is the friendship of Cai Hesen.' No wonder a fellow-student called him a misogynist.

Cai swiftly inducted Zhou into the People's New Study Association at a ceremony in a forest glade outside Montargis. This in turn led Zhou into a weekly discussion group on current affairs organized by the left-wing writer Henri Barbusse, apparently on behalf of the Comintern. Within a short time Zhou was becoming an *habitué* at the Café Pascal on the Rue de l'Ecole de Médecine and another café near the Panthéon. He also joined the Worker–Student Mutual Help Society, of which Cai was a leading member, and which became the focus for the complaints of the Chinese students in France.

Of the many incidents which marked Zhou's time in France the first was the petition by the Chinese students to their Legation in Paris. The Chinese in France had fallen on hard times, often unable to get a job, or even a place of study, or to make ends meet. A group of their representatives asked the Chinese Minister to deal with these problems. He merely passed the request back to the Chinese government, which replied that no further funds were available and students without money or jobs should be repatriated. This angered the students into formally petitioning the Legation on 28 February 1921. The Minister remained noncommittal, and eventually the French police came out and broke up the students' ranks. In this affair Zhou and Cai were two of the four leaders.

The second issue was less parochial. In July the Chinese government sent a delegation to secure a loan from France, overtly for disaster relief but actually for arms. Most of the Chinese students and workers in France opposed this loan, and conferences were held in the summer to protest. As the affair came to a head, the students and workers surrounded the Legation and warned the delegation from China: 'If you sign, we'll kill you.' Zhou's dispatches home were intended to inform opinion in China itself about the loan and create domestic opposition to it. Finally the French government backed down.

But the most spectacular coup was the occupation in September 1921 of Lyons University, where nearly a thousand Chinese students could neither enrol nor work.

The Chinese and French authorities had agreed to set up a new Sino–French university at Lyons, but it transpired that the places would be filled by middle-class students freshly brought from China instead of from the existing ranks of 'troublemakers' in France. When it was announced that grants to Chinese students already in France would stop, they decided to take action. 'The road has ended,' Zhou wrote, 'it must change direction. Our power was weak, our strength minimal, we must unite together.' He called delegates to a meeting in Paris which resolved in mid-September to 'open the Lyons university with no restrictions', and he organized the march on Lyons.

In his old Renault automobile overalls Zhou blended tactfully, it was said, with the French workers. Sitting at a little desk in a Paris hotel room mapping out last-minute strategy, he provoked the comment of a friend watching him: 'You are really getting to look like a car worker, except for that fat briefcase. Nobody at the Renault plant would carry a thing like that around.'

Zhou looked up without interrupting his writing.

'Here, take it,' he said, passing the briefcase to his friend. 'We may need it to while our time away when we get to Lyons.'

As it turned out, they did. They were arrested at Lyons and detained in the barracks where, predictably, they went on hunger strike. The books and pamphlets inside Zhou's briefcase proved most useful.

The French government decided on expulsion, and about a hundred students were put on a train to Marseilles and then on a ship to China. Li Lisan was one of those who found himself prematurely repatriated in this way. Li was two years older than Zhou, Hunanese, and from a poor family. He had gone to Europe as a worker-student a year before Zhou and organized a socialist study group of his own before joining Zhou and others in a new Chinese Communist Youth League in which Li was head of propaganda and Zhou head of organization (positions to be neatly replicated in the Chinese Communist Party itself seven years later). Zhou was to be a faithful supporter of this impetuous and stubborn man, who was also a great orator, when he was running the Party.

Meanwhile, the Chinese Communist Party had been founded in Shanghai, in July 1921. It took some time for the news to filter through to Paris, but Zhou reported to his friends at home that most of the members of the Awakening Society in France had eventually, after long and searching discussions, chosen communism. 'It was only after October 1921,' he added, 'that an official decision was taken.' Writing to his friends in the Awakening Society in Tianjin to describe his intellectual development during his first year in Europe, Zhou explained, 'The creed of the Awakening Society was as a rule not useful enough and lacked light. . . . Only when I came to Europe did I start an inquisitive comparison of all doctrines . . . and now I have already got a firm faith.' Attacking both revisionism and anarchism, he went on, 'The power of balance is held by the bourgeoisie, one's fate is in their hands, how can the working people hope for success? . . . We believe in the principle of communism and also in the two great principles of class revolution and the dictatorship of the proletariat.'

Of the Chinese students then in France Zhou estimated that two in three were potential Communists, with the rest divided equally between anarchism and the Nationalist policies of the Guomindang.

In the spring of 1921, when Zhou had become a member of an informal, five-man Communist group, this represented the first stage, as yet covert, of his commitment to the Communist movement. Meanwhile, he helped prepare for the establishment at the end of 1921 of the Chinese Communist Youth League, which most of the politically active Chinese students in France joined.

Zhou returned to London in early 1922 for a second visit of about two and a half months, later confessing to an American correspondent that he 'did not like it'. On 15 January he reported to the *Yishi Gao* on the British army's brutality in both Ireland and Egypt, and predicted that these troubles would lead to greater ones for Britain in the Middle East.

While Zhou was in London something happened that was to prove very important in his political development. Huang Aiyin, who had joined Zhou's Awakening Society in Tianjin, was shot in a textile strike in Changsha, thus becoming one of the early Communist martyrs. The intensity of the lament that Zhou was to write about his comrade's death suggests a particular closeness between the two men.

Zhou had been under pressure since mid-1921 to join what was going to become the mainstream of Chinese radical politics in the new Communist Party. Yet he obviously had question marks in his own mind about the new philosophy and must have thought very deeply about taking on such a thoroughgoing and stridently self-confident philosophy of life and action. It may be that the death of his friend in the cause that everyone was asking Zhou to join was a decisive factor, supplying the necessary emotional surge to sweep aside any remaining intellectual doubts.

The way in which he wrote about the issues in the months following the formation of the new Youth League is suggestive. Communism, he said in the second issue of *Youth*, the League's journal, was 'a good strategy for thorough reform'. Furthermore,

when one day the success of the revolution is announced, the balance of power will fall into the hands of the working class, and then it will be said that communism is the method for industry to flourish. . . . As things stand in China today, any method to alleviate or correct the situation does not stand a chance. . . .

Even though we are Chinese, we must cast our eyes over the whole world. We must not try to take short cuts, must not be afraid of difficulty or seek momentary comforts, we must divide equally between us the burden of establishing a new society by the world's proletariat.

Somewhere in all these words is a feeling that China might have to accept poor solutions and make the best of them simply because they were being taken up by the rest of the world.

This was during that brief splutter of optimism that coloured the years following the First World War. Few in Zhou's circles asked whether the proletariat was capable of its grand function in a new power structure, or questioned the practicality of the Communist programme for seizing power and transforming society. Marxism was in fashion, and it took a resolute intellect to resist its charms. Marxism was simply scientific, as Zhou put it, to be believed in precisely as one would 'believe in the doctrine of Einstein'.

It was especially difficult for a Chinese, with his main goal the modernization of his backward country to bring it up to the European level, to resist the suggestion skilfully put about by European Marxists that China could save herself much time and suffering by going straight to the next logical stage of Western-style society, bypassing capitalism and heading direct for communism – which a country like China might even, it was flatteringly added, attain in advance of Europe.

– Zhou was a rebel, reacting sharply against the vested interest, privilege and benightedness of China's ruling class. A cast-out from his own family, he deeply sympathized with the unwanted, the rejected of other societies as well as his own. In Europe he gravitated naturally to the company of European rebels against the establishment, and many of these were Marxists. Most of

61

the young Chinese in Europe wanted to get rid of capitalism and imperialism, without putting much thought into a serious investigation of Marxist economics or scientific socialism. Zhou was no exception.

There was another factor. Before reaching France Zhou had idealized that country in his own mind, especially as a result of reading Chen Duxiu's articles, as the fount of all that was modern in the world. But French society in the 1920s could hardly bear the weight of such expectations.

Zhou enjoyed and appreciated many aspects of Paris. Decades later he told a French ambassador to China, 'You are a people who love liberty. When I was in France I noticed with pleasure, all over the streets, that one respects in your country the equality of races.' But French policemen, officials, university teachers, landladies and others with whom the Chinese students had contact were not all particularly modern, nor particularly friendly or helpful to young Chinese visitors. In his disenchantment, Zhou must have been tempted by an ideology that set out precisely to explain that disillusion by analysing the underlying weakness of capitalist society.

What Zhou has to say during his period of conversion discloses an agonizing lack of certainty. It is as if he were saying to his friends at home as well as in Europe: 'All right, if you are set on communism, I will join you and do my best to make it come right. At least it is heading in the right direction, even if it is not exactly what China really needs. But anything to get China into the mainstream of social change.' These half-reservations about Marxism glint through the poem which he wrote in March 1922 for his dead friend Huang:

> A death magnificent,
> A wretched life.
> Don't be hungry to live but scared to die!
> Better to die a death with meaning
> And not take life so seriously.
>
> Parted in life, severed by death
> – That's the worst of punishments.
> Parted in sadness and in pain,
> Or dead for no grave reason –
> Better to say a glorious goodbye.
>
> If no one has sown,
> No one can reap.
> We long for the Communist harvest
> But fail to plant the revolutionary seeds.
> We dream of red flags waving in victory
> But flinch from dyeing them with blood.

Such cheap triumphs are an illusion.
Don't sit and talk
– Get up and do something!
If you hang on to life,
You'll moan its parting.
Life or death will lead you by the nose.
They'll never understand
A touching goodbye,
A heady farewell.

You are the only hope here,
Though the way of life or death is open to all.
Fly up to the light,
It's your choice.
Pick up your hoes,
Open the untilled earth.
Scatter the seeds across the world
And water them with blood.

There have always been partings,
And more farewells will come.
See life and death in calm
And see them through.
Try to make the best of life,
Then try to make the best of death.
What matter if another farewell looms?

There are three themes here. One is sacrifice, the need not to consider life if one's death can be heroic. Another is endeavour: that all is possible to the man who really tries. The third theme is patience: reproaching those who hanker for the fruit of communism but neglect to plant the revolutionary seeds.

In a letter to friends in China introducing his poem, Zhou speaks of it as an act of resolve. 'The news of Huang's death,' he wrote, 'has thoroughly strengthened my commitment to communism. . . . I believe I shall prove worthy of my dead friend.'

Whatever his earlier doubts, Zhou now plunged without visible qualification into a lifetime of continuous Communist work. The fog of doubt was cleared by the loss of a dear one. Zhou gritted his teeth and accepted the fetters of an alien doctrine, reasoning, perhaps, that it was at least modern in spirit and humane in intent. He never wavered, despite occasional rumours to the contrary, for the next fifty years. He thus gave his life a shape, a framework, never to be discarded.

Zhou now became the continent-wide organizer of Chinese students in Europe into Communist groups, and he travelled frequently for the purpose. He went first to Germany, homeland of Marx, in late February or March of 1922, and based himself for about a year in Berlin – in Kant Avenue according to one account, but with a smarter address on Wilhelmstrasse according to another – for a monthly rent of US $12.

He found the Chinese students in Germany scattered among various political groups, and relished the work of drawing them together. One of them described how, at their Chinese student society premises, Zhou 'liked to sit on the sofa by the door of the main sitting room, watching the students play ping-pong. . . .' According to a German-speaking Chinese student from Sichuan, the daughter of Zhou's Berlin landlord fell in love with their handsome lodger. Round-eyed, she told the Sichuanese that although Zhou had paid his rent a year in advance, he only stayed there occasionally. The story is confirmed by another Chinese fellow-student.

Zhou returned to Paris for two important meetings in the summer of 1922. In June or July representatives met for three days in the Bois de Boulogne to set up a Chinese Communist Party organization in Europe. Zhou, there on behalf of the students in Germany, officially entered the Communist Party at last. Once he had taken the plunge himself, he went to great lengths to get his more reluctant friends to follow. He sent a set of documents relating to the Youth League, which he had written in miniature characters to be mimeographed by his young collaborator, Deng Xiaoping, to his old friend Wu in Kyoto. After there was no response, he sent a second set and finally a card saying: 'Twice sent you publications. Did they reach you? Reply please – your younger brother Enlai.' To which Wu, who had been embarrassed by police inquiries following receipt of the documents, replied: 'Our ideas were never compatible. Let us each develop his thinking in his own way but remain friends for ever. Your elder brother Wu.' This was the last correspondence between these two old friends, and Zhou must have felt deeply the failure of their friendship to survive these political differences.

Meanwhile, he did regular battle with the non-Communist Chinese students in Europe. 'On Saturday afternoons and on Sunday,' a colleague recalls, 'Comrade Zhou Enlai would go to the university quarter, the factory quarter and the Chinese workers' quarter in the Parisian suburbs and make speeches in coffee shops where students were gathered.' A few weeks later, the European branch of the Chinese Communist Party was set up by French, German and Belgian contingents with a headquarters at the Godefroy Hotel at No. 17 rue Godefroy, near the Place d'Italie in Paris.* Zhou had his

* Zhou would have been amused by the congregation, just after his death, of about a thousand French and Chinese admirers headed by Premier Hua Guofeng, President Giscard d'Estaing and the mayor of Paris, Jacques Chirac, to unveil a plaque bearing a bust of him at the entrance

photograph taken outside it, looking almost like a broom handle, his thin body squeezed into clothes far too small, so that the cuffs of the coat recede at the wrists and his trouser ends come well above his boots – a picture of deprivation.

It has become a legend how the man who was to become a celebrated general, Zhu De, twelve years older than Zhou and twice as experienced in life's hard school, went to Berlin in October 1922 to persuade Zhou to take him into the Communist Party. Zhu De was an old campaigner who had been through all kinds of uprising against authority, but had been rebuffed by Chen Duxiu, the Party's first Secretary, in his desire to become a Communist. When Zhou's door opened, Zhu De saw 'a slender man of more than average height and with a face so striking that it bordered on the beautiful. Yet it was a manly face, serious and intelligent. . . . Zhou was a quiet and thoughtful man, even a little shy.'

The visitor spurned the chair that Zhou offered and rehearsed his life story: his disillusion with the warlords and the Guomindang who now ruled China, his withdrawal from opium, his conversations with Sun Yat-sen. Zhou listened hard, 'his head a little to one side', and offered to help him find accommodation and become a provisional member of the group until application had been sent to China and been answered.

In the end, Zhu De gained his ambition, but his membership of the Communist Party was kept secret from the Guomindang, to which he still belonged, a precaution which was to prove most useful to Zhou a few years later.

In February 1923 Zhou left Germany to return to France, possibly by way of Belgium. He had already asked his friend Nie Rongzhen, a scientifically inclined student who had not yet opted for communism, to come from Charleroi in Belgium to meet Zhu De – as a result of which he also joined the Communist Party. Now Zhou himself visited the Labour University in Charleroi as guest of his friend Nie, the man who in later years was to become the organizer of China's nuclear programme. Zhou was remembered at Charleroi as a '*beau garçon*', rather silent and often pensive, said to be friendly with the nephew of General Ma, a confidant of the last Emperor Pu Yi, and thus well connected.

Zhou was back in Paris in time for a meeting of the Youth League, which elected him its secretary. From now on, during his final fifteen months in Europe, he dedicated himself to Party and League work, defending Marxism from its detractors and using the journal *Youth* to spread his arguments. He was still following the simple life, often wearing greasy working clothes and making his own meals with the usual bread soaked in water.

---

of this 'rather unimpressive three-storey building', as a local newspaper called it, where Zhou had lived on and off in 1922–24 (*NCNA*, 16 October 1978).

There were also days, however, when Zhou spent a casual evening with his wealthier fellow-students at Sceaux, just outside Paris, sporting a neat jacket instead of oily overalls. If he was early he would go to the kitchen and offer to prepare some northern Chinese delicacy which he could cook well.

That spring he began a new and interesting regular assignment, selecting Chinese students in Western Europe to go to the East Workers' University in Moscow, and personally escorting the successful candidates as far as Berlin. Some of them were senior to Zhou in the local Party hierarchy, so that he himself gradually acquired more seniority in the Chinese Communist ranks in Western Europe. Nobody doubted his dexterity in resolving disputes among the Chinese, ever given to factionalism, or his perennial charm and skilful diplomacy.

'Zhou Enlai,' a colleague later recalled, 'is rather weak in his mastery of political theories, but he can summarize my ideas and re-present them much better than I can. We depended on him to prepare all our public statements, either orally or in writing, because once he handled them they were sure to be accepted by all groups involved.'

It was precisely this kind of skill that was called upon during Zhou's last months in Europe when he was asked to unite all the various bickering groups of Chinese students behind a single patriotic platform. The Guomindang or Nationalist Party under Sun Yat-sen had become the accepted leader of the Chinese republican revolution, supported by most modern-thinking Chinese in the quest to reunify China under the republican banner. Only the Guomindang could offer a plausible programme to challenge the feudalistic warlords who had taken advantage of the collapse of the Manchu imperial system to rule various provinces by themselves for their own benefit. Sun Yat-sen asked the Western powers for help in this formidable task, but they had no time for him. He had no choice then but to turn to the newly created Soviet Union for the material help he needed, and the Russians needed no second invitation. And this in turn meant that the Kremlin, acting through the Comintern, wanted the new Chinese Communist Party to stop quarrelling with the Guomindang and collaborate instead in a national programme for Chinese unity.

In Paris the young members of the two Chinese parties followed these orders, but a third group of anarchistically inclined students were less amenable. Zhou kept revising his draft platform for unity, which was discussed by a general meeting of 400 students in a hall near the Musée de Cluny.

The arguments became so violent that the meeting deteriorated into fist fights, in the course of which two students were taken to hospital and many chairs were broken (one was thrown at Zhou). After this some of the student leaders took to carrying pistols for self-protection.

Zhou had now been away from China for two and a half years, and some of his friends were struck by his ability to do without the company of the opposite sex. On social occasions he exhibited a determination to remain faithful to Deng Yingchao, 'the girl back home', and he underlined these feelings in his letters to her. When an old schoolfriend called and asked whether Zhou had made any 'new discoveries' lately, he replied: 'You mean . . . girls? No.'

'I don't believe it, not with a handsome young man like you and your set-up here.'

'I don't think I want to get involved. It's better to stay single. You get more done that way.'

'How about Deng Yingchao? Haven't you been writing to her every other week?'

'How did you know?'

'She told me. You know, once in a long while I also receive a note from her. . . .'

Thirty years after these events, in 1954, when Zhou Enlai revisited Europe as Premier of the People's Republic of China to attend the Geneva conference on Korea and Indochina, a German journalist sought to reconstruct his life in Germany in the 1920s. His researches revealed that a Chinese student giving his name as Chu had stayed at Düstere-Eichen Weg 18 in Göttingen in 1923, had slept with the pretty young maid in the house, Kunigund Staufenbiel, and duly become the father of a baby boy in April 1924.

Since the family name was so similar, and the birth date of the student was plausible, the journalist assumed that it must be Zhou Enlai. (If Zhou had allowed the outside world to know his exact date of birth, he might have been spared the indignity that followed.) The story was published in *Stern*, and the copious supporting detail suggested that it could not have been wholly invented. Zhou was supposed to have given the girl blankets to keep the baby warm, for example, when the child was sent on the train to her parents' home by her employer, Zhou's landlady. There the boy grew up and later fought in the Second World War, in which he lost an eye. After being fitted with a standard German Army glass eye, he found himself sporting a new blue eye to go with his original brown one. He died in a later battle, however, leaving in turn a son, Zhou's supposed grandson. This young man was still in 1954 living in East Germany, working in a car factory and raising two daughters.

The *Stern* article said that the pregnancy started in the summer of 1923. It was theoretically possible for Zhou to have been travelling at that time between Berlin and Paris, and he could have stopped in Göttingen on the way. But there is no record of such a visit, and it would have been difficult for him to have made any prolonged stay in Göttingen during that autumn, when he was definitely in Paris on a number of occasions. In October, for instance, he uncharacteristically disrupted a meeting of the joint body of Chinese students being held at Philosophers' Hall and started a fight. And at the 10 October celebrations for the Chinese republic (the Double Tenth), Zhou made a surprising spectacle of himself by holding up the Red Flag, strutting round the hall and loudly singing Marxist songs in concert with a dozen comrades.

What does not bear scrutiny is the idea that Zhou was based in any meaningful sense in Göttingen during that winter, as the *Stern* article would have him. His next brief opportunity to visit would have been his second trip to Berlin with the students on the way to Moscow, in the last week of November.

One of Zhou's compatriots working with him in the Youth League at that time declares that no scandal surrounded Zhou's name. 'He led a simple, serious and moral life,' this witness declares. 'His personal morality should not be questioned.'

Yet it would seem plausible, on the face of it, for such a handsome and charming young Chinese to sow a few wild oats during his travels in Europe. And what place more discreet than a town like Göttingen, with relatively few other Chinese students, far from the political hothouses of Paris or Berlin? But then it had to be explained how no other investigator apparently met *Stern*'s informants during the thirty years following publication of the story, so that there was no independent confirmation or subsequent development of it.

Zhou himself gave no definite reaction to the *Stern* story. Was his vanity tickled by it? The outrage of his aides expressed another level of response. Zhou did tell a German delegation when he was Prime Minister that he had never been in Göttingen, and later he mentioned to Pierre Trudeau of Canada that there was a story about his having a German son; if it was true, he went on, he knew nothing about it. This might have been said with the air of a man whom life had cheated of having a son, and would not have been totally disinterested if he had had one who turned out to be German. Eventually the whole story was completely exploded by a diligent Göttingen archivist, who discovered that the true name of the Chinese lodger fathering the child was Chu Ling-gin, with a different date of birth from the Premier's.

Back in the real world, all through that winter of 1923–24 Zhou was trying to argue away the reservations that the anarchist students had about Russia's giving aid to China. They believed that China would lose her independence and come under the sway of these smooth-talking heirs of the Tsars, and they doubted the Guomindang's ability to resist a gradual encroachment of Marxism and totalitarianism into China. Zhou and the other Chinese Communists did not share these fears. They countered with the argument that China had to have *some* foreign help against the warlords, and that the Russians had been more generous and forthcoming in giving arms and supplies to the Chinese republican movement than the Western powers.

The Chinese Communist Party leaders had asked Zhou and his comrades not merely to collaborate with the Guomindang but actually to join it, so that he was in double harness in his last months in Europe. The Guomindang elected him to its Central Executive Committee, so close did the two parties now consider themselves.

When Zhou was charged with insincerity, he resorted to such dramatic defences as bursting into tears – and so touching was his performance that many of the people present believed him. 'They talk and talk about petitions and strikes,' he once said of the anarchists at a Guomindang meeting, 'but when there is a demonstration, who march at the head of the column to face the guns and clubs of the police, get beaten up, arrested, jailed and even butchered? It is we, the Guomindang cadres, not they! They talk about assassination and terrorism, but it is the Guomindang comrades' blood that is shed, not theirs.' Zhou delivered this speech in suitably soiled overalls, to show that the Guomindang–Communist allies had the interests of working people at heart.

In June Zhou received his Party orders. His work in Europe had been invaluable to the Party, especially as an organizer. He had proved himself a leader of a group far more heterogeneous than anything he had had to handle in Tianjin, and he had led them as guests in alien lands. He had dealt with all kinds of problems, from student grants to the propriety of intergovernment loans, the utilization of European educational institutions, harmonizing Communist–Guomindang relations, and the behaviour of European authorities in apprehending Chinese nationals. But now he was to go home to Guangdong Province in south China to work at the front line of the revolution. Of the Chinese Communist leaders who cut their teeth in Europe and survived, almost every one backed Zhou throughout his career – Chen Yi, Li Fuchun, Cai Chang. The so-called French component in the Chinese Communist Party remained influential, if not as tightly knit as others, even after the Cultural Revolution upheavals of the 1960s. And in France Zhou had met not only Li Lisan, an encounter which would prove important only a few years later, but also Ho Chi Minh, the Vietnamese leader – 'already,' Zhou later explained, 'a mature Marxist, and I had just joined the Communist Party. He is my big brother.'

His three and a half years in Western Europe enabled Zhou to come to terms with Marxism and contrive his own personal accommodation with it. All this, together with his rise to the very top of the Chinese Communist hierarchy in Paris, prepared him well for the next phase of his career at home. He left Paris on 20 June 1924.

Six months afterwards, the French police, finding Zhou's name in captured Chinese Communist Party correspondence, decided to investigate him. They knew little about him except his connection with the Communist movement, but on the strength of that were ready to deport him. They were six months too late. The bird had flown.

6

Revolutionary Marriages
1924–25

Zhou returned to semitropical Canton (Guangzhou), now China's revolutionary centre and the capital of Sun Yat-sen's republican movement, in August 1924. Some say that he came home on the Trans-Siberian railway via Moscow, and it was common for the Chinese Communists to return from Western Europe through the USSR. Moreover, it would have been natural for Zhou to want to see his friends and family in north China after such a long absence. Edgar Snow, to whom Zhou confided his life story, states positively that he 'stopped briefly for instructions in Moscow', and a Japanese writer asserts that Zhou not merely passed through Moscow but even 'studied at Lenin University with Tito, Togliatti and Ho Chi Minh'. There is no actual evidence, however, of Zhou in transit in either Moscow or Beijing, and it is just as likely that he returned to China by sea.

His job was to be secretary of the extremely important Guangdong–Guangzi regional committee of the Chinese Communist Party, as well as head of its military affairs department. The office, on the second floor of a building on Wende Road, had no sign, but everybody knew what it was. Indeed, it was the only Communist office publicly operating in China at that time. Barefoot peasants jostled with smartly uniformed officers in the doorway.

The new secretary came to his work ablaze with enthusiasm, full of praise for what the Party had already achieved. 'Many things,' he once wrote, 'can be accomplished in a short time if people work hard. Take the achievements of the Chinese Communist Party from 1921 to 1924.' He was like Alyosha in *The Brothers Karamazov*, whom Dostoyevsky described as 'a young man of our own times, that is, honest by nature, demanding truth, seeking it, believing in it and, believing in it, demanding to serve it with all the strength of his soul, yearning for an immediate act of heroism.'

His ideological view remained less orthodox than that of some of his comrades, however. Soon after returning from France, he wrote,

Imperialism, which has appeared only during the past fifty years, is the extreme development, or ultimate product, of capitalism. . . . As world markets fall under . . . capitalistic monopoly and the living room of the world has been parcelled out, the capitalistic countries will inevitably develop into imperialism and come into conflict with each other. Furthermore, during the lulls between confrontations, the imperialistic countries will form alliances among themselves to exploit the oppressed nations. This is the pattern from which China, a semi-colonial nation jointly controlled by imperialistic powers, cannot expect to escape.

So far so good, but next Zhou borrowed the phraseology of the Confucian tradition in a way calculated to endear his message even to non-Marxists.

When the Great Way prevails, the world belongs to the public. . . . Since one hates to see goods wasted, one does not hoard them for oneself, and since one hates to keep his talents unused, one does not work just for oneself. . . . Thus no robbery or chaos need arise, and no door need be locked. This is the Society of Great Harmony.

Zhou tried firmly to link European Marxism with the utopian ideas of the Chinese thinkers who had influenced his own youth, Kang Youwei and Liang Qichao.

But Zhou was also working for the Guomindang in its marriage of revolutionary convenience with the Communists. It put him in charge of the training department of its national military commission. These were the golden years of cooperation between the Guomindang and the Communist Party, later to ravage China by their fratricidal strife. Soon after Zhou started work in Canton the SS *Varovsky* docked with thousands of Russian rifles and quantities of ammunition for Sun Yat-sen's use. Western neglect of the Guomindang created an opening for Zhou to join revolutionary work that was completely legitimate and not underground.

In the short term the two parties collaborated to consolidate their republican authority in Guangdong Province, while in the longer run they aimed together to annihilate the warlords of north China and restore China's unity.

Both parties in Canton had Russian and Comintern advisers, and the city was a hotbed of revolutionary fervour. Six months before Zhou's return, Sun Yat-sen had convoked the Guomindang's first national assembly and propounded its new Three People's Principles – nationalism, republicanism and equal landholdings – on the basis of which the Communists supported him. The Comintern had recommended the Chinese Communist Party, while taking care 'not to lose its own revolutionary identity', to 'work through the Guomindang, to overthrow the warlords before concentrating on a proletarian movement towards socialism.' The Guomindang had agreed to accept Communist members – like Zhou – on an individual basis.

In fact, Guomindang ranks were themselves divided over the propriety of the Communist alliance, and Zhou eagerly cultivated in Canton the left-leaning among the Guomindang, especially Liao Zhongkai, the Finance Minister and *éminence grise* of the more modernistic followers of Sun Yat-sen. Liao's son remembered how 'one day, a young man with keen eyes and fine, thick eyebrows, wearing a white linen suit', visited his father.

Zhou also became the confidant of General Vasili Blyukher, known in China as Galin, the senior Russian military adviser to the Guomindang. Edgar Snow went so far as to call Galin Zhou's 'real boss'. But Zhou was also guided in these intoxicating days of plotting revolution by another Russian whose personality was remarkably similar to his own, the famous Mikhail Borodin. After a colourful career which included expulsion from Russia by the Tsar, teaching in Chicago, imprisonment in Scotland and smuggling jewels for the Comintern, this 'swarthy and heavily moustached' Jewish Communist was now the USSR representative in China. To add to the galaxy, Ho Chi Minh was in Canton in 1924–25.

In June 1924, Sun formally opened the Military Academy at Huangpu, the new base for China's revolutionary army. The academy was run by Sun's military lieutenant, Chiang Kai-shek, and he, as we now know, was no lover of Communists. Zhou was nevertheless appointed deputy director of its political department, and his Guomindang superior was so busy with other jobs that he left Zhou to act with increasing frequency in his place. Zhou thus found himself in the curious position of being the political commissar of China's Sandhurst or West Point without himself having had a scrap of military training.

Many aspiring and able young men headed for the Huangpu Academy as an entrée into the modern army that would, it was hoped, make China a powerful nation. And many of them fell under Zhou's spell. Some, such as Lin Biao and Luo Ruiqing, later became renowned leaders of the People's Republic Red Army and constituted a kind of informal power base for Zhou's political career. More than eighty of the first batch of students joined the Communist Party. With their successors at Huangpu, they formed an important revolutionary corps for the Party in the civil war that was to follow.

Zhou worked hard among the students, setting up political organizations and launching a newspaper to disseminate Marxism. Every morning he would steam from Canton to Huangpu by river boat to give lectures there, which were always packed, and in the evening he returned for a busy round of political meetings and talks.

But from the beginning there was tension with the rightists in the academy, commanded by Chiang Kai-shek. The student Communist

73

Association was countered by a Guomindang society, and Zhou argued for several hours with a former student of his who had been put in charge of it. 'You've just returned from Russia yourself,' Zhou said. 'You fought with the revolutionary leaders in Russia and you know they are our friends. Who among all the powers gave us guns and ammunition? Only the Russians, and by the shipload too! You were there last year on 7 October when the Russian supplies were unloaded at Huangpu.

'The British sent arms to the Cantonese merchants to fight us. The French, Germans and Americans continue to extort our money, rights and interests through the northern warlords. . . . You of all people should know that the international situation requires us to collaborate with Russia. Otherwise our revolution will be doomed.'

But the young man was well informed, and countered with a question about the Russian Communists' refusal to restore to China ownership of the Manchurian railway. In this particular effort of persuasion, Zhou failed.

He fared no better with Zhou Fohai, a founder member of the Communist Party who now wished to resign. Told of this late one evening, Zhou reached the place where Fohai was staying just before midnight. Fohai handed over his letter of resignation.

'I hope you don't mind,' said Zhou Enlai, tearing the letter up without reading it. 'Comrade Biao has told me what you wanted to do, but I don't think it is necessary at all. May I sit down with you for a moment?' For four hours Zhou Enlai tried to persuade his host that he was making a mistake, while Fohai explained how he now believed that Sun Yat-sen's ideas about equal landholdings were enough to meet the aspirations of the Chinese people without borrowing from communism. But surely, Zhou Enlai argued, the Guomindang had inherited too many problems from the old society, and a more thoroughgoing approach was needed for the revolution.

Once again, Zhou's diplomacy was wasted, but he had to repeat this kind of nocturnal visitation frequently in order to keep his friends in the Party, win new converts, and mediate between extreme groups in dispute. Some of the comrades, not as subtle as Zhou, found the strain of working all the time at two levels, collaborating with the Guomindang on the surface but privately reserving their right to have a second revolution after the first, too difficult.

In 1925, Zhou was already outlining to his students, China's future military officers, some radical ideas about the role of the army. 'The army is a tool,' he asserted in a talk at the academy. 'The oppressors use this tool to oppress people, but the oppressed classes can also make use of this tool to oppress their oppressors and overthrow their power. . . . The West has a proletarian revolution, the East a national one. They can, and will join together to become a world revolution. . . . The army is the vanguard putting our theories into practice.' Then, in that same year, Zhou had the chance, of

74

which every revolutionary dreams, to put his ideas into practice, to commit his Dostoyevskian 'immediate act of heroism'. The Guomindang moved at last against the warlords both in southern and in northern China who were resisting the Nationalist revolution.

The first so-called Eastern Expedition provided Zhou with his opportun-ity. Guangdong could not become a secure base for the republicans until the provincial warlord, Chen Qiongming, whose centre of authority lay inland, was subdued. This was accomplished in 1925 by two military campaigns, the Eastern Expeditions. Two training regiments from the Huangpu Academy took part in the first, with Zhou as a senior political officer at the front. He was responsible for propaganda among the local peasants to convince them to support the campaign. The little army which Zhou helped to lead was only 3000 men strong, but by May it had driven the warlord's soldiers out of the province.

In this important campaign Zhou came through with blazing colours. His propaganda workers organized peasants to line the streets of the towns and villages along the way of the revolutionary army, beating drums and offering food and wine. By the time the soldiers reached the front their numbers had doubled. The peasants were shown how to set up militia groups, distribute weapons, use guerrilla tactics and stir up rebellion against the warlord.

The first showing of the politically motivated Huangpu cadets in action was a resounding success, and Zhou was the man of the hour. Madame Sun Yat-sen remembered afterwards how she had first met him at this time as 'a young but already seasoned and versatile leader, firm and clear-cut in his commitment to revolution.'

Chiang Kai-shek had to promote his Communist junior, and Zhou was put in charge of the academy's martial-law office as well as the political department of the National Revolutionary First Army.

But the disenchantment between the republican right and left heightened after Sun Yat-sen died in March 1925. The rightists in the Guomindang became even more active against the Communists. In May Zhou told a visiting Communist Party comrade that he was optimistic about the future of the Huangpu Academy. He even recommended that Chiang Kai-shek's status be raised after Sun's death, in order to develop the Huangpu cadets more quickly. Chiang was, after all, treating the Communist Party on an equal footing, and taking an apparently pro-Communist stance. Borodin took an equally optimistic view.

In the summer warlords stirred up trouble in Canton, helped by funds from the British in Hong Kong. Zhou was ordered to march his men back to the provincial capital, where he gained peasant and worker support, and saved the day for the revolutionary government.

But demonstrators were shot by soldiers, and there was a strike which went on for more than a year. Zhou egged the strikers on with anti-imperialist propaganda. He was so busy at this time with the two unwillingly allied parties, and travelling between different offices, that he had rooms permanently booked in both the Hsihao Hotel in Canton and the Chiyuan Hotel in Shantou (Swatow).

Zhou now formally took over the political department of the Huangpu Academy. With Soviet advisers in tow, political training had priority, and so Zhou was able to influence many cadets towards Marxism. Among his Communist colleagues on the academy's staff were Ye Jianying, who had joined the Communist Party at Zhou's persuasion against the advice of many of his friends, and became Zhou's closest confidant.

One of the Chinese Communist leaders working with the Guomindang in Canton was Mao Zedong, and a Chinese biographer of Zhou dates the friendship between the two men from this time. They certainly taught at the same peasant education centre, recently founded there by the Guomindang, but no details are known of their actual collaboration in Canton. Conceivably they first began to respect each other through occasional encounters here, but it is unlikely, for they were on such different wavelengths. In the field of military training, for instance, Mao clung to the peasant guerrilla tradition which he was later to use with such success, whereas Zhou lent himself to what a leading historian of the Chinese army calls 'a general effort to regularize, professionalize and routinize a specialist corps of Communist officers' – something which Mao, who considered such goals bourgeois, must have observed with distaste.

Another controversy among the Communists was how to deal with the peasants, who were now being repressed by Chiang Kai-shek and his landlord friends in defiance of Sun's third principle. One group of Marxists felt that the peasants should accept bourgeois leaders, and another believed they should be ignored in order to concentrate solely on the urban industrial workers, as European precepts required. Mao countered both these strategies with his own *Analysis of Chinese Social Classes*, in which he argued that the peasants were an intrinsically revolutionary class in their own right. Zhou remained aloof, it would seem, from these debates, and kept his faith in the potential of the Communist–Guomindang unity.

Zhou's comrades in Canton, finding that he apparently enjoyed Chiang Kai-shek's trust, used him as a channel for making proposals to the Generalissimo. But his key ally within the Guomindang, the liberal-minded Liao, was assassinated on 20 August 1925.

At this point that determined little firebrand, Deng Yingchao, re-entered Zhou's life – for the first time since they had made their farewells on Zhou's sailing to France more than four years earlier. She came down from Tianjin as a delegate to a Guomindang congress, shining even more brightly than

Zhou in this political two-timing which the Communists were called upon to carry out. But there was going to be no two-timing in their personal life. Within a matter of days, quietly and without fanfare, they were married. He was twenty-seven, she was twenty-one.

What was important to both of them was that, in an age when many Chinese still married by the arrangement of their parents, Zhou and Deng had chosen each other – voluntarily, enthusiastically and without dictation from others. They dispensed with formal ceremony, but repeated what progressive comrades called the 'Eight Mutuals' in the presence of friends – to love, to respect, to help, to encourage, to consult, to have consideration for, to have confidence in, and to have mutual understanding for each other. As things turned out, they were one of the few Communist couples to keep their vows. It was to prove one of the most successful, faithful and durable marriages in Chinese public life – a marriage of conviction, a life bond between two Communist revolutionaries from similar backgrounds and of similar mind.

Deng had been born in Henan province in 1903 or 1904 although her father was originally from Guangxi in the south. Like Zhou, she was described by a Chinese biographer as coming from 'a bankrupt scholar's family'. Her father had died suddenly, so Deng, again like Zhou, lacked a father figure and depended in adolescence on an elder of her own sex. An only child, she was brought up rather strictly by her mother, a well-educated and determined woman who gave private tuition in the houses of distinguished families – and who may later have influenced Zhou. The two went to live in the French Concession in Tianjin, where Deng's mother, on a tutor's salary, was able to give her daughter a decent education.

In 1915 Deng had joined the First Girls' Normal School in Tianjin, where she usually ranked about a quarter of the way down her class, being intelligent but not outstanding. Active, eloquent, outgoing, she had a straightforward and open character said to be characteristic of the people from China's central plains.

At the tender age of twelve she had joined the student movement opposing the Japanese demands on China. Within two years, she afterwards claimed, she had 'completed the whole eight years of work given by this school', but as a result of the fatigue brought on by this effort caught tuberculosis. 'The subjects which interested me most were geography, history, music, physics and the Chinese language. I did not like sewing.'

A year before she left school, she joined actively in the May Fourth Movement of 1919. Deng recalled that 'we organized boys and girls separately, because it was more difficult for them to act together. Ours was the Women's Patriotic Association and we cooperated with the boys, one of whom was Zhou Enlai.' But in later life Deng conceded that some of their

77

actions as students had been excessive. 'It was impossible to study in the excitement, and the anti-Japanese spirit was so high that we drove a Japanese teacher away and destroyed his textbooks – I'd now consider this action incorrect, for in order to fight the Japanese, we must study Japanese!'

In the autumn of 1919, the Awakening Society had been set up, and this was where the two future lovers first met. 'Zhou Enlai was then a handsome young man,' a Chinese writer explains, 'while Deng was a popular girl, active in almost all the propaganda and demonstration activities. Their frequent contacts in the Society led to a growing mutual affection.'

In October 1919 in Tianjin the couple was again at the forefront of protest. Deng confessed that they used every trick in the book to foment revolution. 'We exhorted people to save the country and overthrow those who were selling out China. We would cry as we talked, and the audience was moved by this.' Deng also headed a lecture group which travelled about distributing radical student newspapers, including the one edited by Zhou. Graduating in the summer of 1920, Deng joined the staff of a private school in Beijing. She could not go abroad to join Zhou because her mother lost her job and she had to support her.

It is said that it was Deng who first fell in love with Zhou. A German woman who later came to know them both well, Anna Wang, considered Deng plain in appearance so that Zhou 'obviously valued her inner qualities more than her looks' – but that was after the Long March, which aged her greatly.

'I hated the old-style marriage on the one hand,' Deng later reflected, 'and on the other I did not agree with the so-called free love ideas.' Young people had little understanding of these matters, she felt, and so it was difficult to form a successful modern marriage. 'I was not in love with anyone, Zhou Enlai and I were only good friends then. I was only seventeen.'

Her teaching job was demanding. She hoped for a job in a bank, with more pay, so she studied book-keeping at night. Once again, as at her Tianjin school three years earlier, her health collapsed under the strain, so that she had to give up her school work without qualifying for the bank job. After two and a half years in Beijing she went back to Tianjin, to teach in a primary school.

By 1923 she was already receptive to communism, having been, along with Zhou, one of the score of Tianjin student leaders who regularly gathered to discuss the Russian Revolution, and having been much influenced by Li Dazhao, the Communist theoretician in Beijing. China's young women had been so repressed in the past that Western political ideas had a special meaning for them. The brave new promises of freedom and equality may have signified more to Deng than to Zhou.

Deng shared Zhou's interest in both the Guomindang and the Communist

Party, having joined the Guomindang in 1924. She had already met Zhou's revered comrade, Cai Hesen, and in 1924 she joined the Young Communist League, going on to become a Communist Party member a few months afterwards. She was appointed Women's Secretary and when in 1925 the Guomindang selected delegates for its second party congress in Canton, Deng was chosen to represent her area in the north. It was this which enabled her to join the man she admired so much.

She used to tell friends later that they 'fell in love by post' while Zhou was in Paris. Through their correspondence, another writer asserts, love was established between them by the spring of 1922. Now in Canton they were together again.

Deng was described by a Western correspondent as having 'a keen political mind and an objective way of presenting her ideas, combined with good manners and extraordinary tact and graciousness.'

Zhou Enlai, by contrast, was 'by nature frank and open and likely to say exactly what he thinks. His wife makes up for this by being the more expert diplomat of the pair.' Zhou seized on the third syllable of her name and christened his bride 'Little Chao', which became her nickname.

Deng was a valuable assistant to Zhou in his work as well as being a good wife at home. The cadets from the Huangpu Academy and the Party leaders who used to visit the Zhous at their rented house in Canton found it simple, but furnished in good taste. Despite her taxing daily round, Deng never let her guests know that she was busy or tired, and she hospitably tried to make them feel at home. Yet the guests learned from the servants that Deng herself had chosen the furnishings and gave special instructions for making the meals, and they admired the way in which she could double up as both politician and helpmeet. 'After the marriage,' one biographer comments, 'Deng wore the trousers.'

Some would say that she never threw off her petty bourgeois habits – as a result of being spoiled by her mother. Like Zhou's polychrome self-portrait postcards and his smart getaway evenings in Sceaux, this kind of image was a cross which the Zhous would have to bear throughout their lives in the Chinese Communist movement. For all their intellectual convictions they had been born in the elite of the old China and still betrayed many of the mannerisms, values and living styles of that class.

7

Capture in Shanghai
1925–27

If Zhou and his bride enjoyed a honeymoon, it was a short one. Within a few weeks he was back at the front again, playing an even more important role in the second Eastern Expedition against the warlord, Chen Qiongming, starting in October 1925.

Huangpu Academy students made up the nucleus of the First Army, of which Zhou was the political leader. Under his guidance, as before, intense political propaganda was conducted to bring the peasants round to the revolutionary side. The army was given strict instructions not to pressgang recruits or occupy private houses. As a result of Zhou's influence it was said that the political work in four of the army's five divisions was headed by Communists.

Zhou was promoted to be special commissioner in charge of the East River district around Shantou, one of the key cities to be captured in the campaign. 'Now wearing a smart Guomindang army uniform,' a Chinese biographer comments, 'complete with a well-polished Sam Browne belt, Zhou, at twenty-seven, was the political head of Chiang's armed forces and chief administrator of the largest area that had come under Guomindang control.' During the expedition Zhou built up a First Independent Regiment around a nucleus of Communists, and thus boasted for the first time a crack force effectively under his command. The commissionaires at his hotels in Canton and Shantou now saluted him, and even his own Communist Party comrades treated him with more respect. One complained that Zhou's new job in Shantou made him 'so busy that he could not come to Canton', where he was needed to settle disputes with the Guomindang rightists.

These latter had caught Zhou's secretary sending a secret report to the Communist headquarters on the progress of Communist influence in the army. Furious, they had tied the unfortunate man up with rope and bundled him off to Chiang Kai-shek's office for punishment.

Zhou dashed to the scene and spent an anxious hour vouching for his secretary's loyalty. The Communist Party might appear overenthusiastic, but it wanted only the success of the revolution. Surely the priority must be to avoid diversions within the revolutionary ranks when revolt was brewing among various provincial armies? Chiang Kai-shek was sufficiently disarmed to allow Zhou to save his secretary by transferring him to a different division. And when he next spoke to his assembled officers, Chiang ordered the two rival groups on left and right to stand up and salute each other.

Zhou won his critics over with a masterly speech. 'Once I was a Communist Party member myself,' he said, 'but there was neither any committee meeting for me to attend nor any Party dues to pay and I am still here. The Communist Party did not liquidate me.' Laughter eased the tension. Later Zhou told the Comintern representative that he should threaten the Guomindang right wing with the withdrawal of Russian aid if it insisted on acting as a separate rightist association.

When the Guomindang held its congress at the beginning of 1926 the left-wing forces appeared to prevail. Zhou's new wife, Deng Yingchao, was a delegate and Central Committee member, working with Madame Sun Yat-sen.

Zhou's role in the Communist leaders' debate about their tactics at this congress is not very clear. One report has him insisting that Communists should retain their independence of the Guomindang, against Mao's less popular but hard-headed view that the Guomindang should for the time being take the lead in the Chinese revolution. Certainly Mao was present and wrote many articles attacking the Guomindang's right wing. He and Zhou had to judge whether there was enough life left in the Guomindang radical wing to make it worthwhile collaborating.

All these questions were answered when Chiang Kai-shek suddenly showed his hand against the left wing in the so-called *Zhongshan* gunboat incident. The acting commander of the republican navy, whose superior (a Russian) was on leave, received a forged order in March to sail to Huangpu in his gunboat, the *Zhongshan*. When Chiang discovered the unauthorized move he suspected treason and threw the commander and many others in goal, stripped the Russian advisers and Communist commissars of their posts, and declared martial law. 'He also placed me,' Zhou later recalled, 'under house arrest for a day.'

Communist comrades were shaken by Chiang's growing confidence and incipient fascism, but even more disturbed by the incompetence of their own side. 'I know every detail of the 20 March incident,' Zhou afterwards claimed, but he never allowed his analysis to become known, and did not explain or answer any of the charges which his comrades brought against him. As the most important Communist in Huangpu he could hardly shrug off responsibility for an incident in which his own man, the naval commander, had been duped. Zhou's prestige fell, and his embarrassment was plain.

The extent of his power well demonstrated and his point made, Chiang Kai-shek now apologized to the Russian advisers and began to release the Communists, including Zhou. The right wing was going to be in charge, with Chiang using what Zhou later described as 'the treacherous, ruthless methods of a gangster'.

Zhou and the Russian advisers bearded Chiang Kai-shek in his office to demand an explanation. But Zhou's political instincts did not allow him to show any change of heart when face to face with his opponent, and he put on such a pleasant and conciliatory manner that Chiang was astonished.

All the same, Chiang was unrepentant, and now proposed that all Communists be expelled from the Guomindang. On 11 April he dismissed Zhou from his directorship of the First Army political department, and later from his special assignment in Shantou.

When Borodin called the Communist leaders together on 29 April for a post mortem, Zhou reportedly stayed silent throughout. The others apparently argued that in the absence of a Chinese victim, the blame would inevitably fall on Borodin, whose work in China would be hindered – with all that meant for the smooth flow of Russian aid. Zhou was the obvious scapegoat to take the blame and thereby minimize the damage to the Communist cause as a whole. In this way he could appear to those in the know in a heroic light.

But the Communists could not agree on their next move. The Shanghai group, supported by one Comintern representative, were ready to make peace with Chiang and go on fighting the revolution under his cloak. But the more radical Guangdong Communists, backed by Borodin himself, were sickened by Chiang's behaviour and wanted to go it alone. Zhou sat on the fence.

The *Zhongshan* incident was the first open break between Chiang Kai-shek and his Communist allies. But preparations were afoot for the long-awaited Northern Expedition, from which both sides in the Chinese revolution hoped to gain. Without defeating the powerful northern warlords, no republican government in the south, whether left-wing or right-wing, could retain credibility. It was for this reason that Zhou, among others, still tried to salvage something from the *Zhongshan* incident. At all costs, the Communists must be on the Northern Expedition.

Meanwhile he continued his lectures on military affairs, including one on 'The Military Movement and the Peasant Movement', given at the Peasant Movement Training Institute after Mao took over its direction in the spring of 1926.

If the Communists needed Chiang Kai-shek to take them to the north,

Chiang in his turn needed Russian arms for the success of the expedition, so the two parties were still uncomfortably bound together. Chiang allowed Zhou to reinstate many of the purged Communists at Huangpu, his generosity doubtless prompted by his appreciation of Zhou's efforts to patch up the alliance. He not only allowed Zhou to give formal training to the purged Communists, but even gave the Communists an equal opportunity with the Guomindang to nominate commissar candidates for the Northern Expedition. Zhou contested, but there was a deadlock in the voting, broken only when he threw his support to a leftist Guomindang leader – who, after winning, allowed Zhou to recommend candidates for the staff, so that once again it was dominated by the Communist Party.

This was an extremely uncomfortable period for Zhou, having to work day by day with people on both sides who had lost their respect for him. It was a situation, a comrade later recalled, which 'tested Zhou's endurance for the first time and also revealed his genius at handling situations. He never explained or answered questions about what had happened, and on the basis of our decisions, he carried out his training duties at Huangpu nonchalantly and showed even greater respect for Chiang Kai-shek.'

In July 1926 the uneasy Chinese allies with their Russian advisers launched the Northern Expedition to bring Shanghai and Beijing into the republican fold. Zhou was a political officer in the First Army Corps, moving along the coast and arming peasants and workers to support the revolutionary soldiers.

There were personal setbacks in the family. His brother Enzhu was wounded in a battle in September. And it was about this time that Zhou's wife, carrying their first child – a girl – suffered a miscarriage in Canton. It proved to be their last chance to bring a child into the world. In marrying each other they married the Chinese revolution, with all its exacting demands, and their children would be that next generation of China – including some they adopted – whose frontiers of freedom and dignity would be appreciably enlarged by their sacrifice.

At the very end of 1926 the Comintern produced its *Theses on the China Problem*, calling on the Chinese Communists to stay inside the Guomindang and support its left wing against the right. Zhou echoed the Moscow message by telling his comrades to join Chiang Kai-shek's army, strengthen it, fight hard in it, 'but', in a parenthetical submission to the political realities of the day, 'do not carry on independent work there'.

It was time, according to one view, for the Chinese Communists to take a lead in Shanghai, which had the biggest concentration of workers in all China and was now in the line of march of the republican forces of the Northern Expedition. A premature proletarian revolt had fizzled out there in October, but then Zhou arrived to prepare the city from within for its capture by the republican allies. From his mother-in-law's flat at 29 rue Lafayette, in the 'safe' French Concession, he orchestrated, together with comrades from Paris days, the political indoctrination of trade-union leaders and the smuggling of arms for their use.

The Shanghai workers rose a second time at the end of February 1927, when more than a third of a million workers went on strike. The local warlord sent broadswordsmen in to behead people, and this was a signal for an armed uprising masterminded by Zhou and his friends. They had unwisely counted on Chiang Kai-shek's ordering his Northern Expeditionary forces to advance in time to protect the Shanghai workers from the warlords, but Chiang failed to meet this expectation. In any case the workers were not adequately trained for armed seizure of the city, and the uprising collapsed.

Greatly upset, Zhou set about strengthening his political control to prepare for a third rising. He had no formal military training, little acquaintance with the working class, and no insurrectionary manuals or Soviet advisers to point the way. These armed risings were purely the outcome of his own resourcefulness. Zhou still underestimated Chiang's antagonism. In his own mind he may have attributed failure to bad luck or weak communications with Chiang. He wasted no time in recriminations, however, and busied himself with the third and last Shanghai uprising, retraining his workers in a school in the French Concession and supervising frenzied undercover preparations to infiltrate the government's militia and seize more weapons.

Some have held that the character called Kyo Gisors in André Malraux's novel *Man's Fate*, the most famous Western novel about the Shanghai revolution, was based upon Zhou. Kyo is half-Japanese, however, and dies in captivity, and there are other discrepancies. The book may convey some of the atmosphere of these events, but Zhou's own comment on it, later, was that 'things happened quite otherwise'.

Deng was now with him. A mutual friend described her as 'like a snake wrapped around him'. Yet their delight in one another's company was plain for all to see. A comrade's wife once called round for Zhou, to be told by Deng's mother, with some giggles and pointing, 'They're not up yet.' Hearing them call, the lady went into the bedroom to find the couple still in bed behind a white mosquito net, with a newspaper and empty cigarette tin (serving as a spittoon) at one corner of the bed. But Deng could certainly be jealous of her better-looking husband. Once he bought her a particularly beautiful scarf which she adored. Soon afterwards they paid a condolence visit to the attractive young widow of a martyred comrade, and the lady wore an even prettier scarf.

'Where did you get that?' Deng asked.

'Why, Enlai gave it to me.'

Deng gave her husband a look. Over lunch she was very quiet, but afterwards they had a flaming row. She grabbed him and scratched his cheek so that it bled, and then they both burst into tears and separately ran out into the street.

Zhou's headquarters this time was the Shanghai Commercial Press. An 'iron band' of 300 sharpshooters were trained with Mausers smuggled into the city. The left-wing Guomindang government at Wuhan was sending $30,000 a month, to be dispensed by Zhou and his only Communist superior in Shanghai, Gu Shunzhang. Gu was a Russian-trained mechanic, magician and secret-society figure, notorious for his ability to strangle an opponent with bare hands without leaving any telltale marks (he was later to become a millstone around Zhou's neck). They made their move on 21 March with a general strike closing down Shanghai's industries. Some 5000 armed workers seized first the police stations and then the garrison itself.

Zhou led 200 men to take the post office, police headquarters, arsenal and railway station. Out of the alleys and 'rotten holes' of Zhabei, in the words of a foreign correspondent's dispatch, Zhou's 'ragamuffin army of half a million Chinese workers' streamed to victory. The warlord soldiers withdrew and Zhou proclaimed a 'citizen's government'. 'Within two days,' he commented, 'we won everything but the foreign concessions.'

For three weeks the labour unions controlled Shanghai while Zhou nervously waited for Chiang Kai-shek's army to clinch the victory. The Red Flag flew over the city, but it was vulnerable to recapture without the Guomindang armies.

There was now some politicking to increase the pressure on Chiang Kai-shek. On 4 April Zhou went to the customs building in Shanghai to see Wang Jingwei, star of the Guomindang's left wing and chairman of the Guomindang government at that time, who had just returned from France. It was Zhou's mission to use Wang in order to outflank Chiang Kai-shek. He brought a draft joint declaration from Chen Duxiu, the Communist Party leader, for Wang to sign. This joint declaration by the Communists and Guomindang reaffirmed their alliance and denied the two contradictory rumours – one that the Communists were going to set up a workers' government to overthrow the Guomindang, and another that the Guomindang was going to declare war on the Communists and suppress the trade unions.

But as Zhou knew, he was really a green amateur in these matters. About the 1927 Shanghai uprising he commented, thirty years later:

I was responsible for leading the armed revolt, but I lacked experience and was weak in understanding political dynamics. I am an intellectual with a feudalistic family background. I had had little contact with the peasant-worker masses because I had taken no part in the economic process of production. My revolutionary career started abroad, with very limited knowledge about it obtained from books only.

At four o'clock in the morning of 12 April Chiang Kai-shek tardily left his tent to demonstrate who did have the experience and the power. His troops, armed with machine guns, entered Shanghai and fanned out through the working-class quarters. The Communist pickets were caught by surprise. The Guomindang had made a deal with the secret societies, the underworld gangs which were in many respects the real rulers of Chinese Shanghai, and they now gladly struck down the trade-union leaders. By noon the workers' militia was in unceremonious flight, pursued by machine-gun fire. Chiang wanted to wipe out once and and for all the Communist leaders who threatened his own position. He decreed a bloody reprisal in which 5000 Communists were killed. 'Heads rolled in ditches,' an eyewitness said, 'like ripe plums and the weary executioners wielded their swords with the monotonous rhythm of *punka wallahs*.'

Chiang promised $200,000 to the man who captured or killed Zhou Enlai, who was in the Commercial Press building at the time of the attack. He escaped minutes before a Guomindang search party reached the place. One by one the Communist leaders were arrested and executed, often after torture as a result of which they betrayed their comrades. After Zhou's death in 1976, the leftist Yao Wenyuan, one of the 'Gang of Four', alleged that even Zhou had cooperated with the Guomindang in killing Communist comrades during the Shanghai debacle, but no evidence is available for this. Chiang did not need his help at this point to destroy the cream of the proletarian wing of the Chinese Communist leadership. Chen Duxiu criticized Zhou afterwards for not persuading the workers to disarm, and thus giving Chiang's troops an excuse to massacre them. But Zhou replied that the Communists, far from prematurely laying down their arms, should have stepped up their military role in order to assert their independence as a party.

In the calm of the eventual Communist victory in the 1950s, Zhou gave this reasoned explanation of the Shanghai disaster:

Our leadership was inexperienced, and we did not know either how to exploit our success or the tactics of retreat. The Shanghai workers and the peasants of the neighbouring countryside were ready, but we did not have the machinery of cooperation ready. So Chiang was able to crush us.

There was no mercy in the white terror that reigned in Shanghai after the Guomindang came, no trials, no reprieves. Workers suspected of sympathizing with the Communists were shot out of hand, and many of them were thrown into the furnaces of railway engines. But the Communist leadership shillyshallied. Just as Zhou had a few days earlier been parleying with Wang Jingwei in the hope of playing him off against Chiang, so he was now vainly instructed to exploit his old friendships from the Huangpu Academy in order to make contacts with Guomindang officers and secure the release of the arrested workers.

Escape was almost impossible, and when it came to Zhou's turn for arrest he must have assumed that the best he could hope for was a speedy execution. His luck held out, however. It has been said that General Bai Chongxi, that honourable soldier of the old school who commanded the Guomindang force and had now to order Zhou's execution, felt such a debt of gratitude for Zhou's having once saved his brother's life that he pretended not to recognize him when he was arrested. Another tradition has it that the divisional commander's brother, who had been Zhou's student at Huangpu, helped Zhou to escape. A third story says that Zhou, after his death sentence, was rescued by 'somebody who guaranteed his good conduct'. There is a fourth report that after his arrest Zhou was left with other captives in the Guildhouse and succeeded in escaping. Possibly all these stories are true.

At any rate, Zhou did escape – and left Shanghai. He 'shaved his bushy eyebrows off, grew a beard and pushed pads in his sallow cheeks', according to one account, and then boldly applied for a Guomindang passport. Still bearing a pricetag on his head, now said to be $80,000, and dodging the Guomindang police who had distributed his photograph at the railway stations, the disguised Zhou escaped by train to join the other Communist leaders at Wuhan.

In a telling gesture, he stayed at Wuhan in the house of a Guomindang official, an old friend. But the honeymoon was over, not only between the Guomindang and the Communists but also between the left and right within the Guomindang ranks. Chiang Kai-shek's brutal attack in Shanghai was too much for his liberal wing to swallow. He was left controlling a right-wing group with the better army, based in Nanjing, while Wang Jingwei headed a weak left wing at Wuhan. In the end the battle for China was waged between the two extremes on this complex spectrum – the Guomindang right wing and the Communist left wing – and meanwhile the middle ground, where cautious Communists and liberal Nationalists pretended to meet, slowly slipped away. Zhou dropped his Guomindang membership and now devoted his full attention to the Communists. He had shown bravery under battle conditions, and if he had also been naive about Chiang Kai-shek's plans, he was not alone in the Party on that score.

8

The Nanchang Test
1927

Shanghai, which doubled as lively playground of the bourgeoisie and cradle of the industrial workers' movement and Communist Party, had been swept almost effortlessly into the camp of reaction. How had Chiang Kai-shek been able to win such a resounding victory in China's proletarian heartland? The Communist leaders assembled in Wuhan at the end of 1927 to analyse the reasons for defeat.

Chen Duxiu, the senior leader, wanted the Party to concentrate on political work, given the Guomindang's military superiority. Others preferred to take up the military challenge that Chiang had laid down. The dreamy poet, Qu Qiubai, the prickly peasant Mao Zedong and others all put in their recipes for the future. Where did Zhou stand?

Here at the Fifth Party Congress Zhou first used the tactics for which he was to become famous in Party in-fighting. He sympathized with the arguments of the critics, Qu and Mao, but did not actually oppose Chen Duxiu himself, remaining neutral in the struggle for succession. In reward he was made Secretary-General, a post normally ranking second in the hierarchy. Characteristically, he handed it over to his Paris friend, Cai Hesen, while he himself went full time into the Party's military policies – a move which in itself was a vote of non-confidence in Chen's leadership. One thing Zhou did not spurn was a seat on the Politburo, and he continued to serve continuously on that highest policy-making body for the next forty-nine years, right up to his death, a record that none of his colleagues could match. For half a century Zhou was never outside the Communist inner cabinet, amassing a moral authority that no one else, not even Mao, could challenge.

The Communists should at all costs be decisive, Zhou now declared, and press Chiang Kai-shek hard, fighting instead of retreating, and making use of their left-wing Guomindang allies. Not every comrade agreed. A few days later, after an incident at Changsha, the capital of Hunan Province, a left-wing Guomindang commander ordered a hundred Communists to be killed; his Communist commissar denounced him as a butcher, and the fragile alliance between the two parties trembled in the balance. When Zhou saw the posters that the commissar, Liu Ning, was putting up, he upbraided him. 'Are we somebody's concubine?' Liu protested. 'Are we to accept their spitting and beating without any right to speak up in protest?'

'Comrade Liu,' Zhou explained, 'for the sake of our revolution we must be very patient. For the sake of our revolution we can play the role of a concubine, even of a prostitute, if need be.' Zhou consistently argued that they would do better to swallow their pride. 'Withdrawal from the Guomindang,' he said, 'might facilitate the workers' and farmers' movements, but would hinder military progress.'

While the Chinese Communists thus argued to and fro, Stalin and the Indian Comintern representative, M. N. Roy, between them precipitated the final split. The Russian leader sent a telegram on 1 June telling the Chinese Party to go on the offensive by implementing land reform and arming Party members, workers and farmers. For reasons that are still obscure, Roy tactlessly showed this cable to Wang Jingwei, and the shocked left-wing Guomindang promptly broke with the Communists.

The chagrined Communists did not know where to turn. Without the shelter of the left-wing Guomindang they had no military power at all and were vulnerable to the likes of Chiang Kai-shek whenever they made any political move. Borodin, the Russian Comintern adviser they most respected, suggested that they voluntarily surrender their arms to the left-wing Guomindang government as a way of reassuring their former allies that they were not going to follow Stalin's advice and revolt. But many of the Chinese comrades were less trusting. Zhou cut through the middle of this argument by remarking that the 1000 rifles of the Wuhan workers' picket corps were all old weapons and not worth worrying about, so why not give them up? This is what was done, but it meant, of course, that the workers were then at the mercy of the left-wing Guomindang government.

This action of surrendering the picket rifles in Wuhan, along with Zhou's part in it, remained controversial for many years afterwards. The Comintern later criticized the Chinese Party for its 'shameful opportunism' at this moment, but as Trotsky trenchantly observed, 'The Chinese revolution cannot be stuffed into a bottle and sealed from above with a signet.'

Chen Duxiu was dislodged in July as relations worsened with the Guomindang, and the powerful Borodin named a provisional five-man team to run the Party's affairs instead. This included Zhou as well as his old collaborator Li Lisan, and Zhang Guotao, whose career was to intertwine with Zhou's over the next decade. Zhang Guotao came from a Hakka

89

landlord family, and as one of the founders of the Communist Party affected a certain superiority. Many of the Communists prudently moved to safer localities south of the Yangzi River, particularly to Nanchang, capital of Jiangxi Province, where Guomindang power was weak. As the summer reached its height and the left-wing Guomindang began to arrest Communists, only Zhou Enlai and Zhang Guotao were left in charge at the Wuhan headquarters. A comrade wrote this pen portrait of Zhou's work style at this moment:

Zhou Enlai was a tireless worker who did not talk much. He dealt very calmly with complex affairs, both day and night. He took on both work and blame, disregarding criticism. He was responsible for handling most of the work concerned with dispersing comrades. This period also marked the beginning of his being treated with respect by comrades in general, and the growth in importance of his status. In some circles Zhou was being called 'man of iron'.

Borodin was about to return to Russia, and his successor had not yet arrived in Wuhan. During this interregnum, proposals for armed revolt were coming in from Communist leaders in different parts of central and southeastern China, and everything depended on a clear lead from the Politburo in Wuhan. But the left-wing Guomindang was now after Zhou, and once again he had to turn to foreigners for help against his own compatriots. He found sanctuary in the house of the unworldly Bishop Roots in the British Concession in Wuhan, where the Guomindang police could not go. Zhou admitted later that the bishop had saved his life.

By a combination of political indoctrination within the Guomindang armies and a programme of recruiting men directly from the countryside, the Communists could now claim the loyalty of forces numbering perhaps 10,000 – though badly trained and poorly armed. The Communist Party itself had grown in the seven years since its foundation to over 50,000 members, and at this point the spark of revolution seemed to gleam in everybody's eyes. Li Lisan wrote from Nanchang, where the largest number of Red troops had assembled, urging an insurrection to unite workers and peasants not only in Jiangxi but in neighbouring provinces as well.

Zhou jumped at his old comrade-in-arms' proposal but enlarged the target to include the establishment of a new revolutionary government farther south in Guangdong Province (still the psychological centre of the republican movement), in the area of the East River which washes into the ocean at Hong Kong. Zhou had worked there before in the Guomindang's Eastern Expedition two years earlier, and was familiar with the conditions. There were fewer Guomindang forces, the peasant movement was more effective, and supplies from Russia could be cleared conveniently through the nearby port of Shantou on the edge of Guangdong Province. He believed that Russian supplies would be a vital factor in the fight and lobbied strenuously with the Comintern to ensure that they materialized.

Zhou departed for Nanchang on 20 July to organize a front-line committee, not even telling his wife about the plan for an uprising. Just before he left, Zhang Guotao briefed him on the cautious views of the new Comintern representative. Pressed to explain the attitude of the other Russian advisers, Zhou conceded that they were not too keen on the Nanchang uprising plan either.

'So then!' said Zhang Guotao, implying that discretion might be the better part of valour.

'After I get there,' Zhou promised, 'I'll take another look at the situation.' But it looked as if his mind was already made up. There is a strong sense of destiny about Zhou Enlai's progress on the riverboat to Nanchang during those tense days of high summer in 1927. He acted with uncommon dispatch and decisiveness. At one point, coming upon a group of Communist leaders under Li Lisan still arguing about the aims of the uprising, he put a quick end to their deadlock over whether to confiscate the land of large landlords by approving the idea. This was the period when Edgar Snow referred to him as 'the insurrectionist', and there is something magisterial about his judgements and appearances.

He reached Nanchang a few days later in his grey suit, clutching his black briefcase. He stayed incognito at the Jiangxi Hotel. This is where his Berlin understanding with the former opium addict Zhu De paid off. Zhu was in the Communist Party, but had not given up his Guomindang membership or revealed his new colours to his Guomindang superiors. He now served as head of public security and deputy military commander of the left-wing Guomindang forces, in charge of Nanchang; he was brilliantly placed to help his comrades. Zhou immediately contacted him to plan the uprising. Nearby were the forces of Ye Ting and He Long, two other Guomindang commanders friendly to the Communists, as well as a part of the famous 'Ironsides' Fourth Army under General Zhang Fakui, many of whose officers had been trained by Zhou at Huangpu and were sympathetic to the Communists.

The difficult problem was how to treat General Zhang himself, who, while not committed to the anti-Communist campaigns of some Guomindang leaders, had no particular liking for the Communists either. Zhou wanted to go ahead quickly with the uprising while the momentum was up, even at the risk of a clash with General Zhang Fakui, while the Comintern advisers wanted the Chinese comrades to rise in concert with General Zhang to ensure a much larger troop force, and then to break with him if necessary after reaching the Guangdong base area.

But this would have meant spending more time on the delicate – perhaps, in Zhou's estimation, impossible – mission of enticing General Zhang away from his orders.

Zhou, sitting with the by now very excited young Chinese Communist leaders at the Jiangxi Hotel in Nanchang, chose not to wait. The Chinese comrades, with Zhou at their head, for once made a major decision on their own without waiting for Moscow's approval. Would luck smile on them at last?

Having finalized the plan of campaign with his comrades, Zhou's next move was to call on He Long at the Twentieth Army headquarters to show him the whole blueprint. The gamble was a good one. General He, a compassionate man of patriotic vision, responded to Zhou's trust. He agreed to do what was asked, and Zhou appointed him on the spot as the officer in command of the uprising, now timed for 30 July.

All seemed well. But in the middle of the night He Long telephoned Zhou to say that a junior officer had betrayed the plan to the Guomindang command in Wuhan, which was sending troops to suppress the Communists in the area. Undeterred, Zhou ordered that the timetable be advanced by a few hours.

Now came trouble from another quarter. Zhou's colleague Zhang Guotao arrived from Wuhan waving one of those interfering, ill-informed telegrams from Stalin that the Chinese Communists had so learned to fear. It called for a postponement of the uprising.

Zhou, in Nelsonian mood, was ready to disobey the great Russian dictator. 'We must take prompt action,' he insisted. 'The uprising must not be put off, let alone given up altogether.' Zhang Guotao and Ye Ting still preferred to wait until General Zhang Fakui was won over, but the others were hot to get on with the uprising. Zhou gave every imaginable reason why they should go ahead with the plan: some units had already started moving and would be trapped whatever the countermand; if General Zhang disappointed them, the Red officers in his army would do what was necessary.

'This is not in agreement with what the leaders of the Communist Party sent me here for,' he said angrily of the postponement plan. 'I shall have to resign my position . . . if we do not act now.' Zhang Guotao saw this threat as 'the culmination of that tense meeting'. Most of the comrades, having mounted the tiger, were keen to ride it. Zhou was like a petulant schoolboy whose carefully planned treat has been jeopardized by obstructive adults.

It does look as if Zhou, still stinging from the Shanghai betrayal and the ineptitude of Roy, had been determined on this military operation from the very beginning, from the moment he left Wuhan – and that he subordinated all other considerations to bullying and cajoling his comrades into going through with it. In that sense he may be regarded as the architect of the operation. Zhang Guotao, the only participant who has left a detailed memoir of this exciting episode, up to this point praises Zhou's handling of affairs. But henceforth he becomes critical.

Zhou was capable of guiding political affairs, but did not want to. He did not talk much about politics and seldom called a committee meeting. When a meeting was convened important policies were never discussed.

Zhou concentrated his attention on military affairs. Perhaps he was of the opinion that military victory came first in importance, because it would enable rebel forces to get a foothold in the East River area of Guangdong. . . . Most of the important figures in the Communist Party including Li Lisan were of the same opinion, emphasizing the need for uprising and regarding anyone who doubted or opposed as unreliable or irresolute. Such disregard was the basis for adventurism.

But Zhang Guotao slept on it, and went back to the front committee next morning to concede to his 'adventurist' comrades after a few more hours of argument. They resolved to fight at two o'clock that night. But before the day was out, their hand was forced again. News came that General Zhang Fakui was on his way to see the Communists. This sharpened everybody's mind, and at one o'clock in the morning of 1 August the fateful signal was given.

Zhou directed the fighting from a bullet-scarred school hall near the Catholic church in Songpo Lane, surrounded by colleagues who had been fellow-students in Europe – Chen Yi, Ye Jianying, Nie Rongzhen – as well as the military heroes Zhu De, He Long and Liu Bocheng. There is a famous oil painting of them bunched on the porch of their headquarters, with Zhou towering taller than life over the other leaders, apparently giving the men their final orders. There is no doubt whom the official painters of the 1950s regarded as the man in charge at Nanchang.

The fighting in the city itself turned out to be minimal, and calm returned to the city before dawn. Even now Zhou insisted on keeping the channels of the Guomindang alliance formally open. His soldiers kept their Guomindang insignia, and when a revolutionary committee was appointed to rule the city it was under a Guomindang banner (although the Guomindang dignitaries named did not attend).

Liu Ning, the man who had once asked Zhou whether the Communist Party had to behave like the Guomindang's 'concubine', was appointed as head of propaganda for the uprising. He was supposed to draft a statement saying that the Guomindang revolutionary committee in Nanchang was the orthodox branch of the Guomindang and the rightful heir to Dr Sun Yat-sen.

'The people here,' he asked belligerently, 'are all Communists. How can we claim to be the successor of the Guomindang?'

'Aren't we also members,' replied Zhou after a short pause, 'of the Guomindang?' He treasured whatever scraps of legitimacy and formal continuity could be saved from a revolution. But he told Liu to draft a socialist land-reform policy confiscating large holdings.

This should have been Zhou's greatest hour. If it had not been for his ideology, he could by now, not yet thirty, have been well on the way to becoming a successful warlord or Guomindang bigwig. He had proved that he could handle people and organize military actions efficiently. He had even defied Stalin, which few Chinese had dared to do. If Zhou had been lucky in the outcome of the Nanchang uprising, his position as supreme leader in the Communist Party of China would have been assured.

But another act of betrayal snatched victory from his hands. Zhang Guotao recalls how General Cai Tingkai, commanding the 10th Division, had 'looked uneasy' when he came to the headquarters to discuss military plans just before the signal went up. Some officers felt that he was irresolute, but Zhou decided that 'Cai should not be distrusted' and made him commander-in-chief of the left wing of the revolutionary armies – even telling Communists in the 10th Division unreservedly to obey him.

Once on the field of battle, however, Cai took his 10th Division over to the enemy side. Zhou reported to his comrades:

Pretending that he wanted to address the officers, Cai assembled them and arrested and killed . . . the commander of the 30th regiment and about thirty Communist Party members. Only one of our comrades escaped and returned safely, while several dozen others are missing. Therefore our assets in the 10th Division have been completely destroyed. It was my fault, and I should take all the blame.

Zhang Guotao rubbed salt in the wound, commenting that 'it was only natural for Zhou to have a guilty conscience because he had failed to take preventive measures.' Nevertheless, according to his own account, he did not take advantage of Zhou's humiliation at the time. It was, he told Zhou, 'an irreplaceable loss. . . . We were too careless in handling this affair, and we should use it as a lesson. This incident, if it becomes known, will affect our morale: we'd better keep it secret. Don't be dejected at such a critical moment, and don't say you are to blame and wish to resign. You must face it, no matter what's happened.' Zhou agreed to make the best of it.

General Zhang Fakui, on whose partial support the Communists had laid so much store, now turned on them, forcing them to evacuate Nanchang after only three days' occupation. Pressed by superior forces, the Communists had to split, and they did so along lines that were to affect their politics even decades later – Zhu De, Chen Yi and Lin Biao marching southwest through Jiangxi and Hunan, eventually to join Mao Zedong in his mountain fastness of Jinggangshan. Zhou and Ye Ting, by contrast, struck directly southwards to the coast, to the area around Shantou which Zhou knew of old. Not only did they have to battle with Guomindang units there, but the farmers denied them food and water. The Communists suffered huge losses from disease, desertion, mutiny and enemy action.

Why had it all gone wrong? Zhou must have pondered this endlessly on the dispiriting march to the sea. For one thing, the uprising had come too late to capitalize on the wave of indignation that had flowed across China when Chiang Kai-shek massacred the Communists in Shanghai three months earlier. It also came just after the Wuhan government had ended its collaboration with the Communists, so that full use could not be made of that alliance. The Kremlin must take some of the blame, its instructions being confusing and unhelpful. Little effort had been made by the Communists to communicate the goals of the revolt to the peasants or even to their own army. Trotsky himself reproached Zhou on this particular score. He wrote:

A characterization of the Party attitude towards the army was given by Comrade Zhou Enlai in his report. He said to the Party members: 'Go into this national revolutionary army, strengthen it, raise its fighting ability but do not carry on any independent work there.'. . . Our comrades who were political advisers occupied themselves exclusively with military and political work for the Guomindang.

Zhou's comrades could not be said to form an inspiring team. The man heading the revolutionary committee was not a good politician and nobody liked him. Zhou concentrated on the military problems, believing that politics was idle talk without military victory, and Li Lisan agreed. Zhang Guotao had lost his colleagues' confidence. The disagreements within this group seemed larger than the common goals.

And yet there was also cause for satisfaction. The Party in a sense came of age at Nanchang, and 1 August was thereafter observed by China's Communists as the birthday of the Red Army. Zhou was hailed as its founder, and given credit for finally leading the Party out of its parasitic existence within the Guomindang to independence. When the Central Committee met on 7 August, Zhou was belatedly taken to task, in his absence, for the disarming of the labour pickets in Wuhan, an affair that still rankled among his comrades, but he nevertheless retained his Politburo seat.

Zhou's routed forces reached the port of Shantou on 24 September, almost two months after the brave hopes of the Nanchang uprising. Here Zhou received an order from Party headquarters in Shanghai to abandon the city and merge with local peasants to create a new rural base area. Even now he would not give in, insisting on going to the front to take command in one more battle, which was lost. Retreating before Guomindang soldiers and sailors towards Hong Kong, Zhou became depressed and feverish. At a conference at Lusha, Zhou and He Long, whom he had just recommended for Party membership as a reward for his loyalty, decided to send the few remaining armed troops to the nearest Communist base area while Zhou and He took refuge in Hong Kong. Then he had to declare the Communist–Guomindang alliance finally over.

'Why haven't you left, gentlemen?' Zhou declared as he walked into the temple where his colleagues were incongruously assembled. 'We have had orders from headquarters that from now on we Communists will no longer take advantage of the banner of the Guomindang, and, instead, will fight alone under the Red banner. The revolutionary committee of the Guomindang no longer exists. If you gentlemen want to leave us, let's part here.' Zhou had been carried to the temple in a litter and was described as looking 'sick and dejected', but this outburst of sarcasm probably brought the colour back to his cheeks.

Zhou ordered Zhang Guotao and Li Lisan back to Communist headquarters. 'You two,' he said, 'must leave the troops immediately and steal back to Shanghai. I will stay with the troops and take whatever actions are appropriate.'

'Are you feeling any better?' asked Zhang. 'You should leave the troops first, because you are sick. Let me stay in your place.'

'My illness,' Zhou loftily answered, 'is no problem. I think I can hold on. . . . We should not discuss any longer. We had better go quickly before it is too late. The situation at the front was very bad, and I do not know how many of our troops can survive.'

Outnumbered and overpowered, the Zhou Enlai who ordered the retreat to Hailufeng, the tiny Communist outpost on the sea just east of Hong Kong, was only half the man he had been eight weeks earlier. Guomindang soldiers closed in to block his escape route, and in the fighting he lost several dozen baskets of silver dollars, his treasury reserve.

His stretcher-bearers dropped him, and at one point it was only two orderlies, half carrying, half dragging him along a ditch, who got him away. Reluctantly he consented to take a sampan to Hong Kong for urgent medical treatment.

Yet another case of misplaced trust marked Zhou's parting from Zhang Guotao, whom he asked to supervise the soldiers fleeing from the Shantou area. Zhang later discovered that the underground reception centre for these escapees was run by a divorced wife of Zhu De, whose reputation was not good. Zhang Guotao warned Zhou that the centre was not trustworthy because of this 'dangerous woman'. But Zhou would not be persuaded because, in Zhang's view, he wanted to be bold in making use of new recruits to the movement. Zhou always had a soft spot for those whom others had rejected. But a few months later this woman's treachery was indeed exposed, and Zhang regretted that Zhou had continued to trust her.

Zhou reached Hong Kong on a rented boat, penniless, in tatters and, according to one account, unconscious with fever. Once again a Western-governed city offered him shelter from the murderous intentions of his own countrymen. For a few days he shared the simple fare of the rickshaw-pullers at roadside foodstalls, while he regained contact with his friends. Eventually, He Long, Ye Ting and Nie Rongzhen rallied round him, holding an emergency conference in the Queen's Hotel on 15 October. They decided that he should stay in Hong Kong for two weeks for medical attention.

At this point, Zhou's movements become obscure. Some reports suggest that he remained in Hong Kong doing underground work for the Communist Party. Edgar Snow has him moving up the river to Canton to organize the Canton Commune. Snow's fellow-correspondent Agnes Smedley declares that Zhou went to Moscow.

The more plausible assumption is that he travelled, hardly recovered after his fortnight in Hong Kong, to face the Party music in Shanghai, probably in October 1927. The new comrades in charge of the Communist Party, headed by the poet Qu Qiubai, found it difficult to come to a correct official verdict on the Nanchang uprising, which had both positive and negative features. In October, in Zhou's absence, they praised it as a 'splendid record . . . in Chinese revolutionary history'. Yet a month later Qu condemned the episode as 'an unsuccessful experiment in military opportunism'.

Zhou made sure that he would not be penalized because of the change in leadership, expressing full support for the Central Committee and almost exaggerated obedience to the Comintern. In the event, the Central Committee did not punish him for the failure of Nanchang, and he was even allowed to retain his Politburo seat with responsibility for military and secret-service affairs. In all these ways he was treated better than either Li Lisan or Zhang Guotao, his fellow-planners of Nanchang. But then, unlike them, Zhou studiously refrained from submitting extenuating reports about Nanchang to the Central Committee. He managed to appear aloof, rising above the petty quarrels, not representing a threat to any colleague, and this made it easier for him to bounce back again after his temporary setback. Eventually, at the Party Congress in Moscow the following summer, the verdict on the Nanchang uprising was again reversed, and it was accepted as a correct military action against the Guomindang.

After all, in the common eye, Zhou now excelled most of his comrades, a judgement shared by many within the Party and among its Russian advisers. If only he had been trained in Russia rather than in France, he might now have been assured, after a short pause to digest the military failure at Nanchang, of supremacy in the Party. In the end, however, the Comintern preferred to have Soviet-trained trusties in the Chinese saddle. Zhou might have struck a blow for his comrades' independence from the Guomindang, but he had still to reckon with the ideological colonialism of the Russian Marxists.

One of the many Communist leaders who watched Zhou's activities with admiration was Mao Zedong, now several rungs farther down the ladder in terms of experience and qualification. Since their brief encounter in Canton they had had little contact. Mao had apparently retired to his native Hunan, and the Party no longer published his writings. But it was Mao, in fact, who made sure that Zhou's role in the creation of the Red Army was not forgotten.

One of Zhou's new responsibilities was to supervise the infiltration of Gu Shunzhang's secret servicemen into the local police headquarters. Gu, who had been in charge of the disastrous Shanghai rising only eight months earlier, was invaluable to the Party because, as a member of the underworld Green Gang, he could obtain police information before they took action against Communists.

Another responsibility was for the two provinces of Jiangsu and Zhejiang, which formed Shanghai's hinterland. Zhou guided his 'doubting Thomas' Liu Ning into a planned revolt against the local warlord at Hangzhou, the strategic port just down the coast from Shanghai. Liu went there, but found preparations were not up to schedule. He came back to complain to Zhou.

'I have approached the commander of the provincial garrison,' Zhou replied. 'He has about two companies of soldiers and with no more than five or six hundred silver dollars we can get them to start a mutiny for us.'

'But what about the masses?' asked Liu, fearing another Nanchang.

Zhou exchanged a smile with his other colleagues in the room. 'You are new here and you haven't done your homework well enough. In the area surrounding the West Lake we have several dozen trustworthy comrades who enjoy the confidence of more than 10,000 farmers, covering a broad region.'

But when the time came, word of the rising had reached the garrison troops and police, who rushed to the rescue of the local tyrant's family when it was attacked. Liu had to flee, several Communists were arrested and executed, and Zhou's reputation for political assessment took another knock.

But there was one consolation in being back in Shanghai. At the end of 1927 Deng Yingchao caught up with her husband after dodging arrest by the Guomindang in Canton. Things were not much easier in Shanghai, but at least the couple were reunited in the small Western-style house on Weihaiwei Road where Zhou was now living.

9

Regaining Russian Confidence
1928–30

Zhou seemed to drift into a melancholy in the first half of 1928, despite his physical recuperation in Hong Kong, his return to the old familiar haunts of Shanghai, his apparent reconciliation with the new leaders of the Party, and his reunion with his wife. In one single year he had totally misjudged Chiang Kai-shek and thereby exposed the workers of Shanghai to a shocking massacre; he had then gone out on his own, wriggling free from the Russian advisers, and organized a large-scale military rebellion which came to nothing because of pusillanimous leadership and miscalculation of the opposition. Zhou should have been in line for the Party leadership, yet others were favoured instead. But there may have been something deeper.

The shy lad of seventeen who had found Dutch courage behind the robes of stage women, and the twenty-one-year-old whose frontiers of violence were student demonstrations, had matured into a thirty-year-old soldier for whom ordering soldiers into battle, many to certain death, and commanding execution squads to kill opponents, was the norm. Nothing in his childhood and education had prepared Zhou for this kind of violence, and it is quite possible that he now went through a phase of despondent revulsion. For whatever reasons, he went to ground.

There are only two clues to his whereabouts at this time. One is the story that he went to Tianjin to reorganize the Party's North China Bureau. The other report, which may be nearer the truth, is that Zhou went to study at the Advanced Infantry School in the Soviet Union. Could he have said to himself at the end of 1927: 'What I most lack now in order to achieve my goals is the full backing of the Comintern, so I must go to Moscow and make friends there'? If he did spend the first four or five months of 1928 in Russia, he was alone, because Deng Yingchao did not reach the Soviet capital until May, whereupon they both became involved in the famous Sixth Congress.

This was a remarkable affair. For one thing, it was the first time that the Chinese Party had ever held a congress abroad, and while the Chinese comrades were comfortably free from Guomindang harassment they were also very much under Russian surveillance. Even the list of candidates for the Politburo was presented by Bukharin.

The Party was in a bad way, demoralized by falling membership and disoriented by the break with the Guomindang. It resolved to give up trying to overthrow the Guomindang for the time being, and concentrate instead on guerrilla resistance in the countryside and underground work in the cities. Zhou presciently warned the others that if they recruited in rural areas, they would have to fight the corrupting influence of the old-fashioned peasant mentality. But how were the leaders to be united? There were many groups or factions represented at the Moscow Congress: trade unionists, the rural-oriented Red Army leaders like Mao (who was himself absent), the Youth League group, a Trotskyite faction, and finally the three men who were bearing the brunt of the leadership at this time – Li Lisan, Qu Qiubai and Zhou Enlai. One might have expected some sparring over the blame for the Nanchang catastrophe, but instead it was a conciliatory Congress. The three 'big' leaders agreed to tolerate each other rather than give openings to the newly contending factions, led by less well-educated peasants or workers (like Mao), whose non-intellectual backgrounds the three leaders did not trust.

Through a compromise, a virtually unknown trade unionist from Shanghai – the boatmen's leader – became Secretary-General. But the real work was shared by Li Lisan (responsible for propaganda) and Zhou Enlai (initially organizational matters, but later military). Zhou decided to operate as Li's 'right hand', working closely with him for the resuscitation of the Party and the Communist cause in China but allowing him the greater official eminence; this established a pattern for Zhou's future movements in Chinese politics.

They made a good team, just as they had in France. Zhou was so urbane, Li so eloquent, while both shared the same intellectual perception of China's needs. They probably had a tacit understanding that, while Russian help to the Chinese Party was essential, Moscow's influence over the Chinese comrades' actions could, by intelligent manipulation, be kept to the minimum.

But Zhou's errors of the previous year were not to be let go entirely. Like the other leaders, he had to sit through a lecture by Bukharin. 'Comrade Zhou Enlai,' the Russian declared, 'you were in charge of military affairs for the Chinese Party. You should have been able to estimate the strength of your men a little more accurately. If you had done so, there would not have been so many disasters, such blind resort to armed revolt.'

While this was translated, Zhou blushed, according to one report. But he was not expected to defend himself: the Russian moved dispassionately on to a rebuke of Qu Qiubai, sitting next to Zhou.

Zhou nevertheless consolidated his standing among the Russians (on what was probably his maiden visit to the USSR) and was rewarded with a post in the Comintern at its congress, held immediately afterwards. After these political conferences Zhou stayed in Russia, according to Edgar Snow's account, 'for special indoctrination at Sun Yat-sen University', while continuing his military instruction as well. He also investigated a complaint about the Chinese students in Moscow plotting against their administrators: he cleared them all, including Chiang Ching-kuo, the Generalissimo's son who went on to be President of the Republic of China. The boy could be trusted as a revolutionary!

As the man responsible for Party organization, Zhou elaborated his fears about diluting its proletarian spirit, in a letter to all members in November. He listed ten things to avoid, including extreme democratization, personal disputes, working in small groups and mercenary revolutionary mentality – this mostly directed at Mao Zedong and his peasant friends.

Zhou and his wife may have spent the best part of 1928 in the Soviet Union, returning at the end of the year. He now allowed Li Lisan to take the credit for their joint work while Zhou himself got on, undisturbed, with the gargantuan task of reorganizing the Party. He had returned with many new Russian-style ideas for a secret police that could protect his comrades in the difficult years ahead, and now organized a special unit for this purpose, which he put in the charge of his secret-society superior in the Shanghai uprising, the notorious Gu Shunzhang.

The Zhous went to live with an uncle and aunt on Seymour Road, a quiet middle-class haven in the tumultuous city. The lady made Zhou feel at home by using his old childhood name, and she admired his cooking. 'You girls had better not challenge him, I have tasted his cooking a number of times.' It was one of the 'girls' – Zhou's sister-in-law – who later recalled some of these incidents and conversations.

Zhou took up the family duties of his situation as if they had never been interrupted. On the birthday of the departed grandfather Panlong, as the eldest grandson he directed the family preparations for a memorial service, ritually burning pieces of yellow paper with messages for the spirits. 'He really knows all the rules,' the aunt murmured with pride, 'and he does everything right!'

These middle-class relatives professed to be ignorant of Zhou's revolutionary activities, explaining to friends that he was waiting, like many other sons who had done well in examinations, for another government assignment.

Zhou was here reunited with his adoptive brother Enzhu, of whom he was very fond. Since they had last met, however, the younger man had become a notorious playboy. The servants compared the troublesome 'thirteenth young master' with the 'seventh young master who could do no wrong'. Enzhu was now a father of two, and Enlai, who had none, took more interest in the babies than their father did.

Enzhu came home drunk one evening and was scolded by the aunt for spending all his money on a famous Peking opera singer. Zhou intervened, saying to his adoptive brother, 'Of course you mustn't squander the family fortune and waste your time on an opera singer.' Then he turned to the old lady. 'But it is quite all right to learn the music and poetry of it, isn't it, aunt? All the great scholars and statesmen in the past knew these things.'

'I'll go with you to the theatre tomorrow,' Zhou went on, turning to his brother, 'to see just how good the new singer is. Now you'd better go and wash and get something to eat.'

Next morning Zhou put on his long grey silk gown and polished shoes and took his brother out for the whole day, returning with armfuls of opera costumes. He then changed into his blue cotton housegown and led the assembled family in an animated discussion of the art of Peking opera. The aunt listened and frowned and smiled, and never said another word against the theatre.

A few days later Zhou, to humour the old lady, took them all in the family car to see a film chosen by Enzhu's wife.

Zhou tried very hard to persuade his adoptive brother to stop drinking, and often took him out, saying that they were both going to the theatre. Actually he secretly took the young man to Communist Party meetings in the hope that a new interest and dedication would make him forget the old vices.

Zhou plunged eagerly into the new work of the Party, and used his pen to great effect. In various articles, he warned how difficult it might be to 'recapture' the Party's proletarian base, since the peasant predominance made 'fertile ground for the spread of petty-bourgeois ideology'. He castigated those who were frightened to argue:

Our comrades are . . . afraid of any heated debate which they think might cause a schism within the Party . . . and afraid of offending friends, and therefore avoid discussion and tend to gloss over the difficulties. . . . But so long as we can keep our political discussion impersonal, the more intensely we argue, the closer we can come to the truth!

This advice was hard to put across in the Maoist kingdoms. One interesting suggestion by Zhou was that 'the Party should establish production centres . . . and experimentally set up factories.'

But his hopes for a stable leadership collapsed during the summer of 1929, when Li Lisan began to break ranks with him on military strategy and the question of land confiscation. At a Party meeting in September the two men were continually quarrelling. 'I always played their mediator,' recalled the boatmen's leader, who was technically in charge of the Party, but it went beyond his skills.

Zhou was concerned about the danger of the Party slipping away from Marxism. The Fourth Army in particular was exhibiting 'all kinds of non-proletarian ideas, such as a purely military viewpoint, bandit mentality, remnants of warlordism.' A Central Committee letter to the Fourth Army, inspired by Zhou and sent in September, drove the problem home in a way that Mao must have deeply resented. Most of the Fourth Army's Party members were peasants, Zhou said, and most of its ideological problems resulted from 'the selfishness, narrow-mindedness and conservatism of the small peasant economy and from the lack of discipline, vacillation and fanaticism of the petty bourgeoisie. These ran totally counter to the revolutionary principles and organizational discipline of the proletariat.' If such ideas were not eliminated 'the Red Army would meet great danger in its road ahead.'

Mao was obviously the man with leadership potential in Jinggangshan, and Zhou, hoping for the best of both worlds, instructed him to stop sulking and come out to take the lead in reforming the Fourth Army along these lines. He told others to copy Mao's Jinggangshan. 'Many valuable experiences can be found here,' he wrote in a Red Army circular, 'and they are all unique in China, heretofore unseen and unheard of. . . . All the Party branches and Red Army units throughout the country ought to learn from these experiences.' This was bolstering Mao the man, and patronizing his regional leadership, while puncturing his ideas.

Zhou's disputes with Li Lisan worsened. Li, his heart running ahead of his brain, now wanted to prepare the Red Army for a general attack on government forces. In the winter of 1929–30, the two men were having daily arguments about this. Li was increasingly obsessed with his own personal prestige as 'China's Lenin', in the phrase which he himself used to Zhou. In contrast with this megalomania, Zhou was interested neither in personal power nor in reputation. He was concerned with the substance of what could be done, and this is why he did not challenge Li for the leadership of the Party and why he survived so long in the anterooms of power.

By early 1930 Zhou had constructed, from his secret headquarters in Shanghai, a remarkably strong network of military support from the Red Army units under various commanders loyal to him in different provinces. The trouble was that his ebullient comrades on the Central Committee built too many hopes too quickly on his military organization charts. Zhou had to slow down the military build-up and blur the centralization of the Red Army command, for purely practical reasons. And in both respects this disappointed Li Lisan, who wanted direct orders to be given to the troops to get ready for another round of attacks on big cities. Yet Zhou's moderation may well have saved both the Party and the Red Army from disintegration.

It could be said that Zhou, in turning his back on the Li-ist strategy of taking cities, was now moving closer to Mao Zedong, whose situation and policy in Jiangxi was soon to be proved the high road to power for the Communist Party. Such is the argument made by the writer Han Suyin.

This is not to belittle the gifted and dedicated Zhou Enlai, his immense personal courage, enterprise and dedication when he led the uprisings against Nanchang and later Shantou. . . . But the actions against the cities, however significant, were not to lead to the rebuilding of the Party and army.

Zhou was called to Moscow again in the early summer of 1930, for what friends saw as the ultimate offer of the 'crown'. As soon as he had disembarked from the train he was surrounded by Russians wanting to know what was going on in China. They looked up to him as the only sensible and experienced Chinese Bolshevik leader – with Qu Qiubai now distrusted as an emotional littérateur, Li Lisan as an hysterical demagogue. In July Zhou was invited to speak to the Soviet Party Congress – a rare honour, and the first to be accorded to a Chinese. In his speech he dwelt on the 'uneven' development of China's revolutionary situation and the 'uncoordinated' peasant and city-worker movements. The Comintern repeated all this in a new directive, only omitting his provocative declaration – a sop to Li Lisan – that 'the new upsurge in the Chinese revolutionary movement has become an indisputable fact!'

Zhou basked in Moscow's welcome. 'Stalin appreciated him very much,' a comrade recalled, 'praising his consistently fine record in handling military and intelligence work, and prizing his ability and political flair.' And he hit it off with Pavel Mif, the Kremlin's new man in charge of Chinese affairs.

Back at home, Li Lisan busily tied the rope around his own neck. He produced another glamorous plan to capture big cities with Russian military help, and the Fourth Army was told to take Changsha as a preliminary – which it did, but it could not hold the city. Zhou's alleged comment was 'Li Lisan has gone mad.'

At the end of August, Zhou returned to China, enjoying the full confidence of the Russians, who expected him to reorganize the leadership of the Chinese party at a Central Committee meeting in Shanghai in September. Qu Qiubai had been preparing it, but dared not start without Zhou. But the comrades who assumed that the meeting would provide a show-down against Li Lisan were disappointed. Qu took the chair and Zhou, characteristically, the second seat. Neither of them actually condemned Li Lisan, but treated his errors as tactical ones, presenting a report that rebuked him for having 'overestimated the tempo'.

The outcome was a tightening of Party unity with Li Lisan remaining as the most senior figure. A resolution was passed quoting the Li-ist sentence, repeated by Zhou in Moscow but deleted by the Russians in their version of it, that the arrival of a 'new high tide' was indisputable. To mollify the Comintern, however, Zhou engineered the appointment of Wang Ming, leader of a newly returned Russian-trained group of 'twenty-eight Bolsheviks', to a senior position (from which he was to become the next contestant for the 'crown').

Zhou also assured the assembled delegates in Shanghai that they were not at odds with the Comintern. When the Chinese leaders had planned the various Nanchang and Shanghai uprisings, the Comintern had not objected in principle, only 'opposing its being done immediately, today or tomorrow'. In other words, the Chinese Central Committee had made 'sporadic tactical mistakes' only, by overestimating revolutionary development 'in degree and in speed'. As usual, the Russians had misjudged the Chinese instinct for solidarity in the face of foreign criticism.

Zhou then delivered his famous Shaoshan Report, which admirers regard as a key document in the development of the Party. In this wide-ranging analysis of the situation in China which the Communists faced, he discussed first the nature of the disagreement with the Comintern. 'The situation has not ripened sufficiently to warrant nationwide armed insurrections,' Zhou argued. 'Do the errors of the Central Committee lie in a difference in line from the Comintern? Absolutely not! There is no difference in line!' Certainly the Chinese Central Committee had made mistakes.

I myself committed mistakes. . . . We accept the criticism of the Comintern and point out that comrade Li Lisan should shoulder more responsibilities in ideological interpretation. But we must not tolerate irritating remarks by other comrades . . . aimed personally and individually at Li Lisan. . . . We should carry on self-criticism on a collective basis.

This gave Zhou the chance to distract attention away from Li to the improper tactics of Li's critics.

But there was a great deal that was positive in Zhou's report. On the problem of rich peasants – whether to confiscate their land or retain their goodwill – he declared:

There are two leftist mistakes concerning the attitude to the rich peasants, economically to advocate the confiscation of their land and politically to advocate killing them all. Should we treat the rich peasant in this way, the middle peasant would vacillate more. . . . We cannot afford to alienate the middle peasant at this time.

Zhou thus came down in favour of rural revolution *by stages*.

And yet on military questions Zhou was veering towards the old incaution that had swept him off his feet at Nanchang. He was building up the Red Army in Jiangxi and elsewhere by every possible means, bribing bandits and enticing Guomindang troops by propaganda, thus courting the very risks of political dilution of which he had earlier warned. After the Central Committee meeting he boasted to the Party's Military Council that the strength of the Red Army was 'now sufficient for a large-scale civil war'. It sounded as if he was falling into the same trap as Li Lisan, optimistically overestimating the Red Army's chances.

Under the influence of this enthusiasm a new Red Army attack was now made on Changsha, an attack that was ordered by the new Central Committee, apparently under Comintern pressure, but with Zhou, Qu and Li all probably involved. This second failure at Changsha in only a few weeks led Zhou into a confrontation with Mao Zedong. At Ningdu, in Jiangxi province, an officer whom Zhou had once employed and respected was executed; Mao had accused the man of spying for the Guomindang. Zhou was furious, and soon afterwards he treated his Politburo comrades to a stern reprimand of Mao for his hasty attack on Changsha, and for ignoring Comintern instructions to 'consolidate defence positions before advancing further'.

Meanwhile, Li Lisan was called to Moscow to answer for his political errors. For months Zhou had worked energetically to keep the various factions together under Li Lisan's banner, explaining to his colleagues that 'Li Lisan has already admitted his mistakes'. But when the Comintern officially damned him, Li had to be sacrificed for Party unity. Before Li's departure Zhou made him recant in the Politburo and told the other comrades that Li was guilty of 'military opportunism pure and simple', as well as the sin of 'a complete denial of the fact that organizational strength was one of the prerequisites for the maturing of a revolutionary situation.' Zhou also persuaded Mif not to reorganize the Party leadership but rather to leave it to find its own consensus.

10

A Magician Trumped

1931–34

When the Central Committee next met in Shanghai in January 1931, Pavel Mif, in a show of Russian concern about the Chinese Party's irresolute leadership, took the chair himself. When Zhou arrived for the meeting, he sat pointedly between the two mutually hostile groups which the departure of Li Lisan had left as the major contenders for control – the Russian-trained Twenty-eight Bolsheviks under Wang Ming (Mif's own former student at Sun Yat-sen University in Moscow), who had the intellectuals' support, and He Mengxiong, the veteran railway-union leader, who was the grassroots worker and peasant candidate and who liked to pour scorn on 'young students who . . . were taking milk at their mothers' breasts when we were carrying out the revolution.' Zhou's uncommitted stance advertised both his dilemma and ambition.

Mif believed that he had struck a bargain with Zhou, gaining his approval for Wang Ming and the other Bolsheviks to take over the Party, in return for Comintern absolution of Zhou's earlier sins. But Zhou feared the Bolsheviks as representing not only foreign domination of the Chinese Party but also inexperienced leadership. On the other hand, the only other serious candidates were not intellectuals, and Zhou probably doubted if they could be expected to keep the higher universal and ideological goals of the Party in view. And it was from these, the 'indigenous' Chinese Communists like Mao, that the immediate challenge seemed to come. Zhou, Mif and Wang Ming were all apprehensive lest Mao and the trade unionists make a successful takeover, and Zhou's initial assumption of a middle ground between the two soon gave way to an accommodation with the Twenty-eight Bolsheviks in order to keep the uneducated peasants' and workers' leaders out.

For the next three years, therefore, Zhou faithfully supported Wang Ming, just as he had earlier supported Chen Duxiu, Qu Qiubai and Li Lisan, as formal head of the Party. (He was even accused by the ultra-leftists in the Cultural Revolution many years later of having become the 'Twenty-ninth Bolshevik'.) But the deal was far from one-sided. Wang was the Russian candidate, but, having only just returned to China and being still young, he lacked an organization or following within the Party, so in this respect he was dependent on Zhou. And while Zhou played lip-service to Mif and his young Chinese protégé, he assiduously kept most of the strings firmly in his own hands.

Zhou's decision to back the Bolsheviks may have been strengthened by another argument he had with Mao over an incident at Futian in the middle of Jiangxi Province, where Mao had organized a bloody suppression of opponents within his own group, branding these Communists as traitors and having them killed, in December 1930. Zhou had condemned the affair as having 'created fear and suspicion among the Party ranks and reduced our comrades to living under abnormal strain'. Mao seized the opportunity of the Central Committee meeting to give a vigorous defence of himself, to which Zhou responded. On the other hand, Zhou was able to sabotage to some extent the efforts of Mif and Wang to organize a clear rejection of the absent Li Lisan and what they called his 'adventurist line'. The Central Committee members criticized Li, but only halfheartedly, and they went on to reinstate many of his policies. Zhou's position was delicate, because many comrades were annoyed with him for not having taken a tougher line with Li Lisan much earlier; as the only man with any influence over Li, he was criticized for not using it more seriously to correct Li's mistakes. 'Either Zhou was playing dumb,' some said, 'or he could just not be bothered to put in a good word or two.' His detractors called Zhou 'smooth and round by nature', a person inclined to evade responsibility in order to keep out of trouble, who in the end could be likened to Li Lisan ('birds of a feather') in that neither of them, in contrast with the peasant and worker leaders, had ever done any real groundwork at the grassroots to lead the Chinese people into revolution.

Zhou's response to all this was merely to reissue his Shaoshan Report of three months earlier with a new preface but no revisions. 'It may serve as an example,' he explained, 'for those who are tempted to compromise between the Li Lisan line and the Comintern line. I am releasing it so that our Party can identify and renounce my error. And I myself shall also criticize this persistent, serious error in our Party organ.' He thus left it to others to say what was wrong with his report. But even Zhou could not get away with that. He was made to deliver a 'grovelling' confession of his past 'compromise-ism'. All the same, he was the only former supporter of Li who did not have to compose a written repentance, and instead of being prosecuted as his chief supporter, Zhou managed to become a kind of arbitrator, offering judgement on the efforts of others to clear their names.

Zhou entered this Central Committee meeting under a cloud, but the inexperience of the Russians and their protégés, together with the divisions in the other Chinese ranks, allowed him to come out at the end retaining his seat on the Politburo, in charge of the Party's military department as well as its security organization, and also a leading member of the new Central Bureau for the Base Areas. This was to prove an avenue to power at a time when the Chinese Communists controlled large areas of the interior of China as rural bases in the fight against the old government.

But the conference ended on a sour note. The trade unionists, who walked out in a huff, were arrested at their hotel by British police, who turned them over to the Guomindang to be shot. One of them, the leader of the Shanghai rickshaw-pullers, a poet and husband of the writer Ding Ling, had published criticism of Wang Ming, and many comrades wondered whether the new Bolsheviks had not tipped off the foreign police. The American Vice-Consul in Wuhan reported that Zhou had also been 'caught' and executed on the following day by the order of Chiang Kai-shek. Zhou was still very much alive, however, and at the same Oriental Hotel a few days later he briefed his old comrade Zhang Guotao on the meeting, admitting his mistakes in not having renounced the Li Lisan line earlier, and explaining matter of factly what had happened without criticizing anybody, not even Mif or Wang Ming, who had hurriedly returned to Moscow.

The next evening, Zhou took Zhang to see the number two Comintern delegate, a Pole. To his horror, this European threatened Zhang with expulsion from the Politburo if he did not accept the decisions of the meeting he had missed. Zhou interceded on Zhang's behalf, telling the Pole that since there were so many different opinions within the Party, it was important not to drive dissenters away. It was yet another case of the clash in values between the permissive Chinese and the dogmatic European Marxists.

Zhou was beginning now to explain to foreigners why China could not be expected to behave like a Western country. He told a foreign correspondent:

[China cannot plunge headlong into democracy such as America, England and other truly democratic countries enjoy. The people of China have been suppressed for so long that they will require generations of political training before they understand the significance and importance of an honest vote. We are not ready for a thoroughly democratic system. We must have progress slowly.]

He probably made the same point to Mif and the other Russians.

A dramatic example of the difference in values came when Huang Jinghun, a friend and student of Zhou's at Huangpu, suddenly decided to defect to the Guomindang. Zhou first tried to dissuade him, but finally had to brand him a rebel and order his execution because of inside information about the Communists which he would carry to the other side. Zhou told a senior colleague that because the evidence was so concrete and the matter so urgent, he had to make a quick decision to 'kill first, report later'. When his colleague mildly remarked that there was nothing in the Party book about execution, Zhou confessed that he had never done a thing like that before. Although he had lived with violence for the past four years, this was the first time he had had to order the killing of a friend who was not merely holding wrong opinions but, Zhou believed, actually endangering the existence of the Party.

And now Zhou himself was under criticism again from Moscow. A Russian resolution faulted the Chinese leaders for their disunity and for assigning certain Bolsheviks to work in the guerrilla areas. 'In this respect, Comrade Wu Hao [Zhou Enlai] . . . should be held responsible.' But he knew that the Russians and the Chinese Bolsheviks could not do without his organizational support. The grip of the Guomindang on Shanghai was tightening, and Zhou thought it was urgent that Party leaders now scatter themselves inland in the areas controlled by Communist guerrillas. The Politburo, he suggested, should go to Mao's impressive base in Jiangxi Province, while Zhang Guotao should go to the Oyuwan base, just north of the Yangzi River. If the Party went on concentrating itself in the urban 'white areas', it would face continuous difficulty and might well be destroyed. The shooting of the trade-union leaders in February was only the most recent example. The Politburo agreed in April 1931 that Zhou would lead the main body to the Jiangxi area while Liu Shaoqi and Wang Ming would remain behind in Shanghai. Zhou assigned his security chief, Gu Shunzhang, to look after Zhang Guotao's arrangements before going across country to the Oyuwan base.

Gu had by now become a trusted lieutenant of Zhou's. Having once led a strike in the British-American Tobacco Company factory, subsequently undergone training in secret-service techniques in Vladivostok, and then headed the workers' uprisings in Shanghai (although Zhou, technically his deputy, had in fact taken political command), Gu had impressive credentials. Zhou's comrades found Gu able, but with something of the Shanghai playboy in his appearance and manner. Gu was now working as an illusionist from an address in Bubbling Well Road, and he often performed in the roof-garden theatre of the Sincere Department Store. In 1931, he took a troupe of magicians to Wuhan and used the opportunity to set up an espionage network. While there, however, he was recognized at the golf course by a Communist defector, and was arrested by the Guomindang police. Under interrogation he gave away information about Communist leaders and organization, as a result of which more than 800 Communists were eventually arrested. Zhou Enlai himself escaped capture by only ten minutes. According to some sources, Gu was ready to betray his Communist friends because he resented the way in which the new Politburo had turned against Li Lisan. That was no fault of Zhou's, but as the man's immediate boss he had to take responsibility for having trusted someone who in the final analysis proved disloyal.

When a former head of the Party, the boatmen's leader in Shanghai, was executed by the Guomindang on 24 June as a result of Gu's information, the Chinese Communist Party and its head of security – Zhou Enlai – had to act. Zhou decreed – or acquiesced in – a fitting counter-massacre in the Shanghai underworld tradition. Gu's entire family was killed by the Party as a revenge for his betrayal.

This was much bigger than the case of the single cadet whom Zhou had executed earlier in the year. The victims of this secret retribution numbered at least eight – Gu's wife, three children, brother-in-law, sister-in-law and parents-in-law. The corpses, according to one account, were tied together in pairs, head to foot, and then buried ten feet below the courtyard of an empty house in the French Concession.

Zhou's enemies claimed that he killed a hundred members of Gu's family, but even if one included those employed by the family as well as perhaps some others who were wavering in their allegiance to the Party, the total could not have exceeded forty people, and Zhou's Guomindang biographer has concluded, after interviewing the police officers involved in the case, that only twenty-four persons were killed, including the few in Gu's immediate family and others living in the same house.

This information might never have come out if one of the assassins had not subsequently defected to the Guomindang. After interrogation and torture, this Communist was confronted with Gu, his former boss, in the Guomindang prison. 'Please don't blame me,' he blabbed. 'Zhou Enlai told me to do it. You know what the iron discipline of the Party means.' He boasted that he had not killed Gu's son, in spite of the order by Zhou, because at the last minute he felt contrition. As for the other victims (including one European), 'they were all on the Communist Party blacklist. Any Party member, regardless of his position, who disobeyed the orders of Zhou Enlai and the Central Committee, would meet the same fate.'

Eventually the bodies were dug up by Chinese and French police at 11 Aitang Lane on Gaston Road. In the British police reports Zhou Enlai was named as one of the murderers. According to one source, there is a reference in the Chinese Communist records at Yan'an to the effect that Zhou Enlai (under his pseudonym Wu Hào) was in charge of administering the punishment of Gu for his defection.

Both phases of this dreadful affair, the betrayal and Guomindang executions, followed by the Communist reprisals, are grisly episodes in a cruel revolution. The Chinese public was horrified but hardly surprised. Lu Xun, a writer of compassion and Zhou's clansman, wrote that 'bloodshed must be compensated by bloodshed'. 'Our people did some torturing too,' remarks Kyo, Malraux's hero in *Man's Fate*. 'Humanity will have to be very well compensated for that.' The character was not Zhou, but the sentiment could well have been his.

If the Communist leaders needed any further incentive to get out of Shanghai, they had it now. Zhou grew a black beard, in the end five or six inches long. Thus disguised, he was able, as he did once before, to get past the control points at the railway stations and piers where his photograph (in uniform) was now prominently displayed. He could not inform his family where he was going, but merely said that he and his wife were going abroad and that his adoptive brother, Enzhu, would accompany them as far as Tianjin to look for a job.

Deng recalled later that the 'secret work' that she had been doing for the Communist Party in Shanghai had become intolerable. 'Every day I went out, never knowing whether I would not be arrested. The police searched my house in the international settlement. . . . Many good friends were killed and our work became impossible,' so she went with Zhou to the Communist base area in Jiangxi. They left by a small boat that took them down the coast to Fujian Province, and from there they struck inland to the Red base.

The world was left to wonder what had happened to 'the insurrectionist'. A Japanese report said that he had gone to operate from Vladivostok; the Guomindang claimed that Zhou had surrendered. But the bearded Catholic missionary and his wife who arrived at Ruijin, the big market town in Jiangxi Province, just across the Fujian border, in August 1931, were indeed Zhou Enlai and Deng Yingchao, come to elevate the status of Mao Zedong's guerrilla base there in the full expectation that it would become a new Chinese soviet republic.

Zhou had run the blockade of the Guomindang in order to become political commissar to Zhu De, now Commander-in-Chief of the Red Army. He arrived in Jiangxi at a time of tension between the autocratic Mao Zedong and almost every other Communist leader, and soon found himself playing pig-in-the-middle between Mao in Jiangxi and Wang Ming in Shanghai.

On 1 September, Zhou gave orders to the government of the base area that entirely countered Mao's position on strategy, army administration and land reform. He made Mao sign a proclamation rebutting his favoured ideas about how to treat rich peasants, and pushed his own candidates for office against Mao's, utilizing his Party seniority over Mao. Gradually Zhou strengthened his authority in the guerrilla base area, being elected to the Central Executive Committee of the Chinese Soviet Republic when it was founded, on 17 November, with Mao as Chairman (Zhou ranked fourth after Mao, Xiang Ying and Zhang Guotao although he was, of course, senior to all of these in national Communist Party ranking), as well as to the Central Revolutionary Military Council.

Edgar Snow notes that Zhou's local prestige in Jiangxi now began to overshadow Mao's. Yet he was a builder, not a destroyer.

Perhaps it was the unequalled breadth of Zhou's viable connections with all factions that committed him to the role of chief reconciler and balancer of forces rather than to bitter-end struggle for personal leadership attainable only by violent oppression of one or the other element in a core dispute.

He steadily built up the nucleus of an army independent of factions and loyal to the central leadership, even welcoming in December some 20,000 defectors from the Guomindang who had been trained by a tough professional warlord. The Maoist guerrilla ethic began to fade in Jiangxi circles, to be replaced by the 'new school' of Russian military thought, patronized by Zhou and the Comintern advisers, stressing central control over a regular professional military machine.

Early in the new year of 1932 it looked as if Zhou had recognized the entrenched power of Mao, and was seeking to accommodate him. A report by his Central Bureau of Soviet Areas on the Futian incident of a year earlier described Mao's behaviour then as an inexcusably bourgeois act of panic, but the wording was careful: 'The resolute action taken [by Mao] to suppress the Futian revolt was completely correct. But mistakes were committed in recognizing the true nature [of the offending group] and selecting a proper method to deal with it.' By this phraseology Zhou may have hoped to save face for this powerful rural leader whose ambitions he feared, and to gain his future cooperation. But the eventual resolution of the Central Bureau blamed Mao for falling into the 'terroristic and psychopathic state of the petty bourgeoisie' – a more hostile formulation than Zhou's original. Another account suggests that Zhou helped Mao to restore his relations with the friends of his victims at Futian, but that Zhu De and others were adamant in throwing the book at Mao.

Zhou broadened his attack on Mao with a catalogue of 'rightist-opportunist errors'. These, he told the Central Committee, had been committed by

all those who regard the seizure of one or several entire provinces as not an immediate but a distant goal; all those who are sceptical about occupying metropolitan centres and prefer to lead the Soviet regime and the Red Army towards remote areas; all those who are hesitant about a positive outward expansion of Communism to enable the Red Army to utilize its full potential, who prefer to tie the hands of our armed comrades with such assignments as propaganda in the villages and raising funds for the army, forgetting that the principal mission of the Red Army is to destroy our enemies through combat; all those who still linger in a past stage for which a gradual expansion of military action and a defensive and conservative strategy were proper and who are consequently unwilling to move directly to deal a fatal blow to the enemy in the non-Communist areas.

These were precisely the views then being spread by Mao Zedong, vilified soon afterwards by other Party leaders in Jiangxi as 'anti-Marxist, anti-Leninist and anti-Comintern'.

They argued on and on about military tactics. Mao urged mobile guerrilla techniques, such as luring the enemy deep into Red territory and then finishing them off one by one. Zhou's idea was to hold the base area tightly and fight positional warfare behind enemy lines. When the Red Army tried to capture Ganzhou the rival military strategists, Zhou and Mao, collaborated – but with disastrous results.

In May Zhou became more specific in calling for a swift expansion of Red territory, and he accused Mao's group of procrastination. Tension was supposedly released at the Ningdu conference in August 1932, where Zhou took over from Mao as political commissar of the First Front Army, the crack force in the Jiangxi base area, and forced Mao off the military committee of the Central Bureau of Soviet Areas. But Mao was not without support. One comrade recollects that Zhu De and many others now rallied to him.

The leading critic was Bo Gu, one of the Twenty-eight Bolsheviks, who wanted to dismiss Mao altogether. Zhou would not go so far. He was quite willing, however, to tell Mao to his face that the Red Army no longer needed personalized leadership herding a small band of guerrillas in hit-and-run operations. Decades later, Mao complimented Zhou for his role. 'During the Ningdu conference,' he told his followers, 'my critics wanted to expel me but Zhou . . . did not agree.'

Otto Braun, the Comintern military adviser in Jiangxi, described Zhou as a 'hard-liner of the "Stalin Group",' but nevertheless praised his 'high degree of merit' in mobilizing the people of the Jiangxi area and organizing its armed forces. When Wang Ming went off to Moscow, Zhou was left in full charge as the Guomindang armies prepared a series of relentless offensives against the Communists. In the winter of 1932–33 the Guomindang armies' so-called Fourth 'Encirclement' Campaign began to press the Red base hard, and in the middle of it came a further battle of wills between Mao and Zhou.

In between revolutions, in the relative calm of his book-lined office, Zhou was normally a gradualist. But once in the field, with revolutionary forces on the move all round him, he seemed to surrender to optimistic overconfidence.

Zhou believed that rich peasants were undermining the institutions of the base area, and that unless there were more class struggle, the rich peasants and small landlords would cling to their privileged positions. But Mao preferred to play along with the rich peasants for the time being in order to ensure the success of the local economy, and supplies for the Red Army. It was for this reason that observers saw Zhou now as 'far to the left of Mao' – in strong contrast to the usual view of his later role in the 1950s and 1960s.

Zhou had laid down a 'forward and offensive line' under which the Red Army would expand its forces, incorporate local militia and mobilize all possible economic resources. While Mao himself did not disobey, one of his supporters, Luo Ming, did reject these orders, continuing instead to follow the old Jinggangshan guerrilla tactics. Zhou had to discipline Luo and other recalcitrants, dismissing many of them, including Mao's brother and even Zhou's old Paris aide, Deng Xiaoping.

Zhou's military line was vindicated by the Red Army's capture of Zhengzhou in March 1933. Mao retired ill to hospital for several months, and Zhou took over his position as chief political commissar for all the Red armies.

The telegrams that Zhou was now dispatching to the Central Committee from the field of battle were full of colourful detail. He reported on 2 March:

Our forces have been locked in fierce battle with the enemy for three days and nights. It would have been possible for us to go and rout or wipe out the enemy's Eleventh Division on the third day, had it not been for the mountainous terrain, which made it difficult for our forces to communicate with each other and with headquarters. [Nevertheless, the Red Army wiped out another division and the greater part of a third. An enemy column, however, moved to cut off the Communist retreat.] Thus we might find ourselves encircled with the battlefield uncleared, the wounded not yet evacuated and piles of captured equipment stacked everywhere. We will therefore disengage from the victorious battle today and withdraw . . . to regroup and prepare for further fighting.

But now Zhou faced trouble from one of his own men, Kung Chu, who had guarded his life during the retreat from Nanchang. Kung had become Chief of Staff to the Red Army, and he used his rank to take issue with Zhou about peasant policy. When Zhou announced a new 'left' Comintern line dictated by the Kremlin by which the Communist Party would eliminate landlords, confiscate their property, and attack rich peasants, he could win only a reluctant majority for it, because those who had been in the Jiangxi base for any length of time knew how unreal it was.

Kung's relations with Zhou had already deteriorated in the previous autumn, when he had been criticized at a meeting chaired by Zhou. The Communists were taxing the local farmers heavily, while at the same time eating their rice and using their labour to build fortifications. When Kung argued for a softer line which would not antagonize the peasants, Zhou replied: 'But the mass of poor peasants are with us. They are willing to give their lives to defend the land the Communist Party has given them.'

Kung insisted that the peasants might become alienated if labour conscription interfered badly with their work in the fields. To which Zhou retorted that the peasants' education should be stepped up. 'Who told you to *force* them to build fortifications for *us?* Mobilize them to build the pillboxes and dig foxholes to defend themselves!'

Soon afterwards Kung botched an assignment to fortify part of the border with conscripted labour, as a result of which a strategic point was lost. He was summoned to Zhou's presence and given a scathing reprimand. Zhou charged him with lack of class-consciousness and suspended his Party membership. In 'thought-struggle' sessions chaired by Zhou he offered only a mild self-defence which further deepened Zhou's distrust. 'Comrade Kung,' he commented afterwards, 'has not yet recognized his mistakes.' This dedicated Communist, of long and proven service in the Red Army, defected to the Guomindang a few months later. In the course of forcing his city-nourished ideas of revolution onto this rural base and satisfying the demands of the Kremlin, Zhou allowed his judgement in this instance to be warped.

The difficulty faced by a group of highly articulate and ambitious men in forming a collective judgement on the day-to-day tactical events of a military campaign came out strongly in October, when one of the Guomindang units, the 19th Route Army, rose in rebellion against Chiang Kai-shek and appealed to the Communists for cooperation. Although Zhou found himself in a minority in wanting to act positively to make the most of this opportunity, he sent emissaries to Fuzhou to make a pact with the rebels.

Mao, backed this time by the Comintern representations and many Red Army leaders, was sceptical about the value of working together with non-Communists. As a result of his call for caution, Red Army reinforcements were not sent to help the 19th Route Army against Chiang Kai-shek's forces until too late. Zhou's terse comment a few years later was that 'we could have successfully cooperated with Fujian, but due to the advice of [Braun] and the advisory group in Shanghai we withdrew instead.'

As the Fourth 'Encirclement' Campaign of the Guomindang forces against the Red Army unfolded during 1933, Zhou's sway over military policy seemed confirmed. The Red Army captured many weapons, radios and prisoners, and its own organization was further standardized and rationalized. Braun later awarded Zhou 'some credit' for the military successes of this campaign, observing that Zhu De had receded into the background, and it was Zhou who was making the important military decisions.

Zhou nevertheless relied a great deal on his German adviser, discussing military problems with him before conferences and often supporting Braun's suggestions. He did sometimes have to differ from the German, as once in December when Braun went on an inspection visit to the northern front and found a commander who was refusing orders and asking for a new assignment. Braun's reaction was to say no, but Zhou told him that one had to make more allowances. 'This was . . . the subject of a little disagreement I had with Zhou Enlai, who advised me that I must allow for the mentality of such cadres.'

Braun was surprised by the intensity of the antagonism between Zhou and Mao. Mao's friend, General Xiao Jingguang, was accused of disobeying orders and thereby losing the town of Lichao, and also of leading a corrupt and self-indulgent private life: for the first time Zhou personally conducted the prosecution of a high-ranking colleague in the supreme court in front of hundreds of other comrades. If ever a Chinese Communist stood for some kind of rule of law in the Marxist utopia, it was the even-handed Zhou, who now told his fellow-officers how Xiao had used army mules to carry his personal possessions when they should have been carrying wounded soldiers, and how he behaved indecently before village girls. In spite of his good military record in earlier campaigns, Xiao was sent to prison for five years. But the political undertones became clear when Mao re-established his political supremacy eighteen months later and restored his friend Xiao to his former rights.

The jockeying for position came to a head in January 1934, when an important meeting of the Central Committee was followed by the second All-China Congress of Base Areas. Zhou retained his posts, and was also promoted to be vice-chairman of the Central Revolutionary Military Council. In effect, he lost a little influence on the civilian side of the institutions governing the Red base, but gained military voice. Mao, strongly supported in the base-area votes, became chairman of the Central Executive Committee, but could not win a seat on the new Politburo of the Party as a whole, with its nationwide constituency. Mao was nevertheless beginning his political comeback. He was still pleading for more private enterprise in the Red areas as a means of securing the loyalty of the old-fashioned power structure there, leaving the theoretical, bookish reforms of Zhou Enlai to be implemented later when conditions were more appropriate. Zhou by contrast wanted to fight simultaneously against both the Guomindang armies and the greedy landlords. Mao had a thought-out, step-by-step agenda for the revolution; Zhou wanted to accomplish it all in one spectacular effort of will – exactly the reverse of their later positions.

When Chiang Kai-shek's final effort to destroy the Communists, the damaging Fifth 'Encirclement' Campaign, was launched in the spring of 1934, the fighting went so well at first for the Communist side that Zhou began a series of articles in the Party's journal about winning strategic victory through tactical successes in protracted war. He was full of Russian doctrine, lecturing his officers on the latest strategic theories from Moscow. And he expanded the Red Army in every possible way, mobilizing 112,000 Youth Guards whose role proved vital a little later on.

Whether by accident or design, Braun now emerged as the leading military voice in the battle-front campaign. He himself testified to the vitiating escalation of arguments between Mao and Zhou during the campaign. Braun accepted neither Mao's guerrilla tactics nor Zhou's fixed-position ideas, advocating instead his own concept of 'short, swift thrusts'. Zhou, significantly, abandoned his advertised series of articles on protracted war after the first instalment, while Braun took up his pen more and more frequently on military matters. And whereas in previous campaigns Zhou had stayed at the front with the Red Army, during the Fifth 'Encirclement' Campaign it was Braun who directed operations at the front while Zhou stayed at the base capital of Ruijin. It is almost as if Zhou now sensed, months in advance of the event, that the Communists could not hold Jiangxi and would have to evacuate the Red base. His heart seemed no longer in the defence campaign, although his public speeches were still ebullient. In April the catastrophic loss of Guangchang drove him to propose secret preparations to evacuate Jiangxi.

By now the Chinese comrades were able to pin the responsibility for defeat on the German adviser. Braun had throughout been able to communicate by radio, via Shanghai, with his superiors in Moscow, but this link was now cut with the Guomindang's discovery and closure of the Communists' Shanghai office. For the next two years the Chinese leaders had to decide their own fate as they went along, without Russian advice. The Russian-trained or Russian-influenced Chinese Party leaders could no longer invoke the prestige and authority of Comintern advice – something which helped Mao, the native candidate, in his slow rise to power over the following months.

The actual breakout from the Jiangxi trap was masterminded by Zhou, against some opposition from Braun and others. The senior leaders were in a terrible dilemma, not fully agreeing on every aspect of the plan but knowing that secrecy must above all be observed. As the time came nearer for flight, Mao became more and more difficult and was expelled from the Central Committee and put under house arrest by Zhou because of his opposition to the Party line. Yet a month later Zhou was leading a chastened deputation of Zhu De and Luo Fu to Mao's house, where he was down with malaria. Zhou may have been able to say quite bluntly that he had not liked Braun's conduct of the fighting since the winter, and Mao for his part probably urged more careful preparation of the departure from Jiangxi.

The Guomindang pressed them relentlessly, giving the Red Army no rest for days and nights at a time. The loss of the small strategic town of Yiqian, where Zhou had taken personal command, at the end of August was a watershed. Chen Yi was wounded as he and Zhou toured the front together. It was immediately decided that a breakout was necessary. For several days they argued about how to do it – whether to fight one last decisive battle to keep the enemy from following. Everything came to a head on the night of 2 October when Zhou, Bo Gu, Braun and Mao met to decide on evacuating the base. Braun would remain in military control, but Zhou took Zhu De's place as chairman of the Revolutionary Military Council. Many of Mao's supporters were told to stay back to form a rearguard, an instruction that possibly reflected Zhou's irritation with Mao's ambitions. But the positive political goal was enunciated by Zhou: they would seek a new base less vulnerable to Guomindang attack. 'Go north,' he told the other three, 'where our comrades have already carved out a base against the Japanese.'

11

On the Long March
1934–36

Zhou Enlai left the broken dreams of the Chinese Soviet Republic and set out on 16 October 1934 on the strategic retreat of the Red Army that was to become known to millions throughout the world as the Long March. They had no agreed goal save to evade their enemy. As he left the Jiangxi base for the last time with about 10,000 Communists for whom he bore responsibility, Zhou was not to know that the Long March would eventually take him six thousand miles across eleven provinces, across snowy peaks and torrential streams, through swamps and forests, to bandit country, the preserves of hostile tribesmen and waterless zones where they could survive only by drinking their own urine. Zhou was abandoning a base as large as Belgium and embarking on a journey that would last for a whole year, the equivalent of walking from London to Tokyo or from New York to Rio de Janeiro.

Did he feel disappointed, regretful? Once again his hopes of starting a revolution had been dashed. He knew now that he had to make common cause with men whose ideas and backgrounds were all very different, and he probably guessed that any Russian help that materialized was going to have strings, if it came at all.

Once again he was on the road with very little more than what he stood up in. His bodyguard carried two blankets, a quilt, a cover into which he could stuff a change of clothes and a grey sweater to make a pillow, a big brass ink box and the famous rectangular document case in which Zhou kept his precious pencils, maps, compass and magnifying glass for the nightly desk work. His wife, Deng Yingchao, was ill with tuberculosis during most of the Long March, and Zhou himself would have to spend some of the time being carried on stretchers.

Zhou led the central column of the Red Army which included the base areas government apparatus (including a printing press, repair shop and mint) as well as the military headquarters and all the women and children. Mao was also a part of this caravan, which trundled with vulnerable ponderousness through the mountains and valleys of southern China, heading west towards the mountains. One by one the heavy things, like the mint and press, were ditched to lighten the load.

The First Corps was sent out without maps into difficult country and had to come back to rejoin the central column, losing almost a week of precious time and making eventual Guomindang pursuit easier. Mao led the critics who rounded on Zhou, Bo Gu and Braun after each such setback. Zhou calmly answered Mao's complaint by asserting that the mistake was one of faulty intelligence and not something the leaders could help.

The first hazard was the crossing of the River Xiang. Braun and Zhou were keen to get across quietly, but Mao wanted to fight with the local Guomindang. The Revolutionary Military Council split down the middle and Braun won only by the chairman's casting vote. Soon they were in Guizhou Province, where Zhou had a fright one night because the house where he was quartered was set on fire by an enemy arsonist. His guard had to lead him out of the inferno.

They argued again at Liping, just inside Guizhou, about whether to veer northwards and hope to give the Guomindang forces behind them the slip. Mao rejected this idea even more abruptly and insisted on continuing the march westward into Guizhou, where the Guomindang writ ran weaker. This time Zhou joined the chorus of voices against Braun. He was in any case irritated by Braun's personal habits, not only his womanizing (he had brought a 'Chinese wife', i.e. mistress, with him on the Long March), but also his insistent demands for tobacco and liquor which became progressively more difficult and expensive to obtain. Braun had to leave this particular meeting because of malaria, and he recalled that when he asked Zhou about the final decision, 'he responded with an irritation unusual in such a quiet and self-possessed man'.

But they paid for their peace with hunger, since this province had little grain and the local inhabitants fled as soon as the Red Army came in sight.

It was so dark that on night marches they tied white towels on their backs for the man behind to follow. Zhou's guard once tripped and spilt the food which he had prepared in Zhou's three-level container. He rushed up to Zhou, who ordered him to get his cuts and grazes treated. When the guard came back he said apologetically: 'I've still got a bit of burnt rice. Do you want some?'

'Burnt rice?' Zhou responded doubtfully. 'All right, I'll have a bit.' It would be better than nothing.

At the new year of 1935 Zhou walked into the northern Guizhou town of Zunyi soaked with rain. He joined Mao in insisting that Braun stop the march for a fortnight and hold a Politburo meeting to regularize the situation. This Zunyi conference of January 1935 became one of the most controversial meetings in modern communism. At it, Mao succeeded in capturing the leadership of the Chinese Communist Party, at first on a provisional basis, but he made sure that his position was later endorsed, and he never had to give way to any of his comrades again as the number one in the Party.

The Zunyi conference opened with a sustained attack by Mao on the direction of military affairs, principally by Braun but also by the Chinese comrades in charge. General Zhu De followed with a crucial endorsement of Mao's complaints. Bo Gu then got up to defend the record of the official leadership, speaking for the Twenty-eight Bolsheviks and their Comintern link. Only after all that did Zhou speak – when the others, according to one account, had gone on arguing for two days and in a mood of increasing criticism of Zhou's actions.

Whereas Bo Gu had harangued his listeners for not seeing their Party's situation in an international context – with the implicit criticism that Mao's section of the Party suffered from its narrow peasant base – Zhou astonished them all by making a clean breast of the strategic errors of the leadership, including his own. Without waiting for comment, he went on to suggest that Mao should take over leadership of the Red Army while Zhou himself retired from the Military Council. With this, Zhou put himself at the mercy of Mao and made it impossible for the Twenty-eight Bolsheviks to rescue him from the wave of criticism. Instead he subtly distanced himself from his Bolshevik colleagues, who had explained rather too literally and pedagogically the rationale behind the evacuation of the Jiangxi base, including the numerous objective factors then working against the Chinese Party – the international support being given to Chiang Kai-shek, for example, and the weakness of the Communist Party in Guomindang China. Zhou by contrast stressed the subjective factors, including the inadequate political work which the Party had done among the population at large and with Guomindang troops, the ineffective deployment of forces for guerrilla warfare, the various tactical and operational military mistakes. Han Suyin paints Zhou as telling his comrades bluntly that Mao 'has been right all the time and we should listen to him'. Everybody admires a man who is big enough to admit his mistakes, and in this way Zhou squeezed himself out of the dock in which Bo Gu and Braun stood indicted, and made it possible for Mao to focus the criticism of the malcontents in the Red Army on those two while Zhou was spared.

Many historians have therefore concluded that 'a tacit agreement between Mao and Zhou at Zunyi is quite plausible'. One of them even suggests that the entire outcome of Zunyi may have been tentatively agreed between Zhou and Mao before the Red Army ever set out on its long march. Braun's comment was that 'Zhou Enlai, as was to be expected, went over to Mao's side with flying colours.'

The resolution finally passed by the comrades at Zunyi, drafted by Mao, examined 'the mistakes in military line committed by comrades Bo Gu, Zhou Enlai and Otto Braun', and identified their cardinal error as employing a simple defence line against the Fifth 'Encirclement'. A subsidiary misjudgement was to neglect political mobilization during the breakout from the Jiangxi base area on the pretext of security.

Mao lost no time in exploiting his victory, dislodging Zhou as the chief political commissar and *de facto* commander-in-chief and taking this key position himself. But it was a close victory, and one of the participants said afterwards that if only General Zhu De, Mao's long-standing collaborator but also Zhou's long-standing friend, had voted for Zhou instead of Mao, Mao might have lost the day since Zhu carried enormous weight within the Red Army.

One would have expected Zhou to find his new political alliance with Mao embarrassing and uncomfortable, not only because of the several years in which he had officially castigated Mao for his errors, but also because Mao did not represent the kind of leadership of Chinese Communism for which Zhou yearned. He had expected something more sophisticated, more urbane, soaring beyond narrow peasant horizons.

Another comment by Braun, whose view of these things was both close and, as a foreigner, detached, was that when Zhou did go over to Mao's side he became 'at least partly against his better judgement, his most faithful champion'. It was probably an exaggeration to say, as Edgar Snow did a couple of years later, that Zhou never afterwards wavered in his loyalty to Mao. But he certainly kept up a public appearance of loyalty, and some people derided his obvious deference to the new dictator. He became known as 'the most able executor of Mao's blueprints', but was also tagged 'the housekeeper' – meaning the one who carries out the policies of the master of the house. According to one comrade Mao unkindly called his new follower 'little donkey'. Doubtless Zhou pledged his own lack of ambition at Zunyi, and Mao was able to accept him as an 'expert' staff member instead of having to treat him as a rival.

In one respect it was easier for Zhou to cross into Mao's court than might otherwise have been the case, since the threat to Mao's political ambitions came from the Kremlin's chosen candidate for the throne of Chinese communism, Wang Ming, leader of the Twenty-eight Bolsheviks. The rivalry between Mao and Wang was covered up by the need for both unity and security in defeating Guomindang encirclement. Zhou had never been close to Wang, supporting him only for opportunistic or tactical reasons, and Mao was therefore confident of Zhou's independence from the Wang faction.

Another factor influencing Zhou's strategy with his fellow-Communists must have been the relative weakness of his own group of followers at Zunyi, the so-called Huangpu clique. By now this included many able and influential men, notably the Cantonese Marshal Ye Jianying, who in the post-Mao era was to play the role of effective head of state. But during the brief period when Zhou had taken actual command of the Communist forces against the Guomindang, just before the Long March, his patent inferiority to Zhu De as a general and military planner must have eroded the support of the Huangpu cadets for their old leader. It is possible that Zhou may not have been able to count on them in the particular military circumstances of the Zunyi dilemma. The Red Army officers needed a leadership that was skilful on the battlefield, that could make the best of the limited resources dictating guerrilla tactics, and that had a strong feel for the Chinese rural society in which they were going to be embedded for the near future. Mao was the obvious choice, but Zhou was probably not alone in expecting privately that when this great caravan finally came to a halt somewhere and settled into a new base area, a new and politically more sophisticated leadership would be called for.

When two of Zhou's former supporters, Luo Fu and Lin Biao, later reproached Mao for the 'bankruptcy' of his policy of 'flight before the enemy' after Zunyi, Zhou took a philosophical attitude, saying passively that the comrades should 'wait and see' – identifying neither with Mao nor with his critics.

Looking at this astonishing *volte face* from Zhou's point of view, it may have looked like another Shantou unfolding, and when things are going badly on the battlefield it is a clever thing to do to hand over command to your leading critic. He will probably make an even worse mess of it than you, and allow you to make a comeback when it is all over. On top of all that, Zhou was unwell, in no condition to exercise constant executive leadership of the kind needed on a march. Finally, his old friend General Zhu De must have forewarned him that he was going to vote for Mao, and in the narrow balance of factional rivalry that would have been decisive. Zhou had probably steeled himself to this kind of gesture as a means of making the best of what would inevitably follow the vote of no confidence against him.

In any case, despite his many criticisms of Mao, it was clear that Zhou had a certain fascination for this traditional but charismatic character. Probably Zhou's years in the rural-base areas had rubbed the edges off his Tianjin–Paris–Shanghai urbanized view of the Chinese revolution, impressing on him the enormous weight which the Chinese peasants must have in this movement. As the slick city boy he could be of little help in the rural camp except as a handmaid of the authentic peasant leader, his channel to the outside world and the burnisher of his ideas.

Even Zhou's own guards had constantly to be educated into Communist principles. Zhou was once quartered in a big house with elegant furniture, and his men found all kinds of valuables in it. While cleaning, his guard Wei discovered a gold ring. Never having seen such a thing before, he put it on his finger. Next morning when he took a jug of water for Zhou to wash with, Zhou noticed the acquisition and asked the young man reproachfully as he was leaving: 'Wei Guolu, do you understand the three main disciplines?' (These basic rules of Red Army behaviour included the axiom that not a single needle or piece of thread should ever be taken from the people, and that everything captured should be given in.)

Wei protested that he knew the rules well and was applying them properly.

Zhou then pointed to the ring, with the words: 'All right. Then where did the ring on your finger come from?'

The abashed recruit sadly surrendered his bauble.

After their momentous decisions, the Red Army left Zunyi in pouring rain for the west, heading towards the mountains of Yunnan Province. Zhou was kept busy as a member of the new military troika comprising Mao, the neutral Wang Jiaxiang and himself. While Mao was the effective commander-in-chief, Zhou directed the GHQ, but there were few Guomindang troops to face so far inland, and this was a relatively peaceful phase of the Long March.

One night in the mountains of Yunnan Zhou stayed up, poring over his maps and papers, long after everyone else had gone to bed. Finally he went out for a stroll.

'*Kouling*!' (password!) shouted the soldier on duty down the road.

'This is Zhou Enlai,' he replied, forgetting to give the password. But the soldier recognized him and Zhou invited him to his room for a chat and a warm-up at the stove.

About midnight the soldier took up his invitation, noting how Zhou's face had become 'almost buried in overgrown hair and beard'. He asked after the older man's health.

'Not too bad,' Zhou replied. 'The cold I caught shortly after we started last year keeps coming back. It's just a nuisance.'

They went on to talk about the capture of some rich merchants who were now kept marching alongside the Red Army. The soldier wondered if they were being held for ransom, because the officers were treating them so well.

'It's not so much for their money,' explained Zhou. 'Of course, if they have money in excess of their travelling expense to contribute, we would welcome it. But it is even more important for us to have friends. They are rich and influential people from Sichuan, where we are going. Cultivating a little goodwill by showing these people how our Red Army behaves is always a good policy.'

'Supposing they are anti-revolutionaries?'

'In that case we will know how to deal with them. Meanwhile they are learning. They are comparing their lily-white soft feet with our commanders' feet – your feet and my feet – calloused, chapped, just like those of any one of our comrades. . . . Our iron discipline will convince them we are soldiers of revolution, not bandits.'

At another village the bodyguard Wei looked round for food for Zhou's table and eventually discovered a little cornmeal and ten eggs. There was nobody at home to take the money, so Zhou's men decided to cook for Zhou first and think how to pay for it all afterwards.

When the meal was taken to Zhou, he wanted to know where the ingredients had come from and how much they had paid. When they hesitated he said: 'Oh, so you didn't pay?'

They confessed, and Zhou said gravely that they would have to take the things back. But one of the men pleaded with Zhou: 'Would it be all right if we wrote a note to the villager explaining, and left some money in the egg basket?'

Zhou had to agree to this, and that is what they did. One silver *yuan* was left in payment. On another occasion Zhou sat under a pear tree refusing to eat the ripe fruit because there was no way of paying the owner.

In Yunnan their arrival was so unexpected that they easily captured some Guomindang supplies. Three trucks once came trustingly towards them in Yunnan and the Red Army made an easy capture. One was loaded with ham, medicine, tea and military maps.

'The enemy,' Zhou told General Zhu De when he saw all this, 'is the best transportation corps we could ever wish for. They send us whatever we need, and they don't require any payment. . . . We were just worrying about not having maps of Yunnan and here we are with maps sent to us by the enemy themselves. Our wounded men were in need of medicine and now we have all the medicine we could want.'

Everybody laughed delightedly.

Zhou celebrated May Day in Sichuan, in the sombre knowledge that half of the Communist soldiers who had left Jiangxi had been lost in the first six months of the Long March. They all had strange adventures as they now moved northwards across the interior part of Sichuan Province, the part where Tibetans live and the landscape becomes almost lunar in its craziness. Zhou spent one night sleeping on his feet, leaning against a tree, the ground being so wet that this was the recommended way. He had already formed the habit of stuffing any old newspapers he could get hold of around his feet to protect them.

The next obstacle was the torrential Dadu River, which flows down the icy plateau of Qinghai and tumbles through Sichuan Province to become a major tributary of the Yangzi. The current is fast and there are few bridges. The

Red Army first tried to cross at Anshunchang, but there were not enough boats and the Communist troops became exposed to Guomindang fire. After an anxious debate, Zhou and the others decided to make a last attempt farther upriver, over the historic bridge of iron chains at Luding. Zhou made the march along the bank of the Dadu River in pelting rain, but when he got there he found that the planks of the bridge had been destroyed by the enemy and Communist soldiers were crossing at a very slow rate.

'When you cross the bridge,' he advised his bodyguard, 'you have to be careful, keep your eyes on the opposite bank and don't look down to the ravine far below.'

They repaired and replaced planks as they went along the bridge, and by painful, sometimes terrifying steps, Zhou and his group managed to reach the other side. But once he was across, Zhou was made to realize how severely he had been punishing his body. He was suddenly attacked by pains that were later diagnosed as due to a liver abscess. His whole body swelled up, but there was no medicine to take. He had been ill before, with malaria after Shantou, but at least then he had been within reach of big cities and supplies. Here on the Long March through the Chinese interior, Zhou and his comrades faced the entirely novel experience of fighting almost unaided against nature. Small wonder that the survivors afterwards felt a special bond arising from these shared trials.

Next they had to scale the snow-covered Jiajin Mountain, where many of the Red Army men, quite unused to severe cold, simply collapsed and died. One of them was his bodyguard's friend, so Zhou helped Wei to dig out a crevice, put the fallen man into it and fill it up with snow, covering the face with their own clothing. There was a storm of hailstones 'as big as walnuts', and conditions worsened. But Zhou survived.

Food was scarce in these desolate highlands of northwestern Sichuan, and one desperate soldier who ate grass was poisoned by it. When Zhou found him prostrate on the ground he gave him a bowl of wheat flour, his only remaining food from his rations, to take.

When the Long Marchers reunited with another Red Army group under Zhang Guotao in mid-June they should have been delighted to be reinforced by comrades fresher and in better shape than themselves. But Zhang, who had been Mao's senior in the Party, did not hide his unhappiness over Mao's promotion. He also had his ambitions and had become used to being the number one in his own little area and army. Mao feared that unless he took great care, Zhang would unseat him. The other leaders, especially Zhou, initially interceded with Mao and Zhang to get them to collaborate on the remaining stretch of the Long March. In the end Zhang had to be given Mao's post as chief political commissar of a newly united Red Army, though Mao's own men retained the key military positions. Zhou could have been more influential in all this if he had not been confined to his sickbed most of the time. He managed to make a speech calling for unity in the face of Japanese aggression, but when they resumed the march a few days later, he had to be carried on a stretcher for several weeks.

The arrival of Zhang Guotao provided the first major test of the Zunyi compromise, and Zhou must have debated anxiously in his own mind whether this was the moment to begin backtracking on the Maoist leadership, whether Mao's usefulness was not now outlived, and whether the Party should not now prepare itself for a post-survival phase in which comrades like Zhang Guotao and the Bolsheviks and Zhou himself would be the key figures. There are suggestions in the accounts of the continuous meetings which the leaders now proceeded to hold in between marches that Zhang Guotao was initially supported by the Bolsheviks – perhaps with Zhou's tacit acquiescence – in questioning the Zunyi proceedings. Decisions relating to the Party as a whole had after all been taken there by only one group. If Zhou had not been ill at this crucial time, he might have not only backed Zhang Guotao but also lent his talents as stage manager, in which case Mao might not have won.

Seeing the ragged and tired state of Mao's troops, Zhang Guotao decided to assert his own claims to the leadership. One of his lieutenants actually proposed him as the new Secretary-General of the Party. But it was crudely done, and by pushing his claims too brashly, Zhang alienated Zhou and the Bolsheviks, and thus spoilt his chances.

After seeing how Zhang behaved in those first weeks of their reunion, Zhou may in any case have felt that Mao would be more easily manageable, and that the Party would be better off sticking with him.

At one meeting where Mao and Zhang were at loggerheads, Zhou remained totally silent. And when the crucial Politburo meeting came at Maoergai, he was on sick leave with a temperature of 39.5° C. Next day his voice weakened and he was delirious. The doctor told his men to bring down snow from the mountains and soak towels in it to keep his temperature down. Only on the third day did it drop, and on the fourth day it was normal again.

Zhou's guard Wei came down next with malaria, with a bad foot as well, and an infected eye, so that he was blind for a time.

'Don't be upset,' Zhou said calmly. 'Try and find some pig's liver, cook it without salt and eat it with the water you cooked it in. You may also put a little salt in hot water, make a compress of it with clean cotton wool and put that over your eyes before you go to sleep.' It all worked. Zhou put the young man on his own horse when it was time to move on.

The worst horror was the last, crossing the dreaded grasslands at the northern tip of Sichuan. 'For us,' Zhou recalled, 'the darkest time in history was during our long march ... especially when we crossed the great grasslands near Tibet. Our condition was desperate. We not only had nothing to eat, we had nothing to drink. Yet we survived.'

Zhou was physically at his lowest ebb. When the colonel commanding the vanguard came to be briefed, he found that the doctor had ordered Zhou not to receive visitors. Deng Yingchao confided that she was 'deeply concerned about Vice-Chairman Zhou because of the lack of proper medicine.' (The Red Army officers continued throughout the Long March to use this obsolete title of Vice-Chairman of the Revolutionary Military Council of the Chinese Soviet Republic, a sign of affection faintly suggesting that Zhou stood as Mao's deputy in the new hierarchy.) Zhou had to abandon for the time being his custom of conducting military conferences into the night. But he cheerfully contributed to the search for alternative nutrition. Once the soldiers took off their leather belts, softened them by boiling them in water, added wild herbs, and served the concoction at the end of a tough day. Zhou, who must have had a twinge of empathy when he later saw Chaplin's *The Gold Rush*, enthusiastically christened it the 'soup of three delicacies'.

There are rivers in the grasslands, and Zhou and Deng had to cross one of them in heavy rain, at chest height. Because of the rapid flow and the treacherous silt underneath, Zhou told the others to undo their leggings and tie them together into a rope. Three groups got across in this way, but then the rope broke. A second one was made, thicker and taking smaller groups. When it came to Zhou's turn, his men said that he was too weak and that if he got chilled in the water, his illness would flare up again. In the end he gave in to their insistence and was carried on a stretcher, and soon they were among friends again in Shaanxi Province, joining another Red Army base that had grown up there over the past several years.

Both Zhou and his wife survived this one-year saga from Jiangxi to Shaanxi, in spite of his liver and her lungs. Deng claimed afterwards of her tuberculosis, 'strange to say, after a year's extremely strenuous life in the Long March, I was cured without any special medical treatment.'

The best accommodation now was in hillside caves, and for the next few years Zhou became a cave-dweller, first at Baoan and then at Yan'an. It was here that he left behind the long leather coat he had worn for the past twelve years: it still hangs in his old quarters there, preserved by the local Communist cadres. He clung pathetically to his familiar belongings, however old and tattered. At the end of 1935 every Red Army man was issued with a new padded jacket, but Zhou would not accept his. His bodyguard told him that they were now in a Red base area and had won their victory; everyone deserved a new jacket, and Zhou's old one was shabby and untidy. Zhou had to agree, looking at his old coat as if for the first time. But when his guard said that he would get a new one, Zhou still resisted: 'Just wash and repair this old one.'

Mao was not so lucky as Zhou. His wife, pregnant at the beginning of the Long March and actually delivering a child in the middle of it, almost went mad. She was also wounded by shrapnel. She left Mao and went to live in another town where Zhou and Deng Yingchao visited her and tried in vain to persuade her to come back. It was in these circumstances that Mao formed a liaison (one of his major misjudgements) with the pretty Shanghai film star Jiang Qing. But this had an interesting consequence. The less liberated members of Mao's court were indignant when he insisted on divorcing his wife to marry Jiang Qing, whereas Zhou brought a more tolerant and permissive attitude that Mao must have appreciated.

Deng, by contrast, projected herself as the perfect wife, picking out a good cave and turning it into a home in spite of the attentions of a crazed woman in the neighbourhood who used to strut about nude, cursing them. Deng pasted locally made rice paper onto the lattice window frames of the cave and took on a routine of counselling other women on their family problems, modern childcare, tuberculosis, foot-binding and similar problems of the day. Zhou trimmed his beard, in tune with the more sophisticated way of life which they could now adopt.

Once Zhou came home to be welcomed with a cup of coffee out of a can bearing the S & W brand name. 'It's the last bit from this can,' his wife explained; 'old Mao brought it over himself. He said a Western visitor gave it to Zhu De, and it has passed through the hands of many comrades, each taking a few spoonfuls before reaching us.'

Deng relaxed in the evenings by playing rummy and other card games with her friends. It was at this time that the Zhous adopted a daughter, Sun Weishi, one of the many orphaned children of comrades in the Party's care whose parents had been killed or executed by the warlords and Guomindang. Her arrival complemented their more settled way of life, and relieved the prospect of a future without children which Deng's earlier miscarriage had sadly held out.

In the normal event, the Communists could have expected Chiang Kai-shek to organize yet another 'Encirclement' Campaign to destroy them in their new base in a different part of China. But a new factor now appeared to help them. While China's Nationalists and Communists had been fighting each other, the Japanese army had entrenched itself in Manchuria. Now its generals sought to provoke a war with the Chinese National government under Chiang Kai-shek with the goal of becoming master of all China. Zhou had been well aware of the potential significance of Japan's baiting of the Guomindang government, referring to it several times during the Long March. It meant that the Chinese Communists could now offer to collaborate with the Guomindang under a banner of national unity against Japan, and in that guise could strengthen their own appeal to the Chinese public as well as their grassroots organization – while making it more difficult for the Guomindang to fight them.

Zhou undertook the main burden, from the Communist side, of striving to create a Chinese United Front against Japan. He was greatly helped by the fact that two of the Guomindang forces in the neighbourhood of Shaanxi were led by one of China's better warlords, Zhang Xueliang, known by all as the Young Marshal after succeeding his late father, the Old Marshal. The Young Marshal had been an opium-smoking dandy in his earlier days but had now grown in manhood to be energetic and patriotic. He and his generals paid formal court to Chiang Kai-shek as the most powerful leader in China, but felt ambivalent about him. And because the Japanese were so close, the Young Marshal believed that resistance to Japan should take the highest priority.

In January 1936 Zhou sent a letter, co-signed by Mao, to all the officers of China's Northeastern Army, whose allegiance was to the Young Marshal rather than to Chiang Kai-shek and who were potential supporters of a United Front. In April he conferred with the Young Marshal in a Roman Catholic church: they recognized that Chiang Kai-shek, because of his power, was the only plausible leader for China to resist Japanese aggression. Communist units should therefore be integrated into China's national armed forces, and the Communists, for their part, would stop their political agitation while retaining individual political rights. But Communists should also be released from Guomindang prisons. It was reminiscent of the agenda of the mid-1920s when the two rival parties collaborated in the Northern Expedition. When they had agreed, Zhou stood up to shake hands with the Young Marshal.

'Now that's all settled, I am ready to take orders from you at this very moment.' The Young Marshal demurred, preferring to wait for the orders of Chiang Kai-shek.

'I will gladly stay here . . . with you,' Zhou insisted, 'and be held as a hostage.'

'That won't be necessary,' said the Young Marshal. But Chiang Kai-shek took his time responding to this proposed truce, and meanwhile the Young Marshal and the Red Army implemented their own local cease-fire. Eventually Zhou went to Shanghai and later Nanjing to negotiate directly with Guomindang envoys. They agreed on most of the issues concerning a United Front.

But Chiang Kai-shek himself was not convinced of the need for a truce with the Communists, nor did he feel committed to it. He believed that there was still time to destroy the Communist threat to his supremacy before the Japanese threat became serious. He therefore ordered the Young Marshal to move against the Red Army. But the Communists repulsed the attack, and

Zhou sent a confidential reproach to the Young Marshal. 'Chinese do not fight Chinese,' it said. 'Inhuman is he who slays his own brother to feed the wolf!'

Meanwhile Zhou had an encounter which was to prove most fruitful. Walking through a little town north of Yan'an one day in June, he saw a Westerner, then very rare in northern Shaanxi.

'Hello,' Zhou said in English, 'are you looking for somebody?'

It was Edgar Snow, the eager young American correspondent for *Saturday Evening Post* and *Life*, who described his greeter as 'a slender young officer . . . ornamented with a black beard unusually heavy for a Chinese' and tinged with red.

When Zhou found that Snow's mission was to report on the Red Army, he asked him to his headquarters the next morning. This, Snow discovered, was a bomb-proof hut, half-cave, half-building. Despite the $80,000 that Chiang Kai-shek had once offered for Zhou's head, there was only one sentry on the door.

'Inside,' Snow recollected afterwards, 'I saw that the room was clean but furnished in the barest fashion. A mosquito net hanging over the clay *kang** was the only luxury observable. A couple of iron dispatch boxes stood at the foot of it, and a little wooden table served as a desk. Zhou was bending over it reading radiograms when the sentry announced my arrival.'

Zhou told his American visitor that he had been informed that he was a reliable journalist, friendly to the Chinese people and trustworthy. 'This is all we want to know. It does not matter to us that you are not a Communist. . . . You can write about anything you see and you will be given every help to investigate the Communist districts.'

Snow was very taken by this sophisticated figure. He described him in more detail as 'of slender stature, of medium height, with a slight wiry frame, boyish in appearance despite his long black beard, and with large warm deep-set eyes. There was certainly a kind of magnetism about him that seemed to derive from a curious combination of shyness, personal charm and a complete assurance of command. His English was somewhat hesitant but fairly correct, and I was amazed when he told me that he had not used it for five years.' Zhou was handsome, Snow recalled later, with 'a figure willowy as a girl's'.

When Zhou told the American about the United Front plans, Snow went straight to the point: 'Then you're giving up revolution?'

'Not at all,' Zhou replied. 'We are advancing revolution, not giving it up. The revolution will probably come to power by way of anti-Japanese war.'

Zhou gave Snow a horse to carry him to Baoan to see Mao, and the

---

* A bed heated from below.

American then had a unique vantage point from which to compare the two men. Beneath Zhou's urbanity, Snow saw a 'tough, supple mind, but he did not strike me then, nor later, as possessing quite the mental dexterity, vigour and self-confidence of Mao Zedong, nor his gift of the common touch.'

That was in June. As the autumn approached, the United Front question moved towards its climax. Zhou's lieutenants stepped up their indoctrination of the Young Marshal and his officers, and in October Chiang Kai-shek acknowledged the gravity of the situation by rushing back from southern China, where he had been dealing with recalcitrant warlords, in order to stiffen the resolve of the Young Marshal.

12

The Tiger Trapped
1936–40

Suddenly and quite unexpectedly, Zhou's worst enemy, the man who had almost captured him on several occasions and had offered $80,000 for his head, fell into Zhou's power. The independent-minded officers of China's Northeastern Army under the Young Marshal performed the extraordinary coup of kidnapping their superior, Generalissimo Chiang Kai-shek, while he was visiting their headquarters at Xi'an. Chiang, who was hoping to knock the Communists out before turning to face a Japanese attack, was trying to bully the Young Marshal, saying that if the Northeastern Army would not exterminate the Red Army bases in Yan'an, then Chiang would order it south to Fujian Province and do the job himself with loyal troops from elsewhere. But the Young Marshal believed that the Communists were needed to resist the Japanese.

As dawn broke on 12 December 1936, local officers surrounded the historic 'Baths of the Favourite' building where the Generalissimo was quartered in Xi'an. Chiang jumped from his campbed and climbed out of a window, leaving his false teeth behind on the bathroom shelf and losing a slipper. But he was caught. Unlike his hothead colonels, the Young Marshal had never intended to arrest his leader, but now he feared that Chiang Kai-shek might have learned of his secret meetings with Zhou and would punish him. What to do with the tiger in the net? The Young Marshal turned to Zhou Enlai for advice.

Zhou and Mao were jubilant at the Young Marshal's telegram. Their first instinct was to make sure that this enemy of China's revolution should be executed, or at the least stand trial – from which the Communists could derive immense propaganda benefit. But Zhou cautioned his comrades not to expect too much. 'We alone cannot decide what to do,' he warned. 'The attitude of the Young Marshal . . . has to be taken into account.'

134

The Young Marshal's aeroplane, sent to collect Zhou in Baoan, was not able to land in the snow despite a morning-long clear-up by Red Army soldiers. Zhou had to make his own way to Yan'an and board there. His admirers wrote afterwards that he walked the fifty miles from Baoan to Yan'an, braving the north wind and the snow, ordering his delegation to follow him. But another account has Zhou in his grey padded uniform and long black beard riding a burgundy-coloured horse, while the others behind him rode twenty Mongolian steeds. When his aides pressed a new padded coat on him for the night he was to spend in a cave at the halfway mark, Zhou told them crossly: 'Don't treat me like an old man.'

Once they were in Yan'an, the Young Marshal's Boeing got them to Xi'an within an hour, and here Zhou took up lodging at Blacksmith Wong's at the Eastern Gate. His responsibility was formidable. Trusted by the Young Marshal, Zhou was in effect the arbiter of Chiang Kai-shek's fate. He had only to say so, and this man – who had had killed so many thousands of Communists, had on several occasions tried very hard to catch Zhou himself and would have had no compunction in sentencing him to death – would in turn be killed. Guomindang troops loyal to the Generalissimo were on their way, so time was limited. What should be done?

Some of Zhou's own comrades were thirsting for blood, as were many of the Northeastern Army colonels. Zhou's own idea was probably to stage an educational and very political trial. But it soon crystallized in Zhou's mind that while he and his colleagues detested Chiang Kai-shek with a deep loathing, they detested his likely successors within the Guomindang, who would probably sue for peace terms with the Japanese so as to open every gun on the Communists. There was also the Russian angle: Zhou and his friends were in a small minority in China and therefore depended on the Kremlin for support. The Russian attitude was that everything should be subordinated to building Chinese unity against Japan, that the Generalissimo had a role to play. Zhou could hardly ignore this analysis.

Zhou therefore praised the Young Marshal for his courage but criticized him politely for his inexperience in handling the affair. He persuaded the Northeastern Army generals to use this opportunity to force Chiang to accept terms of cooperation with the Red Army in fighting Japan. Executing him would not stop the civil war but escalate it and thus help Japan – so they would have to win him over to a United Front instead.

The Young Marshal had evidently expected Soviet support for his move. It fell to Zhou to disabuse him of this by explaining the Russian viewpoint about Chinese unity. The Young Marshal reacted sullenly by talking of setting up an independent government in Xi'an and imposing sanctions on the Guomindang. In the end, however, Zhou persuaded him that Chiang Kai-shek should be released after agreeing to the terms on which resistance to Japan would be offered. Zhou went on to bring the colonels in the Northeastern Army round to his view. One of his talks to them lasted six hours.

Soon a Guomindang plenipotentiary arrived, and Zhou spent a lot of time with him trying to persuade him to the Communist terms. Just before Christmas Chiang Kai-shek's wife, Soong May-ling, courageously flew into Xi'an. 'Why have you come?' Chiang is supposed to have asked her. 'You know that it is a death trap.' But she had never lacked in courage.

Zhou negotiated strenuously with the Guomindang leaders on the basis of six points, including an end to the civil war and a withdrawal of their central army from areas where they were threatening the Communists, a reshuffle of the central Chinese government to bring in committed anti-Japanese figures, the release of Communist prisoners, and freedom of action for the Communist Party. They eventually agreed. They also paid tribute to this Communist 'foreign minister' – who at the age of thirty-eight had emerged as a brilliant diplomatist. Chiang Kai-shek's closest adviser, W. H. Donald, declared afterwards that, 'Zhou Enlai . . . was actually the one man who enabled the Generalissimo to depart unharmed from the 1936 Xi'an kidnapping.' Only Zhou's trigger-happy critics from within the Northeastern Army withheld their tribute. 'Zhou's amiableness was all false,' one of them commented. 'He was very crafty, and could put on such a lovable manner.' The reputation was to stick.

All this had been achieved by Zhou without even seeing his archenemy. Only on Christmas Eve, after he had been in Xi'an negotiating for over a week, did he actually visit the Generalissimo. The interview was late at night between the two of them alone, and neither said much about it afterwards. One of Zhou's colleagues later insisted that Chiang Kai-shek had refused to speak to Zhou, and in Chiang Kai-shek's account of the Xi'an incident he never mentions actually talking to Zhou. Yet a British correspondent reported that they had three secret conferences, and an American two, and Chiang was said deliberately to have treated Zhou with the utmost disrespect.

There are many different versions of the opening words of this historic interview.

'Mister Chiang, I am glad to see you in good health,' is one variant.

'Chiang Xiansheng' (Teacher Chiang), 'I am your student. So long as we are fighting the Japanese, anything you say will be acceptable to us,' was Zhou's own version, as relayed through one of the Northeastern Army officers.

In yet another account, the Young Marshal 'introduced' Zhou by telling Chiang that a former subordinate of his begged for an audience, whereupon Zhou stepped forward with a smart salute and addressed the Generalissimo as 'commandant', following the old Huangpu custom.

The most elegant reconstruction of this opening scene is: 'Mister Chairman, I have come to sign the articles of betrothal for the remarriage of the Guomindang and Communist Parties.'

Whatever the words may have been, Chiang Kai-shek, still weak and psychologically shaken by his capture, is supposed to have turned pale with apprehension when his former political assistant, whom he had so often sought to expunge from the pages of Chinese history, came through the door. Had the Communists arrived in Xi'an to dispatch him? With heavy insincerity he supposedly pleaded: 'All the time we've been fighting I often thought of you. I remembered even during the civil war that you have worked well for me. I hope we can work together again.'

Zhou implored Chiang to measure up to the call of history, become a genuine national leader and help all the other Chinese to resist Japanese aggression. He catalogued the ideological goals the Communists were giving up in this national cause, and appealed to the Guomindang to be equally patriotic and conciliatory. Zhou's tactic was to exude respect for, and submission to, an outstandingly strong adversary (suppressing his real emotions just as he had done on the Nankai School stage), avoiding coercion so as to make it easier for detailed agreement to be reached later. Chiang spoke in a general way about the desirability of ending the civil war, and Zhou probably read into this a moral commitment which could be translated in later sessions into something more concrete.

Once the tension had eased a little, Zhou is said to have made some social conversation about the Generalissimo's family, confirming that his son, Chiang Ching-kuo (now President of the Republic of China in Taiwan), was enjoying good treatment during his training in Russia. Catching the almost imperceptible sense of regret which the Generalissimo betrayed about his son, Zhou promised to try to bring about a reunion.

But the diplomatic edifice which Zhou was so patiently building fell apart. He had intended to hold Chiang for a few more days to secure the details of the Guomindang–Communist pact. But his grave exhortations for the Generalissimo to be left unharmed and released with conditions were perhaps too successful. On Christmas Day, only hours after Zhou's interview, the Young Marshal took Chiang Kai-shek – whom he had all along respected as a man of honour – with his wife and advisers to the airport for Nanjing. The trap was prematurely sprung, and the archenemy returned to his capital not only physically unscathed but free from any personal obligation. Zhou sped to the airport at the last moment, not having been informed in advance of the release, but too late to prevent Chiang Kai-shek from flying off to safety.

There was even worse to come. Perhaps Zhou vented some of his disgust on the Young Marshal standing next to him in the farewell crowd at the

137

airport. Suddenly the Young Marshal said: 'I am going with the Generalissimo.'

Brushing off Zhou's restraining gesture, he walked impetuously onto the plane to join his former captive – and was never seen again. Chiang Kai-shek was thus able on his safe return home to convict his captor of treason and put him under house arrest – where he remained, first on the mainland and later in Taiwan, for the rest of his life.

Zhou had already cabled Mao full of expectation:

Chiang Kai-shek is ill. When I saw him, he indicated: the suppression of Communists will stop, there will be an alliance with the Red Army to resist Japan. . . . Judging from what has happened, there was a real change in Chiang Kai-shek's attitude. . . . He is sincere in delegating matters to T. V. Soong (a banker, brother-in-law, and key lieutenant of Chiang's) and Soong is really determined to resist Japan. . . . When he was about to leave, Chiang said . . . 'From now on I will never engage in the suppression of Communists.'

Zhou was very shortly to eat those words.

Mao, who had been sceptical all along, now wanted Zhou to cut off their relations with the Young Marshal and destroy the evidence of their earlier negotiations. This was one of those occasions where Mao and Zhou complemented each other, the former spinning his plans inside the camp and the other negotiating outside. 'Mao Zedong,' said one of their mutual colleagues, 'told Zhou all his thoughts and intentions, while Zhou Enlai translated them into action in the light of the actual conditions outside.'

Zhou soon sent another cable to calm Mao down: 'Chiang, with the vainglory of the self-appointed hero, will probably not go back on his word.' The colleague added that this was another poor judgement on Zhou's part.

Could the cease-fire and the United Front against Japan be saved, in this complicated triangular relationship between the Communists, the Guomindang and Northeastern Army? When he learned of the Young Marshal's arrest, Zhou cabled a protest to Nanjing. But the colonels' blood was up, and fifty of them threatened to kill Zhou for his part in losing their Young Marshal. Zhou needed all his skills to disarm their anger. 'You don't want,' he asked, 'to make China into another Spain, do you?'

He was helped by Miao, a tall Manchurian with a booming voice and extreme views, anti-Communist and anti-Guomindang, who sought Zhou's advice on how to secure the Young Marshal's escape.

'It isn't that I don't want to help,' Zhou answered, 'it is just not up to me to dictate the final terms. Besides, the Young Marshal is only one person and there is a whole nation to think about.'

Miao accused Zhou of treating the Young Marshal as expendable for the sake of his revolution.

'No, brother Miao, not for my revolution. It's for our revolution and for those hundreds and thousands of our compatriots who are dying this very minute. . . . You have lived in the Marshal's comfortable headquarters too long. You have not bothered to walk on your own feet for days in western Sichuan and northern Shaanxi and many other out-of-the-way places in our country. You have not seen how most of our people live. They have not lived like human beings for generations.'

Miao insisted that Zhou had no feeling for the Young Marshal. 'I once heard it said that a Communist never sheds tears at a comrade's death.'

'No,' Zhou replied. 'We never shed tears at sadness. We have only tears of anger. And there is a tremendous difference. We are fighting for the people but we have no use for sentimentalism. Our revolutionary experience has been earned with our comrades' lives, and our policy is written in blood that cannot be washed away with a few drops of sentimental tears.'

'You are too old,' Miao taunted. 'You're a damned fool.'

Luckily for Zhou and his professional self-regard, the negotiations on the United Front went forward. A new version sent to Nanjing on 10 February provided the basis for the eventual Communist–Guomindang pact. Evidently, the Generalissimo felt some minimal obligation to honour the terms that had been discussed for his release from Xi'an. The Communists would give up their extreme land reform in return for a recognized place in the joint defence against Japan.

One of the Guomindang emissaries who walked into Zhou's office in Xi'an with a revised set of truce conditions was Zhou's old schoolfriend and student mentor, Wu, the tall Manchurian who had shared his desk with the new boy Zhou at the Nankai Middle School, protected him against bullies during his four years there, and later opened his house in Kyoto to Zhou when they were both studying in Japan. In the seventeen years since then, and since their parting of ways, Wu had risen in the Guomindang government service.

The first handshake was strained, and there was an awkward moment of silence. Neither quite knew whether the old first-name terms should be revived.

'It's been many years,' Zhou began tentatively.

'Yes, we both are getting old.'

'Yes, we are.'

They sadly noted that three of the six 'blood brothers' from their Nankai School gang were already dead.

Zhou fingered his beard, trying to think of the next gambit. 'How is your wife?'

'She manages all right.'

'Any children?'

'Only one.'

'Still the same wife?' Although he said it with a twinkle, Zhou must have realized that this might be taken the wrong way, in the context of Communist allegations about the corruption of Guomindang life. Wu proceeded coldly with the business in hand, and soon those seventeen years rose again as a barrier between two men who, in their youth, could hardly have been closer.

A photographer immortalized the splendid scene of Zhou's triumphal return to the Yan'an airstrip. Flanked by Mao and the other Red leaders, he leans proprietorially against his biplane, hands stuffed nonchalantly in the pockets of his padded flying overall, his white flying helmet on his head and goggles perched on his forehead – the hunter returned with his prey.

Heading for Nanjing some weeks later for yet another round of negotiations, Zhou was ambushed on a mountain forest road in cloudy and windy weather. One of the party was killed, and it seems that because he had one of Zhou's namecards in his pocket the mysterious snipers departed in the belief that they had fulfilled their mission.

When Zhou did reach Nanjing soon afterwards, he had his first taste of a new kind of ambassadorial life, in the full glare of the international media. Also, he was able to visit his old professor, Zhang Boling. 'Teacher,' he is supposed to have said on this occasion, 'are you still willing to take me back as a student?' But he did not mean to be taken literally, and Zhang Boling was unwise to boast to his close friends that he could easily persuade Zhou to leave the Communist Party.

Zhou told a journalist that: 'The influence of the liberals under Chiang Kai-shek is now predominant in the Nanjing government. . . . The success of our plan for cooperation and the cessation of the ten-year civil war is due to the fact that the Chinese people, the Chinese soldiers and the liberals in Nanjing want an end to Chinese fighting Chinese while Japan steals our territory right and left.'

When Helen Foster Snow interviewed him in Yan'an in June 1937, Zhou portrayed the Communist Party as having given up its extreme ambitions, wanting only 'a national democratic system which would include the landowners, bourgeoisie and petty bourgeoisie with the workers and peasants, and exclude only traitors. . . . We want to create a big democratic movement among all classes of the Chinese people . . . for the purpose of the defensive anti-Japanese war.' Now that the Guomindang planned to implement Sun Yat-sen's three principles – of democratic freedom, national emancipation and social welfare – the Communists were ready to help.

Was Zhou sincere in such statements? It is not very helpful to depict him as the man of smiles standing between the frowning Mao and the outside world, as many Guomindang commentators have. Mao had equally breathtaking views to express to foreign visitors about the need for a United Front with Chiang Kai-shek. It was true, however, that Zhou was a consummate actor, whose protests of sincerity, sometimes eased by tears, were so convincing that he won the sympathy and trust of many Chinese who wanted nothing to do with communism.

In his earlier years, for example in his management of the Communist secret service and his handling of revenge against traitors, he had shown himself far from moderate and capable of ruthlessness. The record showed him as a frequent and ardent backer of the intransigent lines of both Li Lisan and Wang Ming in their respective days of power. It was only now, in 1937, that he began to acquire a 'moderate' image, specifically in the way he carried out his brief of representing the Communist cause in the United Front with the Guomindang.

In June Chiang Kai-shek sent his private aeroplane for Zhou to join him and his ministers at Guling, the summer capital of China. Here they discussed the Communist demand for representation in the national legislature. But on 7 July the discussions were interrupted by the outbreak of fighting on the Marco Polo Bridge near Beijing. An apparently unintended exchange of midnight shots between a Japanese patrol and the garrison of a Chinese town on the border of an area militarily controlled by the Japanese was seized upon by adventurists in the Japanese army leadership as a pretext to make demands which no Chinese army commander could honourably accept. On the basis of these, full-scale war between China and Japan broke out. The United Front was no longer a luxury in the inventive mind of Zhou Enlai, but a compelling political necessity which the Chinese people would demand of their political leaders.

Zhou returned to Yan'an for emergency discussions with Mao and the others, and then came back to see the Generalissimo at Lushan, to find him now ready to agree to the political arrangements he had been spurning a few months earlier. In a series of statements Chiang acknowledged the legal role of the Communist Party, the Red Army and the Red base in Shaanxi.

Zhou drafted the Red version of the United Front platform in a burst of mystical nationalism, with the goal of tenacious struggle by 'every patriotic descendant of our common ancestor, the Yellow Emperor, Huang Di, to create a new China, independent, happy and free.' Almost casually it mentioned the Communists' pledge, as their contribution to national unity, to stop confiscating land and cancel the socialist movement in the countryside. There was to be a patriotic moratorium on such ideological activities as arresting trade unionists (on the Guomindang side) and tearing up title deeds to land (on the Communist side).

In August, after the Japanese took Shanghai, Zhou carried back to a Politburo meeting at Lochuan a package proposal which included placing the Communist Party and Red Army under Guomindang orders. Zhou explained that under his deal with Chiang the Red Army would be integrated into the national armed forces but not absorbed, taking orders about their operations and getting planes and arms from Nanjing, but not becoming an organic part of the Guomindang forces. Mao insisted that the Red Army retain total autonomy.

If the Communist Party became active in the war against Japan, Zhou argued, its political status in China would rise. It should keep its word on collaborating with the Guomindang and not disobey orders from the central government. Independence was in any case only relative, and could be expressed in all kinds of subtle ways once the basic agreement was struck with the Guomindang.

When nobody supported Mao, he adjourned the meeting for three days, trying to win over commanders to his view, while Zhou played chess with Zhang Guotao, who had now rejoined the main Red force after the separation at the end of the Long March. As always in an impasse of this kind, somebody set about conciliation, in this instance Luo Fu. Mao really wanted a war on two fronts against both Japan and the Guomindang, and did not accept that this would mean only a halfhearted commitment to each. Zhou said that now was the time for the Party to demonstrate patriotism and to fight with, not against, the Guomindang, rather than lapse back into guerrilla warfare which would spread an impression of Communist weakness. The compromise was to participate in a total war of resistance against Japan, but still primarily through guerrilla rather than mobile operations.

Mao's equivocation and mistrust coloured everything. He agreed with Zhou that the Red Army should learn the Japanese language, military organization and methods. But he did nothing to act on this, and it was left to Zhou to organize training courses for the Communist troops. And when Chiang Kai-shek ordered the Red Army to march to the Shanxi front against the Japanese, Mao kept making excuses: his supplies were not ready, the reorganization was not complete. . . . Even when the Red Army did go to Shanxi, it was not sent all at once in case the Communist military power be annihilated in one battle; the three divisions were dispersed to different parts of Shanxi.

Zhou made his contempt for Mao's tactics known by virtually going to ground for three months and withholding his services. Instead of travelling to Nanjing to liaise with the Guomindang government, as he was supposed to do, he found an excuse to accompany the Red Army on its march to Shanxi, ignoring Mao's numerous telegrams or finding excuses to fail to act on them. He let it be known that the theoretical works of which Mao was so proud, *On Practice* and *On Contradiction*, were not inspiring and might be 'full of errors'.

'By disobeying the order to proceed quickly to Nanjing,' Mao complained, 'Zhou Enlai bungled important matters. How could an envoy be allowed to act at will when he receives an order that he finds displeasing?'

Zhou's presence at the front bore fruit, however, in the battle won by General Lin Biao at the Pingxing Pass, partly helped by Zhou's logistical organization, at the end of September. This was one of the first major Chinese victories over Japan, and although the invaders did not allow themselves to be so easily ambushed in mountain country again, it worked wonders for the Communist image in Guomindang China. Zhou's wife led the celebrations at the Red Army headquarters, singing a song celebrating earlier victories on the Long March.

Agnes Smedley, meeting Zhou again in Taiyuan, the Shanxi capital, in late October, was enthusiastic. 'Of all the men I met in Taiyuan, he was clearly the most realistic, the most able, the most efficient. He is of fine handsome appearance, and in all respects a man of broad knowledge and culture.' She put Zhou on a par with the internationally far better known Jawaharlal Nehru. 'He stood straight, looked men in the eye and spoke with disarming frankness. His knowledge and vision were catholic and his judgement free from sectarianism. . . . If any worthwhile measure such as the introduction of modern medical practice was necessary, it was Zhou Enlai who signed the order and forced the measure through.' Some of the Guomindang hoped to win him over from Communism. 'They never succeeded, for he cared not at all for personal comfort, wealth or power.' Later she tried to teach the Communist leaders to dance. When it came to Zhou, he was 'like a man working out a problem in mathematics'. He would wish to keep control of his environment, and not simply give himself up to an unplanned bodily movement, and yet he had a natural sense of rhythm.

With the war on their doorsteps, huge rallies in Shanxi listened to Zhou telling them that they must become more democratic if Japan were to be defeated. This kind of talk enabled him to win the local warlord's officers over to the Red Army. The British correspondent James Bertram described Zhou in his plain 'Sun Yat-sen' uniform, with short hair and beard, as resembling 'the self-portrait of D. H. Lawrence, an impression which was heightened by [his] intense nervous vitality.' He would have been an artist, Bertram thought, if he had not become a revolutionary. 'His manner was lively, almost gay; and he moved his hands in deft, sudden gestures. He spoke current English with perfect ease, but with an occasional French turn of phrase, or a French word to help out.'

The journalist asked him about the war. 'The Japanese have not enough troops to occupy the whole territory, even if they could,' Zhou replied. 'It is a matter of simple arithmetic. There are more than three hundred cities in north China; the Japanese could never hold all of these, even if they put one company of troops in each city. And if they did, that would be fine for us – we could destroy each separate company in turn!'

But in the short run the well-equipped Japanese made mincemeat of the

Chinese regular defences. In mid-November Zhou took part in the evacuation of Taiyuan, and almost failed to survive. The Red Army tried to move four trucks out on the last night before the Japanese took the city. The bridge across the River Fen was filled with refugees, however, so they had to abandon the trucks and carry what materials they could on foot. Halfway across the leaders realized they had lost Zhou and other senior staff officers. Only later was he found in the confusion, barely reaching the nearest village by the time the first enemy aeroplanes came over the horizon to bomb the city and its bridges.

Zhou was soon back in Nanjing again for his 'ambassadorial' duties, having made it up with Mao. By then the city was being evacuated in anticipation of Japanese attack. He arranged for the American naval attaché, Major Evans Carlson, to visit the Red bases. 'On a day when everyone else was evacuating Nanjing in flight up the river to Wuhan,' wrote Edgar Snow, 'Zhou helped smuggle the big Yankee across Japanese lines by way of the Red underground and into guerrilla territory.'

At the end of 1937, Zhou was comforted by the unexpected return to Yan'an from Moscow of Wang Ming, the Russian-trained intellectual whom he had helped to advance up the Communist Party ladder at the beginning of the 1930s. Zhou was talking to Zhang Guotao at the Communist headquarters one day when they heard the drone of an aircraft, which they took to be a Japanese bomber, but it landed at Yan'an airport, and so they went to see. Zhou had no idea that it would be Wang Ming; Mao had kept the secret to himself. Wang returned as the 'Russian candidate' in the event of Mao's being unseated in the Chinese Party, and he enjoyed seniority in the Party hierarchy over Zhou. Zhou was no doubt pleased that Mao now had somebody much more dangerous to worry about as a potential threat to his leadership, and he took a suitable hedging attitude between the two, at least until the situation clarified.

Wang prided himself, of course, on being not only Stalin's 'man' but also a good Marxist theoretician known to have out-argued Zhou on the Central Committee. Having expounded a United Front line in Moscow for the past two or three years, he now tried to coast on the United Front tide which had been released by Zhou. But Mao found that Wang talked too much and gave away too much, and he was soon criticizing him at Party meetings. When it came a little later to a vital personal letter to Chiang Kai-shek, for example, Mao chose Zhou rather than Wang as the postman – and Zhou did not have to worry about his job after that.

Mao knew now that he could get efficient results from Zhou. Guo Morou, a poet who was now working under Zhou, said that 'his handling of problems is as rapid as electricity'.

There was a telling example about this time of Zhou's diplomatic skill, on this occasion within his own Party. One of his younger confidants, Liao Chengzhi, had been arrested by Zhang Guotao for some supposed offence and kept under guard. Men like Zhang, controlling armies personally loyal to them and with Party Central Committee status to back this military power, could behave almost like independent warlords and there was no rule of law to deter their arbitrary actions. Not every small complaint could be taken up in the Central Committee. Zhou anxiously sought an opportunity to rescue his follower, and one day he saw him by chance in the street. Zhou, who had not seen Liao for a long time, went over to shake his hand but observed Zhang's guard keeping watch, so Zhou said nothing and did not alter his expression. One night soon afterwards, when Zhang Guotao was present at the Red Army headquarters, Zhou sent his adjutant to fetch Liao – which he was able to do by 'pulling rank'.

'Have you recognized your errors?' Zhou shouted sternly to Liao in Zhang Guotao's full hearing. 'Have you fully admitted them and do you intend to correct them?' Liao answered yes to all these questions. Zhou then told Liao to join them for dinner, an order which Zhang Guotao did not dare to countermand because of Zhou's superior rank. Throughout the meal, Zhou talked only to Zhang, but never mentioned Liao, as if there were no problem of any kind among them. Since Liao had confessed errors and promised to correct them in the hearing of many senior officers, Zhang could not kill him, as perhaps he had intended, and there was not much point even in continuing his detention. He was later released, saved by Zhou's impeccable instinct for diplomacy.

The Chiang Kai-shek government, bowing to the Japanese advance, moved farther inland to Wuhan, where Zhou spent most of 1938 as the Communist representative – beardless (though one of his American contacts noted a permanent 'five o'clock shadow' on his face) and smartly dressed in Guomindang uniform, dividing his time between the Military Council offices and the Communist newspaper. He wrote in an editorial: 'The Generalissimo is the rightful and the only person to lead the entire nation to victory, because of his revolutionary experience and dedication.' Some people read this as a signal that Zhou was wavering in his political allegiance. His liaison, both with Chiang Kai-shek and with Chen Cheng, his old schoolfriend, battlefield opponent and new Guomindang boss, was so successful that many people wondered where he really stood.

When Zhang Guotao made a spectacular defection to the Guomindang in April, resisting Zhou's efforts to keep him in the Red camp, Wuhan rumour said that 'Zhou Enlai will be the second Zhang Guotao'. Some predicted that the Generalissimo would exile Mao and rename the Communist Party as the Populist Party under Zhou's supreme leadership – which would, it was presumed, be something less extreme than Marxism. People even asked

Zhou openly at parties whether it was true that he had foresworn communism.

'How could it be true?' he answered. 'If I left our Party organization I would be useless. What good would it do if I were to join the Guomindang?' Asked outright by some junior officials to join the Guomindang, he replied: 'No, the Guomindang has talent at every level. What use would I be there?'

But one of Zhou's former colleagues, Liu Ning, who knew his mind, wrote:

The prediction that Zhou Enlai will be a second Zhang Guotao is not only possible but... unavoidable. The Mao faction's suspicion of, and discrimination against, Zhou has made him uneasy in that environment. At present it may be said that Zhou is vacillating between the Guomindang and the Communist parties. Zhou will not leave the Communist Party in the near future. He has to think about his future and plan carefully. Because of the Zhang Guotao defection, affecting the Communist Party's prestige, the Mao faction attacks on Zhou will be relaxed. A Mao–Zhou rupture and Zhou's defection are inevitable, but they will not come to a head immediately.

All this speculation made Zhou's work in Wuhan much easier, and to that extent he may have encouraged it. It did not help his political status in Yan'an. To foreigners, however, Zhou became the reasonable voice of China which the world wanted to hear, and he cultivated them.

Eventually he was joined by his wife, Deng Yingchao. She had still not quite thrown off the tuberculosis that had afflicted her through the Long March, and in 1936 had gone to convalesce in the Western Hills outside Beijing. The dry climate there, together with good food and rest, had almost cured her when Japanese troops suddenly reached that locality and she had to flee – first to Beijing, where she found Edgar Snow, her old American friend from Yan'an days, whom she begged to help get her out. Since the Japanese were searching all railway passengers and arresting anyone of political significance, Snow suggested he take her to Tianjin as his *amah*. On the appointed day she appeared at the station looking 'the complete *amah*, with her bobbed hair miraculously transformed' (said Edgar Snow), like 'a rather intelligent-looking *amah*' (according to James Bertram, who was helping Snow). Even Jack Service, the American diplomat, who was also on the train and knew Zhou's wife, was not admitted into the secret of the true identity of Snow's '*amah*'.

The danger point was at Tianjin, where the Japanese were picking out any Chinese who looked suspicious to them. A dozen Chinese passengers whose soft white hands, contrasting with their peasant clothes, had aroused suspicion were taken off for questioning. Deng Yingchao hid her hands in her sleeves. 'American,' Snow explained to the Japanese inspector. And, gesturing at Deng Yingchao, '*Amah-san*'. Deng showed herself as good an actor as her husband, dropping her jaw in an idiotic grin. The Japanese contemptuously emptied her luggage on the floor, but passed her without even looking at it. (This is Edgar Snow's description of a very gallant rescue which may have saved Deng Yingchao's life. She herself said many years later that Snow's account was mistaken, but in what detail we do not know. The main outlines of the incident could surely not have been invented by both Snow and Bertram.)

Deng Yingchao soon joined her husband in Wuhan where she took up a bourgeois round of social activities with Guomindang ladies, playing mahjong in front of frilly curtains – with 'just a whisper of a perm in her hair', as one of them described it. She became involved in the New Life Movement, the austerity programme started by the Generalissimo and his wife.

'I don't feel nearly as energetic as I used to,' she confessed to an old schoolfriend, 'since I lost the baby. . . . You know, with all the tension and running.'

'You didn't suffer too much, I hope,' her friend inquired.

'It's all right now, but of course it can never be quite the same again.'

Life in Wuhan was almost like a second honeymoon for Zhou and Deng after the constant interruptions and hardships since their marriage. They hired a beautiful foreign-built villa on the mountainside with a superb orchard of peach trees and a lake nearby. It was the nearest they would ever get to luxury.

They were dining once at the house of Tillman Durdin, the *New York Times* correspondent, when an air-raid warning interrupted the meal. After the all-clear allowed them to return from the shelters, they found that Durdin's house had been bombed to smithereens.

Zhou told the English poet W. H. Auden, visiting China in 1938, that what he most feared was a compromising peace between the Guomindang and Japan at Communist expense. James Bertram followed this up when he went to see Zhou in his office, which was in the former Japanese Concession in Wuhan (he found him sitting on a *tatami* mat before a handsome hanging scroll). Zhou put it to him that the Communist Party's foreign policy was identical with the Guomindang's.

'This is not true just for today,' he underlined. 'We are not opportunists. We believe that China must continue for a long time in her fight against Japanese imperialism before she is successful. In this spirit it is very important for us to have every possible assistance from friendly foreign powers.

'And if in the end we do gain the victory, we shall need all the more the economic and technical assistance of more highly developed foreign countries to rebuild China after the war. Any questions that are still outstanding, such as extraterritoriality and the unequal treaties, can then be settled by peaceful agreement. We shall continue to welcome foreign capital investment and foreign enterprise in China.'

Zhou was once dining with Agnes Smedley and Evans Carlson, the US military attaché whom he had helped visit the guerrilla areas, when Smedley spoke rather sharply about the failure of some foreign journalists to report the true facts. Zhou gazed into space, apparently paying no attention to this tirade. But after a while he sat up, cupped his chin in his hands and rested his elbows on the table in a characteristic pose and observed quietly: 'If the journalists always published accurate accounts of current events, there would be no need for the historians.'

Yet he expressed confidence in the journalists he was meeting in Wuhan. He used to clap Edgar Snow on the shoulder, saying to the other foreign correspondents: 'To us, Snow is the greatest of foreign authors and our best friend abroad.'

Another foreigner whom Zhou came to trust and like was the American missionary, Bishop Logan Herbert Roots, in whose house he had sought refuge a decade earlier and now became a frequent visitor. Zhou used to love talking to the bishop in his study, and after one long session, when the bishop's daughter asked what they had been talking about, the bishop replied: 'I can tell you only one thing: our friend is fascinated by the idea of how to create a new type of man to live in his new society.'

Years afterwards, Zhou told Bishop Roots's son: 'Your father – I loved him.'

When the bishop retired after forty-two years in China, Zhou inscribed some verses for him, from the Chinese *Book of Songs*:

> Brothers fight each other in the house.
> Outside they bar the enemy's attacks. . . .

He meant the strains inside the Chinese United Front, but he might equally have had in mind the quarrelling factions within the Communist Party. Mao was at this point struggling with Wang Ming over military policy. Wang had no more time for guerrilla fighting and praised the regular battle tactics of the Guomindang. Mao still contended that positional warfare was useless as long as Japan was technically so superior. In his view decisive engagements should be avoided, and the defence of Wuhan, for example, should be planned on the assumption that its fall could not be averted. Zhou supported Wang Ming in this particular argument.

A bodyguard assigned to Zhou during one of his frequent visits to the Red base headquarters in the cave city of Yan'an has left a description of his quarters there. He had two rooms built of earth, the outer one used as an office with an old desk, a chair and a long bench. On the table Zhou kept an inkstone and ink, a copper brush holder and two brushes, a red and a blue pencil and an old cup – and next to the table was his veteran rectangular iron document case which had been of such service on the Long March. The inside room was his bedroom, with two old planks lying on top of the *kang*, covered with a layer of straw and an old blanket. The bed was completed with a white sheet and a long-service quilt, with a kitbag as a pillow. These were the home conditions of the man who was the toast of cosmopolitan society in Wuhan.

Zhou left Wuhan for Changsha in the autumn of 1938, retreating with the national government before the Japanese armies. But in November the Japanese reached the gates of Changsha, where the city authorities set the city on fire to deny the enemy use of it. But they did it too soon. Guomindang officials came with petrol to set alight the building where Zhou was still writing at his desk, and he had to escape quickly through a back gate. Zhou turned angrily to look at the blazing buildings behind him. To his credit, Chiang summarily punished his officials for being overzealous.

Zhou did persuade Chiang Kai-shek to legitimize the Communist military forces from Jiangxi which, instead of going on the Long March in 1934, had remained south of the River Yangzi under their commander Ye Ting. The Generalissimo's imprimatur for a New Fourth Army gave the Communists a valuable military base in south-central China from which they could expand in future, and in the spring of 1939 Zhou went on a long field trip to Anhui, Zhejiang and Jiangxi provinces in order to brief the commanders and report on their situation. He told Xiang Ying, the New Fourth Army's political commissar, to expand guerrilla warfare in the area and create the largest possible revolutionary base. Zhou may also have gone to Anhui to reconcile differences between two rival Communist generals leading the New Fourth Army. One story is that he intended to dismiss Ye Ting for decadent behaviour in running off with a woman some years earlier, but was deflected by his good combat record.

This was, of course, Zhou's home country and he eagerly seized the first opportunity he had ever had as an adult to revisit his family seat and childhood haunts. At Shaoxing he called at the Hundred Year Hall of Grandfather Panlong, and then took a sampan along the river, stopping at different villages to see the Zhou clan's burial grounds. Several cousins of his generation greeted him at different places and accompanied him for part of the way. He was, after all, the eldest grandson. He read the family register and inquired after the life and conditions of the members of his branch of the family. Following the old custom, he bowed three times to the head of the clan (although he did not go as far as kowtowing). Wartime restrictions prevented him from revisiting Huaian, his birthplace. But on the evening of 29 March he had dinner with several brothers and cousins at the house of a bank manager in Shaoxing, and after the meal they indulged in their favourite traditional game of composing epigrams for each other.

This incident gives a rare insight into Zhou's psychology, for it shows how within the same few days he could urge total strangers to change their way of life and become democratic and egalitarian, and at the same time relax with apparent satisfaction in the bosom of his unreconstructed family, where his blood relatives were mostly satisfied with their semi-feudal role as a privileged elite. Zhou must have known by instinct and, to a certain extent, by experience that his cousins would be unresponsive to his attempts to convert them to Marxism (Enzhu had been a special case, and not a happy example), and his spring holiday in Zhejiang may have been a simple exercise in nostalgia. Throughout his life he seemed capable of these occasional juxtapositions, although he never allowed his family links to jeopardize his Party career.

When some time in the summer of 1939 Zhou suffered his first serious injury in his active career in the field, it came not from the hand of the Japanese or the Guomindang but from a fellow-Communist. The official story given is that Zhou arrived at Mao's quarters in Yan'an to find him disinclined to take up an invitation to talk on Marxism at the Central Committee's school that evening. Mao had other business to do and asked Zhou to take his place. Mao's wife, Jiang Qing, offered to accompany him. During the short ride to the school Jiang Qing whipped her horse strongly to take the lead as they came to a field of maize where the path at the edge was so narrow that only one horse could negotiate it at a time. Suddenly she reined in her horse so that Zhou, who was immediately behind her, had the choice of colliding with her, trampling on the crops or himself making a sudden halt. He too reined his horse in sharply, the animal reared up and Zhou fell off. To protect his head, he threw out his left arm, and it broke on hitting the ground. Bone could be seen protruding through the elbow and blood came rushing out. Jiang is supposed to have returned to Yan'an pretending to know nothing about the incident, and Zhou said that Mao was not to be told of her part in it. The implication that there was a deliberate intent on Jiang Qing's part to harm Zhou must be taken with reserve, and seen in the context of the campaign to vilify her and the rest of the Gang of Four at the time this story was circulated. It was, more likely, an accident – though a strange one.

Zhou was taken on to the school, where he lay in a cold sweat with a white face and blood soaking through his clothes. He was treated by Dr Kotnis, an Indian volunteer doctor at the Red base, and for several days his arm was clamped between two boards. But it never set properly and remained flexed, giving Zhou intermittent pain and discomfort for the rest of his life, and obliging him to use it as little as possible.

The story of Zhou's accident is highly controversial. For a long time the Communists would not even admit that he had broken his arm. When Edgar Snow was in Yan'an more than twenty years later and asked about the story, his official guide indignantly replied: 'That's an imperialist slander. Premier

Zhou never fell off his horse and there's nothing wrong with his arm.'

Mao decided that Zhou should go to Moscow, where he could have the services of the best surgeons in the world. No doubt there were additional political reasons for this. Mao may have looked forward to a period in Yan'an free from Zhou's presence. Another rationale may have been the Party's need to be better informed about the march of events in Europe, where Stalin had signed a pact with Hitler and war had broken out in Western Europe – while the Russians were negotiating a truce with Japan affecting the eastern Siberian and north China theatres.

Chiang Kai-shek, honouring the spirit of the United Front, sent his private aeroplane to take Zhou on the first stage of the flight to Moscow, where the Generalissimo himself had good relations as the acknowledged national leader of China in the war against Japan. Zhou took his wife and adopted daughter with him.

Mao used this opportunity to send Otto Braun, the now unwanted German military adviser, back to Europe. Braun tried to take his Chinese wife (now legitimized) with him, but Zhou would not allow it. The journey took about three weeks because of bad weather. In Moscow it appeared that Zhou acted, on Mao's behalf, as chief prosecutor of Braun for his 'errors' in the early 1930s. Mao wanted Braun expelled from the Comintern and, according to Braun, 'if possible, liquidated'. From Mao's point of view Braun may have known too much about the legal vulnerability of Mao's leadership claims deriving from the Zunyi conference. In the event Braun was allowed to retire safely to his home in Germany.

Very little has been written about Zhou's six-month stay in the Soviet Union from September 1939 to March 1940. One brief record by a colleague tells us that when Zhou addressed the Comintern, arguing that the realities of Chinese politics must be recognized and the rural areas be seen as the centre of power, 'some comrades of the Comintern, who did not understand the actual conditions in China, were greatly surprised and expressed disapproval.'

The typical tourist, Zhou returned to China in the spring with a new tweed suit, a projector and five films (including *Lenin in October* and *Gorky's Youth*), and bored the pants off the comrades in Yan'an by showing them over and over again. He treated Mao to all five films at one sitting, giving his own impromptu commentary and translating from the Russian soundtrack as the film went on. He ran the projector himself, partly to show that his arm was better, but it had clearly not completely healed. He found it difficult to write, and experienced a dull pain much of the time, in spite of frequent massage.

Zhou was soon back to briefing foreigners about the war situation, as the Communists saw it, in mid-1940. The war had settled into a rut, the Japanese occupying small but key areas and the Chinese lacking the resources to oust them. Zhou told Gerald Samson of Associated Press that the partnership with the Guomindang would go on after the war. And he specifically supported Mao's theories about guerrilla warfare, which, he said, were 'infinitely better suited to the national economy' and calculated seriously to harass the Japanese army's long lines of communication, 'making it obligatory for it to station large and expensive garrisons in the occupied areas'. After years of meticulously clinging to the equal validity of conventional fighting and guerrilla tactics, Zhou was finally conceding to Mao's correctness in emphasizing the latter.

13

Metamorphosis of a Pig
1940–43

The American writer Theodore White was invited in late 1940 to a restaurant dinner with Zhou, at which the main course was a golden-brown, crackly-skinned, suckling pig. When Zhou gestured proudly with his chopsticks, inviting the guest to break the crackling first, White flinched and put his chopsticks down, explaining in his best Chinese that as a Jew he was not allowed to eat the meat of the pig. Zhou's aides, incredulous of these barbarian customs, were appalled by their own *faux pas* and only too well aware that they could not afford to order an alternative dish of comparable delicacy. Zhou picked up his chopsticks again and repeated the invitation, pointing to the dish on the table and telling his guest, with a broad smile: 'Teddy, this is China. Look again. See . . . it looks to you like a pig, but in China this is not a pig – this is a duck.'

White laughed out loud, and everyone else laughed too. The American plunged his chopsticks in, broke the crackling and, in his own words, 'ate my first mouthful of certified pig, and have eaten of pig ever since, for which I hope my ancestors will forgive me.'

Zhou's charming encouragement to break old customs might not have worked with another personality, but on that occasion his diplomatic inventiveness won the day. It was a not untypical evening in the three wartime years from mid-1940 to mid-1943 which Zhou now spent representing Communist interests in Chongqing, the new capital of China's national government. During those three years he built up a curious kind of power, not merely as the Communists' envoy, but almost as the conscience of China's political system, cultivating relations with the Guomindang government and party, while assiduously trying to win over the neutrals.

His headquarters was a dilapidated old house in the heart of Chongqing with no windows onto the street, but a balcony high over an inner courtyard.

On sweltering summer nights he could look out over scores of other roofs descending in tiers down a steep bluff to where the Jialing River emptied its brown waters into the Yangzi.

This was 50 Zengjiayan, described by an American visitor as lying at the end of a slime-covered cobblestone alley, with windows covered by greasy brown paper trapping the stale cooking smells indoors. Theodore White found it 'a shabby place; when it rained, the alley was ankle-deep in mud, which was tracked inside all over the reception room.' Part of the building had been smashed by Japanese bombs.

When Ye Jianying, Zhou's closest lieutenant, came to stay, he had to sleep in the windowless attic, which in Chongqing's climate was stifling. Desperate for air, Ye made a hole in the roof for a window. A Guomindang official who lived on the floor below warned Ye that if it rained the house would be flooded. Sure enough, Ye did not finish the job in time and Zhou's room was drenched; visitors found him sitting disconsolately in bed under an umbrella.

Besides the Guomindang gentleman who lived at 50 Zengjiayan, there were many spies who kept surveillance on Zhou. Outside the gate was the kitchen, where one of the hands reported back on his movements, and every shop and stall in the alley was a front for Guomindang intelligence. The head of the Guomindang secret service himself lived nearby and was able to watch everyone passing Zhou's gate. In this atmosphere of constant spying Zhou remained, as his aides later put it, 'calm and composed in the tiger's lair'.

When they urged him to come home early, he would say: 'One can't think of personal safety when making revolution.' In the same vein, he once chided a guard whom he had asked to wake him, but who let him sleep on until his guests had arrived: 'You know my time is not mine alone. It belongs to the Party, the revolution. I know you want me to sleep longer, but sometimes this may harm the cause of the Party.' As usual, he was sleeping only two or three hours a night.

The food, cooked by the guards, evidently left much to be desired; some guests commented that they had 'tasted the flavour of Yan'an'. Zhou was known to go out to buy a single egg to boil for his breakfast. Other old habits died hard: a guard in Chongqing recalled that Zhou used to take the newspaper into the toilet to read. Some of his books in Chongqing including the *Communist Manifesto* are preserved with his autograph and the date on the cover.

Living in Chongqing brought Zhou closer, perhaps too close for comfort sometimes, to his pre-Communist bourgeois life. Nankai University had been evacuated there, so that he was able to call on Dr Zhang Boling and Kang Nairu, Zhou's former teacher and the Nankai Registrar.

A guest at a lunch in a university house attended by Zhou and his wife described how Dr Zhang 'seemed to take a pride in his former wayward student', the tall, handsome and bushy-eyebrowed politician whose animated talk, anecdotes and graceful table manners won everyone's attention. Zhou was also seen as a good match in drinking bouts with other guests.

He knew how to look after his own staff. At a dinner party in Chongqing he asked the hostess if his chauffeur could also sit at the table. She agreed with something less than enthusiasm, and the chauffeur was brought in from the car where he had been using the time to knit socks.

Zhou emerged physically unscathed from living in the enemy's camp, but the Guomindang circulated stories likely to damage him, such as an alleged romance with the slinky young film star Chen Boer. In spite of such rumours, he succeeded in maintaining his reputation in his own Party for marital fidelity of a high order.

More important, and more painful, was the reappearance of his father Yinen, still living a shiftless existence, staggering from one sinecure to another, and now with a new family – a second wife and two new sons. Penniless and jobless, the old man sought Zhou's help in Chongqing and it is said that Zhou was not very forthcoming, that although he could have intervened to place his father he never did. He did give the old man a modest allowance of $30 a month, but that was not enough even for the daily wine to which Zhou senior was used.

This may be an exaggerated picture, coming from a family member out of sympathy with Zhou. But even if there is only a scrap of truth in it, it suggests some of the pressures operating on Zhou, who could not, of course, appear to his Party comrades to be lavishly helping members of the effete landowning class, especially on the pretext of a blood link which in Marxist theory had no significance. Yet the Guomindang and neutral leaders whom he was trying to court in Chongqing would be highly offended by the notion of a man rejecting his own father. That was just the kind of behaviour which could give the Communists a bad name.

The foreigners in Chongqing were impressed by Zhou. Evans Carlson described him in a report as 'the scion of a mandarin family, and a man of culture and education . . . imbued with a certain nobility of character and humility of spirit.' Influential correspondents like Jack Anderson were frequently invited to dine at the Zengjiayan house. Zhou met Wendell Willkie, the presidential candidate. Some visitors were too full of their own theories to do much listening, like Ernest Hemingway, with whom, an aide reported, Zhou could 'hardly get two or three sentences in'.

Zhou told his new American friends that because Russia was so near it was a menace to China, and for that reason a Communist China would want to be friendly with the USA. Many Americans responded more warmly to Zhou than to the Generalissimo and his colleagues, and this was to make difficulties after the war when Americans at home formed the suspicion that their diplomats in China had been hoodwinked by the Chinese Communists.

Meanwhile, Zhou seized every opportunity to establish relations with other countries, from Korea to India. He regretted missing Jawaharlal Nehru when he made a visit to the Chinese capital, and indeed this was a lost opportunity of some consequence. If these Asian nationalist leaders, comparable in so many ways, had formed a mutual understanding and liking at this stage, when neither was burdened with the responsibilities of government, the Sino-Indian antagonism of twenty years later might have been avoided.

Zhou was soon given a post in the Guomindang government, following the precedent of his collaboration with Chiang Kai-shek in Huangpu fifteen years earlier: he was appointed deputy-director of the agency controlling political affairs in Japanese-occupied areas. Meanwhile, he was secretary of the South China Bureau of the Communist Party, in charge of the Communist underground work in the areas controlled by the Guomindang. He was thus engaged in winning hearts and minds in north China against Japan, while winning hearts and minds in south China against the Guomindang. In addition to these duties, he was responsible for the Communist newspaper *New China Daily*.

Zhou excelled all his Communist colleagues in negotiation, whether with the Guomindang or foreigners. He knew more about international affairs, he was better connected with government officials, his English was more fluent, and his personality was more attuned to this kind of work. Many of the Chinese Communists came to the negotiating table with chips on their shoulders, but Zhou maintained a congenial reasonableness. When things went against him he would put on a resigned air, calculated to win sympathy from the other side.

Theodore White called him Mao's 'scout in the tower'. Yet his political position in the Party at this time was complex. While Zhou was ambassador in Chongqing, others, notably Liu Shaoqi, were busy gaining Mao's ear and helping Mao to build up a Party organization loyal to himself. According to a Russian eyewitness, Vladimirov, Zhou was 'in silent rivalry' with Liu and not too scrupulous about it. The same Russian source has Mao criticizing Zhou as one of the 'subjectivists who have lost the perspective of the Chinese revolution', and on another occasion as an 'empiricist' opposing Mao's own mainstream faction. Yet Zhou consistently proclaimed his loyalty to Mao, and a few months later Mao was quoted as fully trusting Zhou and depending on his support. The same observer reports that Wang Ming, the 'Russian candidate' for the Party leadership, had secured Zhou's support against Mao, and Wang himself recorded that Mao, while praising Zhou's administrative and diplomatic gifts, complained in confidence that Zhou was more popular in the Party than Mao himself. All this is confusing and may not be fully reliable, but it evokes Mao's sense of inferiority and insecurity, as well as

Zhou's instinct for mediation and conciliation. Zhou's acceptance of Mao's leadership was not seriously in question, at least so long as there was a war to wage.

During these years in Chongqing Zhou created the nucleus of what was to become a few years later the Foreign Ministry of the Chinese People's Republic as well as the editorial staff for the media in Beijing after 1949. Exploiting the fact that non-Communists were increasingly alienated by the repressive and dictatorial habits of the Guomindang, he built up contacts with many intellectuals and professional persons who later opted for the People's Republic in 1949, to fill the vast gaps in the Communist administrative, educational and commercial ranks.

The smaller political parties in Chongqing did not at first support the Communists, but after Zhou had spoken to them about the Communist endorsement of such political reforms as direct voting, local self-government and representative democracy from the village upwards, they showed interest. Eventually Zhou helped to organize them into a league which was favourably inclined towards the Communists, and many of them set up shop in the early years of the People's Republic, their fears allayed by Zhou's assurance that his party did not intend to introduce Communism for a long time.

Asked at a press conference whether he was more Chinese or more Communist, Zhou replied: 'I am more Chinese than Communist.'

An American reporter wanted to know if his Party would abolish religion. 'Chinese Communists,' Zhou insisted, 'respect all religions; all forms of worship will be permitted.'

At Christmas in 1940 the Methodist Chiang Kai-shek invited Zhou to dinner to thank him for 'what you did for me', namely saving his life in Xi'an four years earlier. Cupping Zhou's hand in his own two hands, the normally taciturn Generalissimo spoke on this occasion with rare emotion, calling Zhou the most reasonable Communist he knew. 'He laid it on thick,' Zhou later recalled. 'I didn't like the taste of his flattery, and it put me on the alert.' He took the opportunity to complain politely that Chiang was undemocratic.

'Do you know what he answered?' Zhou told a journalist afterwards. 'He said, "You mean you call *me* undemocratic?" '

After the dinner Zhou commented: 'Naturally I was moved; but unhappily human emotion, however sincere, cannot bridge ideological differences.'

A few days after this conciliatory Christmas dinner, the fragile United Front between the Communists and the Guomindang and their joint resistance to the Japanese invasion collapsed. There was a disastrous clash between the Communists' New Fourth Army and the Guomindang troops surrounding it in Anhui Province. Zhou immediately set about telling the world that Chiang Kai-shek had ambushed the New Fourth Army on its way north when it was only following his own orders: its officers and men had been massacred and General Ye Ting imprisoned.

Zhou was speaking at a meeting to celebrate the *New China Daily's* third anniversary when the news of this southern Anhui massacre came through on Yan'an Radio. The Communist newspaper worked all night to incorporate Zhou's articles on the incident, but they were censored by the Guomindang. The paper came out with blank spaces in silent protest – though one of them was filled with a poem which the angry Zhou had composed in the heat of the moment:

> History has never seen a greater wrong
> Then what they did to Ye south of the Yangzi.
> Why do members of the same household
> Take up the hatchet against each other?

Zhou himself helped to sell this issue of the paper on the streets that night, a scene which was to inspire a play entitled *The Newsboys* after his death.

Having made the protest, Zhou hastened to Yan'an to confer with Mao, and himself ran into another ambush when bandits fired on his truck. Zhou was sitting next to the driver, who was so badly wounded that his legs had to be amputated later because of gangrene. Zhou's haste in leaving Chongqing was explained when Mao accused the Guomindang right wing of plotting the arrest of Zhou and his wife and many other Communist leaders.

There was now a total stand-off between Chiang Kai-shek and the Communists. Zhou was particularly bitter because the Generalissimo had personally promised him over that Christmas dinner safe passage for the New Fourth Army on its march northwards. When Zhou had been informed of the incident and had telephoned the Generalissimo, the latter had replied that it was impossible and could not have happened. Someone asked Zhou whether the Generalissimo had been lying. 'No,' Zhou replied. 'Someone was lying to the Generalissimo. But the Generalissimo lies to a certain extent, too. The Generalissimo lies because he wants to strengthen his position among the factions. His success is in utilizing all the contradictions in the country to his own ends.'

Zhou stepped up his talks with the Americans in the hope of bringing indirect pressure on the Generalissimo. When the first Burma campaign was lost in 1942, amid recriminations over the Chinese generals' reluctance to take orders from their inexperienced American theatre commander, Zhou told an American diplomat that if the Generalissimo was ready to agree, he, Zhou, would lead Communist troops in a campaign to retake Burma – 'and *I* would obey General Stilwell's orders!' There were many such deft appeals to American opinion.

In the spring of 1941, back in Chongqing again, Zhou made a stirring open-air address which attracted great interest. In the audience was Han Suyin, the half-Chinese, half-Belgian novelist, seeing Zhou Enlai for the very first time. Zhou was not, she conceded, 'gifted with oratory; but he was immensely impressive through his deep sincerity.' She observed a 'slim, thin-faced man with an abundance of black hair, very calm, very handsome, all his gestures supple.' Her first sensation was 'an almost physical impact of sureness, of self-control and intelligence.' He stood on a table in the hollow between two rises, his eyes moving calmly from face to face. He spoke for almost four hours. 'It was one of the simplest, least complicated, most unrhetorical, almost painstakingly basic speeches one could have heard.' Zhou deplored the Communist–Guomindang quarrels.

'This is *our* country,' he insisted. 'Whatever has happened to cause that fratricidal tragedy must be forgotten. From now on we must look ahead.'

It was in this speech, delivered in a newly pressed khaki uniform without belt or insignia, but in highly polished leather shoes, that Zhou made his famous reference to his adoptive mother's neglected tomb.

'The grave of my mother to whom I owe everything that I am and hope to be is in Japanese-occupied Zhejiang. How I wish I could just go back there once to clear the leaves on her grave – the least a prodigal son who has given his life to revolution and his country could do for his mother.' Here was the actor *manqué*, making everyone cry.

That summer Zhou was suddenly taken ill and had to go to a Guomindang military hospital for an operation on his prostate gland. An American visitor found him 'lying on a bed of rope "springs" ' in a tiny whitewashed room. His bodyguard cheered him up afterwards by bringing him his favourite anchovies, which Zhou enjoyed while complaining of their expense.

Meanwhile in Yan'an Mao had launched an uncompromising Rectification Campaign. Overtly aimed at rooting out wrong ideas in the Communist Party, this degenerated in practice into an operation to ensure Mao's own supremacy when the fateful postwar Party Congress would have to decide whether to legitimize and perpetuate his temporary ascendancy during the exigencies of the Long March six years earlier. He urgently summoned Zhou back from Chongqing for the campaign. Mao and Liu Shaoqi were the only ones untouched by criticism during the sessions of rectification, which went on for a year and a half, leaving Zhou, as the next senior after these two, in an extremely awkward position. According to certain sources, he was named at some of the sessions as an 'empiricist' who deserved to be criticized, presumably because he was not always as abusive of Wang Ming and his fellow-Bolsheviks as the new Mao–Liu partnership required – and the Rectification Campaign was the final phase of the struggle between indigenous Maoism and Russian Bolshevism. Zhou supported Mao, but with a certain passivity which fell short of doing Mao's dirty work for him. In this minefield he had to steer a careful path.

Outwardly Zhou did not hesitate. He firmly nailed his flag to the Maoist mast in a way which set the example for others to follow. The history of the Party, he told his comrades in Yan'an, had vindicated the views of Comrade Mao, and Communism had

gone beyond being a mere body of ideology suitable for China; it has become rather an ideology that is indigenous and has grown roots in the soil of China. Comrade Mao Zedong has integrated Communism with the movement of Chinese national liberation and the movement of improving the livelihood of the Chinese people. . . . Because of his leadership, the strength of the Party has attained an unprecedented height.

Zhou's assessment was that nothing could be gained by a vicious internal fight to remove Mao, and so all the chips could be staked on the hope of being able to 'manage' this cantankerous but appealing peasant leader in the future.

But he did resent Liu's immunity, as became clear when he told the heirs to all this, the young Red Guards of the Cultural Revolution in the 1960s, that the rectification had not gone far enough, had not truly succeeded. Otherwise, how could Liu Shaoqi have risen so high in the Party and gone off on the wrong track?

Zhou took the campaign seriously in examining his own weaknesses, drawing up a list of seven rules for himself. 'Study diligently, grasp essentials, concentrate on one subject rather than seeking a superficial knowledge of many' was the first self-regulation. 'Work hard and have a plan, a focus and a method' was the second. The third was to 'combine study with work and keep them in proper balance according to time, place and circumstances; take care to review and systematize; discover and create.' So far it was *pro forma*. But the last two rules were the result of a deeper self-examination. One was never to become alienated from the masses, and the other was to keep fit and lead a reasonably regular life – two injunctions which Zhou always found difficult, despite his gregariousness and rationalism.

Zhou's Party position was made no easier by his father's death at this time. He placed an obituary notice in the Communist newspaper of the kind which the ancient customs of his family required. Though he did no more than the bare courtesies for a man who had turned him out of the house before he was a year old, even this was frowned upon by Communist Party practice.

Mao sent Zhou back to Chongqing in the spring of 1943 to take up negotiations again with the Guomindang, but in July he was recalled for good. Zhou wheedled some trucks out of Chiang Kai-shek, filled them with files, baggage and bedrolls, and trundled out of the old house on Zengjiayan for the last time.

Had his fulsome protestations of support for Mao been enough for that suspicious Hunanese supremo? Mao not only ended his assignment at Chongqing, but also threw him out of the Politburo Secretariat, installing himself, Liu Shaoqi and the Shanghai Party boss Ren Bishi instead. As his truck rolled through the provinces of China from cosmopolitan Chongqing back to the isolated Communist base at Yan'an, Zhou cannot but have reflected on his own political future and on his wisdom in backing Mao.

14

The World Is Ours

1943–49

Yan'an was in the grip of political hysteria, with Communists saluting Mao like sycophants and mindlessly savaging policies of which he was thought to disapprove. Under the pressure of the continuing Rectification Campaign, Zhou's own past policies were now being discredited. At a meeting welcoming his return, Zhou dutifully chanted that:

Communism . . . has taken root in China after being employed and improved by our Party leader, Comrade Mao Zedong. . . . Our Party's consolidation in the past three years has reached an unprecedented high level after the Rectification experience and examination of cadres.

He readily conceded that he had made 'capitulatory and right-opportunist' mistakes in earlier years, but now in all questions he unhesitatingly yielded to Mao's judgement. He knew when – and how – to climb down. The only exception was the issue of whether to continue the United Front with the Guomindang, but even here, Zhou did not lobby openly for what in Chongqing he had been straining every nerve to achieve; rather, he showed the Party through innuendo and inference how useful for its purposes a working arrangement with the Guomindang was.

At many points in this speech, however, Zhou was tactless. Of the changes in China and abroad during the three years he had been away from Yan'an, he commented: 'We saw this all the more clearly when we were outside.' The implication was that Mao and the Yan'an comrades were in blinkers. And in an undiplomatic reference to Mao's opponents, he noted that 'all those who were opposed to or sceptical about Comrade Mao Zedong's leadership or his views have now been proved utterly wrong.' On the surface that was unexceptionable, but it had the effect of gratuitously reminding everyone that Mao's leadership had once rested on a precarious majority. He came back

162

into line, however, at the end of this equivocal, muddled speech, endorsing the Rectification Campaign, which had 'yielded unprecedented results in ideological remoulding'.

'Comrades! I am back,' he concluded. 'Under the leadership of Mao Zedong I will continue to carry out this policy and fight for it to the very end.'

In the privacy of the Politburo, where Zhou reported on the progress of the war against Japan, he was apparently not allowed to forget his past mistakes. Along with Wang Ming and the surviving Twenty-eight Bolsheviks, he was frequently reproached, and his very survival may have seemed in question to some comrades. The word that was used to describe the errors of all these leaders thought to threaten Mao's supremacy was 'internationalist', a point of view regarded in that witch-hunting atmosphere as pernicious, if not criminal.

Yet Zhou seemed to enjoy good personal relations with Mao, whatever treatment he might get at the hands of Mao's minions. By freely confessing his sins and losing no opportunity to express fervent support for Mao, he did survive, but he had to accept that there were groups in the Party against him.

Zhou had long been privy to the other leaders like Mao and Liu who plunged fully into semi-secret-society methods of gaining and keeping power. He must have been aware of many of their secrets, and by temperament he must have been alienated by them to a great extent, and yet he remained, on the whole, on good terms with them. Did he criticize them in private for their failings? Did they stomach such criticism because they knew he would not follow it up with action? Or was there a conspiracy of silence about it all?

And what were Zhou's private thoughts as he now observed this crude use of Leninist techniques in the Rectification Campaign to secure autocratic power in the Chairman's hands? Did he envy Mao's self-confidence in using old-fashioned methods for a modern purpose, apparently unconcerned about the means tainting the end? Did he consider stooping to such devices himself? Or did he know himself well enough to accept that it was no use building a 'Zhou faction' when his destiny was to serve rather than to lead?

Zhou was unique in Yan'an. An observer noted how neat he was, in contrast with the other Chinese Communist leaders. 'His clothes are not bulky. They are fitted and ironed.' A Russian who saw Zhou at a Yan'an party found that he ate almost nothing, and was the only one not to get drunk. Zhou listened to everything and heard what everyone had to say, sometimes touching affectionately the shoulders or hands of the person to whom he was speaking. Zhou was the hardest worker in the camp, and his private life was exemplary. His wife, Deng Yingchao, together with their adopted daughter, added a homespun quality to his image. Deng described their accommodation in Yan'an as 'the first home they had ever had in their married life'.

163

Zhou's office was a free standing, mud-brick building containing crudely carpentered furniture shining with yellow shellac.

Alone in the Party, Zhou could claim close and effective contacts with the Americans, whom everybody now knew would play the crucial role in China's postwar politics. A Russian comrade noted that, over and above Zhou's American relationships, he 'has even greater sympathies with the British'. He brought with him from Chongqing letters from an English lord to his radical son, who was running Yan'an's radio. He also brought an apparatus of Chinese followers whose competence in economics, politics and international affairs was unparalleled within the Party.

There was now an American military mission in Yan'an – the 'Dixie Mission' as everyone called it* – which became the focus of Zhou's professional work there. Mao needed the American connection to prove his independence from his Moscow-oriented rivals, and Zhou became Mao's indispensable link with the Dixie Mission.

The Americans were impressed by Zhou's sobriety. 'He suggested that Guomindang China was more like a TB patient than a man suffering from . . . cholera; . . . there would continue to be a steady decline but . . . probably . . . no sudden break or collapse.' Zhou described Chiang Kai-shek to them as an opportunistic drifter, 'surrounded by unbelievably stupid, second-rate men'. And he did everything, naturally, to encourage the Americans to give more support to the Red Army to defeat the Japanese in north China.

In the Party hierarchy Zhou now stood above all of the Twenty-eight Bolsheviks, including Wang Ming. Apart from Mao himself, he was inferior only to Liu Shaoqi – who shared with Mao a Hunanese peasant background, and had a genius for Party organization. The antagonism between Liu and Zhou was noted by many observers. The 1940s were a time of faction-building, and while Liu consolidated a huge underground following behind Japanese lines, Zhou headed the south and west Party bureaux, where recruitment had to survive the surveillance of the Guomindang. 'Consequently,' as Edgar Snow observed, 'Zhou's following among the recruits was very much smaller than Liu's.'

Then, in 1944, Zhou looked as if he might be breaking ranks with Mao. It started with a long talk which he gave in Yan'an in March, in which he first explained that when he had gone to Moscow four years earlier to brief the Russians on the new rural thrust of the Chinese Party, they had ridiculed him. This was by way of establishing his credentials as a very early, faithful upholder of the Maoist flag. But then he recalled that 'it also took time for Comrade Mao Zedong to understand this question,' explaining that, until 1925, 'Comrade Mao . . . too believed that our work should be centred on the

* Because southerners predominated in it.

cities. . . . So the thinking of Comrade Mao Zedong underwent a process of development.' He was not going to allow Mao and his acolytes to get away with a myth of infallibility.

There was worse to come. Zhou explained that Bukharin had once wanted Mao to be transferred away from the Red Army, instructions which Zhou duly passed on when he returned to China. In fact, Mao refused to transfer, but the whole thing was soon forgotten because the changing situation in southern China made it necessary for the Communists to expand and Mao was needed. However correct a rendering of Party history, this must have been anathema to the insecure Mao and made him uneasy about Zhou's intentions.

Another dramatic intervention came when Zhou, in the Central Committee secretariat, suddenly attacked the way in which the Rectification Campaign had been carried out by Mao's chief executant, an ugly character called Kang Sheng. Nobody liked Kang Sheng, and now Zhou appeared to be the only man in the Party with the courage and integrity to accuse him openly of going beyond his orders, violating the rules of the Rectification Campaign and resorting to undesirable methods in the attempt to please Mao. In a remarkable pre-run of the Cultural Revolution more than twenty years later, Zhou rallied his comrades: 'You have suffered in vain! You are innocent!'

Mao had given prior tacit backing to Zhou's criticisms, of course, and these did not turn into an attack on the Chairman himself. Mao perhaps sensed that the Rectification Campaign had become counter-productive and was ready to make a sacrifice in order to preserve his own authority – using Zhou as his agent.

Winston Churchill himself, Zhou noted in an October speech, was wondering aloud why China was losing battles in spite of all the American aid she was receiving. The reason was the Guomindang's refusal to make political reforms. The American diplomat, John Singer Service, was in the audience, and observed that Zhou's reception was not as warm as that of General Zhu De, who had preceded him on the platform. Zhou used clear and direct language, but, perhaps because his delivery was rather formal and restrained, it 'did not get the enthusiastic response which General Zhu had seemingly so effortlessly received.'

Another sign of Zhou's new toughness was that he now began to distance himself from his revered headmaster Dr Zhang Boling, who challenged him to say why the Communist newspaper was the only one not to salute a big Chinese (Guomindang) military victory against Japan in the south. Was it a Russian newspaper, not a Chinese one?

As the end of the Japanese war approached, the negotiations with the Guomindang warmed up again, and in late 1944 Zhou flew with the

American Ambassador to Chongqing. At the airport he kissed his wife goodbye, and a foreign correspondent commented that this was 'one of the rare moments when I have seen a proud Chinese display private emotion in public.'* Zhou spent three weeks in Chongqing in the New Year of 1945, but with few results. The Guomindang government would not give any of its political or military power away, even under American pressure.

Zhou had no better luck in his bid to go to Washington to meet President Roosevelt. At the beginning of 1945, the Dixie Mission was informed that Mao and Zhou were ready to confer with the President, but Zhou, in a strange lapse from his usual carefulness, told the American officers in Yan'an to leave Ambassador Hurley out of it, 'as I don't trust his discretion'. Unfortunately for Zhou, General Wedemeyer, to whom this message was addressed in Chongqing, was out of town and told his staff to give his mail to Ambassador Hurley to deal with, so that Hurley read Zhou's comment himself. It was probably not a front runner in any case, but Hurley could be forgiven for not transmitting Zhou's request to the White House until much later, and then as an unimportant postscript to something else. If this had been handled better, Roosevelt, who would certainly have been impressed by Zhou, might have brought more pressure on Chiang Kai-shek to share power.

Zhou's negotiating tactics with the Guomindang and the Americans were otherwise impeccable. A Chinese adversary across the table commented: 'He shifts his line so subtly that it often escapes your notice. Of course, he makes compromises, but only minimal and nominal compromises at the very last moment just to keep negotiations going.'

Was Zhou acting in these situations, as he would on the stage? If so,

then he does it so well that after you leave him you carry with you the impression that his emotional reactions to each development in the negotiating process are genuine, and that he is a man of conviction and integrity. . . . The Communists are winning the mainland not through combat, but across the negotiating table with Zhou at the other side.

On one occasion Zhou could think of no way of rebutting a point made by his opponents on the matter at issue, so he coolly looked at his watch, said that he had to keep another appointment and asked the committee to postpone discussion of the question until the next meeting. When the next meeting duly assembled, a colleague of Zhou's turned up in his place, unable to make any decision because he was not briefed on the issue.

In the spring of 1945 the Seventh Communist Party Congress in Yan'an

---

* On the return flight Zhou told the captain they were off course and heading for the Tibetan wastes and near certain death. 'Have the pilot make a 180-degree turn,' he said, 'and fly till he comes to a river, which will be the Wei, and then north.' His navigation was correct: they arrived safely (David D. Barrett, *Dixie Mission*, University of California, Berkeley, 1970, p. 69).

gave Mao the endorsement as Party leader for which he had worked so hard and unscrupulously. His wariness of Zhou, who was away in Chongqing when the Congress opened, came out when Mao opposed one comrade's candidacy for the Central Committee on the grounds that he had refused to say 'even one word against the address of Zhou'. But Zhou was reaffirmed as a member of the Central Committee, Politburo and Central Secretariat, though he was voted only twenty-third in the Party hierarchy after many less well-known supporters of Mao and Liu Shaoqi. Mao nevertheless sat him down on his left side at the final meeting, publicly assigning him the third position in practical terms after Liu Shaoqi.

After the Japanese surrender on 10 August 1945, Zhou accompanied Mao to Chongqing for a meeting of the two supremos to decide the postwar future of China. China, with Allied help, had defeated Japan. But what kind of postwar China would it be? An observer in Yan'an described Zhou on the eve of the visit as 'active, preparing documents, giving orders and coordinating all matters.' Mao, on the other hand, was 'completely confused and practically keeps away from all affairs.'

En route to the capital Zhou gave Mao his sun helmet to protect his head from the burning sun of south China. And throughout their stay in Chongqing, Zhou worked assiduously to protect Mao from harm in the Guomindang camp. Notwithstanding the Guomindang's guarantee of Mao's safety, Zhou personally arranged Mao's quarters, meals and routes. He accompanied him everywhere and got virtually no sleep as a result. Every dish on every menu had to pass Zhou's scrutiny, and he drank toasts on Mao's behalf in case they were poisoned – or perhaps, as Dennis Bloodworth suggests, to 'keep him sober'.

In six weeks of intensive talks Mao and the Generalissimo gave in to the pressure of Chinese and world opinion and moved towards a compromise on the coalition-government issue. Within the negotiations Zhou reflected the more conciliatory mood of the day. While others in Mao's delegation were blunt, Zhou stressed the positive factors. The Communist Party had, after all, accepted and even supported Guomindang authority for a decade, while 'democratic unification is the current trend of modern countries'.

But he reproachfully indicted his Guomindang opponents for their mistrust, for not recognizing the rights of the Communist Party or the Communist armies. Teasingly, he invited Guomindang delegates on incognito tours of areas liberated from Japanese rule in order to gauge the local support for the Communists.

We'll go unannounced so that you can eavesdrop on the villagers' private conversations and listen to the farmers' songs from a distance, and you will know that they support Yan'an not because they are Communists but because of what we have done for them. And – forgive the illustration – if you catch a militia man and a village girl together, I'll stake my life that you'll find that they may be committing adultery, but never, never rape.

Soon Mao went back to Yan'an, but Zhou stayed on, battling to secure the crucial details of the compromise. He was nearly assassinated at the beginning of October: a poet-editor in the Communist camp, who was driving back from the Nankai campus in Zhou's car, was shot dead. The mystery of this murder was never resolved, but it looked like a conspiracy by some Guomindang factions to kill Zhou in order to sabotage the negotiations. The mistaken-identity killing may have had the opposite effect, because agreement was reached two days later on a consultative conference between the two forces.

In December Zhou led the Communist delegation to the consultative conference in Chongqing and General George Marshall came to be the peacemaker. The Communists and Guomindang agreed on a cease-fire, but Marshall, caught in the middle between Zhou and Chiang Kai-shek, found his role almost impossible. At one point, when he explained to Zhou the Generalissimo's latest demand, Zhou clutched his throat and cried in a strangled voice: 'They want us to commit suicide; they want us to commit suicide!' Zhou knew that such theatricals would not induce the hard-liners in the Guomindang, on whom Chiang Kai-shek depended, to a genuine accommodation with the Communists. He had to be satisfied with the knowledge that his efforts on the Communists' behalf would maximize foreign sympathy, while the successive cease-fire arrangements he was able to make bought time for his party to strengthen its local support, and saved the Red Army from excessive damage at the hands of the Guomindang forces.

On 10 January 1946, the consultative conference was convened. (Deng Yingchao was among the delegates. She was, however, snubbed by the Guomindang in her request to go to Paris and New York for important international women's meetings.) Zhou indulged in some old-fashioned levelling rhetoric. 'Get rid of all old-fashioned and out-dated institutions and working methods,' he urged. 'Rely on the people, realize a government that is truly of the people, by the people and for the people. Only this way can China live up to her name as one of the Big Five.' He reiterated the Communists' willingness to play the junior role in China if their due rights as a political party were conceded. 'We acknowledge Mr Chiang's leadership in this country,' he told the conference, 'not only during the past eight years of war, but in the postwar years as well. . . . We recognize the Guomindang as the largest party. . . . Since the war of resistance began we have never formed another political centre to lead the country.'

Provisions were worked out for ending the fighting between the two parties, reorganizing the government and armies and changing the constitution. It was agreed that a National Assembly should meet in May.

Zhou flew back to Yan'an to confer with Mao, returning to Chongqing two days later. On the two-engined aircraft taking him back was an eleven-year-old girl, the daughter of the New Fourth Army general Ye Ting, whom Zhou was said to have disciplined for slack sexual mores, but who then became a martyr when the Guomindang unjustly imprisoned him. The girl was now going to meet her father on his release from gaol. Over the mountains a mass of cold, mid-winter air encrusted the wings with ice. The aeroplane, already heavily loaded, began to lose altitude and the captain ordered luggage to be thrown out. Zhou helped to throw the suitcases out of the cabin door. Passengers were told to put their parachutes on, and the girl burst into tears because there was none for her seat. According to the story faithfully retailed ever since, Zhou walked across the heaving cabin, untied his own parachute and put it on her back. 'Don't cry, Yang Mei,' he said. 'Be as brave as your father. You have to learn to fight difficulties and danger.' And then they flew out of the cold air and arrived in Chongqing to tell the story.

The gruelling negotiations continued. After one session Zhou accepted a lift in a Guomindang colleague's car, and confessed in an outburst of candour: 'I cannot say that the position of our own side has always been rational. Perhaps we could have made a few more concessions. I really don't know. . . . It is so perplexing.' This is one of the few confirmations of an obvious problem, but one which Zhou took care never to document, namely his frustration with the often small-minded instructions which came from isolated and inexperienced office-holders in Yan'an.

In May 1946, the Guomindang government moved its capital back to Nanjing and Zhou moved there too, staying in New Plum Orchard Village. 'It has been thirty-eight years,' he said at his farewell party in Chongqing, 'since I last saw my old home. The poplars in front of my mother's grave must have grown very tall by now.' From the sweltering heat of Chongqing he arrived in a city with unseasonal snow on the streets. Many of his belongings there – a canvas helmet, a beat-up leather suitcase, a swivel chair and the quilt presented to him by his delegation and which he used for the next eighteen years, together with his black Buick Eight sedan – are all still on public display in Nanjing.

One of his first chores was to take part in tripartite US–Guomindang–Communist mediation just north of Wuhan, where the Guomindang was harassing Red Army units. Zhou's jeep set off in heavy rain but was brought to a halt by a flooded river. He slept the night in an old country house, eating rice porridge and sleeping on a wooden bed. He woke next morning to find that the water level had not yet fallen, but he was determined to cross the mountains to reach the Communist unit which was in difficulty. Local peasants carried his jeep across the river, while Zhou took off his trousers and shoes in order to wade waist-deep almost a hundred yards to the other side.

Back in Nanjing Zhou faced a crisis over the movement of Guomindang soldiers in Manchuria in contravention of the cease-fire agreements. When the American Ambassador brought the Generalissimo's 'concessions' on this to Zhou, he watched how Zhou 'moved to the edge of his chair, listened intently, then bent his head for a long time in depressed silence,' after which came 'a tortured smile . . . and a gentle shake of his head.' Even the best efforts of the Americans with Chiang Kai-shek were no longer enough.

Zhou desperately argued for a total cease-fire. 'During the last twenty years we have fought almost without stop, but also without any final settlement. I can declare without hesitation that even if we kept on fighting for twenty more years we still would not reach any solution. The fighting must stop!'

The frustration at being the middle-man between two parties who did not really want the negotiations to succeed was exhausting. Exposed constantly to the cynicism and self-interest which informed the Guomindang capital, Zhou had begun to forget the self-sacrificing spirit of Yan'an. He may even have lost some of his proverbial patience for issues not central to the day. That is strongly suggested by an encounter which he had with George Fitch, a long-time American YMCA enthusiast in China. Zhou had to go to Zhengzhou for more mediation business in July 1946, and Fitch wrote to ask him to come and see the problem of various Christian institutions near Kaifeng on the Yellow River. They wanted the Communist authorities controlling the area to do more repairs on the dykes.

When Zhou arrived, Fitch took a cot for himself and had his own bed made up for his important visitor, whom he had last met several years before.

'I was somewhat surprised,' Fitch recalled, 'to find him a quite different man from what I had known. . . . Formerly he dressed very simply; now he had a suit of English tweeds of the latest cut. He wore silk shirts, socks and underwear. His luggage was of the best leather and he had a gold-mounted toilet kit.

'Nor did he thank me for giving up my bed for him and taking a cot – quite incredible for a Chinese of the old school who would have protested vigorously against my doing this. His whole attitude was now unfriendly. In our three days of negotiations we got nowhere. He supported the Communist group of advisers to our committee completely.'

– Doubtless Zhou felt that his every energy must still go into the Guomindang negotiation, and that if he made enemies of local Communists on issues that did not really weigh in the big scales of history, he would only be making those negotiations more difficult by weakening Communist unity about them. As for his wardrobe, its improvement no doubt reflected his living in the sophisticated and cosmopolitan capital city where these kinds of accoutrements were a necessary adjunct to professional activity. What is strange is that he continued to wear them on trips to small towns and villages where they were obviously less suitable.

Zhou could not live in Nanjing without contacting his own family again. This was very close, after all, to his birthplace. He had made an early call on his prosperous Sixth Uncle, from whom Zhou learned that his prickly Shanghai aunt had returned home from her wartime retreat, whither they had fled in 1939 because it was rumoured that their relation to Zhou was known to the Japanese. Then Zhou's sister-in-law, the formidable Ma Xunyi, called on him in his office. He dropped all his work to greet her after more than fifteen years apart, even cancelling his appointments that afternoon with General Marshall's office. He inquired eagerly about his aunt's health, about his nieces' and nephews' schooling in Shanghai, and about his adoptive brother Enzhu. She told Zhou that his aunt was unhappy at her son-in-law's having, as she believed, been driven away from home.

The two of them went to call on Sixth Uncle and found him taking his afternoon nap. Zhou insisted that they wait for him to wake up – and that they keep very quiet. 'You know Sixth Uncle's temper and his habit of not napping too soundly,' Zhou warned. 'He could very well overhear you, and that would upset him no end.'

In September, when Zhou moved to Shanghai for the final stage of the doomed talks with the Guomindang, he was even more on his home ground, and he called on his sister-in-law and aunt many times. One day they had news about Ma's father being in trouble. Local Communists were campaigning against rich landlords, and the old man had been put in gaol. Zhou's help was enlisted on his behalf, but Zhou was unmoved. It must have been a misunderstanding, he said. In any case Enzhu had been working with the Communists in that area, so it was scarcely credible.

When, after several unsuccessful attempts, Ma was able to see her father, she returned to say that his dying wish was that she should never again see any member of the Zhou family. The two women, the younger one in mourning, now stormed into Zhou's office. Zhou was made to listen to a bitter harangue over his heartlessness and Communist cruelty. Ma then left her marital home, fell ill, and went to hospital, where the aunt kept her company and would not even allow Enzhu to see his sick wife. Zhou, whose winning ways made him welcome even in the worst of circumstances, became a frequent visitor, sitting with his aunt to help her while away the time, and talking about the children.

Zhou had other troubles in Shanghai. His house on the rue Massenet was under constant Guomindang surveillance and Zhou responded angrily to being followed. When he spotted a suspicious vehicle following his car he

171

told his chauffeur to stop. Stepping out, he admonished the driver behind: 'Your tailing technique is very poor. You are going to lose your job this way.' On another occasion, trying to meet a contact and followed by agents whom he could not shake off, he angrily stopped the car to ask who had sent them. He demanded an apology, and – incredibly – received it the same day from the mayor of Shanghai.

But otherwise it was the same old routine, giving the Communist version of events to the foreign press at midnight conferences where they 'watched and listened to ... Zhou ... speaking in Chinese through an interpreter and pretending that he did not understand English,' as one American journalist put it.

Increasingly Zhou had to criticize the Americans as they became more involved with the Generalissimo. He complained to General Marshall that Guomindang forces were everywhere on the offensive against the Communists, in violation of the cease-fire. Yet when he protested against American arms' supplies to the Generalissimo, Marshall defended them as legitimate supplies to the government of a friendly country. Washington, after all, could deal only with China's legal government.

'Aren't you being a bit mechanically formalistic?' Zhou asked. 'Isn't there an element of hypocrisy when you know – and everybody knows – that anything you turn over to the National government goes to the front facing the Communist troops?'

Marshall, tiring of his thankless task, made a last effort in October to arrange another cease-fire, but Zhou's patience had also run out. When the Rev. John Leighton Stuart, the American Ambassador, invited him to meet a Guomindang representative, Zhou responded: 'There isn't enough time. The Generalissimo cannot be trusted.'

Even the small political parties, hitherto neutral between the Communists and the Guomindang, were bending under the latter's pressure. Three of their leaders brought a compromise proposal about the distribution of troops in Manchuria for Zhou to see. He interrupted their exposition to cry: 'Please don't continue! My heart is broken! Hasn't the Guomindang oppressed us long enough? Now you third parties are joining them in oppressing us! Today's disintegration of peace will start with you! Our friendship of ten years ends today; from now on you will be our enemies.' The three visitors disconcertedly withdrew their idea.

But Zhou did not forget. At a farewell party for one of the independent politicians whose integrity he respected, he said: 'The thought that some day I may find him, and many other good friends like you, on the other side of the fence, has taken away all the flavour of this cup of good wine you are offering me today.'

The Generalissimo was set firm on his course, believing that he had both

Chinese and American support for resuming the extermination of the Communists which the Japanese had made him interrupt nine years earlier. He announced in November 1945 the formation of a National Assembly, dominated by the Guomindang, to which Zhou angrily retorted that 'the door of negotiation has been slammed by the single hand of the Guomindang.' Zhou asked Marshall for a plane, and on 19 November left for Yan'an, taking with him whatever slight hope remained of averting the bloodiest civil war in China's history.

Mao was waiting on the tiny tarmac runway of Yan'an to greet him. Knowing that Zhou would feel the November cold of the northwest he presented him, in return for the sun helmet Zhou had donated to Mao when they went south together, his only overcoat. Zhou now had to face hardship and a reduced life style, as Marshall also sorrowfully packed his bags and the safety catches went off all over China.

For the next four months Zhou participated in the Communists' anxious planning to escape the net which the Generalissimo would now throw over them in Yan'an. It was like the Long March all over again, only worsened by the enormous American armour at the Guomindang's disposal. First the Japanese invaders and then the American liberals had stayed Chiang Kai-shek's hand in eliminating his chief domestic enemies. Now he was no longer restrained, and Zhou and his fellow-Communists were rightly apprehensive.

The Communist leaders divided, so that if some were captured, the others could continue as a credible headquarters. Mao made Liu Shaoqi the head of one group that would strike eastwards across Shanxi Province to the safer mountainous regions of western Hebei. Mao himself took Zhou on a long semicircle to the north. Zhou was thus spared the company of his rival Liu, and was able not only to become more indispensable to Chairman Mao, but also by another prolonged enforced companionship to come much closer to this ponderous peasant who would be his lifelong superior. The two of them were the last to leave, in mid-March 1947, the cave town of Yan'an, whose image as the base of an alternative regime for China they had beamed to the world for a decade. As they set off, there was a muddle about Mao's young daughter, who had been taken by Deng Yingchao to a safer place. The two stayed long enough there for the girl to begin calling her fondly 'Mama Deng' – until Zhou's wife had to leave for more important work.

For the next year, Zhou and Mao were together on the run in appalling conditions and frequently in great danger. Zhou took the pseudonym of Hu Bicheng, meaning 'Certain Winner', but victory seemed far from sure as they marched through difficult country with the enemy at their heels.

For food they had to rely on whatever the local villagers could provide – hard-baked barley cakes, wild greens and 'elm-leaf muffin'. Zhou occasionally raised a morosely appreciative comment: 'Better than anything we had in the grasslands on the Long March!'

On the third day after leaving Yan'an the truck in which they were riding broke down. They switched to horses. Soon afterwards Zhou's nose began to bleed, and would not stop. They had brought only one stretcher with them, intended for the use of Mao and women comrades. But Mao and his wife insisted that Zhou take it. As he clambered onto the litter Mao's wife noticed a big hole in his sole.

'How can you walk in those shoes?' she asked. 'Your sock is showing through.'

'That's not sock,' Zhou explained apologetically. 'I stuck a wad of newspaper in there, and I suppose it will hold out for a while.'

At the Great Wall, stretching across the north of Shanxi Province, they were able in April to take temporary refuge from the Guomindang, but they were almost cornered at the Lu River. They had to cross the river at night in torrential rain over a makeshift bridge of doors; Zhou stood on the slippery river bank in the downpour directing operations until everyone was safely across, and when he gained the other side he helped to carry the wounded. This was their narrowest escape from the Guomindang troops on their trail.

Soon they reached a little village where they stayed for some time in cave rooms halfway up a mountain, dark and stinking of pickles. They were practically on top of each other: both work and sleep were difficult. Zhou found a piece of tree-stump to sit on, cushioning it with his padded jacket and resting his elbows on the earthen stove as he pored over his documents.

Zhou seemed to manage with even less sleep than Mao. Once he came out after dark to look at a big fire which enemy troops had lit across the valley. He ordered the guards to take up good positions.

'Don't tell the Chairman,' he added. 'Let him have a sound sleep. He is too tired!'

Whereupon Mao, who had overheard him from his quarters near at hand, called out: 'Don't worry! Today the world isn't theirs, it's ours.'

Not long afterwards, Zhou was up all night directing a battle by telephone only to find at sunrise, when he was washing his face in preparation for an hour or two's sleep, that stretcher-bearers were coming back with the wounded from the battlefield. Abandoning his plans for sleep, Zhou set about supervising their reception, medical attention and feeding.

On another occasion he sent all the available troops up to the front to clinch a small battle, leaving Mao and himself for a short time within full hearing of the artillery and bombing without any guards at all.

Although he had been stretcher-borne at the beginning, Zhou later turned stretcher-bearer himself. At one point, when two men carried a stretcher through the village where Zhou was quartered, one of them collapsed and no replacement could be found. Zhou could see that the patient on the stretcher was badly wounded in the thigh and needed to get to hospital quickly. Zhou called his own guard to take the sick bearer to a nearby medical station, while Zhou himself is supposed to have picked up one end of the stretcher with the words, 'Come on, let us carry him to the next village.'

During this year of hiding and fighting, Zhou's jowls thickened with bad diet, illness and strain, giving him a quite unfamiliar look. Only after he reached Beijing and settled down to a steady life again did his jawline begin to retrieve some of its old gracefulness. But, by April 1948, at least the running was over. Zhou was able to settle down in the village of Xibaipao in western Hebei, where he and Mao were reunited with Liu's half of the Central Committee. Yan'an had been captured by the Generalissimo, but the Communists were still alive and directing a fierce resistance.

The gathering together of the Communist faction heads brought on a new wave of arguments, especially over the way they should behave towards Russia and America. Stalin had put it on record that the Chinese comrades would do best by holding back on a military victory lest it provoke American intervention and a new world war – at a time when cold-war tensions were rising. Liu Shaoqi supported this position, despite the fact that the Guomindang was demoralized by inflation and Communist resistance, and the Red Army controlled large areas of north China. But Zhou took keen issue with Liu, arguing Mao's view that the American atom bomb was only a paper tiger, and it was defeatist to think a third world war imminent. The Communists, in their first full debate on these high policy matters for more than a year, overruled Liu (and Stalin), opting to press for a decisive military victory over the Guomindang.

Although the Guomindang armies had much new American equipment, the Communists had been able to capture a substantial amount of Japanese arms, and when it came to the point, they were able to out-general and out-fight their Guomindang enemy. Many Guomindang units were inefficient and demoralized, and many field commanders were not convinced that an all-out fight with the Communists was the best thing for China. Within six months the beleaguered Guomindang government was suing for peace again, and by January 1949 things were going so badly for it that Generalissimo Chiang Kai-shek had to resign. The Red Army was on a winning streak. Within weeks the entire Guomindang structure collapsed.

Zhou and Mao, with the Chinese Communist Party and its victorious Red Army, entered Beijing, the city with the first claim to be China's capital, on 25 March 1949. Many assumed at this point that the Red Army would hold China north of the Yangzi, the Guomindang the southern half of the country. But the Red Army troops were not daunted, and they crossed this mighty river to take south China later in the year. The Guomindang had to retreat ignominiously across the water to the island of Taiwan, leaving mainland China itself to its first Communist government. This remarkable outcome of the long civil war surprised even the Chinese. Few had suspected just how rotten the Guomindang had become, and how professional the Communist soldiers under such skilled generals as Lin Biao were. The final victory was a magnificent vindication of the Red Army, whose organization and tactics Zhou had played such a large part in guiding.

After almost three decades of struggle, during which the Chinese Communists had often seemed near to defeat – when Chiang Kai-shek decimated the Shanghai proletariat, for example, in 1927, or when Zhou Enlai led the Red Army in 1934 on what seemed to be the doomed flight of the Long March – and with all the entrenched forces of reaction and conservatism against them, the Communist leaders had won the right to rule China and take it along a daring new path of social experiment. With a Party now numbering over three million, and a Red Army that had grown to over four million in response to the Japanese challenge, Zhou and his fellow-leaders could sit on the emperors' throne, so to speak, in Beijing and proclaim an entirely new doctrine, one which in their youth they had found to be the most modern, with the goal of turning Chinese society around from superstitious elitism to true social democracy. It was probably impossible, and their difficulties were compounded by the reluctance of the outside world (except for the Soviet Union) to recognize the new government of China. But from now onwards Zhou's efforts were directed fully to administering China and wooing its prospective foreign partners. After a lifetime of rebellion, Zhou Enlai at fifty-one years old began to govern.

He set to work feverishly in Beijing to consolidate the new regime and make it as widely acceptable as possible. He warned everybody about the problems which victory would bring. Taking over China would 'require time and qualified personnel, and we must do it in an organized fashion,' he told some of the neutral politicians. 'As for qualified personnel, the Communist Party cannot provide them all, and public figures in all walks of life must participate in the work. . . . We are worried that the work may not be done well.'

In his youth, he added, he and his comrades had 'raised the slogans of overthrowing Confucius and fighting against the feudal family system. But today we realize that if there is anything good in what Confucius says we can quote him for our use. And if our parents come and stay with us we should take care of them.' But the intellectuals would have to change their outlook. 'A characteristic of mental workers in general,' Zhou declared, 'is that they work alone . . . and this can easily give rise to non-collectivist tendencies. Writers and artists should make a special effort to learn the working-class spirit of collectivism.' As for the countryside, he predicted that 'in the near

Zhou Enlai on leaving Nankai School in Tianjin in 1917 (at the age of nineteen)

Members of the Awakening Society in Tianjin at its founding in 1919: Zhou Enlai standing at the extreme right, with his future wife Deng Yingchao in the front row, third from the right

一九二四年攝於巴黎

The French branch of the Chinese Communist Youth League meets in Paris in 1924. Zhou is in the front row, fourth from the left, with Li Fuchun fourth from the right, and Nie Rongzhen at the extreme left. Deng Xiaoping is the short figure at the back, third from the right

Below left: Zhou in the uniform of China's National Revolutionary Army as head of the political department of the Huangpu Military Academy near Canton, 1924–26

Below centre: Zhou Enlai fording a river on horseback in Western China on the Long March, 1935

Right: Zhou returns by plane to Yan'an after successfully negotiating on the Xi'an incident, 1936

Below right: Zhou Enlai, Mao Zedong and Zhu De, the three Long March leaders, in Yan'an in the winter of 1939

Zhou (third from the right) with
New Fourth Army leaders Chen Yi
(extreme left) and Ye Ting (extreme
right) in 1939

Zhou and his wife, Deng Yingchao,
at the Communist headquarters in
Chongqing, 1940

Zhou Enlai leading the Chinese
Communist delegation in Nanjing to
negotiate with the Guomindang in 1946

Zhou Enlai, with Mao Zedong, takes up
residence in Zhongnanhai in old Beijing,
March 1949

Above left: Chairman Mao and Premier Zhou applaud an army athletics competition in the rain, 1952

Below left: Premier Zhou working in his office, Beijing, unaware of the camera

Above: Zhou enjoying the traditional water-splashing festival among the Dai minority people in Yunnan in 1961

Zhou, suffering from cancer, makes his last inspection of the Dazhai model agricultural brigade in the spring of 1973

Grieving Chinese file past Zhou's body, January 1976

future another 200 million peasants will plunge into the tempests of agrarian reform.'

Zhou saw the need to gain support not just from radical but from liberally minded establishment figures as well. He repeatedly tried to persuade Song Qingling, widow of China's first president and the Guomindang's father figure, Sun Yat-sen, to come to Beijing for the inauguration of the new government. He sent Deng Yingchao, her old collaborator, to Shanghai to endorse his pleas, and when Song eventually arrived at Beijing station in September, Zhou – with Mao – was on the platform to greet her and press an office in the People's Republic upon her.

In public Zhou insisted that the new government would be more patriotic than its predecessor and would resist any American pressure against it. 'The Chinese are an ancient people and an heroic people ... brave and ... industrious. What a fine people! It is no wonder we love them! (Of course, other peoples have their good points too, and we certainly recognize that.)' If the Americans went so far as to invade the new China, the Communist government would cut off everything, 'including toilet paper and ice cream', to force them out. Zhou knew his enemies' weak points.

But in private Zhou understood how much the new China needed the recognition and help of the United States. In May he sent a secret message to the American mission in China asking for support in these closing stages of the civil war. If this were given, he argued, it would enable China to serve 'as a mediator between the Western powers and the USSR, and make the USSR discard policies leading to war.' China was on the brink of 'complete economic and physical collapse,' Zhou claimed. The Russians could not supply aid on the scale needed, and so the Chinese Communists hoped to get it from the Americans.

'Zhou is confessedly a sincere Communist,' the US mission's cable to Washington read, 'but feels there has developed in the USA economy something which is outside Marxist theory.' In other words Zhou distanced himself from orthodox Soviet censure of the American economic system. Moreover, the Americans had a genuine interest in the Chinese people. . . . Zhou pulled out all the stops.

He was even bold enough to sketch in the position of his rival Liu Shaoqi. Liu, he told the Americans, was a brilliant organizer of people, but not very realistic and poor at urban administration. For example, Liu was advocating restrictive business laws, which Zhou and his liberals in the Party opposed as 'helpless, hopeless tinkering' with the economic system. 'Zhou appeared very nervous and worried,' the American cable concluded.

When the American diplomats tried to give Zhou the State Department's rather negative and defensive answer a month later, they were rebuffed. Perhaps Liu's men had discovered Zhou's ploy, or Zhou may by then have decided that Stuart, the American Ambassador himself, would be a better confidential channel of communication with Washington.

Stuart was planning to visit Beijing at the end of June. His trip fell through, however, and he received a rather negative personal letter from Zhou puncturing some of his earlier arguments, in which he had maintained that the Americans had already helped China a great deal, particularly in trade matters. Zhou withdrew his invitation to Stuart, and a few weeks later described the unfortunate envoy as 'accustomed to appearing with deceptive countenance falsely covered with affability.'

In retrospect one can detect the contradictory currents in these exchanges. Zhou did sincerely seek American help for the new People's Republic, but could not go too far in that direction without becoming vulnerable to criticism by the Liu-ist and pro-Soviet factions in the Party. And the Americans, for a variety of regrettable reasons, let slip an opportunity to assist in the formation of the new China, which, if grasped, might have allowed both countries to avoid many of the artificial misunderstandings that arose during the next quarter of a century.

Zhou's forthrightness and his unpretentious brand of communism in that strange betwixt-and-between summer of 1949 shone out in a speech which he made about Mao Zedong at a youth congress in Beijing. Mao, he told this next generation of Communists, was a great man but was in no way set apart from ordinary people, and should not be regarded as 'a born leader, a demi-god or a leader impossible to emulate.' Young people should learn from him in the light of his development, not just by looking at his current achievements and neglecting his past growth. 'Yesterday's superstitious child was able to become today's Chairman Mao (of course, I am not saying that every child can become Chairman Mao).' And he repeated his reminder that Mao had once been wrong about the rural question. Yet Mao had already begun to prettify his biography and allow his sycophantic aides to doctor the record. That vitiating tendency had started during the Rectification Campaign seven years earlier, under the star of Liu Shaoqi.

Zhou ended his speech by dutifully agreeing with Liu that the admirable thing about Mao was his successful adaptation of a universal truth to Chinese soil. But, he added, in order to make this knowledge something from which ordinary people could benefit, those ordinary people must first achieve better political consciousness through the processes of education and propaganda. Thus did Zhou correctly foretell the lines of the policy conflicts in China for the following decades, and declare his preference for a pragmatic slow timetable of reforms which would endure, rather than a mad rush to an elusive socialism.

15

A Pair of Blue Pyjamas
1949–52

After a lifetime on the run from enemy bullets, often without a suitcase to his name, Zhou now became what his family had always intended him to be – a mandarin. But China had never seen a mandarin like this before. For the next quarter of a century Zhou was to live in Beijing with the intractable task not merely of running but of radically reforming the largest country in the world. For the rest of his life he worked obsessively towards this extraordinary goal, and became famous for it in every county of China and in every continent of the world. The talents which had ripened in revolt now lent themselves to peaceful administration. The voice which had told the millions to rebel had now to call for obedience.

The first essential was to create the institutions for China's new Communist government and state. In June 1949, Zhou became vice-chairman under Mao of a preparatory committee to draft an interim constitution and bring into being a new 'legislature', the Chinese People's Political Consultative Conference. The CPPCC was the fruit of a year-long campaign by Zhou to bring together leaders of all political groups, including Guomindang splinter groups and exiles in Hong Kong, in a loose consultative framework that would defuse the antagonism and suspicion which many non-Marxists felt about the idea of a Red government.

During this time of preparation for the new state, Zhou also sketched the outlines of China's foreign policy. Non-Communist countries should accept the 'New China' as master of its own house and as fully entitled to the Chinese seat in the United Nations; it was not under any Soviet thumb. Zhou had already declared that his Party was no longer obliged to the Russians, who had 'made too many mistakes for us in the early days,' but now he reassured the Kremlin that 'people will be disappointed if they think there will ever be a Tito in China.'

179

The CPPCC gave formal birth to the new People's Republic of China on 1 October 1949. Zhou stood with his Party comrades on the high balcony of Beijing's Gate of Heavenly Peace – Tienanmen, the scarlet, brass-studded gate through which past bearers of tribute had approached on their knees the emperors' yellow-lacquered throne.

Zhou was appointed Premier of the State Council – the cabinet – and concurrently Minister of Foreign Affairs, and from this moment the world began to know him as Zhou Zhongli – 'Premier Zhou'. In some old-fashioned quarters his skill in getting antagonists to compromise earned him, in the flowery phrasing of an older generation, the soubriquet of First Minister of Great Peace. During a famous argument in the State Council over plans for new buildings which would obstruct Beijing's traffic, Zhou mediated the deadlock with an aptly remembered classical poem: the 'grace' in Zhou's given name of Enlai had at last arrived, fifty years after his father had invoked it.

Zhou's regime as Prime Minister was incessant deskwork, interspersed with meetings, and it never let up for the rest of his life – except for two or three unusual short breaks dictated by illness or exhaustion. He set a pace no one else could match, and attended to an astonishing variety of activities, starting with the weekly meetings of the cabinet to which he delivered countless reports in scrupulous detail. On top of all this he travelled to many different countries almost every year. It was like Talleyrand, a French politician suggested, 'playing the part of Richelieu'.

Following the Chinese tradition that politics depends on consensus, Zhou spent much of his time soliciting and influencing the varying views not only of comrades in the Communist Party, but also of people and interest groups in the bureaucracy and in the country at large. For one occasion, speaking to an important Party Congress, the text of his address went through no fewer than twenty successive drafts. A visitor once asked him whether China's leaders discussed policy. 'We argue continually,' Zhou replied with feeling, and perhaps a tinge of regret. 'We debate everything.'

To his friends who urged rest, Zhou would say that it was right for him to take on 'the bulk of the day-to-day work' in order to leave Mao free for the larger issues. Like Mao, he continued his old habit of working through the night, achieving very often a twenty-hour day. He would commonly sleep from 9 a.m. until noon, and supplement this with catnaps when travelling in his car. 'I have given up,' his wife despaired, 'trying to get him to sleep more.' When he did feel tired he would rub Tiger Balm oil on his forehead. There was always a bottle of this in his briefcase.

Far from being weighed down by this routine, Zhou kept his sparkle. In repose, an American correspondent reported, his face looked 'passive and sullen', but once he unwound, said another, it 'became animated with a thousand expressions as he acted out all the parts of a remembered conversation.' A woman writer from Europe found that 'his eyes, the most startling feature about him, were lustrous and moved quickly; everyone found him irresistible.' But a satirical Chinese author described the five different smiles of Zhou – a beaming welcome with outstretched arms for a Soviet 'elder brother', a broad grin with hands remaining slack at his sides for Mao, a smile a little aloof as would befit a Prime Minister for Western diplomats, a half-grin moving only the upper part of his face for Politburo members, and a mere relaxation of the facial muscles with only the skin smiling for lesser members of the Central Committee.

Zhou elected with his senior comrades to live in a quiet section of the old Forbidden City of the Chinese emperors. It was called Zhongnanhai, in the Park of the South Lake, and here in the complete privacy of a walled compound surrounded by imperial cedars and pines, Zhou led his domestic life with Deng Yingchao. When he first arrived, his new house betrayed longstanding neglect, with blackened walls and crumbling pillars. The ground was damp and there were holes in the windows which they plugged with newspapers during the cold weather.

Zhou regularly fended off the builders and decorators who proposed repairs, so his staff had to seize the opportunity of his travelling abroad to make vital improvements. Once when Zhou returned, he gazed chillingly at new curtains installed in his absence – and ordered the old shabby ones back again. And in the adjoining garage, Zhou would not let them replace a rotting beam, saying that in China's current state of poverty the resources would be better applied in other ways, and it would surely last a few more years if propped up.

Similarly, it was said that the small hall in the Ministry of Foreign Affairs where Zhou worked had insufficient ventilation, and so on experts' recommendation it was decided to alter the roof. 'Who ordered this?' Zhou asked when he heard about it. 'The hall is far better than the caves we lived in at Yan'an. . . . You mustn't alter this small hall while I am the Premier.'

Similar stories were told about Zhou's everyday life. He was notoriously stingy in spending money, even on clothes and food. It was said that when he had finally worn out a facecloth, he would use it for some time as a towel, and when it was rubbed too smooth for that function he would press it into service as a cloth for polishing his shoes. The well-darned socks put on exhibit after his death had been worn, it was claimed, for an unbelievable thirty years, from before the time he became Premier right up to his death. He was once chatting with a Prime Minister from another country when, to the acute embarrassment of the Chinese Foreign Trade Minister who was present, he held out the frayed sleeve of his coat as an example of the poor quality of China's products.

Yet Zhou was no spartan, and he enjoyed his favourite foods – the bony but deliciously succulent crucian carp, for example, anchovies and noodles. But part of the cereals served at his table had to be coarse unpolished grains. He thereby set an example as Premier which many a junior official ignored. According to one report, Zhou's salary in the early 1950s was only $135 a month. Many officials supplemented their income by fees, for example from book royalties. Zhou, however, refused such fees from the People's Publishing House, and he carried correctness to extraordinary lengths when it came to charging for various goods and services incurred on official business. When he went into a photographer's studio one Sunday to get pictures for a foreign trip, he wanted two separate invoices, one for his office and another for himself for the several prints for his personal use. And at Lushan on an official conference once, when he found no curtain to shield the window of his room from the corridor, he paid from his own pocket for one to be installed.

His hosts, friends and admirers had to accustom themselves to traditional gifts being rebuffed. The Communist bosses in his birthplace once sought to honour their famous fellow-townsman by sending local delicacies up to Beijing for his table. Zhou returned them rewrapped, pointedly attaching a copy of the cabinet guidelines on the banning of gifts. When the chef of the Peking Hotel sent half a pound of peanuts to delight him, Zhou returned them with the schoolmasterly comment that foreign guests should be served first, while China in any case needed more peanut oil for its economy. Never had a Chinese head of government behaved like this.

Just as he used to look after his chauffeur in Chongqing, trying to get him into the society dinners to which Zhou was invited, so now as Premier he continued to show concern for the people working under him.

One of his first actions in Beijing was to support a private soldier who had courageously demanded the identification of a high-ranking Party member who struck him in anger. When Zhou suddenly coughed during shaving and his barber cut his chin, Zhou noticed how terrified the man appeared and is supposed to have quickly apologized with the words: 'I should have warned you before coughing.' Probably the most famous story is about the soldier on-guard outside the seaside house where Zhou once stayed, when a great rainstorm suddenly bucketed down. Zhou's wife rushed out, holding an umbrella and carrying something under her arm.

'The Premier sends you this raincoat,' she said. 'Put it on. And he said to remind you not to stand under a tree when there's lightning.'

What the soldiers remembered most vividly was that when they saluted him on sentry-go, he would walk over and shake hands with them, saying: 'We are all comrades together, so don't salute me.'

To a Western reader such stories sound cloying, and perhaps suggest the efforts of an insecure man to make himself more popular. But Zhou was not insecure, and while he may well have enjoyed the popularity which such a life style attracted, the principal motivation was a deep and serious one: to break the mould of the old elitist form of government. This was the first time that anybody had seriously and systematically tried to act in public life in a genuinely democratic manner. As later events were to prove, Chinese society was highly resistant to this kind of innovation, and many of Zhou's efforts were short-lived. But he was the only one of his Party comrades who tried hard to inject egalitarianism into Chinese life at the top, and that is one reason why he was liked and respected by non-Communist Chinese, not only in China itself, but even in Taiwan, Hong Kong and other countries.

The new Premier had his pleasures. Although his wife did not always accompany him to parties, pleading ill health, they were frequently seen dancing together in the early 1950s at the *thé dansant* in the Peking Hotel – before such behaviour came to be considered unrevolutionary. I once saw Premier Zhou busily heeling and toeing on the tarmac of Beijing airport during one of those interminable waits for second-rate foreign dignitaries to which Chinese leaders masochistically subject themselves, as if he was dying for a whirl on the floor.

During the Cultural Revolution Zhou was scolded for having patronized a club where beautiful dancing partners were available and mahjong was played to midnight. Zhou also loved films, his favourite being Chaplin's *The Great Dictator*. Deng Yingchao testified that 'however busy he may be, he would never give up his ping-pong game.'

A foreign visitor once asked him about his drinking so much *maotai*, the fiery Chinese spirit used for toasts, and a key ingredient of Chinese diplomacy. Did not the Premier get drunk? 'Oh yes,' Zhou replied. 'I am only human, and my wife is always telling me not to drink so much. But I have to do it as part of my job. If it gets too much, what I do is go to the toilet and thrust my finger down my throat to make myself sick. And then I come out with a glass of water and go on toasting just as before.' The secret of drinking *maotai*, he confided to one of his officials, was to toss it down like vodka without letting it touch either the tongue or roof of the mouth.

He tried hard to prevent any effort being put into the restoration of his birthplace, as overzealous local officials requested time and again. He instructed the Huaian Party committee many times to pull the house down. 'However,' the posthumous account read, 'in consideration of the people's love for the Premier, the county Party committee did not have his old house dismantled.' According to another report, Zhou issued his fellow-townsmen with a threefold *ukase* about his old family house: 'First, don't allow people to visit it; second, don't have the people now living there moved out: and third, don't mend it when it falls into disrepair.'

Though his family no longer lived there, his relatives continued to embarrass him. A typical story was that of a nephew who studied in Beijing and got a job there after graduating. For ten years he faithfully obeyed his uncle's orders and never disclosed to anybody his blood link with the Premier. When he was invited on his own merits to join the Communist Party, for which purpose he had to reveal the names of his immediate family, the people around him learned for the first time, to their surprise, that he was Zhou's nephew. All that was harmless enough, but then the nephew married a Huaian girl and so his office arranged for her to be transferred to work in Beijing, a common enough arrangement for married Party members. When they mentioned this to Zhou, however, he asked reprovingly why it was, if some arrangement had to be made to live together, that the wife should move rather than her husband? So the couple found themselves later, much to their disappointment, working in the small town of Huaian instead of in the national capital. Zhou made extraordinary efforts to ensure that any potentially embarrassing relatives lived as far away as possible from Beijing, as we shall see later in the case of his niece. He had not, after all, intervened to save that unapologetic landlord, his adoptive brother's father-in-law, and had been less than generous with his own father.

Women were, of course, one of the targets for Zhou's reformatory zeal. 'In a socialist society,' he told a women's group in Shanghai, 'families are very important. You mustn't look down on household duties. No matter what, each of you is responsible for a one-person government. Each of you manages your own family's home and foreign-affairs departments. Whose work could be more important than this?' Here again, a Western reader might find this patronizing, but Chinese men still habitually looked down upon women and this kind of leadership was needed. Women's rights constituted an area of Communist success under Zhou's direction, as his behaviour in his student days with Deng Yingchao had heralded.

Zhou did not have much of an eye for art. He told a Western visitor that if abstract art had no meaning, 'what value has it for the people?' His tastes were demonstrated by the fact that he went eleven times to see that synthetic revolutionary opera *The East Is Red*. Characteristically, he refused to see a play in which he himself was portrayed.

None of this inhibited him from making 'helpful criticisms' to actors and directors, and indeed there was almost no sector of Chinese life into which he did not intrude his restlessly innovatory mind. When the architects were worrying about the design of the new Great Hall of the People, it was Zhou who resolved their problems. The hall had to be big enough to contain 10,000 people, but none of them should be made to feel small or lost or taken over by the building: that was the challenge. It was Zhou's pencil which first drew the oblate or flattened oval shape to meet these requirements, and many of the details of that building originated with his advice. There is a photograph of him looking eagerly proprietorial as Mao is shown the plans.

Another shrewd judgement was the case of the Ling Yin Temple at Hangzhou, where a new 60-foot-high camphorwood Buddha figure was being carved with legs crossed in the traditional posture. The monks wanted the soles of Buddha's feet to be turned upwards, which the artists refused as 'defying anatomy'. Like so many things in China, the controversy eventually reached the accommodating desk of Zhou Enlai.

'What is the image for,' he asked, 'a temple or a museum?'

'A temple,' they replied.

'Then make it as the monks wish,' Zhou adjudicated. But he added a characteristic coda. Having studied the disputed model attentively, he exacted from the monks a price for his judgement, adding: 'And change his hair. Buddha was an Indian; you have made his hair-do Chinese.'

The intensity of his interest even in minor things could make him appear a neurotic old nanny. When it concerned matters of state, this could be forgiven, as when he made a doctor test a new eye ointment on his, Zhou's, own eyes before administering it to Mao, or when he assigned a guard to stand where a water pipe might trip Mao up on his way to a meeting and harshly criticized the poor man afterwards for giving the ignominious job to someone else. Even when Zhou suddenly started to appear on ordinary trains and buses in Beijing one winter, refusing the seats offered him with the words: 'I have come to experience these things with you,' it was to see for himself the problems of commuters. As a result he introduced safety islands and other measures to relieve traffic. Thus far many another conscientious leader might have gone. But when Zhou started to control the traffic himself in places he frequented – at a conference hall or in front of a restaurant hosting some public reception – then one may be excused for thinking that obsessiveness was taking over from legitimate concern.

This side of Zhou was well caught by a Japanese correspondent who wrote of his press conferences:

When he is not talking, his eyes never stop moving. If this had not been Zhou Enlai, I would certainly have regarded him as suffering from a nervous breakdown. He would notice the tiniest thing. He made his interpreter pause, for instance, when a waiter quite a distance away caused a little noise while making tea. He himself moved his microphone to the seat of the interpreter next to him. And then, after a while, he stretched out a hand, leaned forward in his chair and with one swing straightened the microphone wire on the floor. It seemed to make him feel uneasy if things were not exactly right.

On another occasion Zhou pointed out to a photographer quite a long way off that he had forgotten to remove the cover from his camera lens. Clearly he had an observant eye and a marked penchant for tidiness, but these gifts sometimes edged into exaggeration or eccentricity.

His officials complained of his liverish irritability at times, though they usually forgave him when they saw him performing in public. Others described him as mercurial in temperament, a strider and never a stroller, affecting the large, brisk gesture with restless hands and eyes that flickered ceaselessly up and down. At the start of the new regime, Zhou wrote thousands of letters to non-Communist intellectuals and professional men pleading with them to work under the Communist government. Such eminent scholars as the great economist, Ma Yinchu, accepted Zhou's invitation, in the hope of being able to influence policy and help transform China into a modern industrial nation. Perhaps he even dreamed of Zhou's presiding over a constrained but viable system of capitalism, of the kind the Premier had been predicting in earlier United Front days. Like many of the others, Ma died a disappointed man, but all of them probably felt they shared with Zhou the thought that, while Mao's kind of communism was bound to dominate China for a time, it would probably be modified in the future – and the contribution of minds trained in the old China could help to preserve the good values in the interim period.

Zhou used many of China's intellectuals who had been trained in the West and lived in exile but had now returned, in his own office – like Dr Pu Shou-chang, for example, a Harvard-trained economist, who came back to China to become the Premier's secretary. But Zhou could not, of course, control every action of the Party's junior officials and sometimes his invitations went sour. This was the case with Eric Chou, a young writer in Hong Kong, who responded to his appeals for patriotic and professionally trained people to help run China instead of staying selfishly outside in Hong Kong, Taiwan or the West. Chou's editor, a leftist Chinese in Hong Kong, visited Beijing soon after the People's Republic was formed and talked to Zhou Enlai. 'Eric,' he told his staff writer after returning to Hong Kong, 'Premier Zhou remembers you well. He asked about you and I told him that you are with us in Hong Kong. He said he would like to see you personally.' Chou had indeed met Zhou in the mid-1940s as a correspondent in China, and he admired the Premier. His vanity was tickled, and he agreed to go on a short trip to China. But once there, he was detained against his will and in his own account Chinese intelligence sought to recruit him. He eventually escaped without ever meeting Zhou again.

Zhou Enlai tried to portray the new regime as a relatively liberal one, in Communist terms. 'We aren't trying to destroy individuality,' he told two British writers, 'but we are certainly doing our best to destroy individualism. It is a policy of "no man for himself, and every man for others", if you like to put it that way.'

There was one non-Communist individual who did not have to be invited to return to his homeland, but who suffered continuously for the individuality of his political views. That was Zhou's beloved old teacher, Dr Zhang Boling. When the Red Army reached Chongqing, towards the end of 1949, the Communists pressed Zhang Boling to come out in their support. He refused, and returned to Tianjin, where local Communists continued to pressure him into adopting an anti-American stance.

Both teacher and pupil must have drawn the same conclusion from this sad episode. Even a good man at the top cannot prevent crude and uncivilized behaviour at the lower levels. Zhou no doubt regretted that his good old friend of earlier days had become so inflexible, but in private he probably wept when these two irreconcilable forces in his life had their final confrontation and yet another father figure failed him. As for Dr Zhang Boling, he presumably regretted that a pupil of such promise and integrity should have become thus swallowed up by an inhuman political machine. Not long after, he died.

Zhou's comrades' hopes of bringing about a speedy millennium in China were dogged in the early years by foreign interruption. Since the Americans had rebuffed Zhou's and Mao's overtures in the months preceding the Communist victory, it was to Russia that they had to turn for help. Mao flew to Moscow at the end of 1949 to see both the Soviet Union itself and Stalin for the very first time, unwisely leaving his most skilful negotiator at home. But Stalin too could be whimsical, like the Americans, and Mao was kept waiting for long periods without any progress on his requests for aid. Finally he summoned Zhou, who arrived in Moscow on 20 January 1950 with a planeload of experts and a new pair of blue-check flannel pyjamas bought for the occasion. These soon became Zhou's only pair, and he went on wearing them, faded and patched with all the blue and white merged into an indeterminate grey, even taking them on subsequent foreign trips, until the day he died.

Even Zhou with his new pyjamas took almost another month to press the reluctant Russians into a set of agreements which then formed the cornerstone of China's foreign relations for the next decade. Stalin was still angry with the way in which Mao had treated his Comintern and Soviet links in the 1930s, and now the Chinese Communists had to pay for it. On 14 February they signed a Sino-Soviet Treaty of friendship, alliance and mutual assistance, and other pacts affirmed the independent status of Mongolia, provided for joint administration of the railways and ports with which Russia had a traditional connection, and extended a five-year credit to China of $300 million. These were humiliating terms. In order to get a defence commitment and aid which was skimpy compared with the help the United States was giving to other countries or even that Russia gave to East European nations,

Zhou and Mao had to put up with the continuation of the USSR's semi-colonial operations in north and northwest China as well as in Mongolia.

This was the first of six visits which Zhou was to make to Moscow during the 1950s. They began on a bitter note, and the mutual disregard became quickly visible. Decades before, when Lenin had renounced the fruits of former Russian imperialism in Asia, the younger generation of Chinese like Zhou had been exhilarated and impressed. But now that his successor would not honour those promises, no Chinese leader could feel warmth for Moscow. Zhou had to patch up the best possible minimal agreement, something he was well used to from the days of the Guomindang. This was his first emergence on the international stage. For years he had explained to the press of the world – eagerly and in colourful language – that China was not like the Soviet Union, would not follow the Russian example, had been harmed by Russian mistakes, and would in the future be a better country in every way than Russia. This, of course, had been bait for Western, especially American, opinion to give the new China the benefit of the doubt – morally, politically and economically – but to Stalin it had sounded like insult, and to see Zhou now pleading for their roubles both angered and amused the Russians.

For Zhou it was a lesson in the old adage that you cannot serve two masters at once, or that if you say one thing to one man and something different to another, they will both find out and neither will believe you. Zhou had hoped that the Russians would understand the domestic reasons, concerning the Guomindang, why the Chinese comrades had had to resort to such stratagems, and probably he also calculated that an advanced state like the Soviet Union would put its own national and group interests before personal spite. In both suppositions he was profoundly wrong.

Before the People's Republic had had even a year in which to settle down, China became the victim of an unwanted war which made her more dependent upon the Soviet Union, snapped the slender threads with the United States, and led finally to the grisly consequences of field combat between Chinese and American troops – without a single benefit to China. It was precisely the kind of no-win situation which Zhou was trained to avoid, but here he could do nothing. Ironically the Americans believed that China instigated North Korea's invasion into South Korea in 1950. In fact, it seems to have been an independent action on the part of the North Koreans, possibly encouraged to some extent by the Russians (who out of pique would not have consulted China). The war could certainly not have been less opportune from China's point of view.

The Americans interpreted Korea as evidence of a Soviet plan to reduce the West's sphere of influence in every continent. President Truman therefore sent the US Seventh Fleet to protect Taiwan from Chinese

Communist forces. Zhou branded this as an act of 'armed aggression on Chinese territory', so both of them were quickly boxed into a stance of extreme hostility.

From Zhou's office in Beijing it looked as if the world was closing in, with only an untrustworthy Soviet Union to support the new and powerless People's Republic. Ambassador K. M. Pannikar of India and his Burmese colleague vainly tried to persuade Zhou that an important segment of opinion in their countries, and even in countries like Britain, was at least neutral if not positively sympathetic towards China in her struggles with a right-wing American administration.

(Pannikar was most impressed by Zhou. 'What I noticed first about him,' the Indian wrote afterwards, 'were his hands. Not only were they carefully tended, but the fingers were like tender onion shoots, as the Chinese describe them, and he gesticulated with them with great effect.' Zhou's questions were penetrating, though his knowledge about India was sketchy. He was no doubt 'a staunch and convinced Communist and a trained theoretician, but he also has feet firmly planted on mother earth.')

Zhou nevertheless stood by the official Soviet-backed line of North Korea's Kim Il Sung and attacked the United States in public speeches in terms which it would take Washington many years to forgive. On the People's Republic's first birthday, 1 October 1950, for example, he said that the USA had shown itself by 'frenzied and violent acts of imperialist aggression' as China's 'most dangerous foe'. After the Communist liberation the peaceable Chinese people wanted only to rehabilitate and develop their economy and culture. But they 'absolutely will not tolerate foreign aggression nor will they supinely tolerate seeing their neighbours savagely invaded by imperialists. Whoever attempts to exclude nearly 500 million people from the United Nations and whoever sets at nought and violates the interests of this one fourth of mankind in the world and fancies vainly to solve any Eastern problem directly concerned with China arbitrarily, will certainly break their skulls.' This crude language did not advance China's goals *vis-à-vis* the United States. Zhou, of course, had to show the powerful and chauvinistic hard-line section of his own Party that he was no weakling when it came to scolding foreign powers.

Late on the night following this speech, Zhou summoned Ambassador Pannikar, his only available channel to Washington. The Indian found Zhou at this early morning meeting as courteous and charming as ever, not giving the least impression of anxiety. But after briefly thanking Jawaharlal Nehru for his efforts in the cause of peace, the Premier quickly came to the point. If the American forces in South Korea were now to take the offensive and cross into North Korea, as General MacArthur had been loudly announcing, China would have to enter the war. The Ministry of Foreign Affairs served the same desperate warning via other neutral channels to various American embassies throughout the world. But this resort to so many lines of communication made the warning appear as just another propaganda exercise of the kind which Zhou's windy rhetoric had inflated in the past, and in any case Pannikar, the honest Indian who went out of his way to see that China's problems were understood, was by now suspected by American and European leaders as playing the Chinese game.

Nehru duly passed the message to Washington, but President Truman, doubting Pannikar's impartiality, read Zhou's warning as 'a bald attempt to blackmail the United Nations'. *Time* dismissed it as 'only propaganda'. General MacArthur was told that he should feel free to cross into North Korea – and he did.

So Zhou's bluff was called. Mao Zedong paced up and down his room for three days and three nights, while Zhou mournfully warned a meeting of officials that: 'If necessary, we must be prepared to retreat from the coastal provinces to the interior and to make the northwest and southwest the bases for planning a long war.'

Chinese volunteers went in, checked the American advance and eventually pushed them back from North Korea. Then the Americans recovered and drove right up to the Chinese frontier, which MacArthur had made clear he did not regard as something to stand in his way. A desperate Zhou Enlai lent his reputation to the falsification of evidence designed to prove the Americans were conducting aerial espionage over China. In the general alarm which now overtook all the Chinese leaders, Zhou had some kind of breakdown. The official story is that he fell ill from overwork, and Mao suggested he recuperate at the coastal resort of Lüda. (His security guards told him to grow a beard so that he would not be recognized.) It seems that he spent between two and three months with his wife at the seaside convalescing. By the time Zhou came back to resume his duties in Beijing, the Russians had made cease-fire proposals, which eventually led to a belated armistice in Korea two years later.

In fact the Americans refrained from crossing into China or even bombing China. They were not ready to take on the People's Republic at this moment. According to one of his colleagues, Zhou later commented on this in a surprisingly childish vein. 'The leaders of imperialist governments,' he is said to have observed, 'are mean people. You only need to abuse them violently, to attack them, and if necessary give them a colour to look at and they cannot move hand or foot.' Again, on another occasion, he said: 'If you hit the imperialists till they feel it hurts, they will ask peace from you.' This is the language of internal Chinese politics, in which Zhou had to excel in order to maintain his own position, and the language needed psychologically to compensate for China's sense of impotence in world affairs.

All this was a distraction from what the government had designated as a three-year period of rehabilitation and construction for China. It had to reshape China's administrative system as well as deal with continuing opposition to its Communist reforms. As Premier, Zhou could not avoid involvement in the repressive side of the Communists' work. Early in 1951, for example, he had to announce that more than 28,000 opponents had been executed in one province alone during the preceding ten months. He was also in the vanguard of the so-called 'Three-Anti Campaign' which began that year – against corruption, waste and excessive bureaucratic behaviour – at the cost of hundreds of thousands of lives.

The effort required to keep the Red Army in the field in Korea ate remorselessly into China's modest resources, and in the summer of 1952 Zhou went to Moscow with defence specialists to exact the highest possible reparation from the Kremlin for protecting its interests in Korea with Chinese blood. Khrushchev is reported to have described Zhou condescendingly as 'a bright, flexible and up-to-date man with whom we could talk'. By dint of nonstop arguing for several weeks, Zhou persuaded Stalin to agree to give up the semicolonial privileges which had been retained in the first set of negotiations. A further injection of Soviet economic aid was also agreed on, although Zhou could not have felt that its volume in any way corresponded with the sacrifices made by the Chinese soldiers, including Mao's own son.

16

Geneva and Bandung
1953–55

When Stalin, the great Soviet dictator, was buried in March 1953 in the presence of the assembled leaders of world communism, many expected that Mao Zedong, who might now properly claim to be the senior figure in that hierarchy, would make an appearance. But he preferred to avoid further rebuffs of the kind he had learned to expect at Russian hands. Besides, his visit of 1949, not to mention those of his two chief lieutenants Liu Shaoqi and Zhou Enlai, had never been repaid by any high Soviet office-holders visiting China.

So Mao sent Zhou to Stalin's funeral, and the European comrades not only took him as a proxy for Mao but also honoured him in his own right. He was the kind of Communist they liked. At the ceremony in Moscow he was the only foreigner to stand among the Soviet leaders instead of in the foreign contingent, and when the gun carriage bore Stalin's coffin away, Zhou walked immediately behind it on a level with the new leaders of the Soviet State – Khrushchev, Malenkov and Beria.

Zhou had suffered mightily from Stalin's petulant miserliness, and must have relished this unexpected elevation to such prominence in the Marxist world. As he walked with solemn steps behind the dead tyrant's mortal remains, he must have remembered how he had waited on the distant decisions of this man, whose very name made Chinese comrades tremble, how Stalin had guided the Chinese revolution like a policeman atop a skyscraper trying to direct the street traffic below. But Zhou's thoughts of vindication would quickly have moved into the practical sphere. What could he gain for China from the new Soviet leaders who, in contrast with Stalin, had openly advertised the high value they set on Chinese collaboration? There now began a belated honeymoon, which was to last some three years.

Zhou's prominence at Stalin's funeral made him a new figure on the world stage. Everywhere people asked who was this unknown Chinese Premier who exercised so much power in the Communist world? The outside world's appetite to know Zhou better was intensified by his role in the belated armistice in Korea, quickly followed by his remarkable success at the Indochina conference, convened in Geneva in May 1954 to end the war between the French colonial forces and the Vietnamese nationalists led by Ho Chi Minh's Communist Party.

Zhou was one of the three Communist leaders at Geneva, along with Foreign Minister V. M. Molotov and Premier Pham Van Dong of Vietnam. He called at Moscow on his way to the conference, and Khrushchev later remembered him explaining:

Comrade Ho Chi Minh has told me that the situation in Vietnam is hopeless and that if we don't obtain a cease-fire soon, the Vietnamese won't be able to hold out against the French. They . . . want us to help them drive out the French. We simply can't . . . we've already lost too many men in Korea – that war cost us dearly. We're in no condition to get involved in another war at this time.

Khrushchev recommended that Zhou tell a little white Russian lie, and allow Ho Chi Minh to go on believing in the possibility of China's moving troops across the border to help.

In the event, Zhou did not have to take such a defensive position. By the time the conference opened, the Vietnamese had won the battle of Dien Bien Phu and the new French government under Pierre Mendès-France was ready to compromise. But in the process of hammering out the Indochina settlement during the summer of 1954, Zhou unexpectedly made friends with Western leaders and dismayed his Communist allies.

This was his first – and, as it was to turn out, only – return to Western Europe since his student days thirty years before. One of the surprising facts about Zhou's career as Premier is that he never saw with his own eyes the postwar flowering of modern capitalism in its big industrial centres. Geneva and Berne were the only cities he personally observed in the West, and they can hardly have driven home to him the full extent to which China had materially fallen behind.

Geneva did not at first know what to make of him in his wide-brimmed hat and long-skirted coat, all in black. Nervous to begin with, he moved in a knot of bodyguards as if expecting assassination. 'It seemed,' wrote one correspondent, 'he could not look to the left or the right, his face frozen in a mask of contempt.' *Life* magazine portrayed him acidly as 'a Communist who likes luxury', perhaps because his delegation took over one of the best hotels and hired a fleet of cars, while Zhou himself occupied a comfortable villa in which to receive fellow-delegates.

The impression of hostility was borne out by Zhou's early contributions to the conference. He was colder towards the West than Molotov, accusing the Americans of wanting to use South Vietnam as a military base against China.

During the deadlocked early phase of the conference, Zhou came unexpectedly face to face in an anteroom with John Foster Dulles, the dour American Secretary of State, who had publicly questioned Zhou's personal integrity, declaring that he would meet him privately 'only if our cars collide in the street'. Zhou held out his hand to the American, whom he had not met before, and others in the room stiffened to see how Dulles would respond. Deliberately the American shook his head, folded his hands behind his back, turned on his heel, and strode out of the room, muttering like a good New England Christian, 'I cannot.' Zhou gazed at Dulles's receding back, shrugged his shoulders and lifted his hands as if to say, 'What sort of behaviour is that?' It was a *coup de théâtre* which won him friends all over the world. A French official spoke for many when he judged the Chinese 'in simple sandals' as the patrician in this encounter. Afterwards Zhou commented that the US Secretary's discourtesy was 'really carrying even reaction to extremes.' When the business at Geneva was done, it was another American, Dean Acheson, who paid tribute to Zhou as 'the ablest diplomat in the world, not excepting Mr Churchill.'

In the end Zhou rejected Soviet leadership and struck out on his own, apparently deciding that the Soviet–Vietnamese strategy of stonewalling at the conference was going to help Vietnam at the expense of China's interests, both as regards their common border and in the wider arena of East–West relations. He probably saw that Stalin's heirs were in any case preparing a detente with the West. In mid-June, Zhou electrified the conference by telling Foreign Secretary Anthony Eden, and later Prime Minister Pierre Mendès-France, that he would agree to treat the kingdoms of Laos and Cambodia as separate and independent from Vietnam. He had observed how strongly the Indians and other neutrals in the East–West struggle felt about the independence of these two countries and China would have enough trouble dealing with the touchy Vietnamese without the latter inheriting the full writ of French imperialism. Why should the Laotians and Cambodians not be subject to just as much Chinese as Vietnamese influence in the future geopolitics of Indochina? For different reasons, Molotov agreed to Zhou's proposal, but the Vietnamese, who intended to reassert over these two small states the hegemony they had been in the process of forging before the French colonialists ever arrived, were furious.

Eden was struck not merely by the message of compromise, but also by its bearer. Attracted by Zhou's graces, the Briton could not believe that this man had fought as a guerrilla. Zhou hit it off with Eden almost as dramatically as he failed with Dulles. An aide of the British Foreign Secretary wondered if the rapport between the two sprang from their possessing 'the same sort of intuitive, feminine intellect'. Zhou wondered if this suave Briton might not mediate between himself and the Americans.

Zhou was now regarded by almost everyone else in Geneva not merely as a skilful diplomat, but also as a political 'moderate', possibly heading a pragmatic faction of sober administrators in Beijing in contrast with the romantic ideologues like Mao. Dulles's hostile anti-Communist 'brinkmanship' was beginning to alarm the Europeans, who were correspondingly relieved to find that the premier of the country which had given Vietnam its weapons – and made its victory possible – was now willing to compromise. They saw Zhou as a man who drove a hard bargain but could be treated as a partner in building a new era of world peace.

The French, as the operative imperialist power, were in the key position at the conference. 'Not once,' a French official recalled, 'but on several occasions, Mr Zhou Enlai did what he could to bring about a compromise; one of his initiatives was to place his residence at the disposal of the French delegation to meet Mr Pham Van Dong discreetly there.' Zhou travelled to Berne at the end of June to confer privately with Mendès-France, drawing freely on his student memories of France and apparently untroubled by the bad impression this hobnobbing with the French might make on the Vietnamese Communists.

During the recession of the conference in late June, Zhou made more history by paying his first visit to India and Burma, the two countries he had found so helpful, from an ideologically neutral point of view, in negotiating peace in Korea and Indochina. The Indian journey, to meet Nehru, was arranged by the enthusiastic Krishna Menon, India's representative at the Geneva conference.

'What a wealthy country you have!' Zhou said enviously on arriving in India, producing the northern tyro's stock reaction to the tropics. 'You have so much of everything.' But he had a lot of explaining to do. Although India had supported the new Chinese government's various international claims with remarkable sympathy, Nehru had been appalled by the Chinese invasion and military occupation of Tibet in 1950 and had learned from the Tibetans themselves what a hard taskmaster Zhou could be. India understood the Chinese claims of suzerainty over Tibet, but did not see why force had to be used to secure them. Zhou now reassured Nehru that China would not expand its hegemony beyond Tibet. Zhou wanted India and other Commonwealth states in Asia to boycott the forthcoming anti-Communist treaty organization (SEATO) which the Americans were organizing, while Nehru wanted Zhou to keep a restraining hand on the Vietnamese Communists and prevent them from pressuring Laos and Cambodia. They apparently agreed not to talk in detail about their common border and its mysteries. But the most famous outcome of their talks was the declaration of

195

the so-called Five Principles of Peaceful Coexistence, which became the platform for decades ahead of all those countries wishing to align themselves with neither the United States nor the Soviet Union. By co-authoring this document with Nehru, Zhou made it more difficult for other Asian governments, however right-wing, to continue to portray China as a threat and an enemy.

Soon afterwards Zhou visited the great Vietnamese statesman Ho Chi Minh to reassure him about his Geneva diplomacy, though Ho cannot have approved it.

Back in Geneva in July Mendès-France asked Zhou most anxiously how Ho Chi Minh had reacted to the international discussions.

'I found an equal desire for peace,' Zhou blandly replied, 'among all the people I talked to.' But then he added enigmatically: 'Each side would need to step towards the other . . . which is not to say that each has an equal number of steps to make.'

A few days later Zhou was able to reveal to Eden a new Vietnamese concession on the demarcation line, and this broke the deadlock. But the Vietnamese were angry when Zhou was persuaded by Mendès-France to accept a royal (and therefore nationalist) government in Laos instead of a Communist (and therefore Vietnam-leaning) one.

In the final stages Zhou was concerned to obtain from the Americans a commitment not to operate military bases in South Vietnam. He had probably promised Ho Chi Minh at least to ensure that non-Communist South Vietnam would thereby be open to Communist subversion after the Geneva agreement was signed. At one point he summoned the *New York Times* correspondent for an unprecedented interview on the understanding that its contents would be promptly conveyed to Dulles. The message was that Zhou would accept a Vietnam cease-fire provided military bases were barred from Vietnam. But when the 'final declaration' of the negotiating states was issued in July, an event which must have given Zhou great satisfaction, the Americans refused to sign, and Zhou had to settle for a unilateral declaration that the USA would not disturb the agreements made by the other powers.

Years later Zhou tried to defend what fellow-Communists in Asia saw as his naiveté at Geneva in allowing the Americans to get away without a commitment. 'We . . . did not have adequate experience in the field of international problems. . . . How can a country which refused to sign the agreement truly be prepared not to impede its implementation? . . . You can criticize us on these grounds. I, who attended that conference as a member of the Chinese delegation, accept your criticisms.' To the American journalist James Reston many years later, Zhou complained that 'we were very badly taken in during the first Geneva conference.' In making it easy for the

French, whom he so obviously admired, to retire with dignity, Zhou helped to give the Americans a foothold in Indochina.

His weeks in Geneva enabled Zhou to lead China out of the isolation in which she had found herself. His gesture in meeting Charlie Chaplin, one of the most famous foreign exiles in Switzerland and a valued champion of radical causes, was a stroke of genius. Dulles had refused Zhou's handshake; now a much more famous man came to court Zhou.

Chaplin was as innocent of Zhou's diplomatic wiles as Zhou was bewitched by Chaplin's ciné-comic illusions in *City Lights*. Invited to lunch by Zhou, Chaplin was warned at the last moment that the Premier might be detained because of important business at the conference, but would join the lunch party later; yet Chaplin found Zhou on the steps of his residence to greet him when he arrived. He naturally asked what had happened that morning. Zhou tapped him confidentially on the shoulder.

'It was all amicably settled,' he said, 'five minutes ago.'

Another Geneva contact made by Zhou produced later that year a visit to China by Clement Attlee and other leaders of the British Labour Party, now in opposition but lionized by Zhou. He spent, in the words of Morgan Phillips, secretary of the delegation, 'many hours discussing the new constitution of China and the problem of Formosa.'

Stopping in Moscow on his way home from Geneva, Zhou again donned the robes of the supplicant. Having helped to lead international Communist diplomacy at Geneva, he was emboldened to put again some long-standing requests to the Russians.

'Perhaps,' he asked Khrushchev hopefully, 'you could make us the gift of a university?'

'We're poor ourselves, you know,' Khrushchev replied. 'We may be richer than you, but the war has just ended and we are still not back on our feet.'

The new independence which Zhou had evinced on China's behalf in Geneva was also on display in Moscow. At a reception in his honour he proposed a toast in English. 'Why don't you speak Russian, Zhou?' Anastas Mikoyan (later Vice-Premier) complained. 'You know Russian perfectly well' (which was not true).

To which Zhou replied, still in English: 'It's time for you to learn to speak Chinese, Mikoyan.'

'Chinese is a very hard language,' the Soviet leader protested.

'Never mind,' said Zhou gaily, still in English. 'Come around to our embassy in the morning. We'll be glad to give you lessons.'

In Beijing Zhou worked hard to gain support for the Geneva compromise. The North Vietnamese premier, Pham Van Dong, was there in August describing the Geneva conference as merely an initial success waiting to be consolidated and developed. Zhou spoke in quite another vein. The Geneva accord was 'a momentous contribution' towards peace, relaxing world tension and facilitating peaceful coexistence of states with different social systems: 'People are getting increasingly disgusted with those who insist on the so-called policy of strength which seeks armed expansion and war preparation.' Unlike his Vietnamese counterpart, he paid scant regard to the Laotian and Cambodian Communists.

Reporting to the cabinet, Zhou identified the American plan for a Southeast Asian Treaty Organization as the villain in the piece. 'This bloc is being organized mainly against China.' He urged instead, as he had at Geneva, that Asian countries should form their own security arrangements regardless of ideology.

In the autumn of 1954 the National People's Congress had its opening session, attended by Zhou as a deputy elected to represent the city of Beijing. His speeches covered the whole spectrum of government responsibility. China, he said, was now trying to release her productive forces from the oppression of imperialism, feudalism and bureaucratic capitalism. In the process the national economy should develop systematically and rapidly along the road to socialism. The new industrial economy was to be socially and not privately owned. Thus could the material and cultural life of the people be raised and the independent security of the nation strengthened. Reviewing past progress, he declared that the Chinese mainland had now been unified (i.e. through the forcible occupation of Tibet, though still wanting the recalcitrant island of Taiwan), the agrarian system reformed, and the national economy rehabilitated. A First Five-Year Plan was in operation that would bring more than half the peasant households and farmed areas into a cooperative system.

This speech of 23 September also underlined the newly expansive and assertive mood in China's foreign policy. China was willing to establish peaceful relations with 'any country in Europe, South and North America and Australia, provided that it has the same desire and sincerity.' He put China's reasons for this conciliatory departure on the line.

Everyone can see that all our efforts are directed towards the construction of our country, to make it into an industrial, socialist, prosperous and happy country. We work peacefully and we hope for a peaceful atmosphere and a peaceful world: this fundamental fact determines the peaceful policy of our country as regards foreign policy.

A little optimism was permissible, since tensions had eased with the armistices in Korea and Indochina and Zhou had detected in Geneva a receptive attitude to China's claims over Taiwan and for a seat in the United Nations. SEATO could perhaps be countered by some kind of Asian security system rooted in a China–India agreement.

Zhou also lectured his compatriots on how the Overseas Chinese should be regarded. Earlier in his premiership, an Indonesian correspondent had asked him whether the Overseas Chinese, of whom there were several millions in his country, would be a vehicle for Chinese imperialist expansion. One of those present noticed Zhou's 'momentary flash of anger', expressing itself in 'the beautiful flourish of his hands and harsh note in his voice which soon died down.' Zhou had replied that China would not defend its ancestors who had committed aggression against neighbours in the past: the People's Republic pledged that it would never commit such mistakes and never be imperialist. Zhou's anger then subsided. 'He made the listener feel sorry for having been the cause for irritation.'

Zhou had now observed at first hand in Geneva and Rangoon the depth of feeling on this issue: somewhat like the Jews in the Occident, these Chinese quickly dominated the local economy without integrating into the host community. This speech was the first formal acknowledgement that any Chinese government had ever made of the existence of an 'Overseas Chinese problem'. China, he said, was ready to abandon the principle of *jus sanguinis* by which she had previously maintained Chinese citizenship even for those living abroad for many generations, and would settle the status of these twelve million or so people of Chinese origin by agreement with the host governments. Zhou explained:

We are willing to urge Overseas Chinese to respect the laws of the government and the social customs of the countries in which they live. . . . The question of the nationality of Overseas Chinese is one which the reactionary governments of China in the past never tried to solve. This placed Overseas Chinese in a difficult situation and often led to discord between China and the countries concerned.

It may sound like an attitude long overdue, but to many of Zhou's listeners, ordinary Chinese from small towns and villages with no idea about the outside world, only perhaps aware of the useful remittances which poured in from compatriots abroad to their families at home, Zhou's statement was revolutionary. How could a Chinese ever become a foreigner? This is something which is still not accepted by Chinese at heart. Zhou started the process going by which China began to understand the difference between ethnicity and nationality.

To cap Zhou's pleasure at all these developments, Nikita Khrushchev came with Bulganin in late 1954 to attend the celebrations for the fifth anniversary of the People's Republic, the first time the senior man in the Kremlin had visited the Chinese ally. Not only did the new Russian leaders repair their past neglect, but they even put the record right on the awkward issues hanging over from the past, agreeing to withdraw their forces from Lüda, to transfer to China the joint-stock companies they had been operating

199

together, to lend a large sum for Chinese development, and to extend scientific and technical collaboration. According to Khrushchev's memoirs, Zhou pushed his luck a little far by asking if the Russians could leave their heavy artillery behind at Lüda for Chinese use. Khrushchev said severely that the Soviet Union could not afford to jettison this equipment.

Following Khrushchev in October, Nehru made his first visit to Communist China, keen to discuss the Sino-Indian border, which, as shown on Chinese maps, appeared to incorporate a good deal of territory regarded in India as Indian. Zhou responded that the question was not important compared with the others they were engaged in (such as thwarting Dulles and SEATO) and could be shelved for a later occasion when there was more time. Here were the seeds of future discord sown.

Only the Americans, it seemed, would not take Zhou at face value. When the United States signed a security treaty with the Guomindang administration in Taiwan at the end of 1954, Zhou declared metaphorical war on the USA – 'the most arrogant aggressor ever known in history, the most ferocious enemy of world peace and the main prop of all the forces of reaction in the world.'

It was not only SEATO and the American treaty with Taiwan which provoked Zhou's anger. The Guomindang still held a few small and normally uninhabited islets just off the mainland opposite Taiwan, and when the Communists shelled them in September 1954, a prolonged international crisis was sparked. In American eyes this confirmed China's aggressive intentions. Zhou angrily chided the British Ambassador for his government's support of the Americans on this question. Sir Humphrey Trevelyan found Zhou 'in his most emotional and bitter mood'. The Premier concluded with the words: 'Thank you for coming, but I must say it has been a most unpleasant interview.' Eden tried to mediate, asking Zhou to commit his government to a peaceful solution of the problem of these offshore islands of Quemoy and Matsu. He even offered to meet Zhou on the China–Hong Kong border to discuss this further, but Zhou riposted with an invitation for Sir Anthony to visit Beijing – which would have lost the British statesman his influence in Washington. Zhou refused to concede that China should be limited in any action she might take on what she regarded as her own sovereign territory.

In April 1955 Zhou won his greatest diplomatic triumph. The celebrated Bandung conference – twenty-nine African and Asian governments – was convened in Indonesia on the initiative of India, Burma, Ceylon, Indonesia and Pakistan. In Chinese politics Zhou dealt with people whose mentality he knew only too well. At Geneva he had taken on the hard-nosed Europeans and won them over, but they saw China as a distant and currently harmless power whose ancient civilization was to be greatly admired. Now he had to put a Chinese Communist case to an assembly of non-Communist, including some fiercely anti-Communist, Asian leaders, many of whom resented the economic success of the Overseas Chinese in their own countries, and were also apprehensive lest China be tempted to expand her territory or come to the aid of the Overseas Chinese when host governments took action against them.

It was touch and go whether Zhou would be able to attend at Bandung at all, since he came down with acute appendicitis only a fortnight beforehand. But, as soon as the stitches were out, he declared himself ready, and he showed no signs of discomfort during an arduous month in the tropics of Java. In his first week, despite his operation, Zhou slept for only thirteen hours, sometimes in his clothes, without even undressing.

And what the surgeons had saved, Guomindang saboteurs had attempted to bring down. Through the good offices of Nehru, the Chinese had chartered an Indian airliner called *Kashmir Princess* to take their delegation to Bandung. On Easter Monday, this plane, carrying nine Chinese officials, crashed in the sea, and although the facts were never satisfactorily ferreted out, it seemed that a time bomb had been put on board by Guomindang agents in the hope of catching Zhou. His aides had got wind of the plot, however, and Zhou himself went instead by a roundabout route via Rangoon (where he was invited to an advance mini-summit with Prime Ministers Nehru, U Nu of Burma and Nasser of Egypt).

Zhou spoke formally to the Bandung conference on the second day, 19 April, dwelling on the need for peace and an end to colonialism. He could not accept the Pakistan and Philippine statements that SEATO was a defensive pact, because, he said, China had no expansionist intentions. He stressed everything that brought Asia together, especially a common reaction to the colonialism and racial discrimination of the West. 'The population of Asia will never forget that the first atom bomb exploded on Asian soil.' He made it clear that China had confidence in communism, but he was careful to avoid ideological confrontation. Instead, he made gestures of friendship towards the Philippines and Thailand in a skilful, ingratiating speech that could only wound those who were not present. In the words of an American observer, Zhou 'succeeded in creating an impression that there existed a united front of Communists and neutralists, based on the common conviction that Western colonialism and Western military pacts were the only real dangers threatening the independence of the new nations of Asia and Africa.' Nobody remembered that Russia too was white, European and imperialist.

In a gesture which stirred all twenty-nine delegations from two continents, Zhou, having heard the initial addresses from the other leaders, tore up his own prepared second speech and made an impromptu one instead, dealing directly with the issues they had raised. Carlos P. Romulo, the doughty

Filipino, had cursed Communist imperialism as worse than capitalist imperialism, dismissing China as a puppet of the Kremlin. The reporters rushed eagerly to Zhou for his comment.

'I did not come to quarrel,' Zhou blandly replied. 'I came for the success of all the people here.'

And this was the theme of his improvised second speech.

The Chinese delegation has come here to seek common ground, not to create divergences. . . . Differences exist among us but there is also common ground. The overwhelming majority of Asian–African countries and peoples have suffered and are still suffering from the calamities of colonialism. If we seek common ground in doing away with these sufferings, it will be easy for us to have mutual understanding and respect.

As for China's claims to Taiwan, to recognition by other countries, to a seat in the United Nations, these were China's own affair: 'She will not burden the other nations with them.' It was beautifully judged.

Other delegates were fascinated by the subtle relationship between Zhou and Nehru. Both were well-educated mandarins from the upper class, both had swung round to a radical view of politics. They were the aristocrats, sophisticates and internationalists in parties which had been led by those far more earthy and anchored characters, Gandhi and Mao. Nehru had already been of enormous help to Zhou, going far beyond what was called for in the books of diplomacy. It was only to be expected that he should feel superior, his own contacts in the world being so much broader and deeper than Zhou's. He was also nine years older than the Chinese Premier and, as a friend put it, 'naturally he felt rather like an elder brother to him.' Bandung was Nehru's brainchild, and at the conference he naturally felt protective towards Zhou: some observers saw him as chaperoning Zhou around like a protégé. Others concluded that Nehru was deliberately staying in the background in order to give Zhou his head and educate the other Asians into the realities of having to live in China. He saw Zhou's success 'as his own personal triumph'.

For their part, the neutrals tried to defuse Zhou's quarrel with the United States in order to reduce the risk of conflict, and towards the end of the conference he told a small group of his fellow-delegates that China was ready to negotiate with the USA for a detente in the Far East and especially over Taiwan. He thus involved several neutral governments in the problem, motivating them to press the Americans to make concessions.

Meanwhile, all kinds of fences were mended. Following Nasser's conversations with Zhou, Egypt recognized the People's Republic a few months later. Zhou's promise to Prince Wan Waithayakon that China had no subversive designs on Thailand created a huge impression in Bangkok. Similarly, Zhou's talks with Takasaki Tatsunosuke, representing Japan, proved a sound foundation for many informal exchanges in the years ahead. (Zhou suggested that the two countries together simplify their systems of written characters, a statesmanlike proposal which came to nothing because of the pusillanimity of Japan's right-wing Premier Kishi – and the same fate overtook Zhou's hopes of using the Japanese as go-betweens with America over the Taiwan question.)

Not everyone, of course, was swept off his feet. Sir John Kotelawala of Ceylon led those who continued to feel that Zhou could not be trusted. And many must have briefed their aides, as did Prince Norodom Sihanouk of Cambodia, that while friendship at first sight with Zhou was irresistible, they should remember: 'Of course, Zhou is a Communist. Be careful. Since he is so attractive he is more dangerous.' (Still, Zhou told Beijing undergraduates afterwards that the Pakistan and Ceylon leaders had confessed they were not so much anti-Communist as frightened of Indian expansionism, so that he found himself mediating between them and Nehru.)

One investment which paid a big dividend was Zhou's energetic courting of his Indonesian hosts: China signed an agreement on the status of Overseas Chinese in Indonesia which was an unprecedented official abandonment of earlier formal claims on the loyalty of Chinese living abroad. Zhou actually delayed his departure in order to pay a state visit to Indonesia, the first by any Chinese leader of such stature.

It was another triumph. He could hardly move in Indonesia without smiling, patting children on the head, shaking hands with people on either side, accepting flowers and mingling in huge crowds with no bodyguards in view. His popularity reflected the relief that ordinary people felt in realizing that the tough government of the most numerous people in the world could be represented among them by such an engaging and friendly personality. But they also applauded Zhou's lowering of the ideological temperature, his dignity, and his patience in dealing with bad-tempered criticism at Bandung from the leaders of Pakistan, Ceylon and Turkey.

Zhou was affable and approachable, he was willing to negotiate with the Americans over Taiwan and thus remove the threat of a third world war. This was precisely what the Asian public most wanted to hear. 'All Zhou had to do,' one correspondent wrote, 'was to stand his ground and wait with outstretched hands, and they came to him.' Zhou spoke humbly, as no Russian Communist had ever spoken to Asians. The Chinese were suffering, were backward, were afraid of war and should not be feared. 'I'm as violently opposed to communism as ever,' one pro-Western delegate at Bandung admitted, 'but I trust this man.'

The momentum was maintained. In May Zhou declared that China was willing to use peaceful means as far as possible in liberating Taiwan. In August the first ambassadorial-level talks with the Americans began in

Geneva and it looked as if real headway was made in dissolving the mistrust of the Korean War period. Asian visitors began to come to China almost nonstop, beginning with the Indonesian Prime Minister in May 1955, followed in rapid succession by those of Cambodia, Laos, Nepal, Burma and Pakistan, not to mention Nehru and President Sukarno.

Reporting to the National People's Congress in July, Zhou detected a clear desire in Asia and Africa to abolish military blocs, and to open up communication and trade. China would propose a Pacific nuclear-free zone at any future world disarmament conference. 'The Chinese people hope that the countries of Asia and the Pacific region, including the United States, will sign a pact of collective peace to replace the antagonistic military blocs now existing in this part of the world.'

But Zhou also had to reflect the more conservative opinions of his comrades. The three leading Western countries had recently met with the Soviet Union in Geneva and perceptibly reduced international tension. But China should still keep up her guard.

We must preserve our vigilance, we must strengthen our country's necessary defence forces. Only in this way can we protect the fruits of our socialist reconstruction, guarantee the security and integrity of our nation's sovereignty and territory and moreover be of service to enterprises safeguarding world peace.

It may sound as if these sunny years of 1953–55 found Zhou largely preoccupied with foreign affairs, first bringing the new Russian leaders round to a more friendly view of China, and then stunning the world's diplomats successively at Geneva and Bandung. These were indeed relatively quiet years in Chinese politics. But the lines of conflict were already being drawn between Mao's impatient drive towards fast utopian reforms and Zhou's preference for slowly but surely consolidating the transformation of China's peasant farms into cooperatives. The end of 1955 found Zhou deep in discussion with China's non-Communists for a new policy towards intellectuals – another bone of contention between Zhou's rather practical group of administrators and experts on the one hand, and the red-hot ideologues hungry for quick results in attaining a classless society, led by Mao and Liu Shaoqi, on the other. From now on these issues – how fast the peasants should be forced to give up their independent farming, and how far intellectuals should be immune from Party regimentation – would be more and more bitterly fought. The 1953–55 period saw a lull in the domestic upheaval, coinciding with China's breaking out of the circle into the great world outside. Domestically it was a time to analyse socioeconomic problems and draw up alternative solutions, while putting in train less controversial reforms which were long overdue in such sectors as education, the language, legal institutions and national minorities.

From 1956 onwards it was a question of urgent action instead of protracted debate on these central issues, and the Chinese Communist Party came face to face with the intractability of human nature and Chinese society. But Zhou was never so happy as in the golden early 1950s, when he was able without discomfort to wear the mask of communism over his own deep instincts for harmony, peaceful persuasion and understanding. It had fallen to him to present the new image of China to the outside world, and he knew how superbly he had accomplished it.

17

The Hundred Flowers
1956–58

Although the People's Republic had been in business for more than six years, Zhou had not yet given a major policy speech of the kind that his peers and even juniors in the Party hierarchy had enunciated on such crucial issues as land reform or collectivization. Either he cleverly sidestepped such controversial assignments, or else he was regarded as the super-administrator unsuited for them. His only watershed speech for the regime came on 14 January 1956 when he delivered an analysis of the Party's policy towards intellectuals.

Here he set out for the benefit of Party philistines the precise reasons why China's national progress required that the largely non-Marxist scientists, engineers, technicians, doctors and other professional men and women should feel free and comfortable in their work. Moving beyond the industrial revolution of the West based on steam and electricity, which most Chinese laymen supposed they were trying to emulate, Zhou said that China would now have to welcome the far more significant 'new revolution in science, technique and industry produced by automation.' If China was to get anywhere, it would have to 'leap' up to the highest international scientific standards within the coming twelve years.

He was the natural person in the Politburo to present this argument, and to encourage the non-Communist intellectuals to enter wholeheartedly into public life even if they disagreed with Communist Party policies. It was Zhou who had written hundreds of letters appealing to exiles to return, and it was Zhou who now laid down to local Party bosses that these people should be treated properly and given some due. This January speech was in fact a herald of the Hundred Flowers Movement, launched by Mao with Zhou's support in the following year.

Zhou repeated the essentials of his message to the National People's Congress in the summer, in what Han Suyin described as 'an electrifying speech', explaining that intellectuals and the non-Communist parties were needed as genuine partners in the modernization of China, and that the Communist Party must be humble enough to listen to their criticism. Later Han drove through a 'neat avenue bordered with oleanders to a modest pavilion' which was Zhou's home. It was all very simple and lacking in protocol. 'In the living room, many books on shelves, but no antiques, no curios, no priceless furniture. Old worn sofas, rattan chairs, a worn and cheap carpet . . . Spartan. And this was no fake. Zhou simply did not care for any material comfort.' In a China where most Prime Ministers had lived in luxury and accumulated wealth, this was novel. Against a tradition of extravagance in high office, Zhou was setting new standards.

When Han started putting her questions, the Premier grew defensive as he tried to make clear why the Communist government did not have more to show for its years in office. 'There is no going back,' he insisted. 'The door to going back is closed. The power we have will not be lightly cast aside, not in the name of pseudo-liberalism, which will only lead to a tyranny like the one we have just emerged from.' Because of the needs of the nation 'we are prepared to go along even with people who disagree with us, provided they do not sabotage the socialist revolution.' So the new partnership with non-Communist intellectuals was conditional.

'You think there is no dissent in the Party; this is a common subjective view in the West, that the Communist Party is a monolith. . . . If you only knew how much we debate, discuss, argue. . . . We often hold very different opinions.' Han detected here 'a note of passion in his voice'.

Meanwhile the Premier had to take a careful position on the increasingly vehement demands from Mao and the more radical leaders to speed up both collectivization and the growth in production of China's economy, especially in agriculture. He agreed unhesitatingly that it was vitally important to get faster growth than had been realized under the Russian-style First Five-Year Plan. But he opposed a sudden switch to large-scale cooperatives and state ownership as disruptive, and argued that the existing methods of management in China's enterprises should not 'lightly' be changed. Good modes and methods should be preserved as 'historic legacies to be handed down and developed'.

But Mao and the leftists prevailed, and Zhou had to concede, against his better judgement and that of his assembled technical experts, to the 'adventurist' (they were proud of the label) comrades in the Politburo. 'I bore the responsibility,' Zhou later confessed, 'for the opposition to adventurism in 1956 and I made a self-critical examination.'

The Premier's position in the heated economic debate was spelt out in careful language when introducing the draft Second Five-Year Plan at the Eighth Party Congress, which opened in September 1956.

'First,' he declared, 'we should . . . set a reasonable rate for the growth of the national economy, and place the plan on a forward-looking and completely sound basis, to ensure a fairly balanced development. . . . We should set the long-term targets in a comparatively realistic way.' This was such a far cry from Mao's 'adventurism' and the left wing's call for a 'leap forward' that it must have seemed to Mao himself provocative. It would be necessary, Zhou went on, to guard against impetuosity on the one hand and 'timidity and hesitancy' on the other – and his listeners were left to infer that the first of these threats was more to be feared.

'We should make an overall analysis of the objective conditions and . . . make a unified plan of the main targets of the current year and the next year, so that each of the annual plans may dovetail with the next and advance at a fairly even pace.' Large projects should be well coordinated with overall developments so that the different branches of the economy developed in proportion. If departments and regions tried to do everything at once, everywhere and at the same time, 'taking no account of actual conditions and recklessly running ahead', mistakes were bound to be made – and had indeed already been noted earlier in 1956. (Zhou cited the case of the double-bladed plough and the small steam engine, both of which had been ludicrously overproduced, as examples of this incautious approach.) He also implicitly indicted Mao for blindly ignoring the cash limits set in the national budget and thus fanning inflation.

As for the twelve-year agricultural plan which Mao had put forward at the beginning of the year as a charter for rapid change, Zhou warned that there were objective constraints to the raising of food production – flood and drought, difficulties of reclaiming land and insufficient machinery. He stressed that developments in industry must harmonize with those in agriculture, to avoid a situation where industry was held up by lack of adequate raw materials, or not being able to market its products sufficiently to rural consumers.

Outwardly it appeared that Zhou lost nothing in the Party hierarchy at the Congress: he was not only a Vice-Chairman of the Central Committee, but also a member of the six-man Standing Committee of the Politburo. But behind the scenes it was more complex. Zhou and Liu Shaoqi both had reason to criticize Mao, yet they did not like each other. Liu, as Mao's designated second-in-command, was jealous of Zhou's prominence in the diplomatic field, especially when President Sukarno of Indonesia came to China and told his hosts that 'each great nation has its great personages: India has Mahatma Gandhi, Russia has Lenin, China has Sun Yat-sen, Mao Zedong, Zhu De and Zhou Enlai.' Yet Liu himself was scheming to supplant

208

Mao, and it was Zhou who eventually revealed that the resolution endorsing Liu's political report at the Eighth Congress had not even been shown to Mao in advance.

Zhou continued to do the principal work to increase China's diplomatic recognition by foreign powers and to negotiate to remove American influence in Taiwan. About the former he professed to be patient. 'China exists,' he told a foreign correspondent, 'and if there should be some difficulties about recognition, now or later, that does not matter . . . China can wait.' But the question of Taiwan and the small offshore islands was different. 'No one on earth shall tell us what to do with our own territory,' he told another foreign visitor. 'That is infringement of sovereignty.' He pleaded for the Taiwan leaders to view the People's Republic as above party. 'All patriotic people,' he said that summer, 'regardless of whether they joined the patriotic ranks earlier or later and regardless of how great the crimes they committed in the past may have been, will be treated in accordance with the principle that "patriots belong to one family" and a policy of no punishment for past misdeeds.' If Zhou had been in sole control of domestic policy, more Guomindang officials in Taiwan might have responded. But later events were to show them wise to stand firm.

Diplomatic problems were by now so numerous that the Premier felt obliged to undertake a series of foreign visits at the end of 1956. He left Beijing in November, not to return to his desk again, except unexpectedly for a few days in the middle, for three months. Perhaps he reckoned that he was well out of the Party infighting and could safely leave Liu and Mao to do mutually damaging battle with each other.

Zhou began in Vietnam, and proceeded to Cambodia and India, where he had cold exchanges with Nehru. The Indian Premier had brought the border disagreements out into the open, and was keen to discuss them, but Zhou remained curiously unperceptive about the strength of Indian feeling on the subject, assuming that he could continue brushing the dispute to one side. Possibly his military aides would not allow him to negotiate until Chinese forces were actually in command of the territory claimed by China.

Tibet was the other divisive issue with India. Nehru had been dismayed by the bloodiness of the Chinese military occupation of Tibet since 1950, yet now, with an indigenous revolt breaking out against it in 1956, he did not interfere. The Indians had resigned themselves to the notion that China had inherited from earlier times an authority of some sort over Tibet. Indeed, when Zhou told him of plans to liberalize the Chinese stewardship of Tibet, Nehru interceded with the Dalai Lama, the spiritual leader of the Tibetans, who had taken refuge in India, to collaborate with the Chinese.

Such well-meant interference angered Zhou because it showed that the Indians had much better access to the Tibetan leaders than he had. It turned what Zhou saw as an internal dispute within the People's Republic into something wider and less manageable. True, these differences with India were all prompted by China's own actions and ambitions, but Zhou knew that there would be little chance of persuading the blinkered politicians in Beijing, most of whom had never been out of China, to make concessions on Tibet in order to mollify Nehru.

Elsewhere in Asia, Zhou could be more successful in coming to grips with specific complaints. He had already acceded to the pleas of Singapore's eloquent Premier, David Marshall, to declare that when that city-state gained independence from Britain, China would no longer insist on regarding as Chinese citizens the Chinese who took up Singapore citizenship. He merely asked that they be allowed to return to the land of their ancestors to die, and be able to regain their Chinese citizenship. (Marshall, himself a Jew, complained to Zhou about Jews in China being prevented from emigrating to Israel, apparently to placate the Russians. Zhou promised to look into this, and the position was in fact subsequently eased.)

The Overseas Chinese issue was a big one in all the Southeast Asian countries. In Burma, Zhou told his locally resident compatriots that they should 'obey the laws and respect the customs, habits and religious beliefs of their country of residence.' They should learn the local language, marry local people, and become Burmese citizens, at which time they should no longer belong to Overseas Chinese organizations. If they clung to Chinese citizenship, then by the same token they should not take part in local politics, nor join political parties or vote in elections. 'We do not promote the organization of Communist or other . . . parties among Overseas Chinese,' the Premier said in an important commitment. If these people wanted to go into politics, they should either take local citizenship or else come back to China where there would be plenty of politics for them. Zhou maintained throughout his life this clear dividing line between the Chinese of the People's Republic and the Chinese outside it. Sometimes he even told Overseas Chinese to change their religion and become, in the case of Malaysia or Indonesia, Moslem.

In far-off Europe, the Hungarians, who had already defied their Communist Party leadership in seeking a government more independent of the Kremlin, escalated their demands during the final weeks of 1956, to the alarm of the Chinese leadership. It looked as if the Soviet Union might lose control of Eastern Europe, to the immense damage of the international strength of the world Communist bloc. Instead of going on to Nepal and Afghanistan, therefore, in the New Year of 1957, as had been planned, Zhou was recalled to Beijing. Mao Zedong was full of 'I told you so's' about the Hungarian crisis. He had been restless ever since Nikita Khrushchev, Stalin's heir, had spoken in Moscow in February 1956 openly denouncing many of his predecessor's policies and decisions. Mao had good reason to share Khrushchev's dislike of Stalin, but he was long-sighted enough to see that Khrushchev's impulsive discrediting of his predecessor – undertaken without Chinese advice – could strike at the heart of the authority structure within the unruly world Communist movement.

'I told Comrade Zhou Enlai over the phone,' the Chairman explained, that the Russian leaders were 'blinded by their material gains, and the best way to deal with them is to give them a good dressing down.'

Zhou's reaction had been to appreciate Khrushchev's warning of the danger of leaders' creating personality cults as Stalin had done. (He took trouble to apply the lesson at home, telling Party officials for instance: 'In future, when the Chairman comes into a room, you must not stand up and clap. This is not a good thing.')

But the last thing the Chinese Government wanted was a weakening of the world Communist bloc, and so it was prepared to help Khrushchev retain control of Eastern Europe. It was probably Khrushchev himself who asked that Premier Zhou be recalled from India to undertake an urgent impromptu mission to Eastern Europe. Where the Russian voice had lost credibility in Warsaw and Budapest, China, with her reputation for independent experiment in socialist democracy, might still be listened to. Zhou arrived by the Danube in January 1957 – the first Chinese intervention in Europe, as observers were quick to point out, since the days of Genghis Khan.

He undoubtedly acted as a messenger carrying the respective minimum demands between Khrushchev in the Soviet Union, Gomulka in Poland and Kadar in Hungary. His goal was to sell the orthodox Chinese view that the Communist world had to have a leader, that only the Soviet Union could at present fill that role, that the Russians had been too much criticized in this respect, and that any reasonable Communist should basically be satisfied with the Soviet leadership record. But the East Europeans, who had to live with Russian tanks, would have none of it, and as Zhou proceeded with his tour he found it expedient to tone down Chinese support for Kremlin arguments and policies. Nevertheless, his diplomacy helped to shore up the Soviet East European empire.

Back in Moscow Zhou repeated China's doubts about Khrushchev's de-Stalinization approach – that it would weaken Soviet authority, advertise Soviet shortcomings to the world and slow down the international growth of communism. The two sides agreed to differ. 'I pointed out to Premier Khrushchev,' Zhou later recalled of this visit, rubbing salt into his host's wounds, 'that the Soviet Union had taken too much territory, ranging from Japanese territory in the east, to China, the Middle East, Eastern Europe and Finland.'

It was probably during this encounter that Zhou had an acid exchange with

Khrushchev, which was recounted with relish in every Communist capital afterwards. After defending himself for some time against Zhou's reproaches for having adopted 'revisionist' policies unsupported by Marxist doctrine, Khrushchev is supposed to have made an irritated stab at Zhou's class credentials.

'It is all very well your criticizing like this, Comrade Zhou,' he said, 'but you must agree that it is I who spring from the working class, whereas you are a bourgeois by birth.'

There was a short pause, after which Zhou replied very quietly: 'Yes, Comrade Khrushchev. But at least we have one thing in common. We have both betrayed our class!'

Another outlet for Zhou's energies in Moscow was visits to Mao's politically volatile wife, Jiang Qing, then under treatment for cervical cancer in a Russian hospital. On one occasion he brought Borodin's wife and a fashionable opera singer to entertain her, and on another he came directly from a difficult session with Khrushchev to report angrily that the Russian Premier was stubbornly impervious to persuasion. The strain of this hastily prepared journey told in the fact that the letter which he had brought from his own wife to give to Jiang Qing lay in his pocket throughout his visits, and went all the way back to India and China again before it was remembered.

At the end of January 1957 Zhou was able to resume his interrupted Asian tour, visiting Afghanistan, India, Nepal and Ceylon. There was a significant difference in the language of his speeches now from the earlier Asian visits. Before, he had frequently affirmed that China would never exhibit 'great-nation chauvinism', so palpable a snub to the Soviet Union – which all the Asian neutrals were then denouncing for its flagrant intervention in Hungary and Poland – that Khrushchev doubtless insisted in Moscow that he omit it. From now on he talked to his Asian audiences about peaceful coexistence and not about chauvinism. Zhou could suggest China's superiority over the Soviet Union in this matter in private, but not in public.

Meanwhile in India he tried to enlarge the fragile base of understanding about China. Discovering at Visvabharati University, founded by Rabindranath Tagore and the only seat of learning where Chinese studies were then offered in India, a dearth of Chinese books, he promised official help – and shortly afterwards some 12,000 volumes arrived, together with 60,000 rupees. (Zhou was given a DLitt by Visvabharati for his pains.)

He was constantly surprised by the welcome he got, although he should have begun to be accustomed to it after Bandung. 'In the many places we visited,' he said afterwards, 'whether in the daytime or at night, there were always thousands of people coming out, in spite of great heat or bitter cold, to cheer us, to greet us according to their various national customs. . . . A keen feeling of closeness never left us during our visits. . . . We felt very much like being in the homes of close friends, our kinsmen or brothers, and not in strange countries.' If only his capacity to form emotional bonds with foreigners had been matched by an ability to alter their perceptions and ways of thinking.

Early in February he returned to China, staying in the south for several days before returning to Beijing. Perhaps he reported personally to Mao in Wuhan. His colleagues were less interested in hearing about the foibles of the weakling states to their south than in the continuing crisis in Eastern Europe. Zhou's moral there was that the Communist leaders should correct their own mistakes. The Russian comrades' 'criticism of the mistakes and defects of their work,' he told the Central Committee in a staunch deposition for Khrushchev on 5 March, 'has served to advance the life and work in every aspect of the Soviet Union.' Unceasing correction of mistakes would strengthen, not weaken, China's socialist cause. In other words, there should be more rectification within the Party, more purges of wayward officials, more admission to the general public of past mistakes. Zhou warned prophetically that China's youth would rebel in ten years' time 'if we don't change our bureaucratic ways'.

He persuaded Mao to pay attention to the lessons of Stalin's excesses and the chaos it had led to under Khrushchev, but Liu and the others argued that China was quite different from Russia, more disciplined and lacking viable alternative political traditions. They believed that they were in satisfactory command of the political situation and did not need to demean themselves by such measures. But Zhou apparently won Mao's ear for the matter, and it was decided that a big rectification campaign would be launched.

This came in the form of the Hundred Flowers Movement which Mao publicly announced a few days after Zhou's return from Asia and Eastern Europe, and which ran its course in the early summer. (The name of the movement was taken from a classical verse which the Chairman quoted for its theme: 'Let a hundred flowers bloom, let a hundred schools of thought contend' – with echoes of the creative periods of China's golden past.) The Hundred Flowers Movement was unfurled on 1 May, combining intensified explanations to the public about Communist policies, stricter disciplining of Party members who disobeyed orders, and an open invitation to intellectuals to speak out freely and tell the Party what they thought was wrong with its policies. Chairman Mao reassured his doubting followers that giving more scope to non-Communist intellectuals did not threaten the Party's authority.

Zhou stoutly supported Mao's promotion of these liberal policies towards intellectuals during 1956–57, but many other senior leaders, including Liu Shaoqi, Zhu De, Peng Dehuai and Lin Biao, conspicuously dissociated themselves from them. Was Zhou so naive as to believe that tough Communists like Liu and all those second-level leaders whose work in recent years had been entirely directed to building up the largest political party in the world would stand quietly by to be insulted by bourgeois novelists, third-year philosophy students and ivory-tower astrophysicists? His optimism ran away with him on this occasion.

Zhou's rivals in the Party seized on the issue of the economy to embarrass him. Liu stood for the proposition that China's basic problem was economic backwardness, the solutions to which were partly mechanical and partly motivational – that is to say, collectivization – and Party rectification interfered with economic progress. In an otherwise evenly split Politburo, this afforded one of the occasions when Mao would have suffered defeat if Zhou had not voted on his side.

Those in the Party who were jealous of Zhou reminded everyone that he had hobnobbed with non-Communist politicians in wartime Chongqing – as if to say he would be happy to abandon his Communist affiliations now and lead a neutral coalition government instead. Three of these politicians had become Zhou's ministers in what was technically a coalition government run by the Communist Party, and they now came under a barrage of criticism from the National People's Congress. Zhou did not dismiss them as demanded for several months.

A story went round Shanghai about this time in which Mao asked his two quarrelsome lieutenants how they could make a cat eat pepper – which the Shanghai sense of humour saw as a metaphor for making a capitalist swallow socialism. Liu Shaoqi's solution was to hold the animal down while stuffing pepper into its throat with a chopstick. Mao ruled this out, saying that force should never be used. Zhou followed with the idea of starving the cat and then wrapping the pepper in a slice of meat so that the hungry animal would swallow it whole. But Mao threw his hands up at that as deceitful. His own recipe was to rub pepper into the cat's arse so that when it began to burn, the cat would be only too happy to lick it off.

So the Hundred Flowers Campaign began with Zhou's intellectuals speaking their minds as they had not been allowed to for eight years, only to be hounded down by petty-minded Communists who quickly persuaded Mao that the country and Party would crash in pieces if such absurd liberalism continued to reign. By June Zhou was having to manoeuvre to minimize the punishments inflicted on those bravest flowers, now reclassified as 'poisonous weeds'. It was a chastening lesson in the limits to which an inward-looking and poorly educated Leninist-style Party could be marshalled into liberal and cosmopolitan paths, even when told to do so by the charismatic Mao Zedong himself.

Chauvinism was stirring on every hand. There was a growing aversion, for example, to Russian tutelage, encouraged by the antics of the inexperienced Khrushchev. 'Some people,' Zhou defensively lectured the National

People's Congress in June, 'are against learning from the experience of the Soviet Union, and even say that the mistakes and shortcomings in our construction work are also the result of learning from the Soviet Union. This is a very harmful point of view.' China's best course was to borrow wisely from the pioneer socialist state and thereby 'avoid taking many unnecessary detours'. But he was swimming against a nationalistic tide.

Rather desperately, Zhou told his Communist colleagues at the end of June, 'We are not practising democracy for its own sake. We need widespread democracy because we want to rally all the forces that can be rallied to build socialism.' But his listeners did not believe that they needed the help of class enemies. In the very same speech Zhou revealed that one sixth of the counter-revolutionaries who had been put on trial since 1949 had been given death sentences – a figure which allowed foreign China-watchers to estimate the deaths in the hundreds of thousands, even millions.

Yet the fruits of revolution remained elusive. 'Some people . . . ' Zhou sadly concluded, 'say that our living standards have gone down since the liberation.' This was particularly noticed, one could add, by the poorest peasants and their representatives at Party congresses, and yet Zhou found it necessary in this same June speech to justify reasonable differentials in income between workers and peasants on productivity grounds: unthinking egalitarianism should be avoided. That was not the kind of stuff to fire the back rows of Party meetings. Indeed, at the Central Committee meeting later in the year, Zhou's report on wages, strongly plugging material incentives, was withheld from publication. He was now beleaguered by the ascendant left wing of the Party.

Still, he tried stubbornly to lay the foundations of the rational and civilized socialist society for which he yearned. A good example was a long speech he gave in August about the problem of China's national minorities, an exposition which was systematically suppressed by domestic opponents for more than twenty years afterwards because it was too honest. Here he analysed with scrupulous care the Han chauvinism which most Chinese habitually nurse towards the Tibetans and other racial minorities on China's fringe, and the local nationalism which this in turn engendered. Both kinds of nationalism or chauvinism had to be checked. For the Prime Minister to set out to the Han people who formed the vast majority of his constituency the reasons why they were distrusted, even hated, by Tibetans, Mongolians and others was remarkable. He conceded that the Hans had aggressed against the other nationalities in the past, although they had suffered in their turn. He defended the government's long-term goals. 'Assimilation,' he explained, 'is a reactionary thing if it means one nation destroying another by force. It is a progressive act if it means natural merger of nations advancing towards prosperity.'

This was far-sighted, and Zhou spoke like that on a variety of topics. But his reward was an alarming slide in his Party status. Towards the end of 1957 he had to make a self-criticism for opposing the 'adventurism' of the year before, and now he was on the losing side both on the Rectification Campaign and in the Hundred Flowers Movement (where Liu had won) as well as on the economy (where the impatient Mao was finally winning out).

This may have been the reason why Zhou lost his post at the Foreign Ministry in February 1958 to his old friend and colleague Chen Yi. It was quite possible that Zhou finally succumbed to the argument that he ought to give up his double portfolio because of the swelling workload on both sides. But a new mood of nationalism in foreign relations was evident in China, and conciliation – with the Soviet Union, with India, with the West – had now to be gradually replaced by a new sense of strength. Zhou may well have endorsed this, for even after handing over the Foreign Ministry to Chen Yi, he continued to take the lead in foreign policy, making the major pronouncements on the big issues of the day and conferring with the foreign personalities, like Nehru, with whom China had to negotiate. It was still Zhou who led the major Chinese delegations on overseas visits, to Africa later on, and to the Soviet Union, and when the Cultural Revolution came a decade later, it was Zhou who fought doggedly, though as it turned out vainly, for Chen Yi's survival. The decision in 1958 may have been designed to reduce Zhou's own vulnerability to domestic criticism, it may have been an empty gesture to his critics or it may have been a practical administrative improvement – very likely it was a combination of all three. Anyway, he lost face but not authority.

For the rest of 1958, however, Zhou laboured under the cloud of the preparations for the Great Leap Forward (ironically Zhou had originated the phrase) which Mao and a somewhat doubtful Liu now introduced. They sought to inject some vitality into the Chinese economy, which Zhou and his technocrats had guided for eight years along relatively conventional paths, relying heavily on Soviet advisers and experts, but with few exciting results. At the beginning of 1958 Mao won Party backing to institute his so-called Sixty Points for speeding up the modernization of agriculture and industry. Zhou affected a guarded neutrality toward these events.

But there were some ways in which Zhou was pleased to take a public lead. One was the new idea that state leaders should take part in manual labour. In the past, Party officials had estranged themselves from ordinary people in varying degrees, overcome by what Zhou described as 'the bureaucratic, lifeless, spendthrift, haughty and finicky airs with which they were infected in the old society.' In the fresh winds of 1958, Zhou went at least three times to soil his hands in hard labour. The first two occasions were at the new reservoir being built at the Ming Tombs just outside Beijing. Zhou appeared

216

here one May morning with Mao, already dressed in working clothes. According to one account, he 'dug up the soil and put it in baskets, sweat dripping from his forehead. When his turn came to flatten the soil, Zhou Enlai not only levelled it but also hardened it with a hoe.' He then joined the basket-passing line – a big feature of unmechanized China's construction sites. (The foreman predictably arranged for less soil to be put in their baskets, so the visiting leaders had to expostulate.)

A few weeks later Zhou returned to the same site, this time taking 500 of his colleagues from the Party and government departments to stay for a week working on the dam.

When these soft-handed bureaucrats first arrived at the site, the construction workers' leaders welcomed Zhou, who carried a long pole with a big red flag on it.

'We heartily welcome you, head of government.'

'There are no people here,' Zhou admonished, 'who are "heads". There is no premier and no heads of departments of bureaux. We are all ordinary workers.' For a week Zhou lived in a small room with two narrow benches, a board, a coarse quilt, a desk and two hard chairs. He worked and ate with the other workers but hunched over his desk late into the night, studying state files.

For this kind of work Zhou's arm injury told. Yet he managed to trundle wheelbarrows filled with stones along a 15–inch wooden plank. The ordinary workers kept choosing only small stones to pass to Zhou, bringing the containers back to him very slowly so that he could rest – but these stratagems were seen through and countermanded.

A similar atmosphere prevailed in July when a bridge over the Yellow River was washed away. Zhou rushed to the site, walking the final two miles and arriving at midnight. He was offered waterproof clothing but rejected it with the words, 'Aren't we all soaking?' He took the chair at a meeting where the bridge workers made suggestions as to what to do next, and he tried to boost morale. Later in the year he went with Chen Yi to smelt iron in Hebei Province.

But there was another outlet for Zhou's energies. China's relationship with the Soviet Union suddenly became tense. At the Moscow conference of world Communist parties in November 1957, Zhou described his priority as trying 'fruitlessly to persuade the Soviet Union from going too far along the revisionist path.' But he was for once playing second fiddle to Mao, here making his last visit to the Soviet Union, and all kinds of strange betrayals occurred. The Soviet Ambassador to China complained to Khrushchev that Zhou was one of the most vocal opponents of the Soviet Union – which was a poor analysis, to say the least. But Khrushchev, according to his own account, was also told by no less a man than Mao himself about Zhou's failings, with dates, names and specific incidents detailed in a catalogue of sins to discredit Zhou. If he intended to blacken his colleague in order to erase any understandings and concessions which that colleague might have made, and force the other party to start again on Mao's own terms, it fell flat. Alternatively, if he meant to dissuade Khrushchev from discarding himself and putting Zhou in the top seat, it was unnecessary and merely advertised Mao's own sense of insecurity.

Zhou kept quiet in Moscow. But after a few months, the tension which had been continuous between China and Taiwan in the Taiwan Straits that separated them, and particularly over the small offshore islands retained by the Guomindang, escalated into a crisis which looked like drawing the Americans into the fray. Khrushchev flew to Beijing in 1958 to urge the Chinese to stop needling the Americans at a time when he was trying to cajole them into a detente. It satisfied Chinese pride to send the Soviet leader away with a flea in his ear.

The resumed Eighth Congress endorsed Mao's Great Leap Forward, against Zhou's advice but with the acquiescence of Liu Shaoqi. It was obvious to Zhou and his technocrats that the targets Mao was setting were too high: China simply could not double grain production overnight, for example. As the winter of 1958–59 wore on, it became clear to everybody that Mao's goals had indeed been ridiculously high and that his claims as an economic manager were bankrupt. When the Central Committee met for its angriest session at Wuhan at the end of 1958, it was Zhou who discreetly rallied the generals, including Zhu De and Peng Dehuai, to stand with his own group in the Party leadership against the Mao-Liu clique. It was an extraordinary crisis. Mao, seeing how easily Stalin's reputation had been toppled within weeks of his death, had decided to achieve communism in China in his own lifetime. In this first open break with him, Zhou made Mao back down on his policy of insisting on egalitarian communes and a forced march to modernity and socialism regardless of the material and human factors involved.

What would happen now? Would Zhou make his own bid for the leadership? The world press speculated that Zhou might succeed Mao as Chairman of the People's Republic, and that General Lin Biao might take Zhou's place as Premier. Or would Zhou, surmounting his personal dislikes, settle for a continued partnership with either Mao or Liu on a programme of limited communism? The whole future of Chinese communism and Zhou's career hung in the balance.

18

Cleaning Up the Mess
1959–61

'Comrade Zhou,' Khrushchev demanded in early 1959, 'where are all the Chinese steel engineers whom we trained in the USSR . . . ?' To which Zhou had rather shamefacedly to answer: 'In the countryside forging their proletarian consciousness' – while the steels mills were left for untrained personnel to manage. In earlier years Zhou had laboured the theme that one should do manual work in order to shed one's bourgeois airs, but Mao had carried the policy much farther than had ever been intended. And now the Russians were confirming that China's steel mills were in a shambles after the impetuous Great Leap Forward campaign to raise production, which had been undertaken without due consideration for the care of plant and equipment. 'I could tell,' Khrushchev reflected, 'that Zhou himself thought the whole thing was pretty stupid, but there isn't anything he could do about it – the Great Leap wasn't *his* idea.'

Mao had wasted the little Soviet aid he had been given, but here was Zhou in Moscow at the beginning of 1959 asking for more and promising to do better. Perhaps the Russians did hope that erratic, irascible Mao would be finally discredited, and that the urbane Zhou, with whom Khrushchev got on much better, in spite of Mao's dark warnings, might emerge as the central figure in Beijing. Whatever the reasons, this marked the high point not only in Zhou's pilgrimages to Moscow but also in Sino-Soviet relations as a whole. Zhou returned to China with a Soviet commitment to build thirty-one new industrial plants and give $¼ billion in new aid.

Zhou came home to face an atmosphere of steaming recrimination and intrigue. Mao was trying to push some of the blame for the mistakes of the Great Leap onto Zhou, while Liu was fighting hard to ensure that the succession to Mao would go to himself, since he had loyally stood by Mao during the recent crisis. As a result Zhou found himself actually having to defend Mao to some extent, to make the best of things, and to restore face to the Chairman in the hope of being able to keep him under better control in the future.

In April, Liu's claims were endorsed by the National People's Congress, which elected him Chairman of the People's Republic in succession to Mao. (This had been agreed within the leadership some years earlier, but the new circumstances made its significance dramatically different.) Zhou chose at this point to stress the need to democratize Chinese political life. And he did this in deed as well as in word. Driving up to the hotel where the Congress was meeting, he had to wait because another car had stopped at the entrance ahead of him. When a flunky noticed that the Premier's car was kept waiting, he made a great show of ushering the offending car away to give Zhou's vehicle access.

'Why did you direct that car away?' asked Zhou. 'Who is in it?' When he learned that the person who had been unceremoniously moved on was a provincial delegate to the Congress, Zhou told the hotel employee indignantly: 'Please invite him back; he is a representative, I am also a representative.'

Zhou's report on the Great Leap Forward did not blur the judgement he was ready to pronounce. His indictment was couched in polite technical language, but its purport was crushing. It was the technocrats' verdict on an experiment in instant communism that may have caught the world's imagination but left China in the end little farther advanced.

It is quite impracticable to regard the Leap Forward as meaning that the percentage increase of the total value of industrial and agricultural output and the output of every single product must be higher in each succeeding year. . . . Many important raw and other materials, electric power and transport capacity still lag behind the demands of national economic development.

There should be 'ten-day, monthly or quarterly timetables' of production and construction drawn up, and a new corps of inspectors to check on results – a measure that would spell the end of the economic anarchists' paradise. The loss of productivity and the waste in the Great Leap would have to be made up, and the towns would have to disgorge their unskilled labour back to the farms where it was needed.

Not everything had been bad, even in the wasteful development of uneconomic and inefficient 'native' steel-making, however. 'The combination of modern and indigenous methods is a permanent feature, though in content and in form what we signify by "modern and indigenous" will in the future be different from what they are now.' In other words, the quality of goods produced in small village industries would have to be raised. The famous backyard steel furnaces would have to improve their technique, after

which they 'will also play a certain part in iron-smelting and steel-making.'
The emphasis was on the word *certain*. Zhou elaborated the necessity of
injecting more productive labour into school curricula – 'allying theory and
practice and bringing about step by step the fusion of intellectual and manual
work,' so that schools would be 'transformed from day to day into a new sort
of school capable of training new men with a Communist outlook.'

But if Zhou had hoped that the struggle to put China back on course again
was in hand, Khrushchev rudely dictated otherwise a few months later by
cancelling Russia's aid to China's programme to make nuclear bombs. After
Zhou's remarkable success only five months earlier in getting a substantial
new commitment of economic aid, Russian help, it seemed, could no longer
be counted upon.

Mao's Waterloo should have come at a tense session of the Central
Committee at Lushan at the end of July. The big questions were: would he
confess to his mistakes, and what would be the new line-up of leaders and
policies? Mao wavered between swallowing his medicine like a man and
trying to implicate others in the mess. He began by acknowledging that he
had taken over direction of the economy in the past year or so. 'In the past,' he
admitted, 'the responsibility was on others, such as Enlai. . . . Now I am to
blame, for I have indeed taken charge of a great many things.' At the same
time he subtly drew Zhou into the trap. 'Coal and iron cannot walk by
themselves,' Mao told the Central Committee, 'they need vehicles to
transport them. This I did not foresee. I and . . . the Premier did not concern
ourselves with this point. You can say that we were ignorant of it.' And yet he
also had good things to say about Zhou. 'Those who were anti-adventurist
[i.e. against the earlier plans for accelerated development in 1956] at that
time have now stood firm. An example is Comrade Enlai. He has a lot of
energy. . . . Strange that the people who criticized Enlai at that time, this time
find themselves in his shoes.'

But setting his lieutenants against one another could not alter the fact that a
majority of the Central Committee felt that Mao had gone too far. Peng
Dehuai, an old general who had always been jealous of Mao's advancement,
and to whom on a recent visit to Moscow Khrushchev had confided how
much better off China would be without Mao, carried the attack into the
realm of personal recrimination and Party history controversy. This goaded
Mao into a fiercely retaliatory mood as well as alienating some of the people in
the middle ground who did not like to see their leadership decisions
pre-empted in the Kremlin. Mao, threatening to split the Party if it voted
against him, was able to insist on a reconvened session which he packed with
his own supporters. This manoeuvre gave him revenge over those who had
crossed him at Lushan. But the episode fatally weakened Party unity and
encouraged him into further power excesses in the years to come.

After Lushan Zhou was left trying to keep things going on the old basis – with Mao being technically in charge, though greatly discredited, and Liu (now stiffened in ambition) as his deputy. He explained this as best he could at another National People's Congress which followed Lushan, skilfully presenting an even-handed assessment of the Great Leap Forward.

Facts prove that the simultaneous development of large, small and medium industrial enterprises, and the use of both modern and indigenous methods, walking on two legs, have their advantages. . . . The enterprises are widely distributed; it takes less time to build them. . . . It forces an extensive survey of resources and economies in the use of transport. . . . The steel drive is a magnificent spectacle . . . part of the people's understanding of how to transform China from a poor and blank country into an industrial state . . . unparalleled in Chinese history.

But the state of the grain harvest was more difficult to gloss over. 'Due to lack of experience in assessing harvests under conditions of bumper crops, inadequate allocation of labour power . . . which led to rather hurried reaping and threshing . . . the calculations were a bit high.' Yet overall there had been great achievements, and 'the present economic situation is favourable to us and our prospects are bright.'

Zhou repeated this performance a few months later, in a review of the regime's first decade, hailing China's triumphs under communism in becoming the world's seventh largest steel maker, third largest coal miner and second biggest cotton spinner. Under his skilled direction the Party propaganda machine in Beijing unrolled one statistical stratagem after another, conjuring up imagined advances to disguise the dreary stagnation which now beset the land.

The diplomatic front also claimed Zhou's attention. Following a steady rise in hostility in the correspondence between Zhou and Nehru, Indian and Chinese forces clashed in small numbers in August 1959 on the border at Longju, in the middle of the MacMahon Line between Tibet and Nefa (India's North East Frontier Agency). At the end of 1958 Nehru had publicly challenged a road which the Chinese had built in Aksai Chin, as well as the Chinese maps which ignored the MacMahon Line, that old British demarcation line accepted by independent India as its frontier. Then the Tibetan rebellion against the Chinese army had boiled over, the Dalai Lama fled to Delhi, and mutual suspicion between the two statesmen deepened. Nehru insisted on detailed explanations of the position on the Chinese border. Zhou belatedly obliged in September, and Nehru reeled at the revelation that a full 125,000 square kilometres were in contention.

At an earlier meeting, when Nehru had spoken sanctimoniously about the MacMahon Line, Zhou had half-jokingly interjected: 'Who is MacMahon?' He had meant gently to question why a former generation of British

222

imperialists should be dictating the agenda between two sovereign states in the post-colonial era. Zhou was always astonished by the degree to which Indians had absorbed British ideas, institutions and even names. The border question, he now wrote to Nehru, was complicated by history. China's and India's common experience of British imperialism 'should naturally have led them to an identical view' of the border problem. Instead India wanted China to accept the border as it had been unilaterally extended by British imperialism, so that the Indians' benefit from their colonial masters' 'aggression' against a neighbour would be endorsed. Zhou ended by invoking the very five principles which had been so joyously proclaimed to the world by the two statesmen, urging that the *status quo* be peacefully maintained and not changed unilaterally or by force.

Nehru professed to be deeply hurt. He wrote back:

I was greatly surprised and distressed by the suggestion that the independent government of India are seeking to reap a benefit from the British aggression against China. Our parliament and people deeply resent this allegation. The struggle of the Indian people against any form of imperialism both at home and abroad is known and recognized all over the world. . . . It is true that the British occupied and ruled the Indian subcontinent against the wishes of the Indian people. The boundaries of India were, however, settled for centuries by history, geography, custom and tradition.

Even Khrushchev, who passed through Beijing in September in a vain attempt to restrain Zhou's colleagues, was unhelpful. When Zhou started to explain China's stand on the Indian border question, the Soviet leader brushed the proffered maps and documents aside with the words: 'You can't make history all over again.'

At about this time Zhou remarked to a foreign visitor how surprising he found it that Nehru had allowed the map in his own autobiography, published in England, to show the border according to the Chinese claim. Either he was double-dealing, or else Nehru had genuinely not checked his map. Whichever was the explanation, Zhou was astonished. 'Zhou Enlai,' this visitor reported, 'was obviously puzzled by Nehru's character and his reactions. He assumed that Nehru would react in the way an Asian (meaning a Chinese) would react; and he debated whether Nehru himself was fully in control of what he was doing, or whether he was driven to it by the "imperialists".' Zhou mistakenly discounted the role of parliamentary politics in restraining Nehru's freedom of action on the border.

The next year Zhou attempted to solve the Indian border problem by isolating Nehru, concluding border agreements with other neighbouring countries to China's south, and thus pressurizing India to follow suit. Burma signed in January 1960, Nepal in March, and these could in other circumstances have provided precedents for India. But when Zhou and Chen

Yi went that spring on a long tour of Burma, India, Nepal, Cambodia, Vietnam and Mongolia, they found Nehru still obdurate. Zhou now made explicit the bargain at which he had hinted for some time: China would give up the MacMahon Line sector if Nehru would concede the barren reaches of Aksai Chin, where China had built her strategic road linking Tibet with Xinjiang. Nehru was ready to consider the bargain, but Indian conservatives, personified by the powerful Home Minister, were totally opposed. Zhou's visit to New Delhi degenerated into a mutual recapitulation of all the old arguments. When Nehru protested that the proposed Tibet–Nepal highway would for the first time give China access to India, Zhou spiritedly replied: 'On the contrary, it gives India access for the first time to China.'

As well as enduring Nehru's lectures, Zhou had also to submit to the observations of Nehru's deputy, Morarji Desai, whose moralizing manner provoked Zhou into walking out of one meeting. Nor did Zhou get on with Krishna Menon, Nehru's chief confidant and foreign affairs specialist. Little wonder that the gossip in Curzon Bazaar said that relations with China would never improve as long as Zhou Enlai was in charge.

The army of Foreign Ministry officials and the forests of data about which Nehru had been scathing but which Zhou had brought with him to Delhi all the same were not needed. After a week of fruitless discussions, the chagrined Zhou left for Kathmandu. 'I could not move Nehru at all,' he told a correspondent afterwards. 'I think he had made up his mind.'

The more obliging Nepalese signed their treaty with Zhou, and in Cambodia Zhou made such an impact on Prince Norodom Sihanouk at his royal father's funeral that the Prince sent his three sons to Beijing for education.

The last stop was Mongolia where, having negotiated a friendship treaty and aid agreement, Zhou was observed in a sheepskin robe several sizes too large for him, drinking repeated toasts while camelskin drums and bamboo-pipe organs endeavoured to render the 'Internationale'.

There was a reason for taking all this trouble with India and her neighbours. Rebuffed by both Khrushchev and Eisenhower, excluded from both the capitalist and Communist power centres, China looked to Asia and Africa to provide a platform where she could raise her flag. These countries, Zhou had told the National People's Congress in April, 'used to be the imperialist rear' but had now come to the forefront in the fight against aggression and colonialism. 'We are ready to give support and assistance to the full extent of our capabilities to all national independence movements in Asia, Africa and Latin America.'

Yet this was not a happy period for Zhou's Third World diplomacy. He got into a muddle, for instance, when Syria joined Egypt in a United Arab Republic. He found himself backing the Syrian Communists, and thereby antagonizing Nasser, whom he had met so warmly at Bandung and assisted so solicitously in the Suez crisis. Now, said Zhou, Nasser was obstructing 'the cause of Arab national independence'. He was not always as tactful as his admirers believed.

He suffered also from the difficulty that most of the world, certainly the non-aligned states, were enthralled by the Soviet–American detente worked out between Khrushchev and Eisenhower at Camp David. When Han Suyin went to Beijing towards the end of 1959 she confessed to Zhou: 'I too believe that this Camp David meeting is a good thing for the world, Prime Minister.'

'The silence that followed,' she recounted afterwards, 'was one of total immobility. The secretary who took notes froze with pen in air.' Zhou's aide 'stared at me with horror in his eyes. Zhou Enlai's face looked suddenly more tired, a creeping of small wrinkles which began around the eyes.'

'We do not think so,' he said. 'Compromise should not mean selling out the peoples of the Third World. If it does, then it is not peace, only submission and servility. We must decide now whether all the peoples of the world have a right to their national liberation or whether they will be slaves for a thousand years. . . . On this point we shall never compromise.'

To which Han Suyin commented to herself that she now understood what Western journalists called 'Chinese intransigence' – or, one could add, China's self-perceived role as vanguard of the non-European cultures.

But China was starving. Mao's rape of the soil to deliver up more grain was punished by three successive years of unseasonal drought and flood, 'the worst series of disasters,' Zhou called it, 'since the nineteenth century.' While Mao and the others sulked and plotted, Zhou kept the country together in its extremity. 'Zhou . . . ,' a middle-class professional confidently predicted, 'will find a way to clean up the mess. He always does.'

Once his secretary took some medicine into his bedroom where he was half sitting and half lying in the bed, with his glasses on, absorbed in doing sums from piles of forms at his side.

'Wouldn't it be better,' the aide suggested, 'to have somebody else do this concrete, technical kind of work?'

'You think this kind of job is concrete and technical,' Zhou replied, 'but this is not something insignificant. This is a big job which has the great task of feeding millions of people. If I do not do it myself, how do I know the details?' Zhou was in fact calculating the grain ration for the whole country.

'It is not a mere technical job,' he added, sipping his tea.

During those three bitter years, Zhou himself and his family did without meat and eggs, at least in their home. Deng Yingchao claimed to cure herself of diabetes by eating less and dieting.

China's troubles mounted. The already wobbly economy was further weakened by the angry Khrushchev's escalation of the Sino-Soviet dispute in withdrawing all Soviet technicians from China early in 1960. 'The sudden complete withdrawal,' Zhou later explained, 'of 1390 Soviet experts ... abolition of 257 items for scientific and technical cooperation, and since then reduction in large numbers in the supplies of complete equipment' completely upset China's plans and aggravated her difficulties.

Zhou tried valiantly at the time to play down the gravity of it all. He told Edgar Snow in an interview that it was only to be expected that two Communist parties should differ on theory and analysis. 'The return of some Soviet experts,' Zhou went on, 'is a natural thing. Having come to China they are bound to return some day; surely they can't stay here all their lives. They work in China for definite periods of time and have rendered good service. Perhaps it was because many returned this year that it drew the attention of the Western countries.'

This kind of prevarication was not worthy of Zhou, a sign perhaps of the extreme stress under which he was labouring. *Look* magazine called his attempt to cover up the exodus of Soviet experts 'pathetic'.

That winter Han Suyin went again to see a rather different Zhou.

He walked up and down, slowly, looking vaguely about the room. He was obviously under strain. But it was controlled strain. With him, passion and fury exteriorized as lambent ice. His voice shook a little when he was very tired or upset, but it was always cold, restrained and low.

How thin he was! I noticed that his collar was too large for his neck now. He had not slept the night before. . . . Too much work. Nor the night before that. He slept about two hours a day, after lunch; and not always then. But there was a diamond-cutting elegance in his voice when he spoke of 'those who think they can bring us to our knees', who thought that because of China's difficulties she could be threatened and subdued.

He reminded her of the hardships of the Soviet Union under Lenin. 'Nothing is ever acquired without pain.' She could of course travel anywhere in China and would discover problems – 'but not the famines of the past. . . . The Leap has already brought us results that people do not know about. . . . Those who think that China has failed, they will be surprised one day.'

A few days later the Central Committee began a theoretical about-face, committing itself for a start to the proposition, which Mao had rejected earlier, that agriculture was the foundation of China's economy. In future the nation's main investment would be in getting the best out of the land, and only then building up heavy industry.

Also at the beginning of 1961 Zhou addressed himself indirectly to Indian opinion by taking an enormous retinue of more than 400 people – the largest official delegation ever to be sent abroad from China – to Rangoon where the boundary agreement was ceremonially ratified and Zhou signed a £30 million interest-free loan (the largest ever extended by China to a non-Communist government). The implication was clear: India was silly not to follow suit.

By now Zhou's differences with Mao over dealing with the Kremlin were healing: Khrushchev's brusque recall of experts in 1960 had the effect of closing ranks in China. In October 1961 Zhou was given the tricky assignment of representing China at the Twenty-second Party Congress in Moscow. On the first day he left his seat early to avoid having to shake hands with Khrushchev. When the Soviet leader attacked China's ally, Albania, Zhou made a spirited reply. After scorning Soviet naiveté in taking seriously the new Kennedy administration's conciliatory talk of detente, he went on to talk sternly about the unity of the Communist camp.

There should absolutely not be any words or deeds that harm this unity [applause]. We hold that if a dispute or difference unfortunately arises between fraternal parties or fraternal countries, it should be resolved patiently in the spirit of proletarian internationalism and on the principles of equality and unanimity through consultation. Any public, one-sided censure of any fraternal party does not help unity and is not helpful to resolving problems. To lay bare a dispute between fraternal partners or fraternal countries openly in the face of the enemy cannot be regarded as a serious Marxist–Leninist attitude. Such an attitude will only grieve those near and dear to us and gladden our enemies.

Next morning Zhou went to Red Square to lay wreaths on the tombs of not only Lenin but Stalin, a public snub to Khrushchev, who had so denigrated his predecessor. He abruptly left Moscow before the Congress ended, pleading pressure of business at home. He thus made a decisive break with the Russian leaders, and some said that only from this moment did he begin to be trusted, grudgingly, by Mao.

19

The Great Safari
1962–65

After the frenzy of the Great Leap Forward and the misery of its disastrous sequel, Zhou slowed down in 1962. He was formally on sick leave for the best part of a year, while Liu Shaoqi exulted in the belief that nothing could now stop him from inheriting supreme power from a Mao who was run out of the race.

But Zhou was the more experienced long-distance runner, and he shrewdly allowed Liu to set the pace during two years of permissively right-wing reaction against the Great Leap Forward. With his lieutenant, Deng Xiaoping, Liu now attempted to reform the Chinese economy and polity so as to accord more happily with reality – and they did not worry too much if some ideological tenets of the Party were dropped in the interest of economic recovery and efficiency. What did it matter, asked Deng, whether the cat was black or white – as long as it caught the mouse? Zhou was careful not to associate himself with these reforms, and only occasionally drew attention to the ideals for which they were all supposed to stand.

It was to a senior British diplomat with a knack of making friends in the Third World that Zhou now confided his innermost problems. Some of his colleagues, he told Malcolm MacDonald, son of the first Labour Prime Minister and adviser to postwar British premiers, in the autumn of 1962, had been oversanguine about how quickly an equal Communist society could be created in China. These optimists had expected people to accept equal pay uncomplainingly for whatever work they did, since their prime goal should be to serve their fellow-man. So these wishful thinkers had, for example, abolished the private plots which farming families had been allowed to keep in the early stages of collectivization. But they were proved wrong. They were idealists who misjudged human nature. Socialism would have to be attained, Zhou said, step by step, beginning with the education of the masses into 'the ethical rectitude of an egalitarian state'. And in the interim it would have to be recognized that people would remain human, with a mixture of good and bad in them, and must therefore be offered 'the temptation of material reward'. Whereas the wishful thinkers had believed that full economic development could be reached in about a dozen years, Zhou estimated now that China would need another thirty or forty years to become self-sufficient in capital and consumer goods, and up to a century before she could enjoy the same high standard of living as the West.

Zhou stressed to his British visitor his deep belief in the United States' hostility towards China, for all MacDonald's arguments to the contrary. Zhou pointed in proof to the American military bases which ringed China from Pakistan in the west to Vietnam, Thailand and the Philippines in the south, and Taiwan, Korea and Japan in the east. But he regretted these bad relations with the USA, because he hoped that friendly relations would permit China to gain modern technology from America.

He would not permit the conclusion that the Sino-Soviet split was irreparable. 'I see no reason for thinking that the two states should be severed from each other,' he told the general manager of Reuters late in 1963. However, he was soon to challenge Russia vigorously for primacy in the diplomatic arena.

Then, after two relatively quiet years, Zhou suddenly sprang into life again. He left Beijing on 11 December 1963 with Foreign Minister Chen Yi and a huge entourage of officials for an extraordinary seventy-two-day tour, in the course of which he travelled 36,000 miles and visited thirteen Third World countries in Africa and Asia, as well as China's little European ally, Albania. It was an unprecedented safari to countries which had never seen a Chinese leader before, indeed, hardly seen a Chinese at all. The goal was to wean Third World opinion away from the Soviet Union and persuade these countries to look to China for leadership. In particular the Chinese supported a second Afro–Asian conference, on the Bandung model, excluding the Soviet Union because it was a European and not an Asian state. Zhou also expected to detach African nations from their support of the Guomindang government on Taiwan, to promote the case for the People's Republic holding China's seat in the UN, and to sell the novel concept that China's economic aid was preferable to Western aid because Chinese experts, unlike their European counterparts, would live at the Third World standards of living without any privilege.

Leaving China in a chartered KLM aircraft, described unkindly in the European press as a 'very old-fashioned propeller plane made in America and flown by Dutchmen', and inappropriately named *Baltic Sea*, Zhou snatched a quick dinner with President Ne Win of Burma at Rangoon before crossing India to start his main tour in Cairo.

The safari had a shaky start. President Nasser was not even at home to welcome his guest, being still in Tunisia to discuss the best way of handling this awkward intrusion from China. He had shown great interest in China during the Bandung conference, and expressed gratitude for China's very substantial material help during the Suez crisis of 1956, but these positive feelings had given way to nervous detachment now that the Russians were warning everybody against the Chinese. Nasser's men, meanwhile, paid Zhou the dubious compliment of installing him in King Farouk's old palace, and were then tactless enough to take him to see their pride and joy, the Soviet-built Aswan Dam. Zhou was taken ill while climbing the long stairs of the hydroelectric plant. The Premier's nose bled, and one of his aides applied a water compress. He waved aside an American soft drink. 'This happens from time to time,' one of his officials explained. 'It is not serious, but that's why he always has a doctor with him.' His health was not as good as it had been before the 'three bitter years'.

When he finally did meet Nasser, Zhou had his first failure on the Indian border question, on which Nasser strongly supported the Indian position. Zhou told Nasser that China and Egypt could first equal and then surpass the West, and then 'we will lead the centre of the world's gravity back to the East'. But how far east, the Egyptians wondered?

Zhou shortly left for Algeria, where the proposed Afro-Asian conference would be held, Morocco and Albania, where he danced the new year of 1964 in, drinking and celebrating at three separate parties. ('He is an excellent dancer,'one of the participants reported, 'and could do Albanian folk dances on sight. He is also an experienced drinker of toasts.') Then, in Tunisia, Zhou met the first determined opposition to China's ambitions. President Bourguiba told him to his face that 'some of China's attitude had caused doubt in the Tunisian mind, for instance, China's resort to force to settle frontier problems with India and her opposition to the nuclear test-ban treaty. Do you not regard this treaty as a promise of hope for all humanity?' (China regarded it as a licence for the superpowers to dominate the world for ever.)

As Bourguiba explained afterwards to reporters: 'I told him what shocked us in his manner, style and conceptions. I said, "You come to Africa as the enemy of the capitalist states, of the West, of the neutralists and the non-aligned, of India, of Tito, of Khrushchev – of everybody. . . . Others won't tell you straight out, but I will: you won't get far in this continent.' Ironically, Tunisia's recognition of China, which Zhou did manage to negotiate during this visit, was almost the only immediate tangible gain of his entire safari.

Undaunted, Zhou flew to Ghana to begin the first visit of any Chinese leader to Black Africa. Nkrumah's hopes of getting Zhou to endorse his claim to be building socialism, albeit in a rather different form from that followed in

Communist countries, were misplaced. Little occurred during Zhou's tour elsewhere in West Africa.

In East Africa, army mutinies threatened in Tanzania, Kenya, Uganda and Zanzibar. Zhou decided, after brief forays in Ethiopia and Sudan – where he thanked the Sudanese for killing Charles Gordon, the British general who had sacked the Summer Palace in Beijing in 1860 – to call it a day. He left Africa from Somalia – where he made a famous clarion call: 'Revolutionary prospects are excellent throughout the African continent!'

It was all very well for him to tell the Somalis: 'We Afro-Asian people share the same pulsation and are involved in the same revolution. Our common objectives are national independence and development of our national economy and culture.' But the infrastructure for such shared perceptions of common interest was not yet built. The remark provoked a storm of professed dismay on the unrevolutionary continent, where uncertain heads of state felt that any revolution could only be against themselves.

Possibly moved by the passion with which African leaders had spoken to him of their desire to shake free from European influence, Zhou quoted an old Chinese poem:

> A thousand sails pass by the shipwreck;
> Beyond the dead tree stands a forest
> In the prime of spring.

He added his own commentary that 'the ranks of the revolutionary peoples of the world are like a thousand sails floating majestically in the sea winds. The revolutionary cause of the people of the world is like a forest growing in the prime of spring.' Alas, for most Black African countries, the tropical seasons do not provide a temperate spring to symbolize rebirth in the annual climatic cycle. Zhou was talking to himself, just as the Europeans before him had done.

So diplomatic recognition from Tunisia and Ethiopia's promise of it were all that could be claimed as the fruit of this taxing journey. Zhou returned to Asia on 4 February, having missed Iraq, Syria and Yemen, as well as the East African countries. Still, he had lobbied vigorously for the second Afro-Asian conference and for the Chinese argument that Africa could look to Chinese instead of Soviet aid. But he had obviously been unprepared for the extent of support evinced for Nehru's India – and his first act on returning to Asian soil was an unscheduled stop at Rangoon to ask Ne Win to intercede with Nehru on the border negotiations.

The final stretch of his Afro-Asian safari began on 14 February in Burma again, where he told his audience: 'We, new emerging Asian-African countries, have similarly experienced imperialist aggression and oppression and have before us the common task of continuing our fight against imperialism and old and new colonialism.' Everybody realized that 'new' colonialism meant 'Russia', but no one wanted to jeopardize Russian friendship in the common fight against Western imperialism.

Ne Win had by now seen Nehru, but the Indian Premier had rejected the idea of another round of talks with Zhou.

Zhou overflew India once again to go to Pakistan, and ended his long feat of endurance in Ceylon. He told Japanese newsmen that 'revolutionary prospects are excellent in Asia', but the wish seemed father to the thought. This amazing diplomatic marathon has never been matched, and will probably stand as a physical record for any prime minister of any large country, spanning three continents in continuous travel, mostly to new and unfamiliar ground – but the urgent search for influence that motivated it was not wholly successful. Some of the frustration and cultural distaste which all Chinese felt in foreign countries came out in an interview which Zhou gave to the Vienna *Kurier* published a few months later:

We would never commit aggression. It is not just that we lack for this purpose such important weapons as long-range planes and a big navy: this is only one side of it. The other is our people. We cannot win the support of our people for aggression. They would not go along. . . . What do we want in Southeast Asia or India? What can we find there? Only more people, jungle, swamp, mosquitoes and snakes, all things which we Chinese cannot stand. What Chinese would want to go there?

Sometimes it must have seemed that efforts to communicate with the Third World were doomed to failure. The Latin-American poet laureate, Pablo Neruda – a member of the Chilean Communist Party Politburo – noted that Zhou had congratulated a young Chinese for having himself voluntarily sterilized, declaring it an example to be emulated. 'It naturally occurs to us,' lectured Neruda reproachfully, 'that if Comrade Zhou Enlai's father had had this idea, Zhou Enlai would not exist. Is this communism? It is rather a cult, ridiculous, superstitious, unacceptable.'

And then there was Nehru, the man who seemed to have affected and influenced so many of the African leaders whom Zhou was trying to impress. 'I have never met a more arrogant man than Nehru,' Zhou told Ceylonese visitors. 'I am sorry, but this is true.'

Yet he always loved a full-blooded controversy, and when Malcolm MacDonald, his English visitor of a year or so earlier, had firmly spoken up for the Indian case on the border dispute, Zhou said he was 'delighted' at the prospect of arguing with him and proceeded to do so for several hours. Zhou repeated his offer to trade Aksai Chin for the Nefa area south of the MacMahon Line, and wondered why Nehru refused to discuss this with him. MacDonald explained that the fervour of Indian patriotic emotion had been aroused to such a pitch by the fighting that even Nehru could not negotiate to cede any territory to China.

Now, as in the previous year, illness interrupted Zhou's public duties. He was not seen for most of August or September 1964, and diplomats in Beijing said that he had undergone a minor operation and was recuperating at the Beidaihe seaside. When he did come back to his desk in the autumn, it was to preside over the creation of the one thing that was needed to make other countries, whether Russian Marxist, Black African, American imperialist or pharisaical non-aligned, pay attention to China, namely a nuclear bomb. Over the preceding decade Zhou had taken the chair at almost a hundred special meetings of the Scientific and Technical Commission for National Defence, during which this project was discussed and planned. In the previous summer, he had anticipated the achievement of China's own scientists, deprived of Russian help: writing then to world leaders, he proposed a conference for the complete prohibition of nuclear weapons. Now, in October 1964, films and photographs confirmed the successful explosion of China's first nuclear device. Zhou 'clapped his hands happily when he saw the rise of the mushroom cloud', exclaiming, 'We have won,' and inspecting the photographs eagerly with his magnifying glass. Again he repeated his call for a conference to agree 'that the nuclear powers, and those countries which may soon become nuclear powers, undertake not to use nuclear weapons.'

Soon afterwards Zhou was once again in Russia, this time to meet Brezhnev and Kosygin, the new Soviet leaders. Once again the speeches made it clear that they had no concessions for China. Zhou remained dourly silent when all the others clapped Brezhnev's reference to detente with the USA. Nor could he persuade them to call off their proposed international Communist conference, which he saw as a means of reaffirming Soviet control of the world Communist movement. As before, Zhou laid an ostentatious wreath on Stalin's tomb.

Later, when Premier Kosygin flew to Beijing to see Zhou and Mao, Zhou continued his arguments as to why the new Russian leaders should cancel the international conference which Khrushchev had planned and thus demonstrate their radical change of policy. 'You see, Kosygin,' interrupted Mao, who had seemed until then to be dozing, 'our Prime Minister is your friend. He is giving you good advice because he has illusions about you. Not I. I say this: hold your conference and show the world that you are secessionists of the same breed as Khrushchev.'

At home again, the political tensions quickened between Mao and Liu. Receiving Edgar Snow yet again for two separate four-hour interviews at the end of 1964, Zhou tried adroitly to back down from the economic adventurism in which they had all been involved. The American found Zhou fit and laughing at the 'rumours' of his illness, but his hair had acquired grey streaks.

Frankly speaking, as the Premier, I have not fully mastered China's economic construction. . . . I have learned something, but not very well. . . . The laws governing economic development are extremely complicated. We have gained some experience . . . but there are many more laws governing economic development which remain to be understood. We have done quite a few things right in the past fifteen years, but we have also done some wrong things.

Snow asked an awkward question: when would the Chinese catch up with Britain's industrial production, as they had so boastfully predicted they would? 'The overtaking of Britain,' Zhou conceded, 'is no longer the centre of our attention. . . . the modernization of our industry cannot be realized merely through the quantitative increase of a few items of industrial products.'

Zhou spoke out against the disturbing moves to the right which the pragmatic policies of Liu Shaoqi were encouraging in some quarters, but he did throw his full weight behind Liu's education programme, fervently agreeing with the necessity to improve China's schools. At the same time he prevented Snow from interviewing Liu. 'Now why do you want to see Liu Shaoqi?' he asked. In the end Snow found himself invited to a general reception with Liu, Mao and everyone else and their wives. 'Well', said Zhou with his impish smile, 'now you've seen everybody, haven't you?' Snow later decided that the Premier must have been protecting him from involvement with a leader who was about to be in trouble. A less kind interpretation could be that the Premier did not wish to see Liu enjoy the fruits of Zhou's own hard-earned triumphs in foreign affairs and with the foreign media.

As Zhou explained to the National People's Congress in December 1964, the disasters of 1959–62 had represented a political as well as an economic setback. Many people had actively advocated the extension of private plots and free markets, and even the effective decollectivization of agriculture. Zhou for the first time hinted here at the possibility that Liu Shaoqi might have moved too far away from socialism in his concern to modernize the country. 'Serious and acute class troubles exist,' Zhou declared, 'in our urban and rural areas. . . . Such are necessarily reflected inside the party.' So the crux of the Socialist Education Movement, which was then being carried out by the Party under Liu's direction, was 'to purge the capitalist roaders within the Party'.

For quite a long period, the landlord class, the bourgeoisie and other exploiting classes which have been overthrown will remain strong and powerful in our socialist society; we must under no circumstances take them lightly. At the same time, new bourgeois elements, new bourgeois intellectuals, and other new exploiters will be ceaselessly generated in society, in Party and government organs, in economic organizations and in cultural and educational departments. These new bourgeois elements and other exploiters will invariably join hands in opposing socialism and developing capitalism.

Zhou was neither a mindless conservative nor a meek liberal. That was made clear in a prescient and significant declaration: 'No destruction, no construction. Only when there is destruction can there be construction!' This was the earliest signal of the rationale for the Cultural Revolution which was to come a year or so later.

When the visiting European writer K. S. Karol asked Zhou whether China practised Stalinism, Zhou seized the opportunity to make a vital clarification for the benefit of the European left wing:

The Chinese revolution did not make the social classes disappear with a wave of the magic wand. . . . We have taken the means of exploitation from those who use their property to exploit, but we haven't physically liquidated them or deported them. . . . The exploiters, when they were able to defend their privileges with arms, did not hesitate to use even the most extreme methods against us. Now that the power is in our hands we rely above all on education. We tell our exploiters that they can be re-educated if they want to serve the motherland. . . . Repressive measures are used only in the case of grave breaches of the law, when the life of others is involved.

But Zhou was also quarrelling with Mao's men. He urged the Ministry of Defence to lengthen the training period for its army recruits. Senior officers loyal to Lin Biao, Mao's Minister of Defence, rejected this advice and minuted the decision in such a provocative way that Zhou was angry when he read it. Mao ratified what the soldiers had done, not the first time that he had overruled Zhou.

During 1965 Zhou tried to bring about a Communist government in Indonesia under Chinese patronage, and he supported the idea of a rival United Nations which President Sukarno was trying to establish. The existing United Nations, Zhou declared in January, had committed too many mistakes.

It has utterly disappointed the Asian and African countries. . . . It must be thoroughly reorganized. . . . Another UN, a revolutionary one, may well be set up so that rival dramas may be staged in competition with that body which calls itself the United Nations but which is under the manipulation of US imperialism and can therefore only make mischief.

Soon Zhou went to Jakarta to talk further with Sukarno, and it was afterwards alleged that he had signed an agreement whereby China would support Sukarno's project in return for Indonesia's promise to eliminate rightists and anti-Communists. Zhou was also credited by Sukarno with the idea of creating an Indonesian 'fifth force' – an armed peasant-worker militia to function alongside the regular armed forces and provide a left-wing element in the power balance.

Zhou also wooed the Japanese, trying to make them feel ashamed of following the American baton. He had already received a delegation which apologized for Japan's aggression against China in the 1930s. 'Please do not apologize,' Zhou smiled. 'It is we who must thank you. Because you made war on us, you hastened the crumbling of our old feudal system, and through the national war against you, the Chinese people found themselves, became conscious and united.' He told another Japanese delegation: 'East is east, and west is west, and we oriental nations should go hand in hand through the generations for mutual coexistence and prosperity' – for which the Russians tagged him a racist.

That summer of 1965 Zhou took up the African trail once again in pursuit of his will-o'-the-wisp of a second Afro-Asian conference. In Tanzania, making up for the previous year's omission, he obstinately repeated his old call: 'An exceedingly favourable situation for revolution prevails today, not only in Africa but also in Asia and Latin America.' He then went to Cairo to try to mastermind the arrangements for the conference, only to learn with dismay that his 'closest friend and confidant in Africa', Prime Minister Ben Bella of Algeria, had been summarily deposed. Zhou instantly recognized Algeria's successor regime in the hope of saving the conference, but to his fury his diplomats reported that there was no possibility of ensuring a majority at the conference, either to bar the Soviet Union or to denounce the Americans for their latest escalation of the war in Vietnam, a new source of concern to China. Zhou drove in the same car with Sukarno, Nasser and Ayub Khan from Cairo airport to the conference hall to discuss what could be salvaged, but the answer was nothing. The Americans and the Russians between them were still far more powerful and had more friends in high places, even in the Third World, than Zhou Enlai.

If the well-placed Egyptian journalist, Mohamed Heykal, is to be believed, and one would not expect him to invent something out of the whole cloth, Zhou was by this time becoming a little desperate in his international diplomacy. Zhou told President Nasser, Heykal says, that he wanted the Americans to send more troops to Vietnam because that would function 'as an insurance policy against a nuclear attack on China.' China had 'a good portion of their flesh within reach of our nails . . . so close that we could make hostages of them.' Some of the American troops had tasted opium, he went on, 'and we helped them. We planted the better varieties of opium especially for the American soldiers in Vietnam.' This is an extraordinary thing for Zhou to have said, and it does not square with his character. It is probable that he spoke something along these lines in jest or irony, and that the Egyptian misunderstood, taking it seriously.

At the same time it did look as if Zhou badly needed a foreign policy success in 1964–65 to bolster his position at home, and that his luck ran out on him. His frustration was evident to André Malraux, the French Minister of Culture (and novelist about the Shanghai revolution thirty years earlier), who interviewed Zhou in August. The Frenchman found him 'faultlessly urbane' but 'reticent as a cat'. (He must have been the only Westerner to find Zhou '*ennuyeux*'!) Zhou embroidered his theme about the Americans becoming 'the policemen of the world. What for? Let them go home, and the world will have peace again.'

Meanwhile, in China itself, the crisis between Mao and Liu was now approaching. According to one report by a Japanese sinologist, Mao suffered a stroke during a Central Committee meeting in October 1965, in the middle of delivering a diatribe against Liu Shaoqi who, as his deputy, then took control of the meeting. Mao was confined to his house – but after the respective wives had been drawn into the drama, Zhou prevailed upon Liu to let Mao go.

At the same time a new play came out by one of China's best-known dramatists which implicitly attacked Mao and his policies, and one's attitude towards it became the fealty test for the two opposing sides. Mao's economic errors and naive optimism were matters of the past, and Zhou presumably doubted his capacity to spoil things further for China. On the other hand, Liu's pragmatism seemed now to Zhou far more dangerous because Liu appeared to be ready, under the twin pressures of economic hardship and bureaucratic conservatism, to let socialism go altogether.

20

Cultural Revolution
1966–67

Zhou Enlai stood circumspectly on the sidelines for as long as he could while the factional struggle between Mao Zedong and Liu Shaoqi sharpened during 1966. A rumour was put about that Liu was plotting to depose not only Mao but also Zhou, whom he intended to replace as Prime Minister by Deng Xiaoping. When Liu returned from an official visit to Pakistan and Burma, where he had apparently hoped to garner some of the prestige which Zhou was able to extract from such tours, there was nobody to greet him at the airport.

While Chairman Mao was more or less exiled near Canton, the Premier conducted foreign policy more and more independently. There was an awkward moment when some Japanese Communists went to see Mao, hoping to persuade him to be more cooperative with the Soviet Union. Mao delivered a resounding cannonade against Soviet policy only to have them let slip what his own aides had kept from him, namely that the Chinese had already signed a joint communiqué with these Japanese visitors in which Zhou had pledged Sino-Soviet collaboration to aid beleaguered Vietnam. Furthermore, Russian equipment for the Vietnamese army was actually travelling along the Chinese railways. When Mao barked at his own officials, in front of the Japanese visitors, 'You weak-kneed people in Beijing!', it might have looked as if Zhou was in trouble. But Zhou's strength lay precisely in the fact that he, alone among Mao's lieutenants, habitually refused to react to this kind of rebuff by challenging Mao's overall authority and joining his factional opponents. Instead Zhou meekly accepted the rebuke.

And then, in May 1966, Mao launched the Great Proletarian Cultural Revolution, ostensibly with Liu's support. The limited intention at the beginning was systematically to eradicate the 'bourgeois mentality' which had been uncovered during the relatively liberal economic regime over which Liu

238

had been presiding for the past four years. But Zhou had already in a speech on 30 April defined the new movement in its widest terms:

A socialist cultural revolution with a significant historical meaning is now rising in our country. This is a fierce and long-term struggle in the ideological sphere between the proletariat and the bourgeoisie. We have vigorously to promote proletarian thoughts and smash bourgeois thoughts in all the academic, education, journalistic, art, literary and other cultural circles. This is a crucial problem concerning the country as a whole, a problem of development in the socialist revolution in the present stage. It is of the utmost importance, involving the fate and future of our Party and our country.

In May the drama was played out in the relatively small arena of Beijing itself, where the municipal Party committee was led by one of Liu Shaoqi's senior supporters, Peng Zhen. Mao's radical followers tried by every possible means to expel Peng Zhen and other more junior supporters of the Liu-ist line, and to replace them with leftists. The major base for this activity was the campus of Beijing University, commonly known by the abbreviation of its Chinese characters as 'Beida'. Posters began to go up all over the campus criticizing various 'rightists' in Beijing for actions and decisions which the young radicals considered to be neither socialist nor democratic. Since the press and radio were largely under the control of the 'rightists', these posters provided an alternative medium of communication for the young radicals. Students and young workers from other institutions and enterprises would come to Beida to copy the posters down and repeat them in their own premises, so that the aims, strategy and mood of these 'revolutionaries-within-a-revolution' became quickly publicized throughout the city.

And then the Red Guards made their debut, young workers or students recruited by army commanders loyal to Mao to undergo rapid basic military training and then go out to implement the Cultural Revolution on the ground. Not only in Beijing but also in other urban localities, they besieged 'rightist' office administrators or enterprise managers, got in their way and tried to take over their organizations. 'Leftists' were brought in to take the place of the 'rightists' and steer towards a more direct and thoroughgoing socialism.

Meanwhile in the country at large the Socialist Education Movement, begun in 1964, continued, with teams of Communist Party activists going into the villages to correct the bad practices which had sprouted, especially wider discrepancies in earnings and the greater encouragement given to rich peasants than to poor ones. It was the allegedly half-hearted attitude of Liu Shaoqi towards this campaign which had incensed the Maoists.

The second half of June saw Zhou in Eastern Europe, dispensing fine oratory about the Chinese scene. 'We are determined,' he told the Rumanians, 'to liquidate completely all the old ideas, all the old culture, all the old manners and habits through which the exploiting classes poisoned the

239

consciousness of the people for thousands of years' – and to replace them with new proletarian concepts and culture. 'The spearhead of this cultural revolution is mainly directed at the handful of bad elements who have been "hanging sheep's heads while selling dogmeat" (that is, opposing communism under the guise of being Communists), . . . at the handful of bourgeois intellectuals who are anti-Party, anti-socialist and anti-revolution.' But Zhou had to leave Bucharest without a joint communiqué, displaying what the correspondents called 'unguarded anger' with his host, Premier Maurer, who valued Rumania's neutrality between the Kremlin and Beijing. A final rally to see Zhou off was held up for two hours while the two men argued, and in the end he scrapped his farewell speech – bearing what the *Daily Express* correspondent described as 'the look of an angry cobra'.

In Albania he was on friendlier soil and could speak more positively. The Chinese, he said, were using Mao's Thought to smash the agents of capitalism plotting to seize power. 'In our country, proletarian politics is equivalent to Mao Zedong's Thought. Through his genius and creativeness Comrade Mao has completely inherited and developed Marxism–Leninism. Mao Zedong's Thought represents the Marxism–Leninism of an era in which imperialism is heading towards its extinction and socialism is advancing to victory all over the world: it is the peak of modern Marxism–Leninism.' It sounded embarrassingly like Liu's eulogies at the 1945 Congress.

Zhou returned to China to find that the 'socialist re-education teams' being sent out into the Chinese countryside under Liu's supervision were now using arbitrary strong-arm tactics instead of pedagogy – a mistake which the Maoists seized upon as justification for an all-out fight for power with Liu. Zhou was intervening when specific complaints were made to him. Song Qingling, widow of Sun Yat-sen, complained that her parents' graves had been smashed by Red Guards who considered such things out of date. Zhou had them repaired and the memorial tablet re-erected. Again, Red Guards turned upon a famous night-soil collector who had become a congressman, apparently because he had been patronized by Liu Shaoqi. 'Is it the purpose of the Cultural Revolution,' Zhou asked, 'to attack night-soil collectors?' He got the man brought back from farm labour, medically treated and apologized to.

For the most part, however, Zhou's time was spent with the students at the institutions where the Red Guard movement had begun.

His role at this stage was to encourage the students along the right lines and help them to perfect their organization. He arranged for a Red Guard liaison centre to be set up in Beijing, although it was clearly past anybody's ability to make all these young minds think and act alike. He had once said to a friend, 'We must never – *never* – pour cold water on the young.' That was the spirit which informed his nocturnal visits to successive campuses. One day he went at four in the morning to the Foreign Languages Institute to read its posters. 'Chairman Mao asked me to investigate,' he explained. 'I will learn from you.' Did he guess that he would soon be matching wits with these same students for his comfort, peace of mind, dignity and even safety? At another institution where he took lunch he insisted, as always, not only on paying but also getting a receipt. During August he received students from Qinghua University at least twenty times and went to the campus himself four times. 'I have come to fan up the socialist wind.' Three students were killed here in fighting between rival leftist Red Guard factions, in which he tried to mediate.

He went once in the pouring rain to a mass meeting to criticize Liu Shaoqi; he wore his usual grey suit without either raincoat or umbrella. Sloshing through ankle-deep water, he sat on a wet stool on a temporary platform, absolutely soaked. Thousands of dripping students took up the chant: 'An umbrella for the Premier! An umbrella for the Premier!'

Zhou's flattery came to the rescue. 'Didn't you give me a Red Guard armband? You are being tempered in the wind and rain, so let me be tempered with you.'

He sat there for three hours before his turn came to speak. When he did, the crowd was visibly swayed. At the end he led the singing of the Cultural Revolution hymn, 'Sailing the Seas Depends on the Helmsman'.

But Mao's great helmsmanship could not extend to securing a majority in the Party Central Committee for the radicalization of policy which the Cultural Revolution portended. As on earlier occasions when his critics thwarted him, Mao resorted to force. The Defence Minister, General Lin Biao, who was loyal to him, moved troops into Beijing from other commands to ensure that Mao's will would prevail over that of the Liu-ists. Beijing was no longer 'Peng Zhen's fortress'. When Mao himself, in August 1966, joined the poster campaign by writing out and putting up his own alarmingly anarchistic message entitled 'Bombard the Headquarters', the Central Committee, under pressure, endorsed the new line. But not before Zhou's diplomacy had negotiated a number of important explicit restrictions on the Cultural Revolution.

These were the so-called Sixteen Points agreed by the leaders on 8 August, guaranteeing that the economy and the government, including especially the scientists, would be immune from the new movement. A narrow majority for this compromise was achieved in the Central Committee; Lin Biao was designated as Mao's successor; and Chen Boda, Mao's former secretary, became the leader of the group directing the Cultural Revolution. Zhou was left holding his government and administrative functions safe from marauding.

241

Many of the middle-of-the-road intellectuals who normally supported Zhou were now reassured about the Cultural Revolution. 'Obviously,' wrote Han Suyin, 'if Zhou was for it, it *must* be all right.' Another commentator put it more shrewdly: 'Zhou walks with Mao, but three steps behind.' He must have known that the entire apparatus of socialist government and administration which he had so painstakingly built up over the preceding twenty years might still come under threat. Mao wanted to bring it all down about their ears, believing it to be corrupted and unresponsive to change, and it was not evident how much respect would be given to the Sixteen Points. Zhou here performed his characteristic manoeuvre, of waiting until it became quite clear who was going to win in a Party fight, and then joining that winning side on the toughest possible terms to ensure the protection of the administrative structure.

The fluctuations in Zhou's fortunes during the Cultural Revolution of the next three years may appear incomprehensible if the complexity of this extraordinary movement in China is not grasped. At any one moment during these stirring times there were at least two or three quite different major processes in train. Obviously the power struggle between Mao (backed by Zhou and Lin Biao) and Liu Shaoqi was a dominating feature, starting with Maoist attacks on certain writers, then on the Liu-ist mayor of Beijing, finally on Liu himself. But it was waged against the background of a campaign to promote socialist education which was taken with varying seriousness according to the conscientiousness of the leaders involved. At the grassroots, meanwhile, the combination of power struggle and ideological campaign allowed individual units, enterprises and localities across the land to lift the lid momentarily off their own repressed frustrations and rivalries. The Cultural Revolution was a rich *mélange* of anarchy, crusade and duel for national leadership. It was only to be expected, therefore, that Zhou spoke with different voices at different times.

On 18 August 1966 Zhou went to Tienanmen Square at sunrise for the first of the fabulous Red Guard rallies, during which the leadership reviewed a total of eleven million young radicals. At this first rally Zhou was there with Mao, Lin Biao and Jiang Qing to review more than a million people in procession. In the late afternoon he rode with Jiang Qing in the second open car behind Mao through the throng in the square. 'I had to shout so hard,' Zhou recalled, 'that I lost my voice.' (He had still not fully recovered it five weeks later.) He spoke with the full fervour of the new movement, not at this stage emphasizing the reservations and exceptions, the restrictions and regulations.

Chairman Mao has taught us that to make revolution by ourselves we must rely on ourselves. We will educate ourselves, liberate ourselves and carry out the revolution by ourselves. . . . We should set ourselves firmly against monopolizing every undertaking, acting as high and mighty bureaucrats, and standing above the masses, blindly ordering them about.

It sounded as if he did believe that the Sixteen Points would aim the Cultural Revolution against only the Party and not the government machine, that it would be peaceful, and that state economic and technological activities would be protected. But the Red Guards were emboldened by all this flattering attention from Mao and his lieutenants. They began to take control of the cities in the name of Mao, and in the course of that the good resolutions of the Central Committee were progressively forgotten.

Zhou was only an 'adviser' of the Red Guards, without executive authority, but he nevertheless took the lead in expounding the official Party line to them. He constantly reminded them of the limitations set down by the Central Committee. Ministries, for example, should not be picketed or harassed because 'they had work to do'. He told them to be careful what they said in their posters, some of which were revealing to the world details of national security, and also about publication of unofficial versions of remarks by Mao, which might adulterate Mao's Thought. Freedom to bombard the class enemy did not give a green light for indiscriminate attacks. He tried to stop the Red Guards from proliferating their targets. It was Mayor Peng Zhen who was under attack at this point, not those who had made mistakes over the Socialist Education work teams.

It is not difficult to kill a man with a gun – all that is necessary is to aim accurately. It is also not difficult to bruise a man with fists. All that is needed is brute strength. . . . But struggle by violent means merely touches people's flesh. Only struggle through reason can reach their soul.

The Red Guards, Zhou said over and over again, should distinguish correctly between good people and bad. They should not struggle against reformed landlords who were cooperating with the regime, for example, whereas landlords hiding in the cities should be exposed. 'It is necessary to see whether they are engaged in current counter-revolutionary activity. If they have proved themselves more or less honest, we shall have to give them a chance.' Similarly with rightists, if they have 'honestly submitted to reform and accept surveillance, there is no need to prosecute them.'

By all means the bourgeoisie should be criticized, but without destroying or confiscating its property or bank accounts. Hooligans should be punished, but elderly non-Communist politicians supporting the regime should be left in peace; the houses of people of high standing should not be searched or monuments pulled down.

It was no use believing that all power holders were reactionary, that was absurd. At some point the leadership had to be trusted. A person's revolutionary status was not simply reducible to class origins. If the Guomindang had labelled someone revolutionary, for example, that was a good indication, but class origin was not the only criterion for revolutionary acceptability. 'Class determinism is fatalism,' said Zhou, whose own ambiguous class status was insinuated in such discussions. Red Guards should be flexible about middle-class recruits. They could join the Red Guards – though with low priority – provided they had 'turned against their original class and behaved well, because they could not choose their class when they were born.'

The trouble was that while Zhou was talking mainly about the priority of production and about unpopular restrictions on revolutionary zeal, speakers like Lin Biao spoke in far more exciting, apocalyptic terms about 'bombarding the Party headquarters', overthrowing the small handful of bad people who ruled China and getting rid of 'monsters and demons'. That was the kind of language the young radicals had come to Beijing to hear, and it drowned out Zhou's schoolmistressy message. Still, he went on speaking out.

At another rally of a million Red Guards in mid-September, he claimed that the Cultural Revolution was producing the revolutionary impetus necessary to make the economic breakthrough in China's Third Five-Year Plan, which had just started:

Comrades, students! To expedite the normal progress of industrial and agricultural production, Red Guards and revolutionary students of universities and middle schools are not to go to industrial plants and business units, organs and agencies below the district [xian] level and rural People's Communes to exchange revolutionary experience and establish revolutionary ties. . . . Industrial plant and rural villages cannot take a holiday as the schools can and carry out revolution by suspending production. . . . The busy season of autumn harvesting and autumn sowing has arrived. . . . Red Guards . . . should go in an organized manner to the countryside to participate in labour, to assist in the autumn harvesting.

That was a very different and less appealing clarion call than the ones which the Maoists were trumpeting on every street corner. It was the kind of viewpoint which led the most radical students and their patrons in the second and third ranks of the Maoist leadership to plot against Zhou.

The best organized of these was the so-called May 16th Group, which built up a crescendo of anti-Zhou activity during the last four months of 1966, attacking him as a 'double-dealer playing with counter-revolution'. Originating in the Academy of Sciences, although the leadership later passed to the Foreign Languages Institute, it included such senior members of the Cultural Revolution Group as Wang Li and later Chi Benyü, two of the younger zealots on the Central Committee. Ostensibly these were all Maoists, working under Mao's leadership via Lin Biao, Jiang Qing and others. It did not mean that Mao was inciting their hostility to Zhou, but that he was allowing their radicalism to find an outlet because he could not fully control his own followers and risk losing their support for the overall purposes of the Cultural Revolution.

One Red Guard later confessed:

We were told to discover incriminating material against the greatest mandarin of them all. The Directorate would provide us with the documents or we would look for them. These were Zhou Enlai's speeches, talks, interviews. We pored over every word. Each action of Zhou's was scrutinized by us. In 1961 Zhou had said, in a talk on literature, 'there is an evil phenomenon extant among us. A lack of democracy. . . . Many people do not dare to think, to speak, to act. . . .' Was this bourgeois liberalism? We decided it was. He had also said, 'Chairman Mao has corrected his own writings. . . . Great artists correct their own works. . . . Great men acknowledge their errors and mistakes. . . . ' Could this be finding fault with the invincible Thought of Chairman Mao? We coupled stray sentences here and there, from many of his talks, took them out of context and convinced ourselves that Zhou Enlai must be toppled.

Posters attacking Zhou appeared on the streets of Beijing in September. He referred to them in one of his long evening talks with Red Guards which rambled on from ten at night on 25 September to 2.30 the next morning.

I am talking to you very frankly today. What other nation in the world possesses so much freedom? You can print all kinds of posters. Someone even wrote 'Bombard Zhou Enlai'. Of course I am aware of it, but I would not pay any attention to it. . . .

Someone has posted a big-character wall poster . . . demanding the total destruction of Islam. There are many Islamic countries in the world such as India and Pakistan, with populations close on 400 million. How can it be totally destroyed? Answer: It cannot be. . . .

Large meetings . . . may produce worldwide repercussions and we cannot but intervene. Shanghai dragged out 10,000 capitalists to parade them. The Central Committee knew about it, and cabled its objections stating that the scope was far too extensive and likely to influence world opinion. . . . Capitalists should not be dragged out to be paraded around: our country is strong enough to make such things unnecessary. . . .Classes are to be eliminated, but there is not to be physical liquidation of persons.

Zhou criticized these young people for their faulty class analysis, and here he dwelt on his own class status in a way that suggested residual feelings of guilt:

I myself have committed mistakes in line, but that alone does not serve to designate me as revolutionary or counter-revolutionary. At the time of the Nanchang uprising [of 1927] . . . I committed the mistake of going into the cities instead of the villages. But it was not a mistake in line. . . . I also made mistakes during the Fourth Plenum of the Sixth Congress, yet Chiang Kai-shek had orders for my arrest. How can you say that I am unrevolutionary?

At this point he reminisced about his corrupt father, 'a small official from the point of view of class status', and other relatives. 'I do not have any children except for two nephews. One nephew does not work, the other is with the Liberation Army, which has helped to solve his problems. I am the Premier, and yet solution of these problems is not easy.'

Again and again he came back to the economic constraints. 'Production and the service trades cannot be suspended. Otherwise, what shall we eat?'

Never before had the Premier been so fully engaged. When young soldiers came to stay in the Zhongnanhai hostel in Beijing in readiness for the National Day celebrations, Zhou went there at night and tucked their feet in under the quilts. When the Beijing Hotel held one of its endless rival faction meetings, Zhou sat on the steps sucking a bowl of noodles while the two sides argued their case – and when the waiters, fired by revolutionary propaganda, declared that they would no longer clean shoes, answer bells or serve meals, Zhou mildly offered to polish the shoes of foreign guests.

Gradually his government departments became paralysed by the removal of senior and experienced administrative and technical officials, to be criticized, humiliated, beaten or gaoled by the exultant Red Guards. After a few months of white-hot revolution, only one in seven of the staff of the State Council was at work. 'I have no one left to help me,' Zhou lamented at the end, 'except Li Xiannian', the Minister of Finance.

Nothing was too small or trivial to command his attention, and he dealt with all the demands made upon him with apparent equanimity. He ran the normal affairs of government in so far as he could with a skeleton staff, handling everything from the daily supply of oil, rice and firewood to the programme for man-made satellites, the affairs of minority nationalities and the need to receive foreign guests. Parents complained to him about their children being banished to distant provinces, and he invariably promised to investigate their grievances.

Most nights he stayed up until dawn, talking to students, workers, government officers, army officers and provincial representatives, adjudicating between rival Red Guard groups and negotiating for their reconciliation. He ordered the saving of historically significant temples from destruction by radicals. On the long-distance telephone he talked a young zealot out of destroying the historic heritage of the garden city of Hangzhou. Two foreigners living in China at this time described Zhou's activities in accurate terms:

Millions of Chinese believed that he personally was the only man in that enormous country capable of solving the problems in which they all found themselves entangled. . . . What many people looked to him for was his understanding of their personal difficulties, his answers to their anguished letters or to their requests for quilts for their Red Guard children wandering through the cold of North China.

When the National Day came on 1 October, Zhou could still speak with unbounded optimism. The Cultural Revolution had 'deflated the arrogance of the reactionary bourgeoisie, and is cleaning up all the muck left over by the old society', he said. 'A high tide of enthusiastic study of Comrade Mao Zedong's work is now rising. . . . Our 700 million people have taken on an entirely new mental complexion.' But two days later he was underlining the small print of the revolutionary contract once again.

The Red Guards cannot enter organs guarded by the PLA, and Red Guards cannot carry arms or wear military uniforms, because you are not a regular reserve force. . . . Judicial power belongs to the law courts. . . . Propaganda organs, Party newspapers, the New China News Agency and radio stations cannot be used by any Red Guard organization.

He told the Red Guards not to go into Tibet, an interdiction which Jiang Qing quietly countermanded.

The Maoists now decided to raise the stakes and extend the Cultural Revolution right across Chinese society, overruling Zhou's pleas to leave workers and peasants alone and contravening the Sixteen Points of August. Chen Boda, Mao's former secretary, who took charge of the new work within the Central Committee, obviously had Zhou in mind when he denounced people who said that the Cultural Revolution would hinder production, and who thought 'that the masses, once aroused, lack reason'. Those who were 'afraid of the masses,' Chen declared, 'are afraid of revolution.' The Red Guards reported the following exchange between Mao and Zhou at a conference on 24 October.

'Really bad rightists,' Mao suggested, 'make up only one or two or three per cent of the total.'

'More than that, now,' Zhou firmly interrupted.

'Never mind how many more,' said Mao irritably. 'We shall suppress them.'

Later, after the political business, they discussed the 'get-together' which was being arranged for the Red Guards. Zhou took this seriously.

'It should be done with proper preparation,' he insisted. Not for nothing had he been called the housekeeper of the regime.

Mao was indignant. 'What preparation?' he demanded. 'Where can one not find a bowl of rice?'

And that was the difference between these two complementary revolutionaries, one an impulsive man of the people and a genius at improvisation, the other an obsessive planner and puritanical economizer.

Zhou made the clever suggestion that the Red Guards emulate the Long March by making their journeys on foot instead of by train, thus releasing locomotives and carriages for economic work while at the same time tiring out the young radicals before they could do too much damage. He bravely spoke at the centenary ceremony for Sun Yat-sen, the Guomindang founder, and slammed the Red Guards of Shanghai for breaking into Sun's widow's home: 'Some youngsters have acted like hooligans.'

But he had to give ground. Lin Biao blandly announced at the beginning of November that Red Guards could criticize the government as well as the Party, knocking away the final struts of the Sixteen Points compromise of August. Zhou sat silently glowering.

This was the first of several occasions in the Cultural Revolution when Zhou had to put himself on the line and decide whether to be a martyr or a collaborator. It was clear that the movement had gone beyond the bounds previously agreed with Mao and others, which had made it acceptable. From Zhou's viewpoint, what was now happening was wrong, contrary to the ideas of socialism and serving only to discredit, in the eyes of the Chinese themselves as well as those of the outside world, the ideals for which he had given his life's work. The bully-boys in Mao's clique, their ideas still moulded by China's feudal past, were now lustily in command, lashing out indiscriminately at innocent men and women, beating, robbing, torturing and killing people whom they did not like. There was no pretence any more of observing legal or even moral requirements in acting against citizens.

Zhou had two choices, though his success in either direction was gravely limited by his lack of either an organized political following or control of military forces. He could make a stand and demand that Mao call off the campaign or bring the Red Guards to heel. But this would have ended Zhou's usefulness to Mao, and put him unequivocally into the opposition camp of people obstructing the Cultural Revolution. There were those in Mao's entourage who believed that Zhou was already in this category and for Zhou to do this would merely strengthen their position. He would have been hounded out of his position of influence, removed from control of the government and very likely put into the custody of the Red Guards for possible imprisonment, mistreatment and, conceivably, death.

All this might have left Zhou with a better reputation in Western eyes. He would have finished his career as a martyr to idealistic socialism. Such dramatic acts of conscience are not, however, in the Chinese political tradition. The Chinese are more practical and less egotistical than Europeans, and such a gesture on Zhou's part would have seemed merely selfish and theatrical to a people long used to the arbitrary use of power.

The other possibility was to go on pretending to support the movement, while endeavouring to deflect its excesses, blunt its mischief and staunch the wounds it was inflicting. This is the course Zhou chose. It called for a humiliating double act, but one for which Zhou's student histrionics and later political training had prepared him.

248

From now on at official functions, he patiently stood his ground, and had the satisfaction in the end of seeing his point of view vindicated. In the process a large number of innocent people and useful institutions whose fate came into question during the Cultural Revolution were saved. The price Zhou paid was having to endorse Maoist platforms and to be seen in the company of men who were murderers at one remove. For this some Westerners never forgave him, but most Chinese, remembering Confucius's opinion that 'Heaven does not hear a forced oath', were extremely appreciative of the results of Zhou's sophisticated and, in the end, more arduous stand.

The radicals, remembering Zhou's early role as herald of the Socialist Education Movement, thus viewed him as an insincere opportunist who became a turncoat on the Cultural Revolution question the moment things got rough and critical. The liberals hailed him by contrast as a saviour of all that was good and constructive in the regime's philosophy. And the ignorant majority remained bewildered by his apparent wavering.

Zhou sowed the seeds of doubt about Lin Biao's reliability in Mao's mind by taking advantage of an error by General Lin. The Defence Minister had compiled a collection of unofficial and informal statements by Mao and published it, without the Chairman's authority. Zhou was able to obtain an early copy of this book to show to Mao,whose suspicions of Lin then became serious.

It was much more difficult to drive a wedge between Mao and his own wife. Zhou diplomatically seized every opportunity to praise Jiang Qing, and yet he found himself inevitably clashing with her as she more and more openly asserted an authority in the radical cause. In December some of her followers, for example, went to arrest Mayor Peng Zhen, upon which Zhou declared: 'No one is allowed to set a precedent like this, to arrest and take people away at will!' He spirited Peng away to a place of safety. But his ability to conduct this kind of manoeuvre depended on frequent feinting to the left. He had to give his reluctant consent to the Red Guards to interrogate and harass five of his own senior colleagues, all pillars of his efficient government machine. Zhou admitted candidly to visitors from Japan that, at a time like this, personal opinion had to 'advance or . . . retreat' according to majority decisions. One had to 'shift with the wind'. Deng Xiaoping observed when it was all over that Zhou was sometimes forced to act against his conscience in order to minimize the damage.

Zhou was safe from ultimate peril because both Mao and Jiang Qing needed him. Both wanted to use his unique services, even while acquiescing to a degree of humiliation for him. But Zhou did not have the same patronage in high places for his vice-premiers, ministers and vice-ministers who now came under Red Guard pressure. Some, like Tan Zhenlin, the Agriculture

Minister, who had connections with Liu Shaoqi, were not good at accepting criticism or offering self-criticism. Foreign Minister Chen Yi was another outstanding case of a man of indiscretion only too suitable for Red Guard treatment, although he was so important to Zhou's work that the Premier went to enormous lengths to keep him.

So now began the painful process of sacrificing Zhou's valued and trusted subordinates one by one – like throwing Christians piecemeal to the lions, buying time in which to protect himself and his vital organization. In December he had to organize a rally to denounce Liao Chengzhi, one of China's ablest diplomats of the old school, as well as stage a demonstration against another protégé in the Physical Culture Commission. It was a situation where he would tell factories to keep going and Red Guards to keep out of them on one day, only to find the *People's Daily* saying in plain black and white next morning that it was open season for Cultural Revolution in the factories and throughout the country as well as cities.

In the New Year of 1967 the May 16th Group moved into top gear. Huge banners, 15 metres long, appeared in Tienanmen Square on 6 January demanding that Zhou be burned alive. His defenders wrote in the counter-slogan underneath: 'To burn Zhou Enlai is to burn the headquarters of the proletariat.' Another reply, observed in Beijing, ran: 'We want the dog's head of whoever is against Zhou Enlai.' Possibly the open attacks worried the Maoist leadership. 'There are Red Guards,' said Kang Sheng, one of the Maoists, speaking at a radical conference, 'who put up a wall poster criticizing Prime Minister Zhou Enlai in front of the Tienanmen Gate. What is the meaning of all this?'

'It's a counter-revolutionary act,' exclaimed one of the Red Guards.

'Then,' Kang persevered, 'what are you going to do?'

'Catch them.'

'Right!' shouted Kang. Considering that Zhou had led the attack against Kang's handling of the Rectification Campaign twenty years earlier, that was generous.

But Zhou was reduced to defending himself before these youngsters in pathetic terms: 'I have worked for the Party for many years. I have made contributions and I have also made mistakes. I am striving to keep my complete loyalty to the Party during my late years. This is not passive.'

Zhou himself was given a rough time by the Red Guards. When he insisted, against the rising popular demand, that they could 'criticize the bourgeois and reactionary line represented by Liu and Deng, but you must not ask that they are placed in your hands,' he was heckled. To which he retorted, 'I speak here in the name of the Party's Central Committee, and such shouts annoy me.' Chen Yi and other Vice-Premiers had indeed swerved from the Mao line, he added, but had now admitted their faults, were

250

'close to Mao', working under Mao's guidance, and should be given time to prove themselves.

It was even harder for him to intercede for Liu and Deng, but he went on pleading on their behalf all the same. After he defined the object of the struggle as 'the bourgeois reactionary line represented by Liu and Deng', some of the Red Guards in his audience shouted: 'Down with Liu Shaoqi and Deng Xiaoping.'

Zhou instantly turned his back on the audience, which then changed its shout to 'Down with the bourgeois reactionary line', whereupon Zhou turned again to face them.

'There is some difference,' he said, 'in the slogans which you shouted just now. We should thoroughly criticize the bourgeois reactionary line . . . and we should smash it. However, the other slogan is open to question. . . . These two men are still Party Central Standing Committee members. . . . Your shouting that slogan in my face drives me in a hard position.'

As regards his own supporters, Zhou was able to postpone until June the ultimate criticism of the Agriculture Minister, Tan Zhenlin, although the unfortunate man then disappeared from public view. By obfuscating and delaying, Zhou also saved the Finance Minister, Li Xiannian, and the Oil Minister, Yu Qiuli, both of whom went on to play useful roles in the post-Mao regime in the late 1970s and early 1980s. But the remarkable case was Chen Yi's; in defending him Zhou first played for time, then gave provisional agreement to his being attacked but finally appealed to a higher authority to save him. He presided over a mass criticism meeting against Chen Yi, and later agreed to further meetings but only on the understanding that he would take the chair, that specific detailed criticism would be worked out in advance, and that the meetings would extend over three months.

Meanwhile Zhou complained to the Red Guards about the abduction of his Minister of Railways: 'I tried hard to locate him but could not. Who could benefit from this?'

In these circumstances it was an act of courage for Zhou to put out an instruction on 12 January about the 'revival of reputations', paving the way for the reinstatement of leaders who had been subjected to kangaroo courts or suppressed by mistaken criticism.

The New Year saw the full impact of the earlier political decisions by the Central Committee to extend the revolution across the whole of Chinese society. Instead of Red Guards fresh from the classrooms, Zhou's administrators now had to face revolutionary rebels recruited from the industrial workforce. These new entrants into the revolutionary scene had quite different goals, and Zhou had to spend time, for example, drafting and expounding 'emergency instructions concerning wages' which he hoped would satisfy the rebels' demands to abolish the contract system and

251

apprenticeships and implement piece rates instead. Actually, he had to duck this issue and offer only cosmetic improvements for the time being. Luckily these new rebels were workers; they had already learned the discipline of authority and hard work and were easier to deal with through the existing organizational channels. Zhou coined for them the highly appropriate – almost Jesuitical – slogan: 'Power should be seized from below, but only according to Mao's directions from above.'

Nevertheless, social turbulence on such an extended scale was unnerving, to Mao as well as to Zhou, and when it looked as if anarchy was infiltrating almost everywhere, Mao decided to call a halt to the so-called power seizure, finding the dogged localism of the radical attempts to create a Paris-style commune in Shanghai and other cities particularly upsetting. And it was Lin Biao's army, of course, which had to be called upon to stop it all.

Zhou was thrust into the forefront of this new situation by what appeared to be a fortunate accident in mid-January. Jiang Qing and Chen Boda were said to have criticized General Xiao Hua, a senior officer in the People's Liberation Army and a crony of Lin Biao. It seemed that the general had failed to attend a Cultural Revolutionary Group conference on the pretext that he had to meet Premier Zhou for 'some arrangements'. Within hours, Zhou held a dawn conference with more than 900 senior army officers. It is not clear whether he sought to establish the inaccuracy of the reports or to excuse the indiscretions of Mao's wife and secretary. But he had undeniably become the key man in any immediate collaboration between the Maoists and the military – and he doubtless drew heavily on his old Huangpu connections which now gave him special access to former students of his, provincial military commanders all across China.

This was the signal for the overt entry of the P L A into the Cultural Revolution. It was Zhou who made the announcement that the army would in future stand at the side of the revolutionaries in seizing power. And at the end of January Zhou was delighted to find himself conveying Mao's new instructions to a military conference, relishing the new authority (if not the content) of his brief. The 'elderly leaders' of the Party could no longer expect to keep their jobs on the basis of 'past merit' but would have to 'establish new merit'. Furthermore, revolutionaries would be allowed to 'seize power first' and report the results to the State Council afterwards (a reversal of Zhou's old formula of 'business supervision'). Zhou was mouthing policies even more extreme than before, but in the knowledge that he was visibly graced by Mao's approval, making it easier for him to get his own way on a host of minor matters and colour the detailed implementation of policy. Soon enough he was exercising his new authority by giving orders to military units in the field, and ordering commanders, for example, to return to their bases.

The tactical alliance between Zhou and the dour Lin Biao nicely matched their mutual need of the other's skills. Lin had now supplanted Liu Shaoqi as Mao's nominated successor. He needed the civilian diplomacy and negotiating skills of a Zhou Enlai. By the same token, Zhou sorely needed the titular authority of Mao's deputy and successor, in order to press successfully for his way with the recalcitrant revolutionaries and officials whose aspirations, having been so suddenly inflated, could not now be tidily cut back. Zhou invented a new political formula for these events, calling for the streamlining of the Cultural Revolution by means of a triple alliance between revolutionary rebels, the army and the people's organizations. This was a cunning way of wrapping up the hard nut of army intervention with the soft chocolate coating of the young revolutionaries' supposed equality with the power holders.

Like the Chinese weighted doll – *budaowong* – which always bobs up again whenever it is pushed over, Zhou proved again his capacity to survive. The British Sinologist Roderick MacFarquhar described him in the *New Statesman* as being 'like a superb horseman attempting to stay on and ultimately control a bolting horse.' Another English writer, Richard Harris of *The Times*, compared the Premier to a 'referee blowing his whistle, patching up differences, putting a stop to the marching and counter-marching all over China that must have consumed so many billions of man-hours.'

Zhou visibly brightened with his new status. In a famous conversation with Mao about seizing power ('published' by the Red Guards), he elaborated a complex and sophisticated classification of Party officials – and won the Chairman's endorsement:

'Cadres fall into five categories,' Zhou declared. 'First are the influential "black gang" soaked through with erroneous ideology. Second come the "capitalist roaders" in power. Third are those adamantly upholding the bourgeois reactionary line. Fourth are those who admit some mistakes but go on making them, and fifth are the majority who make only isolated common mistakes.'

'Divide the first two categories,' Mao advised, 'and isolate and attack the smallest minority within them. . . . Takeover is in itself a revolution. . . . According to the different circumstances there are five different ways of going about it. You can completely reorganize. Or, after taking over, you can adopt different methods to deal with the faction in authority, such as criticizing them while keeping them at work under supervision. You can suspend them or dismiss them while keeping them at work. Or you could cashier them and punish them.'

'That is a good way,' Zhou replied, 'dismiss them, keep them at work but struggle against them. That gives an opportunity to enlarge and strengthen our own ranks. If the revolutionary rebels take on too much work themselves they will become passive slaves of work. So it is better to keep the faction in authority at work and struggle against them.

'In the Academy of Sciences, incidentally [whence the infamous May 16th Group opposed to Zhou had sprung] the left has grown strong. . . . They let the faction in authority sweep the streets, and after that just go to sleep. They think it is so easy. We must not let ourselves be bogged down by routine business. To take over is a big thing which will touch off a chain of changes. It is a revolution.

'We must be clear about the aim, about the problems involved and about how to go about it. We must have concrete policies. We have seized power but it may be snatched away from us again. In some organizations this tug-of-war might be a discipline in itself. But we must hold on to power and that depends chiefly on the strength of the left. . . . I support the power struggle, therefore.

'After it,' Zhou added in a gentle reminder of real interest, 'we must get down to revolution and encourage production.'

In February Zhou again complained at the slowing down of government work. So many officials were Cultural Revolution casualties that administrative work had to be done by clerks. His own sleep was further reduced and he often worked for thirty hours or more at a stretch, missing his meals, or taking just a cup of porridge and chopped vegetables which he could consume without stopping work. He grew noticeably thinner, and then his doctor discovered that he had heart trouble. But nothing, not even the pleas of Deng Yingchao herself, could slow him down.

On 3 February therefore his staff staged their own rebellion and hung a poster on his door. 'Comrade Zhou Enlai,' it declared:

We want to 'rebel' against your way of working and your habits of living. Only by making some changes to meet your changed health condition [i.e. his heart problem] will you be able to work longer and do more for the Party. We are considering things from the viewpoint of the overall and long-range interests of the Party and the revolution. We earnestly ask you to heed our requests.

When Zhou's wife saw the poster she underlined the word 'changed' in red. Two days later, after discussing it all with Deng Yingchao, the staff wrote out a smaller poster with supplementary suggestions and added it to Zhou's door. Here they urged him to reduce night working, to take breaks between meetings instead of working continuously, to leave some leeway for unforeseen events when making up the daily timetable, to avoid seeing people immediately after returning from meetings in order to get a breathing space, to make meetings short and get people to speak concisely.

The next day, to show respect for the opinions of working people, Zhou wrote at the bottom in neat characters: 'Sincerely accept these suggestions. Will have to see how it works out in practice.' He had no intention of complying.

Three months later his nieces and nephews paid a visit and told the Prime Minister sternly: 'Your actions fall short of the comrades' suggestions. You ought to do as they say, or you're not being a real supporter of the "rebels".' But they got short shift.

Among other things, he was trying to salvage a minimal foreign policy from the chaos of the Red Guards. Between these exchanges about his health with his own staff he spoke at a mammoth rally protesting against Soviet interference with the Chinese Embassy in Moscow. The Red Guards had besieged the Soviet Embassy in retaliation for over a fortnight, and a diplomatic break between the two countries was imminent. Zhou counselled moderation, signalling that the Russian leadership should not be provoked too hard. When he found Red Guards trying to enter the embassy grounds, contrary to all instructions, he cleared them with the use of a megaphone in half a minute. Two days later the Red Guard siege was lifted, and a serious break avoided. A few days later Zhou was telling young rebels in the defence industries that 'the administrative authority of finance, foreign affairs, national defence and industry belongs to the central leadership; no power seizure is permitted to be carried out in these spheres.'

In mid-February he presided over an extraordinary conference to discuss revolution and production with government leaders (both military and civilian) as well as Cultural Revolution Group Maoists. Tan Zhenlin was at the end of his tether. He told the meeting how he had wept bitter tears over his predicament, and on the fourth day he lost his temper. 'Your purpose,' he said, 'is to overthrow the veteran cadres one by one, ruin the families of revolutionaries who joined the revolution forty years ago.' At this point he grabbed his coat and case and rushed to the door, saying that he could not bear it any longer. Zhou asked him patiently to come back, but the outburst released the emotion of other leaders who openly denounced the methods which the Maoists were employing.

At another point in the meeting, Zhou asked the Chairman's former secretary, Chen Boda, whether he had read the pre-publication draft of the editorial in *Red Flag*, the Party's theoretical journal, which, by calling for thorough criticism of the reactionary line of the bourgeoisie, had been used as a passport to violence by the Red Guards. The answer was no.

'Why didn't you ask me to read it, then?' Zhou angrily snapped. 'It is a matter of prime importance.' If Chen had not had time, he should have passed the responsibility to another leader, so that unauthorized interpretation of policy could be avoided.

It was during the course of this important conference, in between its daily sessions, that Zhou was able to exact another crucial commitment from Mao which vastly enhanced his own authority. Mao agreed to Zhou's plan to salvage all the remaining government ministers who were still at their posts, and to forbid Red Guard action against them. 'We must definitely hold to struggle by reason,' Mao wrote belatedly to Zhou, 'bring out the facts, emphasize rationality and use persuasion. . . . Anyone involved in beating others should be dealt with in accordance with the law.'

Within hours there were posters in Beijing describing Zhou as Mao's 'closest comrade-in-arms' – an accolade hitherto reserved for Lin Biao. For his part, Zhou now came out with his first public denunciation of Liu Shaoqi by name, and he even felt strong enough to arrest a high-ranking rebel in the Finance Ministry who had led a seizure of power there, contrary to the new guidelines. Zhou now had to bring out all his powers of persuasion to make the rebels be less arbitrary with office holders and less harsh in their treatment without either stunting their pugnacity against genuine targets or allowing the rightists to take advantage. With the army now participating in seizures of power in the provinces, he understandably found it an extremely delicate operation.

The reinforcement of centralism was, for Zhou, a necessary correlative to the 'mobilization of the masses'. One should not be emphasized to the detriment of the other. He taunted the Red Guards for the death of the Coal Minister, Zhang Linzhi, during a marathon forty-day interrogation session early in 1967, telling them: 'You would not tolerate being dragged in the streets yourselves by the next generation.' When Zhou saw photographs of this Minister being whipped to death, he is said to have somewhat cold-bloodedly exclaimed: 'How am I going to explain to the Party Central Committee? These comrades have all died unaccounted for.' He also said forthrightly that it had been wrong to ridicule Mayor Peng Zhen by putting a card around his neck listing his crimes. In condemning such public humiliation he was implicitly criticizing Lin Biao, who evidently tolerated giving that kind of punishment.

The May 16th Group continued to attack Zhou in wall posters, but was answered by others in mid-March defending him as Mao's 'close comrade-in-arms'. When the Standing Committee of the Politburo met, the other ten members were evenly divided, but Zhou's vote for Mao once again ensured the latter's victory for his policies. Once again, but this time with Chen Boda at his elbow, Zhou told farmers that the spring harvest had absolute priority over power seizure or revolution. He told the Red Guards, with Jiang Qing at his side, that they should go back to school.

You have performed great merits for the Cultural Revolution. No matter how much criticism is levelled against the excess of the Red Guards, it cannot wipe out the great results of the Red Guards.... We hope that you resume lessons and carry out rectification campaigns at the same time.... You must educate yourselves.

In April Zhou went to Guangdong to try to reconcile the warring factions there. He criticized the garrison for manhandling students, while exonerating some of the radical groups, and the net effect was to excite the revolutionaries to fresh violence and upset General Huang, the commander. The Prime Minister was now facing a situation in which no settlement had been reached in negotiations between rival groups in a dozen provinces, and in which the centre was quite out of touch with another seven.

Zhou now began to let fly at Liu Shaoqi, who had refused, he said, to make any self-criticism, had been influenced by Khrushchev and would need to be criticized for his record from 1937 onwards. He was now using Liu's name – and Deng Xiaoping's – quite openly. 'Liu Shaoqi is not a Marxist' and 'must be overthrown.' Red Guards in Canton even claimed that Zhou had actually replaced Liu as president and head of state!

If Zhou's ambition had been so directed, this was the moment when he could most easily have bid for power. The majority of confused generals and functionaries would gladly have rallied round him in an effort to rebuild the state structure, casting both Mao and Liu aside. But it was not in Zhou's nature to seek that kind of prominence, and he knew full well that the divisive consequences of such a venture might have outweighed the healing ones. So he stayed at his post as (publicly) unthanked liaison man keeping the Maoists, the army and what was left of the government in some minimal collaboration.

The poster attacks on him continued all the same. A Red Guard congress in mid-April had to issue a special instruction: 'Premier Zhou Enlai is Chairman Mao Zedong's close comrade-in-arms and you should not harbour any doubts about him. To put up a wall poster attacking Premier Zhou will be considered a counter-revolutionary act.' But the worst was yet to come. Zhou was now to face what he had so far been spared, namely physical danger at the hands of the youthful radicals whom Mao had unleashed.

21

Detained by Red Guards
1967–68

The May Day celebration of 1967 was not a happy one for Zhou Enlai. He had to attend a reception given by Mao for Yao Dengshan, a young Chinese diplomat who had just been expelled from Indonesia for leading a radical power seizure in the Chinese Embassy there, on the emotionally powerful chauvinist platform of protesting against the Indonesian government's discrimination against Chinese residents and openly supporting Communist movements there. Yao openly challenged Zhou's conduct of Chinese foreign policy. To Zhou, this kind of action in Indonesia was not only ineffective, but positively counterproductive in seeking to influence Indonesian government actions. Yet Yao now stood arm-in-arm between Mao Zedong and Jiang Qing, towering above both and revelling in his welcome home. Zhou could only stand by feebly giggling, as Chinese do when extremely embarrassed. That night he was seen clinging precariously to the rail of the moving open truck, in an official parade where he stood halfheartedly waving his *Little Red Book of Chairman Mao's Thoughts* alongside the Cultural Revolution leaders, Jiang Qing, Kang Sheng and Chen Boda.

Another hornet that began to buzz around Zhou's head was Wu Chuanpin, a Guangdong Red Guard hero whom he had unwisely praised earlier but now stigmatized as a 'black character' (even the Maoists later denounced him as arrogant, violent and sexually promiscuous). At a meeting of leftist groups from various provinces, Wu accused Zhou of directing an illicit headquarters to thwart the Cultural Revolution. 'It is not correct,' Wu declared, 'for the head of the government to decide whether the rebels should take power or not in a Ministry. Zhou Enlai . . . must answer for the crimes committed by the "Red Capitalists" like all other high leaders, and not give us orders on how to treat them. . . . His headquarters must be denounced and destroyed.'

Soon Red Guards from the Foreign Languages Institute sent trucks to the

258

Foreign Ministry to raid the archives and bring away classified files, in the hope of finding evidence against Liu Shaoqi, Zhou Enlai and Chen Yi. This happened on at least two occasions during May. The May 16th Group was reinforced by Yao Dengshan, who was made Deputy Head of the General Services Department in the Foreign Ministry.

Zhou was indignant at it all, telling the Red Guards:

I was directly responsible for running the Foreign Ministry, and as a result they seized power from me. They sent telegrams directly to foreign embassies. As a result they were sent back. Yao Dengshan went everywhere making reports and creating trouble. He went to the Ministry of Foreign Trade once. His report . . . was incorrect and was very provocative. I criticized him on the spot. The Central Committee put forward the slogan of 'Down with Liu, Deng, Tao'. He put forward the slogan 'Down with Liu, Deng, Chen'.* How can you as a cadre at the head of department level put forward such a slogan? Who gave you permission? As for sending telegrams to embassies, no one understood this. You rebels always want to do everything in such an absolute fashion.

On another occasion he demanded of these young rebels:

Is China under the dictatorship of you or Chairman Mao? The Party and myself have met with Red Guards . . . on every occasion. You, on the contrary, have carried out your own purposes of your own free will without having any consultations with the Party. You have often broken into government offices in your attempts to drag out anti-Mao elements and have taken away many important documents of the Party and the government. Such thoughtless acts have given nothing but great pleasure and advantage to enemy countries. A flood of news in foreign newspapers has given much advantage to British and American imperialism and Soviet revisionism.

Wang Li, a follower of Mao, took a Cultural Revolution group to mobilize more than 200,000 people, it was reported, to besiege Zhongnanhai, the district of Beijing where government leaders lived. Ostensibly they wanted custody of Liu Shaoqi, but the May 16th Group adherents, presuming that Zhou would come to speak to them, pitched their tents near the south entrance habitually used by the Premier. 'He will come out with Liu Shaoqi,' they told their younger followers, 'and you can kidnap him.' But Zhou would neither yield Liu nor endanger himself, and after three noisy, rumbustious weeks the Red Guards withdrew. A particularly stubborn Red Guard leader, Kuai Dafu, notorious for having resisted even Chairman Mao's blandishments, also turned against Zhou during this month of troubles in May 1967, and swore vengeance on the Premier within one year, for not rubber-stamping his decisions.

* i.e. Chen Yi instead of Tao Zhu.

259

The Foreign Ministry's newspaper busied itself rebutting the May 16th Group, which called Zhou 'a hated gentleman of the bourgeois class'. Even Chen Boda, an untarnished Maoist, came to the rescue. 'Premier Zhou is respected abroad as well as at home,' he said. 'He is a representative Chinese. He is in a responsible position of carrying out the policies of Chairman Mao. . . . No one is allowed to find fault with Premier Zhou Enlai under any circumstances.' The mainstream Red Guards even ranked him as one of China's six 'clean' people – along with Mao, Lin Biao, Chen Boda, Kang Sheng and Jiang Qing.

Under cover of this 'cleanness' Zhou was organizing a highly secretive programme to protect veteran government officials, some of whom had been subjected to Red Guard torture, beatings and humiliation. He instructed his own guards to have a car available at any time to rescue such people, and once even requisitioned a helicopter. Eventually he had twenty ministers under his protection. That summer, when some were spirited away by the Red Guards, others were moved to safety to a place that Zhou's chief guard would not reveal even to Jiang Qing. 'The Premier did the right thing,' Mao commented when he learned of this. 'The garrison commander did well to give protection.'

Meanwhile Zhou recast the three-way alliance which he had established at the beginning of the year, on a new formula of bringing together representatives of the younger, middle and older generations. The original recipe was proving more trouble than it was worth, and it was no longer necessary to camouflage the army's intrusion.

During the summer of 1967, the status of the British Crown Colony of Hong Kong evidently began to give Zhou cause for concern. At an earlier stage of the Cultural Revolution Zhou had told visiting Communists from Hong Kong that no change was contemplated in the status of the British colony from which China earned so much foreign exchange. Since then the radical Hong Kong Communists had taken affairs into their own hands, like the hasty Yao in Indonesia. A struggle developed which Zhou had not wished to provoke, but which he could not now damp down without appearing to confirm the judgement of Yao and the May 16th Group that he was lily-livered in the face of European colonialism. He therefore spoke out fervently for the revolutionary cause in Hong Kong:

Hong Kong and Kowloon have always been China's territory. All proper rights of our patriotic countrymen in Hong Kong, and particularly their sacred right to study and propagate Mao Zedong's Thought, brook no encroachment whatsoever from anyone. . . . The Chinese people, who have scored great victories in the world-shaking Great Proletarian Cultural Revolutionary movement, absolutely will not tolerate the ruthless persecution of their patriotic countrymen in Hong Kong by British imperialism. . . . The destiny of Hong Kong will be decided by our patriotic

260

countrymen in Hong Kong and the 700 million Chinese people, and definitely not by a handful of British imperialists.

It was this kind of extravagant lip-service to untenable policies that moved *The Times* in London to complain: 'In so far as his voice is any longer audible, Mr Zhou Enlai mumbles agreement to the Maoist catechism and takes no part in moderating excesses such as the diplomatic corps in Peking has suffered.'

The May 16th Group stepped up its offensive. 'Ten questions put to Zhou XX', the posters shrieked – 'spokesman for which class?' Zhou was deprecating. 'I do not want to emphasize the May 16th counter-revolutionary group,' he commented. 'There are only a few people involved and it is nothing to get excited about.' (The Guomindang in Taiwan added its own twist with the unlikely rumour that Zhou had opened a personal account with a Swiss bank, because 'he is not feeling secure and is doing something for himself against an unknown future.')

Once again, nevertheless, the skills of the 'bourgeois spokesman' were needed in provincial mediation. Faced with an appallingly antagonistic split among the Communists in Wuhan, in central China, Zhou called in two seasoned Maoists (one of them his avowed enemy Wang Li) to conciliate. But the local commander, General Chen Zaidao, refused to compromise with his young radicals, and arrested the two central conciliators. Zhou immediately went to rescue his comrades and restore the prestige of central authority, whereupon General Chen sent twenty-five truckloads of troops to the airport to arrest him. Luckily for Zhou, loyal air force officers radioed the pilot in mid-air and he was set down at an alternative field on the other side of town where he could begin to knock heads together.

Zhou's solution, as so often, was to find neither of the antagonists right, forcing each to make a concession and thus satisfy the other that he had gained something. A few days later General Chen had to defend himself in Beijing before a nine-hour Central Committee meeting presided over by Zhou. At one point a Maoist slapped the general's face, much to the delight of Jiang Qing, but Zhou snapped crossly: 'We are not three-year-olds and cannot do things like this.' General Chen evidently admired the Premier's talent, and it was rumoured that he and a dozen other senior commanders actually offered to make Zhou China's new leader in place of Mao. But Zhou was probably used to declining such offers tactfully.

Back from Wuhan, Zhou bent every effort to regaining control over the Foreign Ministry. His preoccupation with domestic affairs, coupled with provincial mediation efforts, had allowed his enemies effectively to take over the Ministry, but during August he succeeded, almost by force, in wresting it back. Naturally the Red Guards stepped up their harassment of Chen Yi. At one meeting they hung up a sign saying: 'Overthrow Chen Yi', and Zhou refused to enter until this was taken down. On another occasion when his Foreign Minister was unnecessarily harassed, Zhou indignantly walked out and sent armed guards to escort Chen away.

In order to deflect criticism and strengthen his authority when he wished to assert it over the rebels, Zhou had to take a strongly leftist line in public statements. The radicals in Beijing had told the Chinese embassies in several Southeast Asian countries to organize the local Chinese community in Communist activities to overthrow the host government. Nowhere had this caused more indignation than in Cambodia, whose head of state, Prince Norodom Sihanouk, had considered himself to be on particularly friendly terms with China, despite the fact that his own government was far from being Communist. Zhou had reassured Sihanouk many times before about China's policy of not interfering in Cambodian politics, and yet in mid-August 1967 Zhou told the Cambodian Foreign Minister visiting Beijing that the Chinese residents in Cambodia had the right to 'love Chairman Mao Zedong, to love Chinese communism and the Chinese People's Republic'. Sihanouk was astonished when this was relayed to him, though Zhou also put in a personal word to dissuade Sihanouk from withdrawing his mission from Beijing in protest.

But for a few days Zhou's foreign policy lay in ruins as belligerent young Chinese radicals roughed up foreign diplomats and newsmen in Beijing, evoking memories of Boxer Rising days. The worst incident was the burning of the British Legation in mid-August and the physical assault on many of its officers by Red Guards. When Zhou heard of this he rushed to the scene quivering with rage and commanded the Red Guards to leave – one of the few occasions on which he was seen to lose his temper.

It was more than six months before he felt secure enough to call in John Denson, the chargé d'affaires, to apologize for the incident and pledge financial compensation.

Zhou's foreign policy was also jeopardized by the actions of radical youngsters in southern China, notably Canton, whose representatives he lectured in the capital on 25 August:

You are even more ignorant than children. In order to carry on fighting among yourselves, you looted the munitions which were to be sent to Vietnam as foreign aid supplies. You not only seized guns and rifles, but even anti-aircraft guns and guided missiles. Such actions adversely affected our country's foreign aid plan and greatly damaged our country's prestige.

Then, on 26 August, the climax came when Red Guards flocked by the thousand to surround Zhou and keep him by force in his office for some two and a half days. Neither Mao nor Lin Biao was in Beijing at that point, and Zhou had no way of summoning help or reinforcements. The immediate issue was the campaign against Chen Yi, which the Red Guards again insisted on discussing at length with the Premier. Without sleep, without food, without rest, Zhou argued strenuously with one small group after another until eventually they all withdrew.

Unsurprisingly, a few hours later Zhou suffered a heart attack. (The pilot on one of Zhou's planes had found an oxygen container at his seat, and the nurse accompanying him had explained that Zhou always carried it in case of emergencies.) But he was not long out of the fray.

Zhou had to defend himself against the attacks of the May 16th Group led by Wang Li, which by then had grown into a sizeable ultra-leftist faction hoping to overthrow both Zhou and Lin and to govern with Mao as figurehead. He did so with military help, drawing on his connections with Lin Biao, in a subtle way calculated not to embarrass the Central Committee or the highest leaders of the Maoist group themselves (who, after all, represented Zhou's most valuable future allies in the event of Lin Biao turning against him!). This delicacy was appreciated by Mao and his wife, and the heart attack alarmed them; when Mao returned to Beijing in September he threw himself behind Zhou and against Wang Li, and this was a major turning point for the Premier. He was able to arrange for Chen Yi to make a somewhat perfunctory 'confession', which extricated him from the clutches of the Red Guards. Jiang Qing joined Zhou in denouncing the May 16th Group.

Zhou scolded the Red Guards quite openly for their failings – for not cooperating with the army, and for fighting among themselves. In this transitional period, 'we need the army' to serve as 'the Great Wall that protects our frontiers'. The Red Guards would have to go back to school within a month, otherwise they would not get jobs. As for the rival factions, they represented 'petty bourgeois egotistical ambition' and should be dissolved.

'There is still a certain amount of plundering of houses,' he complained on 20 September, 'indiscriminately grabbing people, holding private courts, beating people, looting archives.' The struggle for order was not yet over.

Early in October Xie Fuzhi of the Cultural Revolution Group gave the most unambiguous bolstering of Zhou Enlai that the Red Guards had ever heard:

The Premier enjoys a high prestige and you cannot oppose him. . . . The Premier is the chief staff officer to Chairman Mao and Vice-Chairman Lin. . . . The Premier cannot be beaten down. The Premier is the representative of our state. . . . The Premier has a fine political style. Your opposition to the Premier will bring joy to Liu and Deng and to the imperialists and revisionists. The imperialists and revisionists are afraid of the Premier.

As if in reciprocity, Zhou spoke with particular positiveness about the Cultural Revolution. It was, he told a rally in Wuhan, 'a decisive victory. Hundreds of millions of people have been truly aroused. Mao Zedong's Thought has been popularized on a gigantic scale. The handful of Party persons in authority taking the capitalist road have been ferreted out. The power they usurped has come back into the hands of the proletariat.' Yes, there had been 'disturbances, but they were nothing to be afraid of. . . . Bad things can be turned into good things.' As for the 'drop in production', it had been 'transient. We took this into account in advance. . . . The revolutionization of the thinking of the people is bound to be transformed into a tremendous material force.'

'Today,' he told bickering Red Guards from Canton when they came to the capital in November, 'we shall have a little less democracy. We must . . . not arrest any people.' A fortnight later he was exhorting the railway workers, who were also still squabbling among themselves for the new patronage and office holding which the Cultural Revolution had opened up:

Transport is a very important matter. Chairman Mao and Vice-Chairman Lin are very concerned about it . . . 3,600 rail cars are still not in operation. Coal and petrol are not being transported from the northeast. This has a very serious effect upon the construction and production of our motherland.

In January 1968 Zhou lost his temper in public again, this time with Red Guards who had interfered with the production of vital equipment and supply of arms. Deploring the conflicts in some of the industrial ministries as well as in the Commission for Science and Technology, Zhou described with mounting anger how the Red Guards had seized rifles and ammunition and, in a clash between rival factions, 'fired into the air thousands of shells that should have been sent to Vietnam.' In a rare outburst, he shouted: 'I am indeed very much upset, very much upset.' He reprimanded Red Guards who were gambling and 'thinking of love' when they should be pursuing revolution.

It was a time for the surfacing of strong emotions. In March (near his seventieth birthday) Lin Biao's henchmen found a way to pressure Zhou's most trusted bodyguard, who had been with him for decades, to leave Beijing rather than face interrogation. Zhou ate with him before he left, and then gave him a firm handshake, saying: 'Take care of your health, try to stand the tests. There will be work to do in the future.' But later when it was all over Zhou confessed: 'Since I grew up with the smell of gunpowder on the battlefield, I seldom wept before. But at that time I could not help shedding tears.'

Zhou could not defend his friends beyond a certain point. When almost a hundred Foreign Ministry officials put up a wall poster defending Chen Yi

264

and attacking the ultra-leftists, Zhou rebuked them. 'This big-character poster,' he declared, 'is mistaken in principle. It is an interference from the right.' Similarly, he had to come out in public deploring the rash of 'revisions of verdicts' by which several victims of the Cultural Revolution were securing reinstatement. If the balance went too far in either direction, the fragile stability of the regime was threatened.

When Lin Biao's followers asked Zhou to help them find articles written by Jiang Qing in the 1930s – in the hope of discovering unfavourable material – Zhou was put in an awkward position, but agreed to undertake the search, and then claimed to have found nothing of any real interest. Even Zhou's own followers sometimes unwittingly laid traps for him. In April the organization in Canton bringing rival Red Guard groups together, which Zhou had been instrumental in launching, celebrated its first anniversary, and did so by honouring Zhou for his visit to Canton the year before. He cabled immediately to say that he had been acting then in accordance with Mao's directions, and that the meeting of 'a small number of people' to celebrate the anniversary 'by giving prominence to my name' had constituted 'a big mistake . . . contrary to the spirit of the Cultural Revolution. I firmly oppose it.'

But while keeping a low profile and leaving the less politically experienced giants – Lin Biao and Jiang Qing – to battle it out, Zhou also sought obstinately for ways to reduce the nationwide chaos of the Cultural Revolution. His best effort came in March 1968, when at a mass meeting with Chen Boda and Jiang Qing present, he accused Liu Shaoqi (falsely, it would seem) of having deserted the Communist Party forty times and entered the Guomindang – an accusation which, if true, meant that targets of the Cultural Revolution no longer had to be treated as internal deviators within a Party continually vulnerable to revisionist infection, but more simply as infiltrating members of an enemy party. Treason was a more manageable concept for Party officials than the grey shades of ideological polemics.

But the factionalism would not die down. The stubborn Red Guard leader Kuai Dafu ordered a final assault on his rivals in May partly as a means of 'settling accounts politically with Premier Zhou Enlai'.

The flavour of Zhou's further meetings with Red Guards is conveyed in the following report of a meeting with Guangxi Province Red Guards visiting Beijing on 25 July 1968. They had caused a two-month suspension of the railway linking the centre with, among other places, Vietnam, and they were suspected of arson and all kinds of disobedience to central orders – a reputation that had preceded them to Beijing.

'You have to admit,' Zhou lectured them, 'that in spite of the many telephone calls and telegrams we have made and sent to you, and in spite of the notice which was sent to you more than twenty days ago, railway traffic is still held up and trains cannot get past Liuzhou. Have you really divided among yourselves the ammunition destined for Vietnam which you looted?'

One Red Guard leader admitted that his railway rebels had seized 'more than 4000 cases', but insisted that the rest had been grabbed by a rival group, the 'Rebel Grand Army'. 'We ask to be forgiven.'

The Premier then asked whether the two rival factions could cooperate, and a spokesman for the second one replied: 'Things can be settled. But there is no guarantee for our safety.'

Zhou continued to address himself to the first spokesman. 'Is your black boss* still directing you from behind the scenes? . . . You must tell me the truth. Can you guarantee that neither side will obstruct the restoration of traffic?'

The young man denied that they had ever obstructed traffic, but an official interjected that they had used a device to derail a train.

'Yes, that's right,' said Zhou. 'Had the PLA come fifty seconds later, the train would have met with an accident.'

'It was done,' came the explanation in self-defence, 'by a student who could not foresee the consequences.'

'What do you mean,' Zhou exclaimed, 'not able to foresee the consequences? It was a counter-revolutionary incident!'

Zhou now spoke to the leader of the 'Rebel Grand Army'. 'Let me ask you this. You took part in the looting of ammunition destined for Vietnam, but can't you hand over what you looted? You have seized 11,800 cases, that is no small matter. . . . You must return all the loot within one or two days. You know very well that the train was carrying supplies in aid of Vietnam. . . . Don't you know how the loot was divided?'

An official observed that they had seized the ammunition chauvinistically, knowing that it was going to Vietnam – to foreigners! – and another said that the looting had been well organized, and all over in less than an hour.

'How can you try to deceive us,' Zhou persisted, 'and get away free? How can you tell lies and try to get away with it! There are two things which you must do: first, all the looted ammunition destined for Vietnam must be returned. Second, you must restore the railway traffic . . . and guarantee through traffic. . . .

'Now,' Zhou went on, 'let us discuss the problem of Guilin.' Here too there were rival factions, and the leader of one of them immediately said defensively that they would guarantee that their men who were occupying the prison in Guilin would evacuate it by three o'clock that afternoon.

Zhou Enlai called on them to telephone home to ensure that one faction withdrew from the prison while the other refrained from attacking it during

* Zhou referred to an anti-Communist organization which had taken advantage of the Cultural Revolution anarchy to operate in south China.

the withdrawal, upon which one side pointed out that the other had seized more than 6000 rifles.

'The mistakes of both factions are great,' Zhou pronounced. 'You are now at the brink of the precipice. Some of you have already committed crimes. You are now given a chance to mend yourselves and redeem yourselves by doing meritorious service.' He turned to one of the Guilin railway bureau rebels.

'Is it true that your men took away the locomotive of train No. 45?'

'Only one,' came the reply.

'Oh, "only one"! But one is serious enough! The locomotive driver came from Tsitsihar especially to help, because you two factions were too busily engaged in struggle with each other. You threatened the driver with a machine gun and took away the locomotive. You also broke open the doors of the carriages and the tool box and took away an axe. It was only after I called ... over long-distance telephone and gave up a good night's sleep that you returned them. Why don't you criticize yourselves for such a serious mistake, why do you prefer to accuse others?'

Such was the detail into which the Premier had to descend in the effort, often useless, to scale down the vicious factionalism of the Red Guard movement, and to preserve some of the basic functions of government and diplomacy which were carelessly put at risk when these young revolutionaries interrupted production, transport and commercial life for their own local ends.

In August 1968, Russian troops marched into Czechoslovakia to provoke yet another East European crisis. The Chinese leadership strongly supported those elements in the Czechoslovakian Communist Party which wanted a less restrictive regime, more free from Soviet pressure, and at this stage of their own cultural revolution they found it convenient to underscore the bellicosity of the Soviet Union – before which the Chinese should patently preserve their own unity in order to be secure. Zhou lost no time in denouncing the Soviet invasion as 'the most bare-faced and most typical specimen of fascist power politics played by the Soviet revisionist clique of renegades and scabs.'

Perhaps encouraged by this reminder of outside threats, Zhou endeavoured to wind up the Cultural Revolution, drawing some tentative balance sheets in September. During the twenty months since the Shanghai proletariat had seized power from the capitalists in the Party, 'we have finally smashed the plot of the handful of top Party persons ... to restore capitalism,' he told a mass rally. This was to celebrate the creation of the last two revolutionary committees which now straddled all the Chinese provinces on the basis of collaboration between all the legitimate political elements. 'We can say with certainty that the old world is going to collapse.'

From now on until the end of his life, Zhou was to be seen in public with his neatly tailored tunic bearing only a single small red badge bearing Mao's picture with the principal Cultural Revolution slogan: 'Serve the people' – his favourite.

Zhou had played many roles during the Cultural Revolution. At the beginning he was out in front with Mao, urging on a political movement with whose ideals he was fully in sympathy. Provided this most ambitious Socialist Education Movement could be correctly managed, so as to preserve the economy and science on which the future of the population would depend, he fully favoured subjecting huge numbers of Party members to this most rigorous and soul-searching of tests and reforms. (Indeed, he was audacious enough later on to place it on the official record that it was Lin Biao, not Zhou himself, who had sought to slow down the motor of revolution in order to develop economic production.)

But Zhou was the supreme conservator, protecting human beings, institutions and even property whose destruction was not truly necessary for the advance of the political movement. He sheltered his comrades, not indiscriminately but as generously as his own political circumstances would allow. His bodyguard compared him to 'a big tree reaching the sky under which the elite was protected'. Certainly history's indictment sheet against the Cultural Revolutionaries would be far graver and bloodier had not Zhou limited the sacrifices made to them through his combined moral authority and political skill.

Tragically, his lifeline could not extend to those dearest to him. In October 1968, Zhou's adopted daughter, Sun Weishi, died under Red Guard torture. She had become a theatre director and Jiang Qing grew jealous. The story is told that Zhou was either powerless to intercede – or else held back because he believed the Cultural Revolution took priority over family loyalty. Only when the news of her murder broke did he rush a team of doctors to perform an autopsy. They were too late – her body had already been cremated and all the personnel concerned dispersed.

So complex were the events of the Cultural Revolution that it almost defies brief analysis, but the clearest way to look at it is to re-examine the three quite distinct phenomena which fused together under its label. To begin with there was indeed an ideological campaign to alter the old-fashioned, feudal, pre-socialist mentality of the majority of the Communists and others in China. To this crusade for a higher level of democracy, socialism and collectivist spirit, Zhou was an eager adherent.

It was in this context that Zhou afterwards explained that the Cultural Revolution had been only the first of a series. It 'could not possibly solve all the problems at once,' he told Felix Greene a few years later. 'Such a revolution must be conducted again and again, each time to a more advanced stage and each going deeper than the one before.' There was no real contradiction here. This was the socialist zealot in Zhou speaking, and presuming in his usual optimistic way that, next time, anarchy and power struggles could be avoided.

The Cultural Revolution was also, and at the same high level of leadership, a straightforward 'palace' struggle wherein Mao reclaimed his leadership from the challenge of Liu Shaoqi by gathering such powerful allies as Lin Biao in the army and Zhou himself. Among Western commentators, Zhou is often considered a moderate, but in this particular struggle he lined up with Mao rather than with the more pragmatic Liu – presumably because he trusted, respected and even liked the first more than the second. Both Mao and Liu were secretive men who played their cards close to the chest, but Mao had the redeeming quality of humour and the rare skill of political genius. Zhou had worked intimately with him for thirty-five years, whereas Liu he hardly knew.

Finally, there was a lower level of the Cultural Revolution far away from Beijing which was a lifting of the normal restraints of law and order, to allow local scores to be settled and leadership rivalries fought out, factionally and individually. In small doses this might have appeared as a helpful periodic bloodletting, but in the end it spelt nationwide anarchy, and Zhou pitted himself against it with determination and final success. His talk with the Guangxi rebels represented only one tiny episode in this work which he conducted from Beijing over a three-year period.

'We can still say,' Zhou told Edgar Snow later, 'that what we gained was far, far more than what we lost.' The Cultural Revolution had purged less than 1 per cent of Party membership (perhaps 200,000 persons!). But on the tough material criteria which sceptical outsiders tend to invoke, Zhou had to be defensive. 'As a result of some struggles in factories, disruptions in traffic and lost labour hours, industrial production in 1967 and 1968 did decline somewhat.' And the programme to reduce China's population growth had been set back by Red Guard permissiveness.

There was another casualty. The Cultural Revolution, which would have killed a lesser man on his feet, tired Zhou Enlai out. He never again recovered his old sparkle. There was one major coup left for him to pull off in the international sphere, but otherwise his final seven years were to be spent rather quietly, assiduously repairing the damage from the Cultural Revolution while fighting to retain his own political place in the aftermath.

269

22

Disciple in the White House
1969–76

Fighting between Chinese soldiers and superior Russian troops on the tiny island of Chenpao on the frozen Wusuli River at the north end of the Sino-Soviet border in the spring of 1969 dramatized Chinese vulnerability. China's neighbours had not taken advantage of the years of rampaging Red Guards, when defences were weak. But Zhou and his administrators recognized that communications with the outside world had to be repaired. These had been interrupted even in a very literal sense: during this Chenpao crisis Premier Kosygin vainly sought to speak to Zhou Enlai on the hot-line telephone, only to find the Chinese telephonist refusing to connect him as a 'revisionist'.

The chance for diplomatic amends came in the autumn of 1969 when world Communist leaders assembled in Hanoi for the funeral of President Ho Chi Minh of North Vietnam. Kosygin pointedly departed before Zhou's arrival, but eventually doubled back to Beijing for a four-hour session with him – in an airport lounge, since Zhou would not allow him into the city – of acrimonious argument about the issues that had brought the two nations to arms on their common border.

Zhou insisted that Russia recognize the moral unfairness of the 'unequal' Sino-Russian treaties of the nineteenth century, but he promised that China would make no claim to the actual territory which had been wrested by Russia from China under them. The treaties would be taken as the basis for settling the boundary question anew along broadly the same demarcation line as before. Meanwhile both sides should keep the *status quo* by withdrawing forces to an agreed distance and undertaking not to use force or to make public criticism during these substantive negotiations. Kosygin apparently accepted all this verbally, but the public denunciation of China was renewed when he returned to Moscow.

Meanwhile, China's Ninth Party Congress in April 1969 settled the post-Cultural Revolution political hierarchy. It was a strange Congress, with Lin fidgeting wanly, Zhou showing uncharacteristic irritation, and only Mao apparently composed as ever – three men in uncomfortable harness. Zhou was elected Secretary-General of the Party, and was listed third in the new five-man Politburo, higher than Chen Boda and Kang Sheng of Cultural Revolution notoriety. A new constitution proclaimed Lin as the heir to Mao. Zhou did not choose to fight this patently improper provision: 'Do not discuss it too much,' he was reported to have told his followers, 'let it pass.'

He still held on to his alliance with Lin Biao and the Maoists as the only possible basis on which a reconstruction of China was possible. But it was hard and tedious work. As an admirer wrote: 'He was able to work even with the devil, and extract some good out of him.'

That autumn Zhou was the victim of an interesting conflict of cultures when the British newspaper man Anthony Grey of Reuters was released by the government after almost two years' imprisonment in China. His detention and psychological harassment by Red Guards had become a *cause célèbre* in Europe, and everybody welcomed his belated release, which Zhou had only now been able to engineer. At the next diplomatic banquet Zhou eagerly approached the British chargé d'affaires.

'Well,' the Premier said in his slow English, 'Grey is out, he is free.'

'Yes,' Denson replied. 'But he's not out of China yet.'

'Well, he can stay here if he likes.'

'I'm not sure he'd want to.'

At this Zhou moved away, but then returned to ask if Grey was present. He was not, but Zhou asked the same question at the next reception and seemed ready to make some amends for the suffering of the young Englishman, perhaps by giving him a personal apology or an exclusive interview.

Mao began to call Zhou Enlai 'the manager', which was a good appellation. A European diplomat once observed that if China were a family, 'Zhou, who was loved by the people, would have played the role of mother; and Mao, who was at first respected, and later feared, that of the father.' During this time he was quietly rehabilitating his vice-ministers and senior officials after their torments at the hands of the Red Guards. He gained ground in the summer of 1970, when Lin Biao and Chen Boda went out on an extreme limb which Mao would not support. Lin wanted to be head of state, and Zhou took some enjoyment in frustrating this particular ambition, although in his physical condition he found it exhausting. On his way to a meeting one morning he collapsed in the corridor. After an hour he came round, realized that he had an important meeting to attend, got up, called a car and rushed out against everybody's advice, insisting that he was all right.

Now came the most famous feat in Zhou's diplomatic record. There were not likely to be any further developments of importance in the Soviet relationship under Zhou's stewardship, after his meeting with Kosygin, but the United States was another matter. Most of the generals under Lin Biao still preferred to lean towards their former mentors in Moscow. Mao and Zhou did not take issue with this – until Lin's overweening political ambitions in late 1970 stimulated them to become more serious about a possible rapprochement with the United States. Moreover, Zhou's experts calculated that a major realignment had taken place in world affairs, making the Americans a lesser threat than the Russians. Zhou mused about the possibility of high-level talks with the United States – if only Washington would take the initiative.

Edgar Snow was given a hint of this in August, when he interviewed Zhou at a ping-pong tournament in Beijing – 'his hair faintly beginning to silver, wearing a summer sports shirt and grey slacks above sandals and white socks.' Zhou was extremely inquisitive about American politics, and reminded Snow of the threat to China from the north, i.e. from the Russians.

'If China sought a detente,' Snow asked, 'would the possibilities be better for negotiating with Russia or with the United States?'

At that time the question was still almost unaskable, and the questioner might well have simply been shown the door. But Snow's timing was impeccable.

'I've been asking myself the same question,' came Zhou's disarming reply.

The next act in this little public-relations play came at the National Day parade when Zhou went up to Snow, tugged his sleeve and took him and his wife to stand for a time next to Chairman Mao on the crowded reviewing stand, thus giving millions of Chinese and Americans a clear hint of what was to come.

A few weeks later Zhou gave the American correspondent a substantial interview, defending China's economic situation, explaining the reasons for its costly grain imports, painting a picture of a worthy and hard-working people badly in need of American technology. China, he concluded proudly, had no internal or external debt. His glowing portrait – of a country where the best lessons of the Cultural Revolution had sunk in and the worst excesses had been made up for – was duly reproduced in the American press. Finally, he said that China was ready to negotiate the United States' 'armed aggression' in Taiwan.

One of the sessions with Snow lasted from dinner until six the next morning, by which time the American was tired out.

'I must let you get some sleep,' he mumbled.

Zhou threw back his head and laughed. 'I've already had my sleep,' he said. 'Now I'm going to work.'

Zhou's letters to President Richard Nixon, and the American replies, had to go, in the absence of a direct channel, via the respective Pakistani or Rumanian missions. In one such message, reaching the White House early in December, Zhou emphasized that he spoke for Mao Zedong and Lin Biao as well as for himself in saying that China 'has always been willing and has always tried to negotiate by peaceful means. . . . In order to discuss the subject of the vacation of the Chinese territories called Taiwan, a special envoy of President Nixon's will be most welcome in Beijing.' Nixon agreed to send his National Security Adviser, Henry Kissinger, covertly to China to lay the groundwork for a later presidential visit.

At home Zhou's quarrel with Lin came more and more into the open. When the Prime Minister flew back from a visit to Vietnam in March 1971, Lin allegedly tried to eliminate his enemy by ordering his plane to be shot down on its return to Chinese airspace. But the general who received the order held his fire when he saw the plane's civilian markings, forcing it down instead. A puzzled Prime Minister stepped out to be handed Lin's telegram, which Zhou carried home with him, giving it to his wife, it is said, to show to Mao after his own death. Or so, at least, the story went in Beijing.

Zhou was left to mastermind a coalition with the many provincial generals who neither liked nor trusted Lin Biao, on the basis of a foreign policy of detente with the West and an economic policy of decentralization – a recipe which Mao finally, if reluctantly, endorsed during the summer of 1971.

Chen Boda, meanwhile, became ever more extreme in his radical-fascist ideas, and Mao turned completely against his former secretary. He was purged in April 1971, by a group under the chairmanship of Zhou, who skilfully managed to spread some of the opprobrium onto leading supporters of Lin Biao. The situation was well expressed at the May Day celebration – where Mao made the first ceremonial entrance, followed by Lin waving his *Little Red Book of Chairman Mao's Thoughts* with a shy grin, followed in turn by Zhou, not in his usual close proximity to the two great men but instead three paces behind and a little to one side.

Meanwhile Zhou made his first overture to the United States by inviting the American ping-pong team to play in China, a move that was accompanied by enormous publicity. 'You have opened a new chapter in the relations of the American and Chinese people', he told them. 'I am confident that this beginning again of our friendship will certainly meet with the majority support of our two peoples.'

When the stunned athletes failed to respond, Zhou prodded them. 'Don't you agree with me?'

They burst into applause and invited the Chinese team back to the USA. As Kissinger noted, Zhou Enlai 'knew how to make gestures that could not be rebuffed.'

And now Zhou deployed, for the first time since his Nanjing days of 1946, his full deftness in diplomacy through American journalists and professional visitors. Typical was a dinner with Seymour Topping of the *New York Times*, William Atwood of *Newsday* and Bob Keatley of the *Wall Street Journal* on 21 June, during which he brilliantly defended China's current situation and policies, and cleverly teased American pretensions to being the world's policeman.

Zhou elegantly reminisced about his youthful years in Nanjing. 'Now, as Premier, I am not so free. For instance,' pointing at one of his guests' notebooks, 'I say just one word and you note it down.'

But would he visit America?

'I am certain that day will surely come,' he replied.

Recommending the *maotai* wine, he observed: 'This liquor won't go to your head, although you can light it with a match. . . . Actually, after drinking for thirty years, I am giving it up. . . . In spirit I am always young, but my material base is getting older and older.'

For all that, he nevertheless knocked back his *maotai* toasts with gusto, calling: 'I will not pretend to drink, let me have real liquor.'

Zhou's humanity won all hearts. Topping asked him about the population growth, and Zhou explained how in some parts of China it was still like the old days, where a couple would go on having children until they had the son, on which every traditional family insists. They might produce nine girls. 'By then the wife is forty-five, and only then can she stop trying for a son. Is this equality?'

Topping confessed at this point, slightly embarrassed, that he was himself the father of five daughters.

'No sons?' asked the Premier, raising his thick black eyebrows.

'Topping is tired,' an irreverent member of the American party broke in.

'No,' Zhou briskly snapped. '*Mrs* Topping is tired. I am talking on behalf of women.'

There were to be many more such encounters, and they were, as always, two-way communications. Zhou articulated China's policies, needs and successes to the foreign press, while at the same time he absorbed from these seasoned journalists a more intimate and 'inside' version of American politics. 'He questioned us rather extensively,' reported an amazed American biologist, 'about the chances which various candidates might have in the 1972 elections.' Zhou told the Briton, Malcolm MacDonald, 'with a broad grin', that he well knew that one of Nixon's motives in visiting Beijing in 1972 was to gain prestige with voters before the next presidential election, but he hoped China might thereby win some 'partially useful concession' from the Americans without having to do much in return.

A month later an American scholar was warning a US Senate hearing in Washington not to be euphoric over Zhou Enlai as a pragmatist and a man of reason. 'Actually,' said Professor Franz Michael, his record showed him 'as a ruthless and cruel leader, quite capable of the brutal slaughter of the families of Communist agents who revealed information when captured.' But Michael was representing a view that was losing its majority in American opinion. Zhou's superior skills were telling, not only over the Lin Biaos and Chen Bodas of China, but over those who stood against him in other countries.

Kissinger, in Asia on a diplomatic mission, secretly flew to China from Islamabad (where the world believed him to be ill in bed with a stomach ailment) on 9 July. His diplomatic illness became a painfully real one in China, but all discomfort was forgotten when, four hours after his arrival, Zhou came to the guest house for their first discussion. They were to spend seventeen hours talking and these two representatives of rival ideological camps simply fell in love with each other. It is rare for the spokesmen of two giant opposing blocs at the highest level to be able to speak and understand each other's language as Zhou and Kissinger could. Kissinger greeted the Premier at the door and ostentatiously stuck out his hand. Zhou took it with a quick smile – they were both thinking of Dulles. 'It was the first step,' Kissinger commented afterwards, 'in putting the legacy of the past behind us.' He sensed the ambivalence in Zhou's position – negotiating with China's archenemy of twenty-five years, while the Vietnam war and Taiwan's recalcitrance still echoed loudly in Chinese ears.

This was 'reflected in a certain brooding quality of Zhou's, in the occasional schizophrenia of his presentation.' Yet Zhou was never impatient or let slip any sign that he had other things to do. 'We were never interrupted by phone calls or the bureaucratic necessities of running a huge state,' the American observed. And whereas Kissinger had voluminous documents to hand for the talks, Zhou, on this as on subsequent occasions, bore only a single sheet of paper.

What captivated Kissinger was Zhou's innate sense of the cultural superiority of his ancient civilization, which allowed the edges of ideological hostility to be softened 'by an insinuating ease of manner and a seemingly effortless skill to penetrate to the heart of the matter.' He admired Zhou's

air of controlled tension, steely discipline and self-control, as if he were a coiled spring. He conveyed an easy casualness which ... did not deceive the careful observer. The quick smile, the comprehending expression that made clear he understood English even without translation, a palpable alertness, but clearly the features of a man who had had burned into him by a searing half-century the vital importance of self-possession.

For Zhou, this unusual guest concealed beneath the brash fascination of American power the depths of matured European wisdom and knowledge.

Gossiping with visiting Americans on the eve of another later Kissinger visit, Zhou would sometimes grin with delight and clap his hands together. 'Oh, that's very good, that's something I can use with Kissinger.' Both of them evidently took boyish pleasure in engaging the other in diplomatic duels of wits. Nevertheless they made mistakes at their first encounter. Kissinger perpetrated the classic blunder of the first-time tourist by referring to China as 'this beautiful, and to us, mysterious land'. Zhou instantly held up an admonitory hand. 'You will find it not mysterious. When you have become familiar with it, it will not be as mysterious as before.' And on later visits he referred to this early cliché.

But then, when Zhou wanted to know how large President Nixon's party would be when he came to China, he made the mistake of guessing that it would be about fifty people, earning the condescending pity of American officials: the correct answer was that Nixon expected to come with 700.

For Zhou to have tempted the National Security Adviser onto Chinese soil, to have engaged him in many hours of policy discussion and to have established with him the agreement in principle that President Nixon would visit China in person and in public represented a remarkable success on Zhou's part. The brittle General Lin Biao, who had played no part in it, was riled by Zhou's triumph. 'If Zhou can invite Nixon,' he was said to have boasted (or threatened), 'I can invite Brezhnev.' Perhaps he felt that Zhou had gone too far. At any rate, he soon made his last attempt to achieve supreme power in China, but the circumstances even today remain controversial and obscure. It seems that in August 1971 he planned to bomb Mao's train while the Chairman was travelling in central China, but Lin's daughter told Zhou just in time to save Mao. Then, on 12 September, Lin Biao with his wife and son and some senior officers were on holiday at the seaside at Beidaihe. Late that afternoon Zhou discovered that Lin had ordered two Trident aircraft to go to the Beidaihe airfield for an unauthorized night flight. His suspicions were aroused: one lurid rumour in Beijing had it that Zhou Enlai actually strangled Lin 'at the turn of a dim corridor of a villa in Beidaihe'. But this is fanciful.

The official Chinese government story was that Lin tried to flee to the Soviet Union, perhaps in the hope of securing Russian intervention in China, but that his plane crashed in Mongolia in the night. As Zhou put it in his subsequent official report, Lin 'fled as a defector to the Soviet revisionists, in betrayal of the Party and country.'

Yet another story given out by Chinese officials was that Zhou tried to arrest Lin Biao on suspicion of foul play against Chen Yi. In the course of resisting arrest, Lin was killed by a carelessly ignited grenade, leaving only his son, deputy chief of the air force, to make the flight to Russia.

Twelve years later an even more extraordinary version of Lin's plot and death was published, claiming to be based on official documents, in which Zhou is seen blackmailing Lin Biao's son-in-law by threatening to circulate information about his reactionary Guomindang landlord father – as a result of which Lin's plot was revealed to Mao before it could be carried out. Zhou then participated in what he called the 'last supper' for Lin at Mao's residence, where they drank 480-year-old rice wine and ate succulent tendons of tiger before waving Lin off to his death by mortar fire on the wooded driveway to Mao's villa. There is no way of knowing which version, if any, is correct.

In any event Lin was now dead, and the major threat to Zhou's succession to Mao was removed. The delighted French Ambassador undiplomatically toasted the Premier at an embassy dinner party with the words: 'The hour of Zhou Enlai has come, and it is a good hour for China.' Those were certainly the feelings of a very large number of Chinese.

The timing of Lin's death was awkward, however. There were rumours that Guangdong Province might secede, after its leading generals were quickly purged for their pro-Lin sentiments. It needed all Zhou's skill to ensure that no touchy Communist 'warlord' or PLA provincial commander felt elbowed out by his rivals. And, of course, Zhou still had to cope with his only slightly less distasteful allies, the radical Maoists symbolized by Jiang Qing, Mao's wife, who with Zhang Chunqiao, Yao Wenyuan and Wang Hongwen (all from Shanghai) came to be known as the infamous Gang of Four.

Zhou's programme for rehabilitating his old aides gathered pace, with Liao Chengzhi gaining reinstatement in August, Dong Biwu confirmed as deputy head of state, and with old comrades like Zhu De and Nie Rongzhen back in their old jobs in the Military Commission and nuclear programme again. To win all this while the Gang of Four was still active and powerful took some doing.

But for some of his friends it was too late. In January 1972, Chen Yi died, having never recovered from his Cultural Revolution experiences. 'We should . . . transform our grief into strength,' Zhou said in his funeral oration. After the ceremony Mao remained rooted to the spot, staring vacantly at the wreaths, as if he could not understand why such things had to happen, or perhaps he was lost in some kind of remorse, until Zhou eventually took him by the arm and gently led him away.

'All of us, including myself,' Zhou told American visitors, 'have made mistakes. . . . How can there ever be absolute authority? . . . Mao Zedong may be an authority on some questions, but as to questions that are not in his field, how can he be an authority on them? . . . There is also a question of time. You may be an authority today, but does that mean you are an authority tomorrow?'

This was a frightening time for anyone responsible for China's safety. The country was disunited, and on bad terms with all the powers around it. Who could say what adventures the Lin Biao affair might not have encouraged the Kremlin to consider? 'Suppose,' Zhou put it to American journalists, 'the Soviet army goes straight to the northern bank of the Yellow River, the Americans go to the southern banks of the Yangzi River [presumably from Taiwan or Indochina] while Japan invades and occupies Chingdao in Shandong and India joins in and invades Tibet?' He told another visiting writer: 'We have made full preparations to be attacked by all four at once.'

Kissinger came again to Beijing in October to work out the final details for Richard Nixon's visit to China. He found an English-language propaganda bulletin in his guest room calling on the people of the world to 'overthrow the American imperialists'. He gave it back to the Chinese with the dry remark that it must have been left there by the previous occupant. When Zhou received the American party a few hours later, he explained away the leaflet as 'firing an empty cannon', and said that it was China's actions rather than its rhetoric which warranted attention. Meanwhile he had been doing his homework. He had seen the film *Patton* after hearing that Nixon admired it, and, as usual, he had memorized so much about the background and careers of the American government Sinologists whom Kissinger brought with him that they all went away feeling warm and flattered.

This time Kissinger was struck by Zhou's 'extraordinary grasp of the relationship of events. He was a dedicated ideologue, but he used the faith that had sustained him through decades of struggle to discipline a passionate nature into one of the most acute and unsentimental assessments of reality that I have ever encountered.' Zhou knew that statesmen cannot invent reality, and often quoted the old Chinese proverb: 'The helmsman must guide the boat by using the waves, otherwise it will be submerged by them.'

Kissinger fell, however, for an old diplomatic trick which Zhou played. They had agreed that the American draft for the communiqué to be issued in China during Nixon's visit could serve as a basis for discussion, so the Americans were expecting no trouble about it. At the last moment, however, Zhou came with a 'scorching one-hour speech' delivered, he claimed, at the express direction of Mao himself. The American approach was not acceptable, he said, and unless the communiqué set forth the fundamental differences between the two sides it would be 'untruthful'. It was wrong to pretend to illusory agreement, better to face the reality of discord. Kissinger would have none of this, but then came a well-timed break for roast duck. With stomachs duly filled, Zhou put a new draft on the table which stated the Chinese position but left blank the space for the Americans to insert theirs. Kissinger was at first appalled, but then came to be attracted by the novelty of the idea and accepted it.

At this point Kissinger scored his compensating success over Zhou with his famous formulation that: 'The United States acknowledges that all Chinese on either side of the Taiwan Straits maintain that there is but one China. The US government does not challenge that position.' This was actually lifted from a State Department document of the 1950s, but Zhou was impressed. Although that did not actually commit the United States to a change in policy, it seemed to say exactly what the Chinese wanted. So they agreed on the main outline of what was to become the Shanghai Communiqué.

When Kissinger left for the airport, Zhou said to him in English: 'Come back soon for the joy of talking!'

A few hours later the United Nations General Assembly voted for the Chinese People's Republic to take China's seat in the UN, ending twenty-two years of boycott. This was a deserved triumph for Zhou, after his sustained diplomacy. John Service, the American diplomat who had been with the Dixie Mission negotiating with Zhou in Yan'an all those years ago, happened to be visiting Zhou in Beijing that day, and he joked that he hoped to see the Prime Minister when he came to New York. Zhou turned very quickly with that sudden positive movement that he often displayed. 'Never, never,' he said. 'As long as there is a Taiwan Ambassador in Washington, you will never see me in the United States.' He knew the limits of his successes and the length of ground that was left to cover.

One of the factors in China's success at the UN was, of course, the growing acceptance of China's claims among the Third World nations. As he had repeatedly proclaimed during his trips to Africa and Asia, and as he told visitors from Zambia in 1971: 'We are all developing countries and we all belong to the Third World.' But his solidarity was a responsible one. When a deputy for Colonel Qadafi of Libya came to China to buy an atom bomb – 'just a tactical one' – Zhou informed him politely that they were not for sale. China would gladly help in the research, but for the actual production of such a weapon the Libyans would have to rely on themselves.

On 17 February 1972 President Richard Nixon himself stepped out of his plane into the cold air of Beijing winter, the first American President to visit China. When Nixon was halfway down the steps, Zhou Enlai, standing hatless at the foot of the ramp, began to clap. Nixon paused for a moment, and then returned the Chinese gesture. At the bottom Nixon extended his hand. 'When our hands met,' he wrote afterwards, 'one era ended and another began.' Zhou stood with his pelvis tilted forward slightly, shoulders back and head and neck firmly erect, the whole posture giving the appearance of slight casualness, a kind of 'oh-its-you!' attitude, contrasting markedly with Nixon's overeager air. Zhou's comment as they drove into the city together was: 'Your handshake came over the vastest ocean in the world – twenty-five years of no communication.' The ghost of Dulles was very much present.

It was the crowning achievement of Zhou's long career as a diplomat to have enticed the most powerful political leader in the world, head of a nation which for so long had been implacably hostile to Chinese communism, not only to pay an official visit to China – which his government did not even recognize – and negotiate on outstanding bilateral issues, but even to regard the event in the same highflown language used by Zhou himself, as a breakthrough of joyous proportions in international relations.

They soon relaxed into the usual banter of such occasions. Kissinger's secret visits and his droll suggestion that his absences should be explained away as having romantic reasons provided obvious material for wisecracks. Nixon said that, as President, he would get into trouble if he used girls as a cover. 'Especially,' Zhou added quickly, 'during an election.'

That the trip to China might be part of Nixon's re-election strategy was obviously in Zhou's mind. When the President remarked that the Chinese orchestra was playing a song he had chosen for his inauguration three years earlier, Zhou raised his glass immediately with the toast: 'Here's to your next inauguration!' He was also delighted to have scooped Nixon from the Russians. 'You have come here first,' he boasted, 'and Moscow is carrying on like anything!'

Nixon was not quite so enthusiastic as Kissinger about Zhou's personality, and the fifty hours they spent in each other's company gave him insights into the Chinese Premier's limitations. Despite his 'brilliance and dynamism', Nixon found Zhou's perspective 'badly distorted by his rigid ideological frame of reference.'

For example, Nixon noted, Zhou saw the French intervention in the American War of Independence as having been made by volunteers under Lafayette rather than by the French government. Again, he saw Lincoln as a man who had prevailed because he had the people on his side – whereas Nixon perceived him as a total pragmatist who had fought the Civil War and liberated slaves as a tactical military manoeuvre (not, for example, freeing slaves in the northern border states).

But at the level of political confidences, the two got on famously. Nixon disclosed to the Premier that 'our State Department leaks like a sieve', which Zhou reciprocated by explaining that the acting Chinese Foreign Minister Ji Pengfei 'has his limitations'. But Zhou was baffled by Nixon's giving him a pen with which he had signed into law some minor bill or other. He had never heard of this custom and did not like it when Kissinger explained – it sounded too much like interference in American internal affairs. Perhaps the Americans could give him another pen instead, after they got home?

The big question was Taiwan. Kissinger's formulation for the communiqué allowed the two governments to come together without having Taiwan as an obstacle, although a full solution to the question of Taiwan remained on the agenda. 'We, being so big,' Zhou counselled, 'have already let the Taiwan issue remain for twenty-two years, and can still afford to let it wait there for a time.' And that is where the position remains even today.

At the final banquet Nixon told Zhou: 'There is no reason for us to be enemies. Neither of us seeks the territory of the other; neither of us seeks domination over the other; neither of us seeks to stretch out our hands and rule the world.' Zhou echoed him in a more subdued vein – possibly influenced by anxiety among his colleagues that he should not take detente with the United States too far.

Seen as a *coup de théâtre* that would vastly increase China's bargaining power with the nation from which she had most to fear, namely the Soviet Union, this rapprochement with the United States was brilliant. Seen as a demonstration to restive non-Communists in China that the United States, for all its self-righteousness, was not going to insist on communism being swept away before talking to the Chinese government and helping the Chinese economy, it was astonishing. Seen as a vindication of the hopes, so long nursed by modernistic Chinese from Chairman Mao downwards, that contact would some time be regained with the country that had, after all, done more to modernize the world than any other, it was moving. And seen as vivid proof that China was no longer isolated, for all her historical peculiarities and ideological rigidities, it was a towering success for Zhou Enlai. It was in no small measure responsible for the visibly greater ascendancy of Zhou in the Chinese political spectrum at this time, contrasting with a decline in the power and prestige of the Gang of Four.

One of the minor themes which recurred in Zhou's meetings with Nixon concerned his own age. He was particularly struck by the youth of the people in Nixon's entourage. The Presidential aide Dwight Chapin, for example, was then only thirty-one and looked less. 'We have too many elderly people in our leadership,' Zhou complained. 'So on this point we should learn from you.' Although he remained alert and attentive during the long negotiating sessions (when some of the youngsters on both sides got drowsy, especially after the duck), Zhou occasionally faltered. When they went to the opera (devised by Jiang Qing), he mentioned to Nixon that seven years earlier Khrushchev had come to the same opera and sat in the same seat. But suddenly he flushed and corrected himself. 'I mean Kosygin, not Khrushchev.'

The Americans noticed that Zhou often took some small white pills, which they guessed were for his high blood pressure – though he confided to Nixon that it was a case of bronchitis. At one point Zhou expressed the hope that both Nixon and Kissinger would continue in office so that the fruits of these negotiations could be fully harvested. But, he added, 'various changes may be bound to come. For example, if I should suddenly die of a heart attack you would also have to deal with a different counterpart.'

And indeed Zhou's health was precarious. A few days after Nixon's departure from China, Zhou's doctor broke the news to him that he had incurable cancer. Everybody noticed the change in the Premier. 'Zhou is getting almost transparent,' one of his Western aides said at dinner one night. 'He works too hard. How can we stop him working?' Zhou confided to a visitor that his doctors did not want him to fly any more. And the BBC correspondent, Anthony Lawrence, observed how Zhou's eyes, which used to dance – 'they were so intensely alive' – had become 'dull, half-shut'.

Yet Zhou did not give up his pleasures. He continued to recommend *maotai* wine by personal example, and told American visitors in July: 'You are all afraid of cancer, so you Americans don't smoke, and your cigarette packets carry a warning, but it hasn't yet been shown that smoking shortens your life.' In the same month he told the head of Beijing University to develop a department of theoretical science, and followed this up a few weeks later with a letter urging that there should be no further delay in strengthening the study of basic theory in the Science Academy.

Small things can weigh heavy in such a mood. On the evening of 3 August Zhou's car knocked over a girl cyclist. He sent her for an X-ray, telephoned solicitously for the result, ordered the police not to trouble her, replaced her torn clothing and sent no fewer than three aides next day to inquire how she was.

But in the same month Zhou was still astute enough to lay a trap for Jiang Qing by recommending to her Roxane Witke, an American Sinologist – 'young and enthusiastic for China' – who came to Beijing with a project to interview Chinese women. Zhou led her to the number one woman, doubtless anticipating – correctly – that the lady, given such an opportunity, would say too much.

In October 1972 Zhou read to some American guests a poem by another famous Chinese Prime Minister written in the third century AD:

> Though it lives longer than most,
> The tortoise, too, comes to an end. . . .
> The aged hero has the wish
> To aim high at the last. . . .
> Heaven may not decide how long
> The span of human life will be.

If his focus became sharpened, in his extremity, on the essential agenda for the long term, he could also be realistic about just how long that term was going to be for China's advance towards the kind of American standards he had been able to observe in Nixon's entourage.

'China has made some progress,' he told an American friend, 'but we still have a long, long way to go even to approach the material standards of your country. It will certainly never happen in our lifetime – nor, in all likelihood, for several centuries.'

In 1973 Zhou further consolidated his political position at the Tenth Party Congress, where the younger Cultural Revolutionaries in the leadership skirmished with him for political preferment. A newspaper article criticized him in veiled terms: 'The class enemies in society, and in particular the chieftain of the opportunist line in the Party, have always attempted to revive Confucianism in order to prevent the establishment of the revolutionary line of Chairman Mao.' (In the symbolism of the day, Confucius represented Zhou to many Chinese, and it was easy to get the press to publish articles criticizing Confucius.) But the old sleight of hand was still there. In prosecuting the concluding case against Lin Biao, Zhou declared that his old enemy had not only capitulated to Soviet revisionism, but betrayed himself as a rightist rather than as the ultra-leftist that earlier analyses had made him out to be. It was Lin who had turned his back on socialism in order to develop industrial production, not Zhou! It was only needed for Zhou a little later to link the 'criticize-Confucius' and 'criticize-Lin' campaigns together to take the sting out of the Gang of Four's attack. He knew the value of rewriting the charge sheet after your opponent is defeated.

In the Congress photographs Mao is flanked by Zhou (taking the seat formerly filled by Lin Biao) and Wang Hongwen, the youngest of the Gang of Four, from Shanghai: Mao looks to Zhou as if to indicate his approval of Zhou's being next in line. But the cunning old Chairman until his dying day prevented any potential successor from enjoying total security, and continued to give tacit support to Jiang Qing and her Gang of Four on some matters while approving Zhou's line on others. He ostentatiously absented himself from the Congress discussions, while Zhou restored that peppery little autocrat, Deng Xiaoping, to the Politburo. The man who only a few years ago had been reviled as the odious lieutenant of capitalist-roader Liu Shaoqi was now presented as the saviour to come. Zhou admired his ability and could live with his pragmatism, and he was popular with the army.

The Premier adroitly told the Congress that its policy discussions had been pre-empted. 'Chairman Mao has laid down for our Party,' he explained, 'the basic line of policies for the entire historical period of socialism and also specific lines of policies for specific work.' There was no need for argument, and no one could accuse him of denying Maoism. But by inference he indicated how Maoism had failed its promise: 'Economically, ours is still a poor and developing country.' In fact Zhou was reverting to his excellent but largely ignored policies of the 1950s. 'Planning and coordination must be strengthened, rational rules and regulations improved and both central and local initiative further brought into full play.' And the new constitution omitted the claim that Mao Thought was the Marxism–Leninism of the present era. Mao was being quietly brought down to lifesize again, however flattering Zhou's personal references to him sounded.

Only in Zhou's report on the international situation did a defensive note creep in, suggesting that his dalliance with Nixon was still not appreciated by some Party members.

> Wind in the tower
> Heralds the approaching storm.

He quoted this poem to show that there was 'a great disorder on the earth' which China should welcome because it threw her enemies into confusion. The disorder made it important for Third World countries to form a united front against the two superpowers, a theme Zhou continued to stress during his last years. China's approach to the USA was only a tactic in this long strategy: 'Relaxation is a temporary phenomenon, and great disorder will continue.' Zhou quoted Lenin on Soviet Russia's Brest–Litovsk peace treaty with Germany in 1918 as a precedent for the compromises China found it useful to make with the Americans, and he found it necessary to point out that Lenin had been in a minority of one in the Council of People's Commissars on that question. Was Zhou's majority for the Nixon detente too small for comfort? He left his Chinese listeners with the kind of image they appreciated: 'China is an attractive piece of meat coveted by all, but this piece of meat is very tough and for years no one has been able to bite into it.'

It was also in 1973 that Zhou made his formal peace with the surprisingly large number of Western experts living in China, most of whom earned a living by helping to edit and translate propaganda material for publication in foreign languages – some of them had become more Maoist than the Maoists and had unwisely taken part in the Cultural Revolution, others of whom had been more circumspect but had suffered from the anti-foreign chauvinism of the Red Guards. On Women's Day Zhou gave them a big reception and conceded that many evil things had been done to them during the recent past; on behalf of the government he apologized and promised redress, walking round the tables shaking hands and hugging these foreign friends. Typically, he pleaded with them to regard their ordeals as a fulfilment, because they were an organic stage in the creation of a new world in China. The only one whom Zhou would not forgive was Sidney Rittenberg, the American leftist writer, who was 'a very bad person' and had 'duped' him in the Cultural Revolution.

Zhou acknowledged the existence of chauvinism and racialism in the way that foreigners were treated in China. 'What is wrong,' he asked, 'with a Chinese and a foreigner getting married?' To stand in the way of such a thing would prevent China from making her proper contribution to mankind. But everybody knew that a vast majority of the officials in the government and the Party who were responsible for carrying out the day-to-day decisions on these matters felt differently.

Out of interest in devising a world strategy to curb the superpowers, especially the Soviet Union, Zhou now became an unexpected champion of European unity. 'America and Russia are not to be trusted,' he advised Dutch visitors. 'Europe must build up her own strength.' He hosted President Georges Pompidou of France and dozens of other European luminaries in the hope of curbing their intra-European bickerings and strengthening their defences against Russia.

It was bad luck for Zhou that Nixon's Watergate crisis rendered his effort with the American President largely wasted (in terms of the personal relationship with a foreign head of government which the Chinese so value). In October he manfully told the *New York Times* that Watergate would not affect Sino-American relations, was an internal affair of the Americans and was not even known about in China because it was not reported in the Chinese press. It was better not to discuss it, he believed, but he hoped nevertheless that Nixon would overcome his difficulties.

When Kissinger came for another visit that autumn he found Zhou somewhat insecure. 'The old bite and sparkle were missing.' But Kissinger himself was unusually tactless. Apparently ill briefed about the 'anti-Confucius campaign' from which his host was still suffering politically, Kissinger observed that Maoist China was surely still a Confucian polity. Such philosophical sallies would have delighted Zhou a year or two earlier, but this was too close to the bone. Zhou delivered an agitated rebuttal even before the poor interpreter could translate Kissinger's remark. It was the only time that he lost his composure with Kissinger.

This was the strangest period in Zhou's relationship with Mao. It was almost as if Mao backed his actual policies but begrudged him the credit. The Chairman's feelings towards his own wife, Jiang Qing, implementer of the radical half of his schizophrenic mind, seemed equally ambiguous.

At some point during the autumn of 1973 Mao learned of Jiang's interviews with Roxane Witke, and of what seemed to be her obvious ploy of projecting her political personality in the way that he himself had done back in the 1930s through the enthusiastic pen of Edgar Snow. Mao apparently decided to divorce Jiang, but Zhou realized that this would throw the radicals in China into a complete uproar and there would be no containing them, so he vigorously opposed an act which would so publicly advertise the disunity of the Party and might sting Jiang into desperate measures. A few weeks later Mao wrote a bitter dissociating letter to his wife which contained the sad remark, 'I do envy the Zhou Enlai marriage.'

Not only was Zhou Enlai's marriage faultless, but the way in which he kept his relatives from doing anything which might conceivably be construed as trading on his own eminence was extraordinary. His nephew wrote to say that after five years of exile in the rural areas he would like to come back to his pre-Cultural Revolution life in the city. Zhou refused to help on the ground that he could not be seen to favour his own family.

Early in 1974 the leftists behind Jiang Qing intensified their effort to topple Zhou – to them simply an old man in the Prime Minister's office who represented the past. Under cover of the campaign to resist the teachings of Confucius, the Gang of Four became more and more audacious in saying things that could only have been meant to apply to Zhou Enlai, and they gloated over his suffering.

Once, when Zhou was conversing with a foreign guest, Jiang Qing declared provocatively: 'I have never studied the "four books" and the "five classics" [tomes with which anyone of Zhou Enlai's education would of course be well acquainted]. Probably the Premier is the only one among us here who has.'

Zhou evaded the trap by asking Zhang, the best educated of the Gang of Four, whether he had not studied these classics, only to receive the mendacious reply: 'No, I haven't. Now, I have to study them in order to destroy them.'

But 'the greatest Confucianist mandarin of them all, who is negating the Cultural Revolution' (as Zhou was labelled), was able to turn the tables on the Gang of Four by the stratagem of taking command of the campaign against Confucius himself and identifying it with the campaign against Lin Biao's ideas. Zhou accomplished this so vigorously that he took the wind out of the Maoists' sails and raised doubts in everybody's minds as to whether he really was the target of wrath.

Yet some of the damage could not be undone. Many of the cultural contacts which Zhou had encouraged with Western countries were spoiled. The Italian film-maker Michelangelo Antonioni, who had been invited with Zhou's support to film in China, and several artists who could no longer defend themselves, like Beethoven and Schubert, fell victim to attack. Even Zhou's policy of importing complete factories to start new industries was disparaged as an example of the 'worship of things foreign' and 'a slavish comprador philosophy'.

Nevertheless, the Gang of Four had to concede that Zhou was immoveable, although they succeeded in robbing him of some fruits of his victory by making it in one way or another difficult for him to schedule the daily conversation with Mao on which he relied so much politically.

During the spring of 1974 Zhou's health deteriorated and he was sent to hospital. In June he suffered one heart attack and in July a second. He went on working from his bed, and continued to receive foreign dignitaries – though no longer for the old three- or six-hour conversations on which he used to thrive.

Characteristically he fought his way back to a public appearance at the Army Day reception in July, moving rather slowly and overstraining himself so that on 9 September he was back in hospital. There he saw Senator Mike Mansfield a few days later and told him: 'The door between our two countries should never have been closed.' The regrets of what-might-have-been were uppermost in his mind.

Four days later General Gowon of Nigeria was told that Zhou was recovering from an operation. The foreign press claimed that Zhou had stomach cancer, but the Foreign Ministry denied it. *The Times* of London reported that he was being treated with cobalt radiation.

The diminutive Deng Xiaoping tried mightily to fill Zhou's chair when President Bhutto and other foreign leaders called to visit Mao in his study. Zhou's enemies rallied hopefully. The Gang of Four called on its followers to write articles against 'the present-day Confucian'. One provincial newspaper duly denounced 'a landlord element who constantly pretends to be wholly honest and sincere . . . but subverts the youth with his false "benevolence".' A film was produced in which a trusted old Communist peasant (Mao) was led astray by a clever convert who came from outside (a reference to Zhou's training in France).

Wang Hongwen, the youngest of the Gang of Four, rushed to Mao's southern retreat near Changsha to inform him of a new 'plot'. 'Although the Premier is seriously sick,' he said, 'he is "busy" finding people to talk to. Those who often visit the Premier's residence include comrades Peng Zhen, Ye Jianying and Li Xiannian' – all Party technocrats of long experience who had been dislodged during the Cultural Revolution, and were now rein-stated by Zhou Enlai. But Mao did not react to this tale-telling.

A Japanese visitor was told in December by Deng Xiaoping that Zhou had been in hospital for eight months, and was being informed only of very important matters. Yet there was one last piece of business which the Premier was determined to conclude in his own inimitable way. The Fourth National People's Congress was scheduled for the middle of January 1975, and this was Zhou's last opportunity to cement into place, beyond the grasp of the Gang of Four's itchy and destructive fingers, a new government machine capable of carrying China into its next phase of development. To do this Zhou had to make his last airflight, to Changsha, to win Mao's imprimatur. 'Emaciated, his hair turned grey,' an airline official recalled, 'he had difficulty in walking and his hands trembled. He needed help to get into the plane.' Asked about his health, he replied: 'One must fight it . . . I haven't flown for a year, and I've spent eight months lying in bed, but I'm much better now.' He could hardly unwrap the sweets which the stewardess gave him, so much did his hands shake. But on 26 December Mao evidently approved Zhou's draft constitution and new proposed appointments, while reserving for himself the outlet of issuing 'important instructions' on theory to keep radical ideas alive without interfering with state business.

Zhou's Congress report on 13 January 1975 was his political testament. He justified the Cultural Revolution as anti-bourgeois and he did not set the economy above politics, since class struggle and social revolution were still necessary. 'Only when we do well in revolution, is it possible to do well in production.' He proceeded to outline a breathtaking programme to 'accomplish the comprehensive modernization of agriculture, industry, national defence and science and technology before the end of the century, so that our national economy will be advancing in the front ranks of the world.' These were the so-called Four Modernizations, with which China has been concerned ever since. The new constitution guaranteed that in each commune, the basic unit of rural life, there would be the maximum incentive for the smallest sub-unit (the production team) and security for private plots and private sideline occupations, thus ensuring a mixed-economy approach to China's development.

It was the first National People's Congress for ten years, and Zhou drew attention to the interruptions of the Cultural Revolution by going back to the early 1960s to cite Chairman Mao's pronunciations then as authority for the new policies of the 1970s. In practical terms Zhou's triumph meant that most of the army commanders had rallied behind his government bureaucrats to support a blueprint for China's future that required steady and palpable progress more than ideological effervescence. Deng Xiaoping was named First Vice-Premier and effective deputy to Zhou, and also Chief of General Staff. Mao remained aloof, preferring not to lend his legitimizing presence to the affair, though he was well enough to receive a leading politician from West Germany while the Congress was actually in session.

This was probably Zhou's biggest regret, raising as it did the possibility that the Gang of Four still had enough hold on Mao to upset these new plans. Most people still assumed at this point that Zhou would outlive Mao. The Chairman was four years older than Zhou and had not, on the whole, been as healthy as the Premier. Yet Zhou must have now known of the death sentence which his own doctors had pronounced upon him, and wondered what would happen if Mao survived him. Could the carefully constructed edifice under Deng Xiaoping, whom Mao disliked, stand up to the assaults of a senile Mao manipulated by his wife and the rest of the Gang of Four?

Zhou was now being treated by foreign as well as Chinese specialists, and in February 1975 he had another operation. He told his doctors afterwards that they should do more investigation of the incidence of lung cancer among

288

the tin miners of Yunnan in southern China. In the final stage of his illness his life was prolonged for several months by a uraemia prescription using Chinese herbal medicines invented by a young doctor who subsequently defected to the United States. Zhou would not have his own barber in for a shave or haircut in the terminal phase of his illness, because it would upset them both too much.

Foreign visitors streamed in. Premier Kukrit Pramoj of Thailand was given a stirring message by the dying Premier. 'Go back home and tell everyone, especially your children and grandchildren, that China will never attack Thailand.'

Kukrit was quick-witted enough to ask Zhou to commit the pledge to paper for him. 'My hand shakes,' Zhou sadly confessed. 'I am too ill to write it down.' Yet it was an agreement about diplomatic relations with Thailand on which he put his last shaky official signature. That was in July.

A few weeks later he was informed, ironically by a foreign cancer specialist who had come from abroad to treat him, that a new political campaign had been launched in China against the old romantic novel *Water Margin*. Mao used to admire this book, but now saw it as 'a portrayal of capitulationism'. Zhou realized how cut off he was from political currents, that only from a foreigner did he learn what was going on. It was his effective political demise. He would no longer be consulted, even by Mao.

'I am afraid my illness is beyond cure,' he commented.

There was another kind of consulting, which was not so welcome but which he had to endure. The Party had a supervisory committee for Zhou's medical treatment which was headed by Wang Hongwen of the Gang of Four. 'Premier Zhou,' one of the doctors later recalled, 'was hounded to the day of his death. . . . They would allow him no rest. . . . Even while we were giving him a blood transfusion, Jiang Qing would ring up and *order* that the transfusion be stopped while she talked nonsense to him, calling it "matters of state".' This doctor alleged that treatment recommended by the best cancer specialists in China was not followed.

But the old man would not bow out. He appeared, incredibly, at the Beijing Hotel in the centre of the capital one day in November 1975 for a meal. But did he rest? Oh no, there were documents which he pulled out from his case to read!

On 31 December 1975, he was back in hospital for the last time. Two poems by Mao were published that day which the Chairman had written on the eve of the Cultural Revolution, and Zhou spent many of his last hours listening to them. One was about revisiting Jinggangshan, where Mao had established his guerrilla base in the 1920s. It ended with the couplet:

> Nothing is hard in this world
> If you dare to scale the heights.

The second was an image of the Sino-Soviet relationship, lampooning Khrushchev-style goulash communism, and it ended with the phrase: 'Look, the world is being turned upside down.'

At one point in his sleeplessness, induced by pain, it is said that Zhou uttered the word 'poems'. Everyone at his bedside realized that he meant Mao's poems, so they took turns at reading them out. At the end of the second one Zhou laughed out loud – the first time he had been able to laugh for some time.

This story may have been invented by his followers, who wanted to counter the Gang of Four's propaganda about Zhou being hostile to Mao. Or, if it was true, it may have been Zhou himself, play-acting to the end, trying to ensure the same result – and in which case, there was doubtless a strong fellow-feeling for Mao's gusty idealism, which in its better moments had after all inspired Zhou himself.

But the same cannot be said of a document with which Zhou's very last hours became lumbered, an alleged political will and testament which he supposedly dictated to Deng Yingchao from his deathbed, but which shows traces of having been invented by Soviet or Guomindang propagandists. For Zhou to say at the end, after all his careful efforts, that 'an error like the Cultural Revolution must not be repeated', or to describe normalized relations with the Soviet Union as 'the great diplomatic target', is highly improbable.

It is a little more difficult to deal with the story, equally unverifiable, that Mao Zedong spent several hours with Zhou in the hospital during his final days. One report has it that he was there until only half an hour before the death. Other stories said precisely the opposite, that Mao had snubbed his old colleague, just as he had done at the Fourth National People's Congress but more painfully, by not coming to his bedside at all.

There is even a description of how at the last moment Zhou in agony sang the 'Internationale' in a very low voice to his wife sitting by his bed.

That is as may be. But that he died finally at 9.57 a.m. on 8 January 1976, at the age of seventy-eight, the best loved, the most accomplished, the most successful and the most unerring political leader in twentieth-century China, is fact. The curtain is not to be lifted on the private penultimate days, and neither his poems nor his singing nor his testament are to be taken literally. They may only show that this life was too important to other politicians and to the ordinary people of China to be left to be snuffed out without advantage to someone.

Epilogue

As the man died, his legend was born. The Gang of Four could hardly believe their luck in having their most powerful opponent leave this world before their reluctant patron, Chairman Mao. The first battle therefore was over the corpse itself. Could it be made to disappear without fuss?

Six days of official mourning, minimal in the circumstances, were declared, and in the middle of them a small ambulance, white with blue stripes, took the simple black coffin from the hospital through the wide streets of Beijing, followed by only a few cars carrying Deng Yingchao and some old comrades. There was no guard of honour, no music, only silent citizens – some say as many as a million and a half – who came, having learned through word of mouth, to watch the late Premier pass. In the cold winter air, twelve degrees below zero, of that sorrowful evening, they waited dumbly.

The ambulance, draped with black and yellow streamers and laden with wreaths, circled round Tienanmen Square and then drove down the Avenue of Eternal Peace towards the Western Hills and the setting sun to Babaoshan, to the cemetery of revolutionary heroes.

It was rumoured that cremation had been ordered by the Politburo to prevent Zhou's role in Chinese history from being properly commemorated, perhaps as a prelude to disavowing his policies. His widow had to leave her car to assure the people that Zhou himself had asked to be cremated. There was no funeral announcement, but many Chinese came with traditional mourning bunches of white silk-paper chrysanthemums. The body had lain in state for only two days, and 10,000 favoured 'representatives of the masses' had been allowed to pay their respects. (Mao's body was given very different treatment nine months later.)

Zhou's ashes were brought back to the old Imperial City to rest for three days in a magnificent hall where emperors had once worshipped. Chinese and foreigners alike walked through the vermilion and yellow courtyards to climb the stone steps where they could stand in silence for a few seconds before the carved red-lacquer casket containing the ashes, half-covered by the Party flag and with a photograph of Zhou (aged fifty) behind.

The ashes went next to the Great Hall of the People, where Zhou had spent so much of his working life, for a memorial ceremony on 15 January. Here Deng Xiaoping read a eulogy to a small group of officials and delegates. Mao was conspicuous by his absence, although he had attended a similar ceremony for Chen Yi and other old comrades, had received a good ten foreign visitors in the preceding weeks, all of whom reported him very much alive, and would receive Richard Nixon for almost two hours a few days afterwards. Then came an order to end the period of mourning, and foreign visitors were asked to do nothing in Zhou's honour – 'out of consideration for Chairman Mao's feelings'.

The final act was the scattering of Zhou's ashes, following his request, in the rivers, lakes and seas of China and on its land – a revolutionary stipulation breaking the fetters of deep-seated tradition in Chinese life. (Even Taiwan was not forgotten since part of the ashes was strewn in the Taiwan Straits.) Zhou had specifically stated that there should be no memorial built for him.

Deng Xiaoping's funeral oration acquired a significance, since it turned out to be his last major public appearance for several years. Whereas Mao had stood fast against serious attempts by his wife and the Gang of Four to get rid of Zhou, he had no such scruples about Deng, whose opinion of socialism had been advertised by his famous dictum that it did not matter whether the cat was black or white as long as it caught the mouse. The Gang of Four propaganda machine swung eagerly into action. A complete set of revisionist programmes lay behind the Four Modernizations, it announced. Zhou had been a 'capitalist roader' – and much more in the same vein. But Zhou's admirers retaliated with astonishing demonstrations of affection during the annual Qing Ming festival in March-April, when the dead are remembered. More than 10,000 wreaths for the late Premier were placed on the Heroes Monument in Tienanmen Square. 'Qing Ming is for ghosts,' the Party propagandists vainly exhorted, and commemorating the dead was 'an outmoded custom'. But still home-made wreaths in white, red and yellow continued to pour into the square.

'He left no inheritance,' one eulogy went, 'he had no children, he has no grave, he left no remains. His ashes were scattered over the mountains and rivers of our land. It seems he has left us nothing, but . . . he has hundreds of millions of children and grandchildren and all China's soil is his tomb.'

Soon the base of the monument was smothered with wreaths piled fifty feet from the ground. Thousands of poems were read and posted during this spontaneous commemoration:

[A generation of heroes created our world;
Millions of people are worried;
Who will succeed them?]

Or:

Ah! This is the hope
Our beloved Premier placed in us
His millions of sons and daughters.
And this is the ideal
To which I, a young Communist,
Will dedicate my life.

Or again:

The ashes are not yet cold,
Song oppresses the sounds of sadness.
There is an empty seat on the stage. . . .

Some admirers of Zhou sensed what might follow:

His work is yet unconsummated:
Demons run amok
But where to seek another pillar to shoulder the skies?
Throughout the land,
Eight hundred million share
The same endless thoughts,
The same intense emotions.

By 5 April the radicals had had enough. They sent their men in just before dawn to tear down the wreaths and repress by force this unwanted commemoration. It looked as though the Gang of Four had won, but not across the board – because it was Hua Guofeng, a relatively unknown recent arrival from provincial leadership, whom Mao chose as compromise Premier, in preference either to Deng Xiaoping or the Gang of Four candidate, Zhang Chunqiao. When the Chairman himself was carried off the stage at the end of the year, however, the forces of moderation and the right banded together to make a definitive exclusion of radicals for the next several years – under the energetic leadership of the ebullient Deng Xiaoping and the banner of Zhou's Four Modernizations.

On the first anniversary of Zhou's death thousands took his portrait, draped in black, to Tienanmen Square to swear fidelity. 'Zhou is alive!' some of them shouted. 'He is among us!'

A Summing-up

Zhou Enlai is often portrayed as a brilliant middle-class student who wandered into the Marxist camp by accident and then spent his life passively implementing the extreme policies of his proletarian comrades – but never threatening their supremacy in terms of power because he felt psychologically inhibited from running a Communist Party himself.

Zhou was certainly unusual in the Chinese Communist movement because of his sophisticated and Westernized urban ways, and to some extent he resigned himself to being of marginal influence in policy making, at least in public – though probably less so in the privacy of committee meetings.

But the full picture is more complicated. Explanations must begin with childhood, where Zhou's singular experiences go some way to elucidate his subsequent uniqueness on the Chinese political scene. As James MacDonald, the British Sinologist, once perceptively commented on the published interpretations of Zhou Enlai, his diplomatic abilities cannot be attributed merely to his Chinese cultural tradition but 'must have other origins – probably in early life. In finding them, we might also find the root of Zhou's self-abnegation, . . . and with it the reason why he chose communism.'

Like most Chinese, Zhou was brought up in one of those large family households within which he and his parents constituted only one sub-unit, so that there was sufficient support to ensure a minimum collective security for everyone. Whatever crises might occur, someone would help. Within that communal protection, however, Zhou was dashed by heartbreaking losses and rejections, firstly by his natural parents giving him up when he was only a few months old, then by his adoptive father dying before he could come to know him, and later at the age of ten by the deaths in quick succession of his two mothers. While it is unwise, because of the over-arching nature of the Chinese

294

family unit, to place an ambitious Freudian interpretation on all this, it seems obvious that Zhou must in his early childhood have come to miss the availability of an exclusive father figure. It is legitimate to go on to guess that he probably nursed retrospective anger, particularly against his natural father, who by unhappy chance was the least responsible, the least caring of all four of his parents, and yet was also the one who survived to badger him later in his adult professional career. The hints of later neurosis – the obsessive tidiness and providence, the irritability, the unbelievable devotion to work – may also find their origin here.

The early adult Zhou thus emerges as a patriot and radical, good at manipulating people to his ends. 'You make friends,' he once observed, 'in order to isolate your enemies,' and for the revolution one should be 'ready to play the prostitute'. Despite his universal reputation, in China as well as abroad, as a man of honour, [he resorted, no less than other politicians, to deception as a stratagem of state,] rearranging the evidence, for example, about American airmen shot down over China in the 1950s to make it appear that they were spying, and leading Nehru up the garden path over the Kashmir question. Yet, by the yardstick of his comrades, he stood out as exceptionally honourable.

This radical and patriotic Zhou then lights upon Marxism and takes it to his heart, as the most modern and fashionable doctrine for changing society. Zhou was always inquisitive about the outside world, much more so than Mao or his other Communist colleagues. As Professor Lucian Pye has observed, 'he lived more years abroad than all of his colleagues on the Politburo combined.'

Zhou was also taught by a Westerner at home at a very early age, thanks to his enlightened adoptive mother. He absorbed Western political science as a schoolboy and tried consciously to go to schools or universities which were Western-influenced. It is hardly surprising that he was attracted by Marxism as the latest trend in Western thinking, believing that for a China fallen so low, only the best would do.

Zhou continued to pile up debts to the West throughout his life. He was educated at Dr Zhang Boling's Nankai School with Western help, and then drank at foreign wells in Japan, France, Belgium, Germany and the Soviet Union. Not only that, he made dramatic use of the tiny pockets of Western rule on Chinese soil to escape the attentions of his Chinese opponents. This started with the May Fourth Movement student meetings at his mother-in-law's house in the French Concession in Tianjin in 1919, and was resumed eight years later by the use for revolutionary plotting of the same francophile lady's premises in the French Concession in Shanghai – followed by Zhou's use of Bishop Roots's Wuhan house as an asylum later that year, and his brief recourse to the British flag at Hong Kong after the Nanchang uprising of

1927. Without these recuperative forays into imperialist-ruled territory there would be no life of Zhou Enlai to write:

Then there is Zhou's dependence on the Russians, through the Comintern, for instance in the implententation of the Nanchang uprising. Nanchang was a high point in Zhou's career as a Communist revolutionary. He put his distinctive stamp on it with remarkable determination. In the short term it flopped, but it did establish a new model and momentum for Communist risings which ultimately succeeded. But that was the only moment in a long career when Zhou behaved – and was treated – as if he were on top.

Even before Nanchang Zhou had begun his famous series of refusals to accept the leading position in the Chinese Communist Party. At the Fifth Congress he had surprised his friends by deferring to Chen Duxiu instead of going along with the latter's critics. A year later he supported Li Lisan and in 1930, without joining in the condemnation of Li, he supported the poet Qu Qiubai as leader. Then came the rise of Wang Ming, whom Zhou backed in 1931 while keeping *de facto* direction of Party affairs behind the scenes. Even in the People's Republic, when some groups wanted to make him president over Mao Zedong, he turned them down. Indeed, just as he earned the displeasure of his juniors in the 1930s for not intervening to curb Li Lisan's excesses, precisely the same thing happened with Mao in the 1960s. In the latter case he could plead lack of power, but the former instance suggests there was more – that he felt psychologically handicapped from telling his formal superiors what to do.

Zhou assessed himself as being born for administration, rather than a symbolic supreme representative of the people. He had good occasion to observe how the latter do not last long (there were four of them in as many years in the Chinese Party in 1927–31), and he was a workaholic who was happier filling his time with productive effort rather than politicking which necessarily preoccupies the highest leader.

At Zunyi in 1935, Zhou made his dramatic switch from being Mao's superior and critic to becoming his servant and supporter. Hints of this remarkable relationship, which was to determine the whole shape and course of the People's Republic, had been dropped before; Zhou's way of dealing with the Futian incident at the end of 1930, and his role in the Ningdu conference in 1932 had shown that his criticism of Mao was always tempered, that he sought out things to praise about Mao and that he was never vindictive in the way that Mao's fiercer critics could be. Mao, therefore, had reason to be grateful for Zhou's fairness and flexibility, and he said as much later on.

The immediate problem at Zunyi was military tactics. It was obvious that Mao's guerrilla ideas were then more suitable than Zhou's conventional approach. But Zhou could have sought to ditch Mao once the guerrilla methods had served his turn, or once circumstances brought the Party to a happier, more normal situation. Such could have become the case in Sichuan, in the later phase of the Long March, when Zhang Guotao joined the main force; yet in the end Zhou backed Mao against Zhang. Another moment of choice came during the Rectification Campaign in Yan'an in 1943–45 when Wang Ming was once more a contender for power – but Zhou would not support him. Since Zhang Guotao and Wang Ming had been Zhou's earlier collaborators, and since Mao had always cut an uncouth and ungainly figure in Chinese Communist circles – of the kind one might have expected a man of Zhou's quality to find distasteful, even risible – Zhou's loyalty to Mao after the Long March has to be explained. After a period of enforced companionship Zhou was possibly impressed by Mao's intrinsic authority, his authentic charisma.

In the ten years since the Communists' first experimental urban uprisings in Shanghai and Nanchang, Zhou had learned at first hand of the immensity of the challenge of the peasant revolution in China and the reasons for its primacy over urban revolution. There was no better leader for this than Mao. Zhou may also have found Mao to be more educable than others in many areas of policy and Party work. From the very beginning they complemented each other, as other comrades witnessed when they saw Zhou, having abdicated at Zunyi, calmly assuming the role of deputy to Mao in military leadership in the remaining stages of the Long March.

In the People's Republic Zhou had to cope with threats to Mao's supremacy from Liu Shaoqi and Lin Biao. He proved indispensable to Mao at the very beginning of Liu Shaoqi's chequered career as Mao's deputy – supporting Mao against Liu, for instance, in a crucial vote at Xibaipao in 1948 about whether to resume the civil war against the Guomindang. He backed Mao against Liu in the Hundred Flowers Campaign in 1957 and the Cultural Revolution in the late 1960s, and against Lin Biao in the 1970s. Only in the Great Leap Forward of 1958 did Zhou take direct issue with the Chairman. So strongly did he feel about the economic unwisdom of this policy that he uncharacteristically stage-managed opposition from various quarters, concerting it in such a way that Mao had to give in.

But their partnership survived. With hindsight one can detect some of its unwritten rules. One of these seemed to be that while Zhou enjoyed a very good personal working relationship with Mao, it was left to him to make his own peace with Mao's followers. It was for this reason that Zhou had difficulty in the Rectification Campaign of 1943 and again in the Cultural Revolution in 1967. By the same token Zhou evidently preserved his right, indeed duty, to prevent Mao from degenerating into a deity to be worshipped and manipulated by pressure groups within his following. The record is remarkably full of Zhou's exhortations to the younger generation in the Party to keep their critical faculties alive and not to let Mao, or Mao's myth or image, take over the decision-making which only they individually should accomplish. When Mao was being raised on a pedestal, as was particularly the case in the rectification of 1943–44 and again in the Cultural Revolution, this advice was easily misunderstood and made enemies for Zhou.

Another ground rule was that while Zhou could argue heatedly with the Chairman and even disagree with him in the Central Committee, he would never organize a faction against him. Zhou never had a formal clique of his own in Party politics, though he did have a large, loose following which he could orchestrate to some extent when needed for a particular purpose, as at Wuhan in 1958. An enormous number of people in leadership positions felt loyal to him, not in any old-fashioned sworn blood-brother sense, but simply out of admiration and gratitude for Zhou's past teaching, advice or preferment. This pattern goes back to Paris, where the Communist adherents among the Chinese students were almost all influenced by Zhou – people who subsequently came to fill many important posts in the Chinese government and army, including Deng Xiaoping and Zhu De, whom Zhou inducted into the Party.

Also, although Zhou never commanded an army in the field, he did teach most of the Red generals in the Huangpu Academy and then in later years administered them and provided them with military theory. As a result he was almost never at a loss for a useful military friend in any region of China. These sympathizers were particularly important in the late 1960s, when Zhou came under personal threat from Lin Biao. But they were not people who would support him at all costs, whatever the issues, whatever the circumstances. He never did more than ask them to act on their own consciences, and this, in a Party filled with power factions of various kinds, was important to Mao Zedong.

Zhou could demonstrate that he had no ambition to unseat Mao. He formed no faction, he published no volumes of 'selected works' (the tome published after his death was a miserable ragbag of undistinguished ephemera), he consistently made public deference to Mao's personality and leadership. Edgar Snow described their relationship as symbiotic, while Alain Peyrefitte saw Mao as the Holy Ghost acting through 'the very Roman pontificate of Zhou Enlai'.

Of all the men who had been senior to Mao in the Party hierarchy, only Zhou survived as a continuous member of Mao's team. It would be going too far to say that Mao trusted Zhou, but over the years the two did grow to need each other more and more. Zhou accepted that the vitality of Chinese Communism would have to come from a rural leader who knew how peasants lived and thought. Mao, for his part, needed a diplomat who could represent the movement to the world. Zhou did not flatter Mao, but he was able to appeal to the middle ground of Mao's personality, which on the one hand distrusted sycophancy, yet on the other hand was apprehensive about potential betrayal. Zhou could skilfully assuage these insecurities, while Mao supplied that bedrock father figure of unyielding judgement for which Zhou's childhood had perhaps made him yearn.

In the end their relationship proved resistant even to the stresses of the Cultural Revolution. Zhou's *modus operandi* in Chinese politics was so clear-cut, executed so patently in the interests of the movement rather than for any one clique or individual, that he gained a certain immunity from criticism which enabled him to survive that holocaust. 'No one will believe anything against Zhou,' said Chen Boda, who ought to know, 'not even the old man.'

And so Zhou and Mao were able to dispense with ceremony. A Frenchman recalled an audience he had with Mao where Premier Zhou sat on the next chair, idly turning over the pages of a newspaper and apparently paying no attention to the exchange. 'Imagine anyone reading a newspaper next to De Gaulle,' the visitor commented.

Underneath his high regard for Zhou, however, Mao may well have nursed an envy of his superior skills, graces and knowledge – and that may be why he churlishly stayed away from Zhou's funeral. Mao needed Zhou, he used him and appreciated him; he even came gradually not to feel threatened by him, but he never perhaps liked him. By the end of his own life Mao may have felt that he no longer had to do things which he did not really enjoy, or which did not serve his surviving purposes. But this can only be speculation, and it is quite possible that his wife simply succeeded in keeping him away, as she had every reason to.

Zhou never committed the mistake of elevating policies into principles, or condemning himself to going into opposition or disgrace, when confessing 'errors' would enable him to hold down his job. It is possible that he suffered from a certain self-deprecation, not valuing himself highly, and was for this reason induced to throw his life into the betterment of others, using an ideology in which individual fulfilment was played down, and developing a skill in manoeuvring and manipulating others to serve his ideals. As James MacDonald has noted, the two roles in which Zhou excelled, as adviser before the policy decision was taken, and as implementer thereafter, are both 'the functions of servants'. And this in turn can be linked to the ministering side of Zhou, his occasional delight in what the Chinese men of his generation insensitively termed 'women's work'.

The rejection of the infant Zhou may also be the source for his capacity to sympathize and identify with society's minorites. It is striking that he often made friends of people in minority groups – Ma Jun the Moslem, and Dr

Zhang Boling the Christian, both at Nankai School, and Bishop Logan Roots the missionary in Wuhan. No other Communist leader in China had so many European or American friends, and Zhou's ability to get to know people from other countries and cultures was outstanding.

But none of this means that he was soft or moderate when it came to the cruelties inherent in the Communist Party's accelerated solution to social problems. Zhou had demonstrated as early as 1931 in Shanghai, a city used to secret-society thuggery, that he could accept responsibility for cold-blooded executions necessary for Party discipline. The Dalai Lama later found Zhou a much tougher customer to deal with than Mao, and those admirers charmed by Zhou's manners and modern ideas had to come to terms with his direction of the secret police and his ultimate responsibility for official excesses throughout his giant bureaucracy. Zhou never watered down Communist policy except at times when the Politburo had agreed to do so – for example during the various United Front periods – and in concert with Mao Zedong and other leaders.

Zhou did sometimes disagree with Mao and the others about the timing and priorities of social and economic reforms – when Zhou wanted to go faster and Mao stood for a slowing down, or vice versa. But these disagreements related to the means or pace by which the agreed ends of socialism could be attained, not to the desirability of Communism itself, about which both men were equally clear. If Mao was the brilliant but erratic navigator, Zhou was the patient boatswain who kept the engines going, the crew busy and the victuals furbished.

The proof that Zhou was not a 'moderate' in Western political terms came with the Cultural Revolution, when he delivered in November 1964 the speech which, with its cry of 'No destruction, no construction', heralded the chaos to come. He was to reaffirm on several occasions the underlying objectives of the Socialist Education Movement which he saw as the crucial element in the Cultural Revolution. When he called on China, as he did in April 1965, to 'smash bourgeois thoughts', he was being serious about the Cultural Revolution in a way that even Mao did not always manage to be. He tried harder than Mao to keep the Red Guards on track, on target, in the hope of not discrediting the whole movement.

Where Zhou thwarted Mao, for example during the Great Leap Forward of 1958, his opposition sprang not from any dislike of campaigns to increase production as such, but from a conviction that the whole idea of such campaigns would be damaged by putting political capital into one that strained for impossible targets and had been inadequately prepared. Zhou had a volatile blend of idealism and practicality, but they were kept in appropriate channels.

Idealism means optimism, and Zhou was human enough to make mistakes because of overconfidence, especially in mid-spate. At the Huangpu Academy he was overoptimistic about Chiang Kai-shek's future intentions towards the Communists. His incompetence in the *Zhongshan* incident in 1926 and in the Shanghai rising of 1927 may be attributed to the same fault, although we do not really know enough about them to be sure. But there were many instances thereafter of his misjudging actors on the political stage, such as Chiang Kai-shek again during the Xi'an incident in 1937.

Zhou bungled his attempt to visit Roosevelt in America in 1946, and misjudged the Indian border question with Nehru in the 1950s. Again, excessive optimism led him to support the Hundred Flowers Movement in 1957, not realizing that Liu Shaoqi and the other apparatniks would never allow the Party organization to be assailed by non-Communists. In the foreign-affairs field he was too optimistic in his hope that Anthony Eden could influence Dulles over the Quemoy crisis and SEATO, and yet he was simultaneously pessimistic in believing that the Americans might invade China.

Zhou's career can thus be painted in negative colours. He grasped a superficially stirring but unsuitable ideology; he placed himself at the beck and call of a succession of Communist supremos whose competence was often in doubt; he then found that even on basic matters like economic growth the combination of the chosen doctrine and his own best implementing skills could not bring the hoped-for results. He himself recognized in the 1940s that communism would not work in China until millions of people had been successfully educated into changing their beliefs in a cooperativist and collectivist direction. But once he was heading the government of his giant nation he felt impelled to go full tilt towards all the Communist goals at once.

This is not, however, the last word. If Zhou fell down on his promise, failing in his own lifetime to bring China decisively into the modern world with a markedly better standard of living and higher stage of industrial and technological development, it was not strictly his fault. It was more the obduracy of the subject. Anyone seeking great progress from such a low base across such vast ground would have met frustration. Yet instead of petulant surrender or melodramatic reaction to the inevitable setbacks, Zhou stolidly held his ground to provide the only major force for continuity of reform in Communist China. And he did so not in the dour ungiving way in which Liu Shaoqi might have proceeded, but in an unfailingly cheerful, very democratic vein which constantly inspired others to rally round and help.

When his successor, Deng Xiaoping, is finished, and when *his* successors have come and gone, it is Zhou's work and personality that will be remembered before Mao's or anyone else's. Ironically, since Mao combined the roles of China's Lenin and China's Stalin but must now be discredited, there may be a move to assign the unimpeachable 'Lenin role' posthumously to Zhou – though his contribution to Party building was quite different. A few years after his death far more Zhou badges were visible on Chinese lapels than Mao's or any other kind. Zhou's China is a China lifting itself up by its own bootstraps with a very human and patient thoughtfulness. Mao stands for gargantuan leaps forward, which as often as not left the Chinese back where they had begun. It was exciting, perhaps, to stay up all night for a few weeks at a time making low-grade unusable steel, or to rampage into municipal offices to bully, humiliate and torture local officials. But when these activities did not actually produce measurable progress, let alone the millennium, Zhou's less exciting but more sensible gradualism acquired appeal.

Zhou did not sell communism short. It is rather Mao Zedong and his like who should be seen as out of step, the ones who lost their sense of balance between ends and means, who were greedy for results faster than nature could provide them, ready to bring out the worst in human nature in the magical belief that it could lead to its opposite. That was not communism, it was an infantile dream of grandeur. It is Zhou who was the Communist, while the others merely provided the political leadership of which he was incapable. He had the reforming fecundity of a Napoleon, combined with the political tenacity of a Metternich.

Zhou was true to his beliefs, just as he was true to China and to his enduring sense of humanity. And this is what singles him out among all the leaders of China in this century. It is true that he failed to understand Nehru just as he failed to understand Khrushchev or Kosygin. But there are others in the West who suffered the same misfortune, and one should not read too much into that. The occasional signs of embedded chauvinism one glimpses in Zhou's dealings with foreign nations are minute by comparison with those exhibited by his peers in China; and the extent of his understanding of the outside world was in a quite different class. We in the West may see him as an earnest of our future collaboration with what still appears a nationalistic, culturally ethnocentric country. To come away from a meeting with Zhou was to feel reinvigorated about the future potential for working together with China in a single world order. To the extent that he left like-minded persons to carry out his twin visions – of modernizing China and guiding her to a responsible role in world affairs – we can feel grateful for the life he chose to lead and hopeful for the China he left behind.

Acknowledgements

Over the past ten years I have pestered almost everyone in the modern Sinological field about Zhou Enlai, and invariably, at least in the West and Japan, I have been helped. In this space I can only thank those who contributed substantially, beginning with Michel Oksenberg, whose ideas on sources and strategies gave me a good start. For the numerous translations that were called for, I was most lucky to have the services of Calliope Caroussis, Donald Clark, Gail Eadie Duggett, Caroline Mason, Beth Mckillop, Linda Trew, Clio Whitaker and Zhang Ning from Chinese; Setsuko May from Japanese; a Russian official who must be nameless; and Wolfgang Deckers from German.

On the research side I am grateful to all those scholars who opened their work to me, especially Genevieve Barman, Marianne Bastid, Ogawa Heishiro, the late Hsu Kai-yu, Helga-Maria Kühn, Li Tien-min, Roderick MacFarquhar, Lucian Pye, Tom Robinson, Stuart Schram, Nora Wang and Rhoda Weidenbaum.

Those who very kindly read and commented on parts of my manuscript before publication include, apart from scholars already mentioned, Sally Backhouse and Sybil van der Sprenkel.

Among the many who wrote and talked to me about Zhou, I should like to thank: Sir John Addis, J. Chester Cheng, Pei-kai Cheng, Tillman Durdin, John K. Emmerson, Eto Shinkichi, H. D. Fong, Kimirou Fujita, Mae Jean Go, Han Suyin, Dieter Heinzig, William Jenner, Khwaja Mohammed Kaiser, K. S. Karol, the late Malcolm MacDonald, Oba Sadanobu, Pu Shou-chang, John Roots, Ilsa Sharp, Lois Wheeler Snow, Tang Tsou, Lord Trevelyan, Warren Unna, Tarzie Vittachi and Zhou Erliu.

Finally I thank Elisabeth Sifton for her scrupulous editing, and Janet Marks for the typing. Without Adam Baillie, who saw the book through from its inception, collating and storing material, researching and administering, it would never have seen the light.

Glossary of Personal Names

Pinyin	Wade-Giles	Pinyin	Wade-Giles
Bai Chongxi	Pai Ch'ung-hsi	Liu Bocheng	Liu Po-ch'eng
Bo Gu	Po Ku	Liu Shaoqi	Liu Shao-ch'i
Cai Chang	Ts'ai Ch'ang	Lu Xun	Lu Hsun
Cai Hesen	Ts'ai Ho-sen	Luo Ruiqing	Lo Jui-ch'ing
Cai Tingkai	Ts'ai T'ing-k'ai	Ma Jun	Ma Chun
Chen Boda	Ch'en Po-ta	Ma Xunyi	Ma Hsun-yi
Chen Duxiu	Ch'en Tu-hsiu	Mao Zedong	Mao Tse-tung
Chen Zaidao	Ch'en Tsai-tao	Nie Rongzhen	Nieh Jung-chen
Chi Benyu	Ch'ih Pen-yu	Peng Dehuai	P'eng Teh-huai
Deng Xiaoping	Teng Hsiao-p'ing	Peng Zhen	P'eng Chen
Deng Yingchao	Teng Ying-ch'ao	Qi Benyu	Chi Pen-yu
Dong Biwu	Tung Piwu	Qu Qiubai	Ch'u Ch'iu-pai
Gu Shunzhang	Ku Shun-chang	Ren Bishi	Jen Pi-shih
Guo Morou	Kuo Mo-jo	Sima Qian	Ssu-ma Ch'ien
Guomindang	Kuomintang	Song Qingling	Sung Ch'ing-ling
He Mengxiong	Ho Meng-hsiung	Sun Zhongshan	Sun Yat-sen
Hua Guofeng	Hua Kuo-feng	Tan Zhenlin	T'an Chen-lin
Jiang Jieshi	Chiang Kai-shek	Wang Fuxin	Wang Fu-hsin
Jiang Jingguo	Chiang Ching-kuo	Wang Hongwen	Wang Hung-wen
Jiang Qing	Chiang Ch'ing	Wang Jingwei	Wang Ching-wei
Kuai Dafu	K'uai Ta-fu	Xiang Ying	Hsiang Ying
Li Dazhao	Li Ta-chao	Xiao Hua	Hsiao Hua
Li Fujing	Li Fu-ching	Xie Fuzhi	Hsieh Fu-chih
Li Xiannian	Li Hsien-nien	Yao Dengshan	Yao Teng-shan
Liao Chengzhi	Liao Ch'eng-chih	Ye Jianying	Yeh Chien-ying
Liao Zhongkai	Liao Chung-k'ai	Ye Ting	Yeh T'ing
Lin Biao	Lin Piao	Yu Qiuli	Yu Ch'iu-li

Pinyin	Wade-Giles	Pinyin	Wade-Giles
Zhang Boling	Chang Poling	Zhang Xueliang	Chang Hsueh-liang
Zhang Chunqiao	Chang Ch'un-ch'iao	Zhou Enlai	Chou En-lai
Zhang Fakui	Chang Fa-k'uei	Zhou Fohai	Chou Fo-hai
Zhang Guotao	Chang Kuo-t'ao	Zhu De	Chu Teh

Glossary of Placenames

Pinyin	Former conventional spelling	Pinyin	Former conventional spelling
Beijing	Peking	Shandong	Shantung
Chongqing	Chungking	Shantou	Swatow
Guangdong	Kwangtung	Shanxi	Shansi
Guangxi	Kwangsi	Shenyang	Mukden
Guangzhou	Canton	Sichuan	Szechwan
Hebei	Hopeh	Tianjin	Tientsin
Henan	Honan	Xi'an	Sian
Huangpu	Whampoa	Xiamen	Amoy
Jiangsu	Kiangsu	Xinjiang	Sinkiang
Jiangxi	Kiangsi	Yan'an	Yenan
Lüda	Dairen	Yangzi	Yangtse
Nanjing	Nanking	Zhejiang	Chekiang
Shaanxi	Shensi	Zunyi	Tsunyi

A Note on Sources

'None of us kept a diary,' Zhou Enlai told James Reston in 1971, near the end of his life, 'and none of us want to write our memoirs' (Helen Foster Snow, *The Chinese Communists*, Greenwood, Westport, 1972, p. xv). True, Mao Zedong volunteered a brief autobiography to Edgar Snow in 1936, and allowed his birthplace in the central province of Hunan to be commemorated and visited. He even allowed a Chinese writer to publish an account of his early revolutionary activities during his own lifetime (Li Jui, *The Early Revolutionary Activities of Comrade Mao Tse-tung*, Sharpe, White Plains, 1977 – the original was published in Beijing in 1957). But this was justified by the need to have a limited cult of personality for the one supreme leader. Zhou Enlai was made of sterner stuff, and unswervingly rebuffed all Westerners – Edgar Snow, Jack Belden, John Roots – who sought to write the story of his life, just as he systematically prevented writers in China from publishing anything personal about him. There was a convention, as the Sinologist Simon Leys put it, that Zhou 'was born without a navel' (*Chinese Shadows*, Penguin, London, 1978, p. 82).

Zhou travelled abroad more frequently and met more foreigners than any of his Chinese Communist comrades, and some of those foreigners published impressions of him. But such open handling of state information (defined by the Chinese to include the private and family life of the politician) is not possible within China itself. The Chinese cultural tradition, reinforced by Communist authoritarianism, dams up the flow of data outside the channels of state needs. If Zhou had allowed even such basic and uncontroversial facts as his date of birth to be known, he might have avoided the mistaken-identity embarrassment of the notorious *Stern* article of 1954 about the Chinese student romance. Similarly it was possible for a London broadcaster, Arthur Mathers, to tell the world in 1954 that Zhou had not been on the Long March ('London Calling', 17 June 1954). Now, after the repressive silence of Zhou's lifetime, China has produced a host of conflicting memoirs – with no one able authoritatively to pronounce between them.

Edgar Snow was the most successful in prising personal information out of Zhou, although what he published fell short of what he could say about Mao Zedong, for example. Snow's own notes of his original 1936 interviews with Zhou, some of which remained unpublished, seem unfortunately to have disappeared.

The starting point for any inquiry into the life of Zhou Enlai must be the biographies by two Chinese writers, Hsu Kai-yu and Li Tien-min, who intended to collaborate in exploring the Guomindang archives on Zhou but eventually published two separate books. Hsu Kai-yu's *Chou En-lai, China's Gray Eminence* (Doubleday, New York, 1968) was the first and more readable of the two, while Li Tien-min's *Chou En-lai* (Institute of International Relations, Taipei, 1970) is perhaps the more informative. Hsu's book, when published in Chinese translation by Mingbao in Hong Kong in 1976, had some additional material included (his name in pinyin is Xu Jieyu). Inevitably the hostility of these two writers to communism influences their assessment of Zhou, but one could equally say that as Chinese they are also tempted here and there to exaggerate his good points. Their use of the memoirs of Zhou's sister-in-law, Ma Xunyi, who chose Taiwan rather than communism, has been criticized by some, but Ma was not wholly hostile to Zhou and some of her testimony on family matters is plausible.

Then there are more anecdotal treatments, such as Yen Chingwen's *Biography of Zhou Enlai* (Po Wen Books, Hong Kong, 1974) and more pictorial ones, such as Ed Hammonds's *Coming of Grace, An Illustrative Biography of Zhou Enlai* (Lancaster Miller, Berkeley, 1980). There should also be mentioned John Roots's *Chou* (Doubleday, New York, 1978) which is useful for the 1930s and 1940s where there is some first-hand material. Jules Archer's *Chou En-Lai* (Hawthorn, New York, 1973) adds little that is new.

Zhou's collected poems were first published in Beijing after his death, soon followed by an English-language translation by Nancy T. Lin (*In Quest, Poems of Chou En-lai*, Joint Publishing, Hong Kong, 1979). But there is a dilemma in translating Chinese poetry into English. If you translate literally the result remains partly incomprehensible because of the frequent assumption by the poet that his reader will understand allusions to – or even quotations from – the Chinese classics of many centuries ago. If you translate freely, on the other hand, you make the poem over to yourself, forcing it into only one of the many channels of meaning which the poet may have intended. Nancy Lin puts literalness first, and for this reason Zhang Ning and I attempted the entirely new joint translations which appear in this book. The poems themselves are not considered to be very good – not nearly as successful as Mao Zedong's.

The *Selected Works of Zhou Enlai* began to be published in Beijing in 1980, with the first volume in English translation coming out the following year. They are dull, sometimes surprisingly ephemeral and infuriatingly incomplete, but they remain indispensable. It cannot be emphasized sufficiently that publishing in China is a political act, almost always furthering a political purpose – on the part of the government or Party, or some group therein – which is contemporary and often distorts the subject matter. The China-watcher has to weigh such official or semi-official matter along with data from unofficial sources (refugees, intelligence-gatherers in Taiwan and Hong Kong, foreigners in or visiting China, etc.) before coming to tentative conclusions.

Slightly less official collections include the *Quotations from Chou En-lai* (Chih Luen

Press, Hong Kong, 1969), put out in eye-catching yellow apparently as a rival to the more famous *Little Red Book of Chairman Mao's Thoughts*, and various symposia of transcripts of Zhou's speeches, interviews and press conferences with foreigners, e.g. Song Lianze (ed.), *Talks with Zhou Enlai* (New Communications Press, Hong Kong, 1978).

A number of books on the earlier part of Zhou's career have recently been published in the People's Republic. Those by Hu Hua and Huai En, for example, have interesting if often contradictory data. Those by former bodyguards to Zhou, like Lung Feihu's *Eleven Years with Vice-Chairman Zhou* (PLA Press, Beijing, 1959) or Wei Guolu's 'With Vice-Chairman Zhou on the Long March' in *Hong Qi Piao Piao*, vol. II (China Youth Press, Beijing, 1959) are more superficial but occasionally yield an interesting description or conversation. Since they relate only to certain periods I have cited these works in the notes that follow for the relevant chapters.

Japanese writers have been prolific in dealing with Zhou, and Matsuno Tanio's *A Leader of China – Zhou Enlai and His Age* (Doyusha, Tokyo, 1961), Nishikawa Takeshi's *The Path of Zhou Enlai* (Tokuma Shoten, Tokyo, 1976) and Arai Takeo's *The Practice of a Revolutionary, Zhou Enlai* (Cho Shuppansha, Tokyo, 1979) are all helpful. Matsuno's book first appeared as a series of articles in the *Asahi Shimbun*.

Among the people I interviewed about Zhou Enlai, who knew him and worked with him, and whose first-hand information is used at several points in this book, are: Chen Nikia (Zhou's fellow-student in Europe in the 1920s, interviewed in Brussels, June 1977); Jen Chohsuan (Zhou's Communist Party comrade in France in the 1920s, interviewed in Taipei, June 1980); Wu Dager (with Zhou at Nankai School and in Japan, interviewed in Taipei, June 1980); Anna Wang Martens (knew Zhou in Yan'an, interviewed in Hamburg, June 1977); Okada Akira (dealt with Zhou at Bandung in 1955, interviewed in Paris, October 1982); Okada Haruo (involved with Zhou in Sino-Japanese relations from 1950s, interviewed in London, October 1982); Jack Service (the American official who got closest to Zhou in the 1940s, interviewed in Berkeley, June 1980); Liu Wuchi (who knew Zhou in the war years in Chongqing, interviewed in Menlo Park, June 1980); Chun-ming Chang (a Nankai University teacher who met Zhou in the 1940s, interviewed in New York, May 1980); and Okazaki Kaheite (frequent visitor to Zhou on Japanese affairs from 1960s, interviewed in Tokyo, April 1982).

Notes

What follows is a documentation of the major sources for the main incidents and quotations in the text of the book. These notes are not numbered, because numbers dotting the text of the book might distract or put off some readers. Instead, each note is introduced by one word or phrase in bold letters.

The first note to Chapter 1 is **Birthdate**, for example, and any reader wanting to find further details of the sources for this, sometimes with a discussion of them and additional points of interest, will find what he needs in the note under this heading. The notes are designed to give the maximum information in the minimum space, and books which are cited more than twice are therefore abbreviated to a single word or phrase, which is always italicized. The list of books which now follows gives all these works with their abbreviations in alphabetical order. To go back to the first note, **Birthdate**: the first reference here is *Tienmin* 32. This means that the reference is to page 32 of the book listed as *Tienmin*, which is an abbreviation for Li Tien-min's *Chou En-lai*.

Other abbreviations used in this book are as follows:

CB	*Current Background* (Hong Kong)
CQ	*China Quarterly* (London)
CR	*China Reconstructs* (Beijing)
JPRS	*Joint Publication Research Service: Translations on Communist China* (Washington)
NCNA	New China News Agency (Beijing)
PD	*People's Daily* (Beijing)
SCMP	*Survey of the Chinese Mainland Press* (Hong Kong)
SWB/FE	*BBC Summary of World Broadcasts, Far East* (London)

List of sources most frequently cited:

Arai Arai Takeo, *The Practice of a Revolutionary, Zhou Enlai* (Cho Shuppansha, Tokyo, 1979)
Birdless Han Suyin, *Birdless Summer* (Cape, London, 1968)
Bloodworth Dennis Bloodworth and Ching Ping, *Heirs Apparent* (Secker & Warburg, London, 1973)

Braun   Otto Braun, *A Comintern Agent in China* (Hurst, London, 1982)

Chang   Chang Kuo-tao, *The Rise of the Chinese Communist Party*, 2 vols., vol. I: 1921–1927; vol. II: 1928–1938 (Kansas University Press, 1971 and 1972)

China 2001   Han Suyin, *China in the Year 2001* (Watts, London, 1967)

Communists   Helen Foster Snow, *The Chinese Communists* (Greenwood, Westport, 1972)

Deluge   Han Suyin, *The Morning Deluge, Mao Tse-tung and the Chinese Revolution 1893–1953* (Cape, London, 1972)

Ekins   H. R. Ekins and Theon Wright, *China Fights for Her Life* (Whittlesey, New York, 1938)

Elegant   Robert S. Elegant, *Mao's Great Revolution* (World, New York, 1971)

Enduring   *Enduring Memories of Premier Zhou* (China Youth Publishing House, Beijing, 1978)

Eventful   Liu Jiuzhou, Peng Haiguei and He Qian, *Eventful Years* (People's Publishing Society, Tianjin, 1977)

Foreign Devils   Richard Hughes, *Foreign Devils* (Deutsch, London, 1972)

Garside   Roger Garside, *Coming Alive, China after Mao* (Deutsch, London, 1981)

Goodstadt   Leo Goodstadt, *Mao Tse-tung: The Search for Plenty* (Longman, Hong Kong, 1972)

Griffith   Samuel B. Griffith II, *The Chinese People's Liberation Army* (Weidenfeld, London, 1968)

Guillermaz   Jacques Guillermaz, *The Chinese Communist Party in Power 1949–1976* (Westview, Boulder, 1976)

Harrison   James Pinckney Harrison, *The Long March to Power* (Macmillan, London, 1973)

Hinton   Harold C. Hinton, *Communist China in World Politics* (Macmillan, London, 1966)

Hsu   Hsu Kai-yu, *Chou En-lai, China's Gray Eminence* (Doubleday, New York, 1968)

Hsu II   Hsu Kai-yu *The Biography of Zhou Enlai* (Mingbao, Hong Kong, 1976)

Hu Hua   Hu Hua, *The Young Comrade Zhou Enlai* (China Youth Press, Beijing, 1977)
   see also Hu Hua, *The Early Life of Zhou Enlai* (Foreign Languages Press, Beijing, 1980)

Huai En   Huai En, *The Youth of Zhou Enlai* (Sichuan People's Press, Chongqing, 1979)

Hutheesing   Raja Hutheesing, *Window on China* (Casement, Bombay, 1953)

Johnson   Hewlett Johnson, *China's New Creative Age* (Lawrence & Wishart, London, 1953)

Journey   Edgar Snow, *Journey to the Beginning* (Random House, New York, 1958)

Karnow   Stanley Karnow, *Mao and China* (Viking, New York, 1972)

Khrushchev   *Khrushchev Remembers* (translated by Strobe Talbott), 2 vols. (Deutsch, London, 1971 and 1974)

Kissinger   Henry Kissinger, *The White House Years* (Weidenfeld, London, 1979)

Long   Edgar Snow, *The Long Revolution* (Hutchinson, London, 1973)

Matsuno   Matsuno Tanio, *A Leader of China – Zhou Enlai and His Age* (Doyusha, Tokyo, 1961)

Mortal   Han Suyin, *A Mortal Flower* (Cape, London, 1966)

Museum   *Commemorative Materials on Zhou Enlai* (Chinese Historical Museum, Beijing, 1977)

My House   Han Suyin, *My House Has Two Doors* (Cape, London, 1980)

Nishikawa   Nishikawa Takeshi, *The Path of Zhou Enlai* (Tokuma Shoten, Tokyo, 1976)

Nixon   *The Memoirs of Richard Nixon* (Sidgwick & Jackson, London, 1978)

Other   Edgar Snow, *The Other Side of the River* (Gollancz, London, 1963)

Panikkar   K. M. Panikkar, *In Two Chinas, Memoirs of a Diplomat* (George Allen, London, 1955)

Payne   Robert Payne, *Chiang Kai-shek* (Weybright, New York, 1969)

Random   Edgar Snow, *Random Notes on Red China* (Harvard, Cambridge, 1957)

Robinson   Thomas W. Robinson, 'Zhou Enlai and the Cultural Revolution in China', in Thomas W. Robinson (ed.), *The Cultural Revolution in China* (University of California Press, Berkeley, 1971)

Roots   John Roots, *Chou* (Doubleday, New York, 1978)

Rue   John E. Rue, *Mao Tse-tung in Opposition 1927–1935* (Stanford University Press, California, 1966)

Selected Works   *Selected Works of Zhou Enlai*, vol. I (Foreign Languages Press, Beijing, 1981)

Service   John S. Service, *Lost Chance in China* (Vintage, New York, 1974)

Smedley   Agnes Smedley, *The Great Road* (Monthly Review Press, New York, 1956)

Star I   Edgar Snow, *Red Star Over China* (Gollancz, London, 1937)

Star II   Edgar Snow, *Red Star Over China*, revised edition (Bantam, New York, 1971)

Stories   *Stories of Premier Zhou* (People's Press, Tianjin, 1977)

Strong   Anna Louise Strong, *Letters from China*, vol. I: nos. 1–10, 1962–63; vol. II: nos. 11–20, 1963–64 (New World Press, Beijing, 1963 and 1964).

Swarup   Shanti Swarup, *A Study of the Chinese Communist Movement 1927–1934* (Oxford, London, 1966)

Tienmin   Li Tien-min, *Chou En-lai* (Institute of International Relations, Taipei, 1970)

Topping   Seymour Topping, *Journey Between Two Chinas* (Harper, New York, 1972)

Trevelyan   Humphrey Trevelyan, *Worlds Apart* (Macmillan, London, 1971)

Turning   *The Great Turning Point* (Foreign Languages Press, Beijing, 1962)

Vladimirov   P. P. Vladimirov, *Vladimirov Diaries* (Doubleday, New York, 1975)

Wang   Wang Ming, *Half a Century of the CCP and the Treachery of Mao Zedong* (Political Literature Press, Moscow, 1975)

White   Theodore White, *In Search of History* (Cape, London, 1979)

Whitson   William W. Whitson, *A History of Communist Military Politics 1927–71, The Chinese High Command* (Macmillan, London, 1973)

Wind   Han Suyin, *Wind in the Tower* (Cape, London, 1976)

Witke   Roxane Witke, *Comrade Chiang Ch'ing* (Weidenfeld, London, 1977)

Women   Helen Foster Snow, *Women in Modern China* (Mouton, The Hague, 1967)

Yen   Yen Ching-wen, *Biography of Zhou Enlai* (Po Wen Books, Hong Kong, 1974)

Youth   *Premier Zhou and Youth* (China Youth Press, Beijing, 1977)

1   The Much Adopted 1898–1913

In the opening chapters of this book, three works have been especially helpful: Hu Hua, *The Young Comrade Zhou Enlai* (China Youth Press, Beijing, 1977) (hereinafter referred to as *Hu Hua*); Huai En, *The Youth of Zhou Enlai* (Sichuan People's Press, Chongqing, 1979) (*Huai En*); and *The Story of Premier Zhou's Childhood* (Liaoning People's Press, Shenyang, 1978) (*Childhood*). All have a certain cachet as being published in the People's Republic of China. That does not mean that they may be relied upon unquestioningly (they contradict each other in several respects), but rather that all the matter in them can safely be considered as genuinely possible. While Zhou was alive no one dared to publish such material, and after his death there was no authority left who dared to judge their truth or falsehood. When Ogawa Heishiro, who had first become interested in the early life of Zhou when he served as Japanese Ambassador to China in the 1970s, visited Zhou's birthplace in 1980 he was given information which sometimes contradicted that of Hu and/or Huai: see his two articles in *East Asia* (Tokyo) entitled 'A Visit to Premier Zhou's Old Home' and 'Zhou Enlai's Early Years and Family' of August 1979 and July 1980 respectively – hereafter referred to as *Ogawa*.

Birthdate   *Tienmin* 32 assembles sources giving 1896, 1898 and 1899 as Zhou's year of birth, and he opts himself (14) for 1899! Even Edgar Snow adhered to 1899 in both editions of *Red Star Over China*. But 5 March 1898 is unequivocally stated in *Huai En*, and this is followed by *Ogawa* writing after his visit to Huaian. Zhou's Kyoto University application form was also obtained by *Ogawa*.

Father   *Star II* 72 (states wrongly that Yinen died when Zhou was an infant); Su Shuyang, *The Son of Great Earth, A Story about Zhou Enlai* (China Youth, Beijing, 1982) 8. Dates from *Ogawa*. 'Monthly income' (speech by Zhou of 25 September 1966): translated in *Robinson* 303.

Family   'Bankrupt Mandarin': *Star II* 71; 'fallen feudal': *Hu Hua* 2.

Mother   *Ogawa* gives her dates as 1877–1904, but *Huai En* says she died when Zhou was nine and other evidence supports a 1907 death (*Hsu* 5 and 236 seem to agree). Her father's death: *Ogawa*.

Grandfather Panlong   There is much confusion about the career of this man and the number of his sons: see *Hsu* 3 and *Tienmin* 14–15.

Shaoxing   'My home': *Robinson* 303. *Bloodworth* 29 may be misleading Western readers when he declares 'Chou comes from Shaoxing'. It may be doubted how religiously the boys made this annual pilgrimage, for all the publicity later attaching to it.

Uncles   Here is a rich muddle of conflicting materials. Yinen is often described as the youngest of seven brothers (*Hsu* 4). Two recent sources in China put him as second of four, however, and I prefer this.

Adoption   *Hu Hua* says Zhou was adopted when one year old after the uncle had died, and other Chinese publications support this. But *Ogawa* was told at Huaian it was before the child was one, and before the uncle's death. 'Ineffective parents': *Hsu* 6. **Adoptive brother** (Enzhu): *Hsu* 7.

Adoptive mother   *Star II* 72; *Hu Hua* 3; *Hsu* 7; *Tienmin* 17; *Nishikawa* 14. 'I feel grateful' (talk of 28 April 1946): cited in *Tienmin* 18. **Wet nurse** (Jiang): *Ogawa*. **Huaiyin** *Ogawa*, *Hu Hua* 2 and *Huai En*. It was a student biography of Zhou using an incorrect placename for Huaiyin, which was subsequently misidentified, which probably led to the myth (repeated in the *New York Times* obituary, 7 January 1976) that Zhou spent part of his childhood in Shanghai, but this is denied in Huaian: see *Ogawa*. **Pawnshop** *Hu Hua* 4.

Mothers' deaths 'My aunt': *Star II* 72. *Hu Hua* 3 says both died of grief.

Move to Shenyang *Ogawa* summarizes the contradictory evidence well. 'Talked and manoeuvred': Zhou's sister-in-law Tillman Durdin, *New York Times Magazine*, 24 April 1960.

Shenyang 'Pigtail': cited in *Hsu* 221; *Huai En* 15; *Hu Hua* 9. 'So that China': *Childhood* ch. 1 and *Hu Hua* 9. Teachers: *Hsu* 8–9; *Tienmin* 16. Footbinding: 'My mother' (interview of 19 July 1971): *Bulletin of Concerned Asian Scholars* (San Francisco), summer 1971, vol. 3, no. 3, p. 35. Cut queue: *Tienmin* 8; disillusion: *Childhood* ch. 1. Little Southerner: *Hu Hua* 6. 'I came': speech of summer 1966, quoted *Hu Hua* 6. 'Advantages': *Huai En* 27. Battlefield: *Hu Hua* 8. 'Keep this': *Hu Hua* 9.

'Donated house' Speech of 25 September 1966, in *Robinson* 303.

2 Slinging Satchels in Tianjin 1913–17

Examinations *Roots* 111; *Nishikawa* ch. 1; *Matsuno* 4; *Hsu* 10. **Five poems** *Huai En* 28.

Nankai *China Reporting Service* (Hong Kong), 30 June 1969; *Hu Hua* 11–12; *Tienmin* 20–21; *Hsu* 11–14.

Wu Dager is the form of romanization ultimately preferred by Han Dager as he is presented in *Hsu*, *Matsuno* and other sources. He was interviewed by the author in Taipei in June 1980 for the purposes of the present book. This first meeting with Zhou is from *Hsu* 11.

'Daintiness' Author's interview with Wu Dager. **First-year essay** *Childhood* ch. 1. **Fees** *Huai En* 55; *Hu Hua* 12. 'No help' from family: *Star II* 72–3.

Dr Zhang Boling A good impression of the esteem in which Zhang Boling came to be held by Chinese and American fellow-scholars can be gained from *There Is Another China: Essays and Articles for Chang Poling of Nankai* (Columbia University, New York, 1948).

Dramatics *Hu Hua* 16; *Hsu* 26; *Huai En* 52 and further information from Wu Dager. 'Effeminate': *Hsu* 227; *Hsu II* 245; also Chih Meng in Rhoda Sussman Weidenbaum, 'Chou En-lai, Creative Revolutionary', PhD thesis, University of Connecticut, 1981, p. 63. **Homosexuality** ibid. 32 and 68. **'His art'** *Hsu* 228; Tillman Durdin, the Chinese-speaking American correspondent, described Zhou's voice in the 1940s as 'strained and high-pitched' (*New York Times Magazine*, 24 April 1960). 'Teacher, times changed': *Hsu* 14–16.

Zhou's reading *Hu Hua* 12. 'You can fool': *Huai En* 30–31. **'Insurrectionist'** *Star I* 59.

'My alma mater' Speech of 24 February 1951, *Huai En* 58; see also *Hsinhua*

Fortnightly, 1957, no. 9, p. 8, for 10 April 1957 speech in Tianjin with similar references.
Zhang *Tienmin* 20–21. *Matsuno* 4 uses 'adore' to express Zhou's attitude to this teacher.
Romance *Hsu* 237.

3   Treading the Sea 1917–19

Kobe reception Matsuno Tanio in *Asahi Shimbun* (Tokyo), 8 February 1980. Hosei University: *Matsuno* 5; also Okamoto Ryuzo, 'Zhou Enlai as a Student in Japan', *Asahi Shimbun*, 23 January 1969, and 'Premier Chou En-lai', *Asia Review* (Tokyo), autumn 1970, p. 28.
Tokyo accommodation *Huai En* 64.
Police apology Kuroda Yoshiharu, in *Matsuno*. The police chief was from Kagurazaka.
Wu invited *Hsu* 18. Arguments, wine bottle: *Hsu* 19, and author's interview with Wu, June 1980. 'How can you get really angry?': *Hsu* 227.
Arashiyama poems (5 April): Fukumori Hideo of the Kyoto Metereological Observatory informs me that the cherry probably began to flower in 1919 on 5 or 6 April, and the full blossom would have come about mid-April or a little later. The poems may therefore be attributed to the early stages of cherry-blossom viewing.
'I didn't study' (interview with Japanese trade unionists, 12 July 1971): *Nishikawa* 31.
Takasaki Author's interview, October 1981, with Okada Akira, who had interpreted between Takasaki and Zhou at Bandung. Hayashi Fujio tells a similar story of Zhou's saying *konnichiwa* to him in 1956 when he was Japanese Consul-General in Bombay, 'Impressions of Premier Zhou Enlai', *Bungei Shunju* (Tokyo), June 1972. But Okada remembers instances of Zhou correcting the Japanese interpreter.
'Bean curd' (in interview, 15 April 1970, with Japanese trade delegates): *Nishikawa* 31. **'Awed'** Author's interview with Wu Dager.

4   In Prison 1919–20

Return to Tianjin This was probably in late May or early June. Zhou told Ogawa Heishiro (to whom I am indebted for this information) that 'the cherry blossom was over when I returned' to China, which sounds like late April or May at the earliest. The Nankai School alumnus magazine of 30 April 1919 reports Zhou's undated, possibly merely intended, return from Japan: it is here that the welcoming (undated) tea party is also mentioned. Zhou is first listed as actually being present in China on 9 June, participating in a patriotic-oath mass meeting.
Dr Zhang Boling Wilfred V. Pennell, *A Lifetime with the Chinese* (South China Morning Post, Hong Kong, 1974) 89.
Undergraduate? *Ogawa*; *Hu Hua* 41. 'My name' (speech, 12 December 1957, to Shanghai students): *Chinese Youth Press* (Beijing), 7 January 1958.
Finance *Star II* 73.

Newspaper *Hu Hua* 27–8. Tolstoy: *Hsu* 23. 'Lenin II': *Tienmin* 26. Polevoy: *Hsu* 24.

Deng 'The youngest': her 'Reminiscences of May Fourth Movement' in *Women of China* (Beijing, 1959) 94.

Zhou's routine *Tienmin* 25; *Hsu* 22. 'Wasn't like that': Pan Shilun in *Huai En* 80. 'Oh compatriots': *Hu Hua* 31. Mixed organization: *Hu Hua* 38–9.

Deng 'only fifteen' (a remark by Zhou to visiting American scholars, 19 July 1971): *Bulletin of Concerned Asian Scholars* (San Francisco), summer 1971, vol. 3, no. 3, p. 32; also Song Lianze (ed.), *Zhou Enlai Talks* (New Navigation, Hong Kong, 1978) 22.

Another girl *Nishikawa* 45 describes this in passionate terms as Zhou's 'first love': the quoted comments are his. See also *Hsu II* and *Hsu* 25. According to *Yen* 34 Zhou was bitter over losing this girl.

'I read' *Star II* 73. 'Police should': *Hu Hua* 41. Kang Nairu: information from Wu. Pseudonyms: *Huai En* 95.

Gate Incident *Hu Hua* 45–55. In prison: *Hu Hua* 55–67. Trial: *Hu Hua* 68–72.

Donations *Hsu* 26. 'Everyone knows': *Hu Hua* 75.

5   Commitment in France 1920–24

SS *Porthos* I am indebted to Adam Baillie and Lloyds Register of Shipping for this clarification: *Tienmin* 37 and *Hsu* 27 have the ship as *Borthos* and *Hu Hua* 77 as *Bordeaux*, without exact dates. The *Porthos* was at Hong Kong from 10–11 November, Saigon (15th–18th), Singapore (20th) and Colombo (25th) en route to Marseilles. Zhou's memory must have failed when he told Edgar Snow he sailed in October (*Star II* 73). The voyage: *Hu Hua* 77–8; Xie Shuqing in *Zhou Enlai's Youth* (Tianjin, 1980) 9.

Château Thierry *Nishikawa* 54. Beer: *CR*, March 1979, p.22. Billancourt: *Hsu* 30. Zhou's places of residence are still uncertain, with no definite evidence for either Château Thierry or Billancourt (Geneviève Barman has investigated).

Catholic paper Zhou apparently arranged to write for four separate newspapers, two in Tianjin and two in Shanghai. The fifty-one despatches sent between 1 February 1921 and 10 March 1922 to the *Yishi Gao* are reprinted as a collection, and it is from these that these extracts are taken: *Zhou Enlai Tongzhi Lu Ou Wenji* (Wenwu, Beijing, 1979).

London *Huai En* 140 implies Zhou was in England at the end of February. *Hsu* 27 says Zhou failed to make 'the right kind of contact' in England. Address (on letter): *Zhou Enlai Lu Ou Wenji* (Wenwu, Beijing, 1982) 71 – I am indebted to Geneviève Barman for this reference. The building has since been pulled down. I could not authenticate the story that Zhou lived in east London and supported Arsenal Football Club.

Austerity *Huai En* 182; coffee bills: *Asahi Shimbun*, 18 April 1957, and *Matsuno* 83.

Finance 'Many old': *Star II* 73; Yan Fansun's proverb: *Star II* 74. Comintern: *Hsu* 33. In June 1977 Chen Nikia told me at his home in Brussels that Zhou, with whom he was then working at Renault as a turner and fitter, had probably been receiving 500 roubles a month from the Comintern, equal to some 2500 francs. He was also getting 800 francs a month from the Belgian Catholics, since Father Vincent Lebbe, a

Belgian Lazarist whom Zhou had met in Tianjin, had now returned to Paris and was helping to finance students. With another 300 francs from Renault, this would have made a total income of 3600 francs a month which is certainly too much. In 1982 Chen was interviewed again on my behalf, and this time he stated that they were not paid by the Comintern, and would have lived better if they had been. It seems that the memory of this contemporary of Zhou's may, in his old age, have become confused. Postcard: *Hsu* 30 and *Nishikawa* 30.

Renault   Snow says that Zhou did manual work at Renault but adds that he was also studying labour organization there: *Star II* 74. *Elegant* 323, *Hu Hua* 82, *Huai En* 140 and *Matsuno* all agree that Zhou worked at Renault. *Nishikawa* 30 cites He Zhanggong, *Memoir of Work-Study Life* (1958), to assert that Zhou did simple casting and moulding, for a small wage and in silence. Another Chinese then working at Renault, Chen Nikia, has told me that Zhou did unskilled work for less than 300 francs per month, for a twelve and a half hour day. 'This is not': *Tienmin* 38; Zhou's denial: K. S. Karol, *China the Other Communism* (Heinemann, London, 1967) 9; 'laughed': *PD*, 10 January 1976; Lille: *Elegant* 323; *Hu Hua* 82.

Notre Dame   *Nishikawa* 55–6, citing He Zhanggong. Montargis: Siao-yu, *Mao Tse-tung and I Were Beggars* (Souvenir, Syracuse, 1959) 185–7. Barbusse: *Nishikawa* 54; *Hsu* 28.

Legation protest   Cai Chang in *Women* 238; *Hu Hua* 86–8. Lyons University: *Hu Hua* 89–92; *Huai En* 139–50. 'Fat briefcase': *Hsu* 32.

London again: 'Did not like': *Star II* 73.

'You are a people'   (to Etienne Manac'h): *Le Monde*, 10 January 1976.

Germany   *Zhou Enlai's Youth* (Tianjin, 1980) 10–11; *Hsu* 33. The Sichuanese student is Huang Naiyuan. The second Chinese student confirming this story is an anonymous informant of Li Tien-min. It is wrong, of course, to link this romance with the later alleged affair in Göttingen. Writes to Wu: *Hsu* 35–6.

'On Saturday'   He Zhanggong in *Hu Hua* 98.

Zhu De   *Smedley* 151–2; *Huai En* 184.

Belgium   *Ta Kung Pao* (Hong Kong), 29 May 1958; *Tienmin* 49; *La Nouvelle Gazette* (Charleroi), 21 January 1967, and letters from J. Willequet and J. Lanotte.

Sceaux   *Hsu* 43. 'Weak in theory': *Hsu* 229. 'Girls?': *Hsu* 33–4.

Göttingen   The *Stern* article by Gerd Heidemann was published on 1 October 1954. The story was widely carried, e.g. in *Asahi Shimbun*, 4 September 1954, *Daily Telegraph*, 23 November 1971, and *Nan Peichi* (Hong Kong), 16 March 1976; and also in *Yen*. The mistaken identity was established by the Göttingen archivist Dr Helge-Maria Kühn in a paper of 18 October 1976. She noted that *Stern*'s romantic Chinese student in Göttingen was called Tschu, in the German system of romanizing Chinese names, not Tschou. She discovered that his real name was Ling-gin, and he was born on 18 July 1898 in Shanxi Province. Search of the residents' registry and university rolls showed that no Tschou Enlai had studied in Göttingen. Several statements have now been made to the effect that Zhou never visited Göttingen, including one by Zhou himself to a German delegation under Dr Gerhard Schroder in 1972. I am grateful to the Europe–China Association for its help in obtaining this information. Heidemann, the journalist responsible, resigned from *Stern* in 1983 when his story of the so-called Hitler diaries was proved to be based on a forgery.

A spectacle *Tienmin* 44. Trudeau: information from John Small.

No scandal Comment to author by Jen Cho-hsuan, a colleague of Zhou's in Paris, in interview in Taipei, June 1980. 'Talk and talk': *Hsu* 42–3.

Ho Chi Minh Zhou to Nixon in *Nixon* 568; *SCMP*, no. 1418. According to William Duiker, *CQ*, April 1972, no.50, p.475, Ho was in Paris from about the end of 1918 to mid–1923.

French police I am indebted to Nora Wang for this information based on Chen Duxiu's correspondence. It is curious all the same that no French police dossier on Zhou has come to light.

6   Revolutionary Marriages 1924–25

Russia *Star II* 74, *Matsuno* 64 and Tillman Durdin (*New York Times Magazine*, 24 April 1960) all say that Zhou returned by way of the USSR. Durdin adds that he met Borodin, Stalin and Zinoviev there, and *Matsuno* mentions 'another view' that Zhou studied at Lenin University with Tito, Toglietti and Ho Chi Minh. *Hsu* 241 records that 'some say' Zhou went first to north China on his return from France, which would fit in. *Tienmin* 51 says Zhou returned 'directly to Canton'. But then *Huai En* 204 has Zhou sitting on the dais for the Huangpu Academy opening ceremony in June 1924 when he was clearly still in Europe!

Canton office *Chang* I 449. 'Many things': 19 July 1971 talk to American scholars. 'Imperialism': *Hsu* 213; Zhou inconsistently criticized Chiang Kai-shek later for seeking the utopian 'Great Harmony' of idealistic Confucianism (speech of 16 August 1943, *Selected Works* 168).

Liao *Arai* 167–70. **Galin** *Star II* 74 (this is one of Snow's many rewritten passages since *Star I*). **Borodin** See Dan N. Jacobs, *Borodin, Stalin's Man in China* (Harvard University Press, Cambridge, 1981).

Ho Chi Minh Dennis Duncanson, 'Ho Chi Minh in Hongkong 1931–32', *CQ*, January 1974, no. 57, p. 91.

'You've just returned' *Hsu* 51–3. **Zhou Fohai** *Hsu* 50–51.

'The army' *Huai En* 207–8. **Eastern Expedition** *Huai En* 212 and 218.

Madame Sun *CR*, April 1977. **Zhou optimistic** *Chang* I 451. Mao friendship: *Mortal* 62. 'Regularizes': *Whitson* 40.

Deng's career is taken from her autobiography as told to Helen Foster Snow in *Communists* 254–8, supplemented by *Star II* 500, *Bloodworth* 31, *Women* 250–53, *Tienmin* 28–31 and *Matsuno* 80–82. 'Wore the trousers': *Yen* 39.

Zhous at home *Matsuno* 81.

7   Capture in Shanghai 1925–27

Eastern Expedition *Huai En* 212–30; *Hsu* 48–50. **'So busy'** *Chang* I 477. Dilip K. Basu of the University of California at Santa Cruz has written a research paper on 'Micropolitics of Local Insurrection: Zhou Enlai in Shantou 1925–26'. **Secretary incident** *Hsu* 54–5.

Guomindang congress *Tienmin* 79–80.

Zhongshan incident *Tienmin* 66 and 74–6; *Huai En* 245–7; *Hsu* 58–9. **'Tested'** *Chang* I 500 and 510.

Brother Guo Moruo, 'A Poet with the Northern Expedition' (translated Josiah Barnett), *Far Eastern Quarterly* (Menasha, Wisconsin), February 1944, vol.3, no. 2, pp. 139 and 166.

Miscarriage *Women* 251; *Matsuno* 81. His conventional friends suggested that Zhou remarry in order to have children (on which Chinese tradition sets such store). He is supposed to have replied: 'No, all the children of China are my children': *Arai* 62–3. **Shanghai** *Hsu* 61.

Malraux Jean Lacouture, Malraux's biographer (*Malraux, Une Vie dans le Siècle*, Du Seuil, Paris, 1973), says that Malraux, writing *La Condition Humaine* in Paris after a visit to Hong Kong in August 1925 and a brief tour of China in 1931, based Kyo Gisors on Kyo Komatsu, a young Japanese writer in Paris in the 1920s who had known first Ho Chi Minh and then Malraux there. Zhou was 'probably unknown' to Malraux then (p. 129), but W. Frohock and others claimed to notice a similarity between Kyo Gisors and Zhou; the *New York Times* obituary to Zhou in 1976 lends credence to the identification, if thinly disguised, and Lucian Pye also accepts it (*Virginia Quarterly Review*, spring 1977, p. 222). Malraux, wringing advantage from the misapprehension, writes in 1956 in his *Antimemoirs* (Hamilton, London, 1968, p. 367) of the Zhou Enlai he is about to meet: 'He knows as well as I do that in the United States he is thought to be the original of one of the characters in *La Condition Humaine*.' Zhou's comment on that book to Edgar Snow was 'things happened quite otherwise' (*Star II* 420). I am obliged to David Baker for helping me to disentangle this knot.

Deng *Matsuno* 82; scarf: 40. **Still in bed** *Yen* 40.

Shanghai uprising *Star I* 60–75; *Huai En* 258–84; *Star II* 75–6.

Wang Jingwei *Hsu* 65–6; *Tienmin* 82.

'I was responsible' *Comrades Liu, Zhou and Zhu in the Midst of the Masses* (Beijing, 1958) 27, cited in *Hsu* 2. See also *Chang I* 589. **'Heads rolled'** *Ekins* 50–51.

Yao *Mingbao* (Hong Kong), 31 October 1976.

Chen Duxiu *Deluge* 183. **'Our leadership'** *Pannikar* 91.

Escape *Elegant* 324; *Tienmin* 85–6; Robert Payne, *Chiang Kai-shek* (Weybright, New York, 1976) 122–3. (Payne says Zhou disguised himself initially as a woman after his escape.)

8 The Nanchang Test 1927

Fifth Congress *Hsu* 64. **'Concubine?'** Matsuno in *Asahi Shimbun*, 23 January 1976; *Nishikawa* ch. 9; *Tienmin* 89; *Hsu* 68–9. Wuhan pickets: *Chang* I 649–50 and II 42; *Tienmin* 90.

'A tireless worker' *Chang* I 659. **'Man of iron'** *Smedley* 199.

Bishop Roots *Roots* 51.

Party membership *Harrison* 454. **East River plan** *Chang* I 660–62; Martin C. Wilbur, 'The Ashes of Defeat', *CQ*, April 1965, no. 18, p. 54. **'So then'** *Chang* II 47; also *Chang* I 671.

Nanchang Jacques Guillermaz, 'The Nanchang Uprising', *CQ*, July 1962, no. 11, pp. 161–8; *Chang* II 3–35; Stuart Schram, *Mao Tse-tung* (Penguin, Harmondsworth, 1967) 105–7. General Zhang Fakui: *Whitson* 437.

He Long *Eastern Horizon* (Hong Kong), May 1977, pp. 34–5; *Hsu* 72.
Stalin telegram *Tienmin* 90; *Hsu* 69–70. **Zhang Guotao criticizes** *Chang* II 10.
Liu Ning *Hsu* 73; *Tienmin* 103. **Cai Tingkai** *Chang* II 17.
Trotsky *Problems of the Chinese Revolution* (Pioneer, New York, 1932) 421.
Shantou *Chang* II 29–30. **Lusha** *Chang* II 31–2. **Zhe De's wife** *Chang* II 46 and 60–62.
Hong Kong *Hsu* 75 and 248; *Tienmin* 119. It is curious that Zhang Guotao does not mention his Hong Kong meeting with Zhou in his memoirs. Some writers credit Zhou with helping to create the Canton Commune at this time – see James Bertram, *First Act in China* (Viking, New York, 1938) 133, *Deluge* 209 and *Johnson* 148, where the late Dean declares flatly that workers organized the Canton Commune in 1927 'under Zhou Enlai'. But there seems to be no indigenous evidence for this.
To Shanghai *Hsu* 77 (or to Moscow? *Smedley* 209). Politburo: Hsiao Tso-liang, *Chinese Communism in 1927* (Chinese University of Hong Kong, 1970) 105; *Chang* II 45.
Hangzhou *Hsu* 78–9.
Deng *Communists* 258.

9 Regaining Russian Confidence 1928–30

To Tianjin *Elegant* 114.
To Russia *Deluge* 211; *Chang* II 127. **Sixth Congress** *Chang* II 76; *Harrison* 522.
Bukharin Liu Ning in *Tienmin* 124; *Hsu* 80. **University** *Star II* 461; *Whitson* 36.
Chiang's son *Chang* II 87.
Gu Shunzhang *Hsu* 94.
Uncle and family *Hsu* 98–102; *Roots* 55–7. **Enzhu** *Hsu* 100–101.
'Our comrades' *Hsu* 219–20. **'Mediator'** *Tienmin* 142. **Fourth Army** *PD*, 19 January 1981, and *SWB/FE*/6630. **Mao** *Hsu* 82.
'China's Lenin' *Deluge* 261. **Han Suyin** *Deluge* 209. **Moscow** *Hsu* 87–8. **Li 'mad'** *Deluge* 266.
Shanghai (conference, August 1930, and Third Plenum of Central Committee at Lushan, September 1930): *Chang* II 157–8; *Hsu* 88; *Tienmin* 133. **Shaoshan Report** *Swarup* 121; *Hsu* 89.
Military questions *Whitson* 40; *Hsu* 83.
Changsha James P. Harrison, 'The Li Li-san Line and the CCP in 1930, Part II', *CQ*, July 1963, no. 15, pp. 148–9. **Ningdu execution** *Hsu* 90–91.

10 A Magician Trumped 1931–34

Shanghai Central Committee January 1931 (Fourth Plenum): *Hsu* 91–2; *Rue* 236–44; *Star II* 462; *Swarup* 242–6; *Tienmin* 136–9; William F. Dorrill, 'Transfer of Legitimacy in the Chinese Communist Party', *CQ*, October 1968, no. 36, p. 59.
Futian incident *Chang* II 276; *Matsuno* 98–9.
'Playing dumb' *Chang* II 155. **Shaoshan Report** *Hsu* 91. **'Grovelling' confession** *Rue* 244. **American Vice-Consul:** in O. Edmund Clubb, *Communism in China:*

As Reported from Hankow in 1932 (Columbia University Press, New York, 1968) 89.
Zhang Guotao and the Pole   *Chang* II 144–6. **China and democracy**   *Ekins*
126. **Executing a friend**   *Chang* II 150–51; *Tienmin* 157.
Gu Shunzhang episode   *Tienmin* 150–55; *Hsu* 94–6; Li Ang, *The Red Stage*
(Chongqing, 1942) 115–16; *Chang* II 175–6 and 261; *Rue* 245; *Matsuno* 36; see also
Bloodworth 32. 'Comrade Wu Hao [Zhou Enlai] was in charge of administering the
punishment' – cited from Yan'an archives in *Tienmin* 155. Zhang Guotao attributes
the decision to the Central Committee and comments that it resulted in 'the total
liquidation of Ku's family': *Chang* II 261.
Kyo   In André Malraux, *Man's Fate*   (Methuen, London, 1948; first published as
Storm in Shanghai, 1934).
Bearded   Zhou leaves Shanghai: *Matsuno* 36; *Nishikawa* 136; *Tienmin* 157; *Hsu*
102–3. **Deng**   In *Women* 258. **Vladivostok**   In *Harrison* 222.
Zhou as reconciler   *Star* II 462. **Welcomes defectors**   *Whitson* 57; *Hsu* 112.
Report on Futian   and Zhou's catalogue of errors: *Tienmin* 166; *Hsu* 105–7; *Braun*
102.
Ningdu conference   *Braun* 28; *Harrison* 229 and 566. Mao's remark (of 24
October 1966) in Stuart Schram, *Mao Tse-Tung Unrehearsed* (Penguin Books,
Harmondsworth, 1974) 268; Braun's in *Braun* 37 and *CQ*, June 1971, no. 46, p. 282.
'Left of Mao'   *Swarup* 129. **Zhou as commissar**   Dieter Heinzig in *CQ*, June
1971, no. 46, pp. 279–80. **Telegrams**   *Selected Works* 72.
Kung Chu affair   *Rue* 259–60; *Hsu* 113–14; *Tienmin* 178.
19th Route Army   Kung Chu, *The Red Army and I* (Southwinds, Hong Kong,
1954) 364; William F. Dorrill, 'The Fukien Rebellion and the CCP', *CQ*, January
1969, no. 37, p. 34; *Braun* 26–8. Zhou's remark: in *Random* 60.
'Some credit'   *Braun* 105. **Braun's 'little disagreement'**   *Braun* 69.
General Xiao   *Whitson* 266; *Tienmin* 171; *Hsu* 115.
Fifth 'Encirclement'   Chi-hsi Hu, 'Hua Fu, the Fifth Encirclement Campaign
and the Tsunyi Conference', *CQ*, July 1970, no. 43, p. 33; Jerome Ch'en,
'Resolutions of the Tsunyi Conference', *CQ*, October 1969, no. 40, p. 23.
Radio   Dieter Heinzig in *CQ*, June 1971, no. 46, p. 285.
Evacuation   *Hsu* 111; *Swarup* 257; *Deluge* 306; Chi-hsi Hu, 'Mao, Lin Piao and the
Fifth Encirclement Campaign', *CQ*, June 1980, no. 82, pp. 261–2.

11   On the Long March 1934–36

This chapter draws upon the author's earlier book *The Long March 1935* (Hamilton,
London, 1971); Wei Guolu, *With Vice-Chairman Zhou on the Long March* (Foreign
Languages Press, Beijing, 1978) (cited hereafter as *Wei*) and also the immense
scholarly literature that has built up about the controversial Zunyi conference,
analysis of which must be regarded as only provisional in view of recent new evidence
prompting reinterpretation.

River Xiang   *Braun* 160–62. **Liping**   *Braun* 167.
Braun's habits   Shi Buzhi (alias Kung Chu), *Chingkangshan de Fenghuo* (Ng Hing
Lee, Hong Kong, 1964) 82–5. **Zhou's 'irritation'**   *Braun* 168. **Burnt rice**   *Wei*

24–6.

Zunyi conference *Harrison* 569; *Tienmin* 186–8; *Deluge* 322–3. 'Tacit agreement': in Jerome Ch'en, *Mao and the Chinese Revolution* (OUP, London, 1965) 189; Chi-hsi Hu, *CQ*, July 1970, no. 143, p. 31; and *Swarup* 257.

'Flying colours' *Braun* 189. Resolution: in *Tienmin* 186–9; Jerome Ch'en, 'Resolutions of the Tsunyi Conference', *CQ*, October 1969, no. 40, p. 23.

Zhou as Mao's champion *Braun* 106. As executor and housekeeper: *Deluge* 362. Donkey: in *Wang* 185. **Luo and Lin criticize** *Braun* 125. **Zhu De's vote** *Wang* 367.

Gold ring *Wei* 15–16. **Password!** *Hsu* 118–19. **Paying for eggs** *Wei* 32–3. **Trucks captured** *Wei* 28–30.

Luding bridge *Wei* 36–7. Liver abscess: *Stories* 31.

Jiajin Mountain *Wei* 47. **Giving flour** *Arai* 112.

Zhang Guotao reunion *Chang* II 378–92; *Whitson* 63; *Braun* 229. **Zhou silent** *Chang* II 410. **Maoergai** *Tienmin* 192 and 196; *Chang* II 412. Zhou and Wei ill: *Wei* 54–5 and 75–6.

Grasslands Zhou's comment in *Other* 83. Deng's comment: in Yang Chengwu, 'Crossing the Grasslands', in Liu Po-cheng, *A Single Spark Can Light a Prairie Fire* (San Lien, Hong Kong, 1960) 175. River crossing: in *Wei* 64–5.

Deng's tuberculosis *Birdless* 318–19. **Mao's wife** *Witke* 161.

Zhou's tolerance Lucian W. Pye, *Mao Tse-tung, The Man in the Leader* (Basic Books, New York, 1976) 210. **Coffee** *Hsu* 130–34.

Young Marshal *Hsu* 130–34.

Edgar Snow *Star II* 68–71. This is a longer and more detailed version than in the original *Star I* 59. See also *Journey*.

12 The Tiger Trapped 1936–40

Zhou Enlai and the Xi'an Incident by Luo Ruiqing, Lu Zhengcao and Wang Bingnan (hereafter cited as *Luo*) was helpful in this chapter; so were James M. Bertram, *First Act in China: The Story of Sian Mutiny* (Viking, New York, 1938), and Mi Zauchen, *The Life of General Yang Hucheng* (Joint Publishing, Hong Kong, 1981).

Xi'an incident Zhou's first reaction: *Chang* II 479–80. His journey to Xi'an: *Eventful* 11; *Stories* 50. His idea of a trial: *Random* 1–14. The restraining factors: *Payne* 217. **Soviet** attitude: *Chang* II 486. Zhou addresses Young Marshal: *Luo* 44; also article by Young Marshal's aide in *PD*, 6 March 1979, translated in *SWB/FE/*6063. Chiang's remarks to wife: *Payne* 217. Donald's comment (to *Associated Press* on 25 February 1945): cited in Gunther Stein, *The Challenge of Red China* (McGraw-Hill, New York, 1945) 17. Zhou **'crafty'** In words of the wife of Miao Jianqiu (political adviser to Young Marshal), cited in *Hsu II* 247 – she presumably reflected her husband's views.

Interview with Chiang Bo Gu, who was there, confirmed the interview to Edgar Snow (*Star II* 438) though he apparently denied it to Braun (*Braun* 334). *Luo* 54–5 also confirms. Robert Payne, *Mao Tse-tung* (Weybright, New York, 1950) refers to three secret meetings, and see also *Payne* 217. Opening words – first version: *Mortal*

381; second version reported in *Hsu* 136 as having been told by Zhou to Miao Jianqiu; third version: *Chang* II 488; fourth version: *Elegant* 326. Chiang's apprehensiveness: *Star II* 388.

Chiang's son   *Chang* II 488. Although Chiang himself does not admit seeing Zhou, the fullest biography has Zhou interviewing Madame Chiang and promising to secure Chiang's release (Keiji Furuya, *Chiang Kai-shek, His Life and Times*, St John's, New York, 1981, p. 519).

Zhou cables to Mao   *Selected Works* 89–90. Zhou complements Mao, sends second cable: *Chang* II 497. **Talk with Miao**   *Hsu* 140–42; *Random* 7–8. Wu: *Hsu* 137–8.

Ambush   *Luo* 78; *Eventful* 13; *Chang* II 509–10.

In Nanjing   Zhang Boling: *Hsu* 15. On the liberals: *Ekins* 187. Helen Foster Snow: *Inside Red China* (Doubleday, New York, 1939) 209–11.

Yellow Emperor   *Selected Works* 93 (declaration of 15 July 1937).

Lochuan conference   The best account of Zhou's role is in *Chang* II 537–8. **Mao's 'errors'**   At third hand from Teng Fa via Sheng Shih-tai in Alan Whiting, *Sinkiang: Pawn or Pivot* (East Lansing, Michigan, 1958) 229–31. **Zhou 'bungled'**   *Chang* II 557. **Smedley's comments**   *China Fights Back* (Gollancz, London, 1938) 73–4 and *Battle Hymn of China* (Gollancz, London, 1944) 124. See also T. A. Bisson interview of 23 June in his *Yenan in June 1944* (University of California Press, Berkeley, 1973) 43. Dancing: ibid. 123.

Bertram interview   James Bertram, *Unconquered* (John Day, New York, 1939) 150–53. **Taiyuan evacuation**   Smedley, *China Fights Back* 205–6; *Hsu* 151.

Carlson   *Journey* 186.

Wang's return   *Chang* II 565; *Braun* 408; *Hsu* 152.

Guo Moruo   In his *Hung Po Chu*, cited in *Tienmin* 225. **Liao**   *Arai* 170. **Five o'clock shadow**   *Roots* 85. **Editorial on Chiang**   Cited in *Hsu* 147; see also *Tienmin* 359.

Zhang defects   *Hsu* 256–7. Zhou's comment: *Hsu* 150.

Liu Ning   Quoted in *Tienmin* 224.

Deng Yingchao   Snow's rescue: in *Journey* 189; confirmed in Bertram, *Return to China* (Heinemann, London, 1957) 6; see also John S. Service, 'Edgar Snow, Some Personal Reminiscences', *CQ*, April 1972, vol. 50, p. 213. Deng's perm and conversation: in *Hsu* 149. Wuhan peach trees: *Yen* 263.

Durdin   In *Women* 253. **Auden**   In W. H. Auden and Christopher Isherwood, *Journey to a War* (Faber, London, 1939) 171–72. **Bertram**   *Unconquered* 296–7.

On journalists   In E. F. Carlson, *Twin Stars of China* (Dodd Mead, New York, 1940) 134. **On Snow**   In Freda Utley, *China At War* (Faber, London, 1939) 74.

Bishop Roots   In *Roots* 182. Zhou's inscription: *Roots* 149.

Supports Wang   (on Wuhan defence): Gregor Benton, 'The Second Wang Ming Line', *CQ*, March 1975, no. 61, p. 87; Warren Kuo in *Issues and Studies* (Taipei), July 1972, vol. 8, no. 10, pp. 42–51; Warren Kuo, *Analytical History of the Chinese Communist Party* (Taipei) 1968, vol. III, p. 44.

Zhou's Yan'an quarters   *Eventful* 5.

Changsha fire   *Eventful* 29.

Zhou's tour   *Braun* 435–6; *Tienmin* 33 (citing Guomindang archives) and 228; *Hsu* 4–5.

Breaks arm *Eventful* 31 and 34; *My House* 587 identifies the doctor as an Indian, and Indian sources have told me he was Dr Kotnis, leader of the five Indian doctors who had volunteered for duty with the Chinese Communists. 'Imperialist slander': *Other* 466.

Moscow The journey: *Service* 351; *Braun* 475. The reasons: *Vladimirov* 349 (the Vladimirov diaries are suspect because the author cannot be identified, but some of their material is plausible and it is that which is occasionally cited in this book). Speech: *Selected Works* 177–9; also *Worker's Daily* (Beijing), 29 December 1980, and *SWB/FE/6619*.

Russian films *Eventful* 34; *Stories* 55. **Gerald Samson** *Warning Lights of Asia* (Hale, London, 1940).

13 Metamorphosis of a Pig 1940–43

Theodore White, *In Search of History* (Cape, London, 1979), is a frequent source for this chapter, hereafter referred to as *White*; also, for this and the next chapter, John Paton Davies Jr's *Dragon by the Tail* (Robson, London, 1974), hereinafter cited as *Davies*.

Pig In *White* 119–20.

Zhou's Chongqing quarters From author's interview with Chun-ming Chang in New York, 1980; *White* 120; *Eventful* 39–47; the memoirs of Liu Wuchi; *Roots* 91 (the American visitor was Jack Anderson); *Red Flag* (Beijing), January 1977, and *SWB/FE/5409*. His comments on sleep: *CR*, April 1977. His food: *Eventful* 79. Reading newspapers: Liu Jiouzhou in *Eventful* 79.

Dr Zhang From memoirs of Liu Wuchi. **Chauffeur** In memoirs of host's son Liu Wuchi.

Romance *Tien Wen Tai* (Hong Kong), 10 December 1958, cited in *Tienmin* 36. **Father** *Hsu* 6.

Evans Carlson *The Chinese Army* (Institute of Pacific Relations, New York, 1940), p. 40. **Willkie** *Davies* 255. **Hemingway** In Anna Wang, *Ich Kämpfte für Mao* (Holsten, Hamburg, 1973). **Americans** e.g. *Service* 174.

Koreans In *CQ*, January 1962, no. 9, p. 189. **Nehru** *Pannikar* 90. **'Scout'** *White* 120.

Liu *Vladimirov* 414. **'Subjectivist'** *Vladimirov* 23 and 59 (diary entries of 9 June and 21 October 1942). Mao's later and more trusting view: *Vladimirov* 92–3 (entry of 25 March 1943). Zhou supports Wang: *Vladimirov* 62. Wang's report: *Wang* 63. **'More Chinese'** *White* 118.

Chiang dinner ibid. 114; *Roots* 89.

New Fourth Army incident Poem: *Hsu* 153–4; Zhou sells on street: *Red Flag*, February 1977; also *SWB/FE/5409*; *Eventful* 69.

Ambush *Braun* 438 (Braun, incidentally, writes that sources in Yan'an attributed Zhou's broken arm to this incident rather than the fall described earlier).

Zhou bitter (in interview with Theodore White, 1 February 1941): in *White* 117.

Stilwell *Davies* 247, and Barbara Tuchman, *Sand Against the Wind, Stilwell and the American Experience in China 1911–45* (Macmillan, London, 1970) 320.

Zhou's speech *Birdless* 215–16; *Roots* 88. Han Suyin's quoted comments on Zhou's oratory: in *My House* 165. Zhou on mother: *Hsu* 8.
Operation *Eventful* 93–7; *Davies* 247.
Rectification Zhou as 'empiricist': *Wang* 59 and 150. Speech on Mao: *Hsu* 157–8. Remark to Red Guards (of 29 November 1967): in *Harrison* 343.
Seven rules (of 18 March 1943): *Selected Works* 144.
Father's death (on 10 July 1942): *New York Times*, 9 January 1976.
Departure from Chongqing *White* 166. **Recall** Vladimirov suggests that Zhou was permanently recalled to Yan'an for his 'allegiance to Wang Ming's group' (*Vladimirov* 150) but I prefer to utilize this slightly doubtful source for relatively concrete facts than questionable judgements.

14   The World Is Ours 1943–49

The Great Turning Point (People's Publishing Society, Tianjin, 1977) is relevant to this chapter, hereafter referred to as *Turning*.

Zhou's Yan'an speech (of 2 August 1943): *Selected Works* 151–9. His role in rectification: *Vladimirov* 147–8 and 249–50; Stuart Gelder (ed.), *The Chinese Communists* (Gollancz, London, 1946) 173–80.
Neat clothes *Vladimirov* 192. Russian on party: *Vladimirov* 479–80 (entry of 9 July 1945).
'First home' Deng to Tillman Durdin, *New York Times Magazine*, 24 April 1960. Daughter: mentioned in *Vladimirov* 269. The Zhou Enlais are also said to have adopted 'as godchildren' several other of their comrades' children, including two of Zhu De's ten, and to have paid for the bringing up of yet more. Another goddaughter was Zhou Xiaoyen: *Arai* 63; *Bloodworth* 31 and 320.
Zhou's office Adolph Snehsdorf, *New York Times*, 11 January 1976.
British *Vladimirov* 275. Lord Lindsay's letters: Michael Lindsay, *The Unknown War* (Bergstrom & Boyle, London, 1975).
'Dixie Mission' Zhou's remarks on Chiang, etc.: *Service* 258–62.
Snow *Red China Today* (Random House, New York, 1970) 333–6.
Talk by Zhou (in two parts, 3 and 4 March 1944): *Selected Works* 177; passage cited is from p. 201.
Kang Sheng *Vladimirov* 250 (entry of 6 September 1944).
Churchill (speech of 10 October 1944): in Harrison Forman, *Report from Red China* (Holt, New York, 1945) 181–7; and *Service* 281.
Dr Zhang (17 October 1944) *Hsu* 16. **Kiss** *White* 204; also David D. Barrett, *Dixie Mission* (University of California Press, Berkeley, 1970) 64.
Roosevelt Visit bid: *White* 123; *Wang* 198–200; *Foreign Affairs* (Washington), October 1972, pp. 44 and 55.
Negotiating tactics Anonymous Guomindang official: quoted in *Hsu* 163–4; postponement ploy: *Tienmin* 271.
Seventh Congress Mao's wariness: *Wang* 171. Rankings: *Harrison* 594. On Mao's left: *Wang* 170.
Chongqing Zhou on eve: *Vladimirov* 509 (entry of 26 August 1945). Sun helmet:

Enduring 20. Toasts: *Red Flag*, January 1977, and *SWB/FE/5409*; Dennis Bloodworth, *The Messiah and the Mandarins* (Weidenfeld, London, 1982) 77. On democracy: *Tienmin* 254. 'Go unannounced': *Hsu* 168. Editor shot: *Smedley* 425; memoirs of Liu Wuchi. 'Suicide': Tillman Durdin in *New York Times Magazine*, 24 April 1960.

'Rely on people' *Quotations from Chou En-lai* (Paul Flesch, Melbourne, 1969) 4. 'Acknowledge Chiang': *Tienmin* 259. **Parachute episode** (of 29 January 1946): *CR*, April 1977; *Stories* 64–8; and *New York Times*, 31 January 1946. **Zhou's candour** *Hsu* 174. Leaves Chongqing, **mother's grave** *Hsu* 8.

Nanjing Zhou's set-up: *NCNA*, 8 January 1977, and *SWB/FE/5411*; *Dawn* (Karachi), 8 January 1978; and recollections of bodyguard Yen Tailung, *Survey of People's Republic of China Magazines* (Washington), 1977, no. 23, p. 22. Wading river: *Eventful* 104–7.

Chiang's 'concessions' *Roots* 97. 'Fighting must stop': *Hsu* 176. **YMCA** George A. Fitch, *My Eighty Years in China* (Meiya, Taipei, 1967) 301–2. **Sixth Uncle** *Hsu* 185.

Shanghai Ma's father: *Hsu* 97. Using interpreter: Robert Shaplen in *Foreign Devils* 279. 'Hypocrisy': *Hsu* 183. 'No time': *Hsu* 183. Small parties: *Tienmin* 272. 'Cup of wine': *Hsu* 184. 'Door slammed': *Griffith* 87. **Overcoat** Lung Feihu, *Martial Flags Flying in Northwest Highlands* (Military Society of the PLA, Beijing, 1978) 5.

On the run *Roots* 99–100; *Strong* II (30 December 1969). Mao's daughter: *Witke* 201. Hole in shoe: Yen Chang Lin in *Turning* 92–3. 'World is ours': *Turning* 99–100. Stretcher-bearer: *CR*, April 1977.

Debate with Liu *Harrison* 402.

'Require time' *Selected Works* 357.

Secret US bid *Service* 86–95; see also Yu-ming Shaw's 'John Leighton Stuart and US–Chinese Communist Rapprochement in 1949: Was There Another "Lost Chance in China"?' *CQ*, March 1982, no. 89, p. 74. The intermediary was Michael Keon, the Australian journalist.

On Mao *Selected Works* 370 (report of 7 May 1949).

15   A Pair of Blue Pyjamas 1949–52

Russian mistakes *Harrison* 384. 'No Tito' in Derk Bodde, *Peking Diary* (Cape, London, 1951) 199.

Prime Minister *Elegant* 18. **Talleyrand** Alain Peyrefitte, *Le Monde*, 10 January 1976. **'We argue'** *Mortal* 90. **Deng on sleep** *New York Times*, 9 January 1976. **Tiger Balm** *Museum* 232. **Face 'passive'** Tillman Durdin, *New York Times Magazine*, 24 April 1960; 'animated': *White* 122. Eyes lustrous: *My House* 164–5. **Five smiles** Yao Ch'ien, cited in *Bloodworth* 27. Repairs: *Enduring* 76 and *Arai* 39–41. **Facecloth** *Enduring* 75. Poor products: *New York Times*, 9 January 1976. **Salary** *Hutheesing* 190. Fees: *Eventful* 121–2. Photographs: *Enduring* 2–3. **Curtain** *Eventful* 32. **Home delicacies** Radio Beijing, 5 January 1977, and *SWB/FE/5409*. **Peanuts** *Youth* 140. **Identification** *Eventful* 115. Shaving: *Stories* 121–2. **Raincoat** *CR*, April 1977, p. 39. **Salute** *Red Flag*, January 1977, and *SWB/FE/5409*.

Dancing *Pannikar* 106; Clare Hollingworth, *Daily Telegraph*, 10 January 1976; *Tienanmen* (student journal of Beijing Physical Culture School), March 1967; Watanabe Ryusuke also describes Zhou dancing in Beijing in 1949, 'Premier Zhou Enlai's Waltz', *Bungei Shunju*, December 1972. **Chaplin** Joris Ivens, *Le Monde*, 10 January 1976. **Ping-pong** *Japan Times*, 12 April 1979. **Drinking** Information from Okada Akira; also K. C. Wu in Derek Davies, *Far Eastern Economic Review* (Hong Kong), 15 October 1982; but *Asiaweek*, 23 January 1976, reported Zhou substituted Chinese tea for *maotai* when toasting guests.

Birthplace Radio Beijing, 5 January 1977, and *SWB/FE/*5409. Nephew: ibid. and *Stories* 115–16. **Landlord** *Other* 298 (Snow refers to him as Zhou's 'older' brother's father-in-law, presumably a confusion). Ma Xunyi, the landlord's daughter, commented: 'I don't believe that he personally had anything to do with my father's death because I knew he truly rejected our Chinese traditional ethics and morals': *Hsu* II 247.

On women *Hsu II* 248. **On art** *Other* 283. **Opera** *Youth* 140. **Play** (*The Storm of 1 August*): *Youth* 170. **Temple** *Strong* II 114. **Mao's ointment** *Zhou's Life* (Xinshong Tushu, Hong Kong, 1977) 246. Commuters: *Arai* 27–30. **At press conference** Kadota Isao, *Asahi Shimbun*, 23 May 1980, cited in *Matsuno* 264. Photographer: ibid., *Matsuno* 264. Ma: *CQ*, April 1961, no. 6, p. 58. **Pu** *Hutheesing* 47.

Eric Chou *A Man Must Choose* (Knopf, New York, 1963) 25–7 and 44–7. **Individualism** Stuart and Roma Gelder, *Long March to Freedom* (Hutchinson, London, 1962) 133; see *Johnson* 107 for a good report of Zhou's policies requiring Chinese Christians to assert independence from Western churches. **Dr Zhang Boling** *Hsu* 16 and 236; *Tienmin* 22. Pyjamas: *Eventful* 131.

Korean War *Pannikar* 78–9. Fighting: *Griffith* 110. Burmese: *Pannikar* 106–7. 'Frenzied acts' and 'whoever attempts': *NCNA*, 1 October 1950; also *Griffith* 119–20. Pannikar again: *Pannikar* 110–11. Propaganda exercise: *Trevelyan* 65. **Truman** *Years of Trial and Hope* (Doubleday, New York, 1956) II 362; *Time*: 9 October 1950. 'Prepared to retreat': Chow Chingwen, *Ten Years of Storm* (Holt, New York, 1960) 193–5, and *CQ*, April 1960, no. 2, p. 105. **Zhou's breakdown** *Eventful* 118. On imperialists: Chow Chingwen, op. cit. 491–2.

Executions Cited by *Guillermaz* 22. **'A bright'** *Khrushchev* I 372 (Khrushchev's memoirs are doubted by some experts, but where they are plausible they are drawn upon in this book).

16 Geneva and Bandung 1953–55

I am grateful to Sir John Addis and Okada Akira for their personal first-hand recollections of the Geneva and Bandung conferences respectively.

Stalin's funeral David Floyd, *Mao Against Khrushchev* (Praeger, New York, 1964) 18; *Hinton* 227–9; and *Guillermaz* 184.
Geneva conference Generally, see Guy Wint in *CQ*, January 1960, no. 1, p. 64. 'Comrade Ho': *Khrushchev* I 482. 'Face frozen': *New York Times*, 8 March 1967. 'Likes luxury': cited in *Matsuno*. **Dulles** *Topping* 393; Zhou's comment: quoted

Johnson 245. Zhou's concession of **Laos**   Georges Chauvel in Alistair Buchan (ed.), *China and the Peace of Asia* (Chatto, London, 1965) 38. Eden: information from an observer. Residence at disposal: Chauvel, op. cit. 41. **India 'wealthy'**   Cited in *My House* 103. **On Tibet**   *Pannikar* 105. **Meets Ho**   Jean Lacouture, *Ho Chi Minh* (Vintage Books, New York, 1968) 193. **Mendès-France**   ibid. *New York Times* correspondent: *Topping* 146. Zhou's self-criticism: in *New York Times*, 8 May 1971. And to Reston: in *Topping* 152.

Charles Chaplin   *My Autobiography* (Bodley Head, London, 1964) 520–21.
Attlee   In Morgan Phillips, *East Meets West* (Lincolns-Praeger, London, 1954) 42; *Trevelyan*, 119.
Moscow   'Gift of a university': *Khrushchev* I 465–6. Speak Russian: Harrison E. Salisbury in *New York Times*, 11 January 1967; also his *The Coming War between Russia and China* (Secker & Warburg, London, 1969).
Geneva 'contribution'   *Guillermaz* 173.
On SEATO   (report of 11 August 1954): *CQ*, April 1967, no. 30, p. 161.
Efforts in construction   *Guillermaz* 186.
Overseas Chinese   Victor Purcell, *The Chinese in Southeast Asia* (OUP, London, 1965) 482–3; also *CQ*, October 1970, no. 44, pp. 14–15. Indonesian question: *Hutheesing* 52–4.
Khrushchev   *Khrushchev* II 247. **Nehru**   See Margaret W. Fisher and Joan U. Bondurant, 'Indian Views of Sino-Indian Relations', *CQ*, April 1967, no. 30, p. 166; *Hinton* 284; *Guillermaz* 176. 'Arrogant aggressor': *NCNA*, 30 December 1954; *Trevelyan* 142–4. **Eden**   *Trevelyan* 144–6.
Bandung conference   Appendicitis: Huang Shutze, 'The People's Great Premier', in *Tiyu Pao* (Beijing), 24 February 1978; also *JPRS*, no. 70910; and *PD*, 11 January 1977, also *SWB/FE/*5412. *Kashmir Princess*: see *Trevelyan* 156–61; and Gary Catron, 'Hong Kong and Chinese Foreign Policy 1955–60', *CQ*, July 1972, no. 51, p. 406. Frans Schutzman, then manager of the Raffles Hotel in Singapore, insists that Zhou stayed there on his way to or from Bandung, but in the absence of supporting details it seems prudent to suspend judgement on that (I am grateful to Ilsa Sharp for this information).
Zhou's first speech   (19 April 1955): *Guillermaz* 175; *CQ*, July 1961, no. 7, p. 6. American comment: Richard Lowenthal in Zbigniew Brzezinski (ed.), *Africa and the Communist World* (Stanford University Press, 1963) 151. **Second speech** and Romulo: *CQ*, ibid. Nehru: *Asiaweek*, 23 January 1976; Richard Wright, *The Color Curtain* (World, Cleveland, 1956) 165; Sarvepalli Gopal, *Jawaharlal Nehru*, vol. II (Cape, London, 1979) 241. **US relations**   Guy Wint, *CQ*, January 1960, no. 1, p. 64. **Prince Wan**   In David A. Wilson, 'China, Thailand and the Spirit of Bandung', *CQ*, July 1967, no. 31, pp. 97–8, *Hinton* 421. **Takasaki**   *Asahi Shimbun*, 4 April 1967, and information from Okada Akira. **Sihanouk**   Via Song Le in *Museum*.
Indonesia   Lee F. Williams, *CQ*, July 1962, no. 11, pp. 187–8. Zhou's popularity there: *New York Times*, 8 March 1967. 'Stand his ground' and 'I trust this man': Wright op. cit. 161 and 164.
NPC speech   (of 30 July 1955): *CQ*, July 1967, no. 31, p. 112, and *CB*, no. 342.

17 The Hundred Flowers 1956–58

Roderick MacFarquhar's books, *The Hundred Flowers Campaign and the Chinese Intellectuals* (Praeger, New York, 1960), which he edited, and *The Origins of the Cultural Revolution* (OUP, London, 1974), are both germane to this chapter: the latter is hereafter referred to as *MacFarquhar*.

Speech (of 14 January 1956): *NCNA*, 29 January 1956; *CB*, no. 376; *Wind* 80–81 and *China 2001* 107; *MacFarquhar* 34–5; *Hsu* 209. Richard Solomon calls this speech 'Maoist' because it stresses opposition to rightist ideology, in *Mao's Revolution and the Chinese Political Culture* (University of California Press, Berkeley, 1971) 273. **Han visits** Zhou's home: *My House* 170–73. Do not 'lightly' change (speech of 30 January 1956): *MacFarquhar* 24–5. **Zhou's self-criticism** and **Eighth Congress** speech (of 16 September 1967): *MacFarquhar* 89. On cash limits and twelve-year plan: *MacFarquhar* 123–4. **Sukarno** Cited in *MacFarquhar* 356. Zhou revealed: *MacFarquhar* 101. **On Taiwan** James Bertram, *Return to China* (Heinemann, London, 1957) 89; *My House* 172. NPC speech of 28 June 1956: in *MacFarquhar* 85. **India** See *My House* 262 and *Hinton* 449. Marshall of **Singapore** In Joseph and Lynn Silverstein, 'David Marshall and Jewish Emigration from China', *CQ*, September 1978, no. 75, p. 652. **Burma** Stephen Fitzgerald, 'Overseas Chinese Affairs and the Cultural Revolution', *CQ*, December 1969, no. 40, p. 106. **Mao on phone** *Selected Works of Mao Tse-tung* (Foreign Languages Press, Beijing, 1977) 365. **'Must not clap'** Chow Chingwen, *Ten Years of Storm* (Holt, Rinehart, New York, 1960) 84. **Khrushchev** requested?: *MacFarquhar* 175–6. First Chinese intervention: *Other* 384. 'Too much territory' (speaking to Japanese visitors): *SWB/FE/*1624. **Jiang Qing** *Witke* 270. Visvabharati: *CQ*, July 1961, no. 7, pp. 96–7. 'Thousands to greet': report of 5 March 1957 to CPPCC in *CQ*, June 1979, no. 78, p. 331.

'Criticism helps' *MacFarquhar* 180–82 (MacFarquhar roundly concludes: 'Zhou, it is clear, was Mao's principal supporter in pushing the "liberal" policies of 1956–57' – *MacFarquhar* 195.) Rebellion predicted: *PD*, 26 April 1957. **Cat and pepper** Karl Eskelund, *The Red Mandarins* (Alvin Redman, London, 1959) 150–51.

Learning from Russia *Goodstadt* 19. 'Need democracy': in NPC report, 26 June 1957, *Quotations from Chou En-Lai* (Paul Flesch, Melbourne, 1969) 5, and Stuart Schram, *Mao Tse-tung* (Penguin, Harmondsworth, 1967) 247. **Wages report** Franz Schurmann, *Ideology and Organization in Communist China* (University of California Press, Berkeley, 1966) 199.

On minorities (speech of 4 August 1957): *Beijing Review*, 3 March 1980. Self-criticism: *MacFarquhar* 315. Loses **Foreign Ministry** Guy Wint, *CQ*, January 1960, no. 1, pp. 16–17; *China News Analysis* (Hong Kong), 21 February 1958, p. 217. Lost face: phrase from *MacFarquhar* 74.

Economy 'haughty airs': *Goodstadt* 194. Ming Tombs: *Guangming Daily* (Beijing), 1 January 1977; *Arai* 15–27; *Enduring* 39. Yellow River flood: *Museum* 198.

Russia Fruitless persuasion: *Topping* 353; *Khrushchev* II 243 and 253. Wuhan (Wuchang) conference: Richard Hughes, *Sunday Times* (London), 22 March 1959.

18   Cleaning Up the Mess 1959–61

Khrushchev   On steel: *Khrushchev* II 274–5. Car incident: *Youth* 133. 'Impracticable' report on **Leap**   *PD*, 19 April 1959, and *CQ*, January 1964, no. 17, pp. 27–8. 'Allying theory': *Guillermaz* 213.
Lushan conference   Mao on Zhou's role: Stuart Schram, *Mao Tse-tung Unrehearsed* (Penguin Books, Harmondsworth, 1974) 142 and 138.
'**Facts prove**'   *Wind* 164–5; see also *Goodstadt* 114. **Decade review**   *A Great Decade* (Foreign Languages Press, Beijing, 1959).
Nehru   *My House* 256. McMahon: information from Tarzie Vittachi. **Letter to Nehru**   (of 8 September and reply of 26 September 1959): *CQ*, January 1960, no. 1, p. 113. **Khrushchev's view**   *Wind* 168–9. Nehru and map: *My House* 256–7.
Bargain   *CQ*, April 1960, no. 2, pp. 120–21. 'India access': *Foreign Devils* 201. Desai: *Asiaweek*, 23 January 1976. Nehru: *My House* 264 (Zhou had been grateful for the results of Nehru's conciliation in the Korean armistice talks of the early 1950s, but rejected his 1958 offer to mediate with the US over Taiwan – see *Wind* 167.)
Mongolia   *Hsu* 201.
On Third World   (report to NPC on 18 April 1959): *CB*, no. 559 and *CQ*, July 1961, no. 7, p. 9: **Nasser**   *Guillermaz* 275. Han Suyin on **Camp David**   *My House* 258.
'**Worst disasters**'   *Other* 621. Clean up: *My House* 290. Ration figures: *Youth*. Deng's diabetes: *PD*, 18 September 1960.
Withdrawal of Soviet experts   (report of 4 December 1963): in *China 2001* 76–7. 'Natural' (talk to Edgar Snow, 30 August 1960): *Other* 19. Han Suyin (December 1960 interview): *My House* 306–7.
Twenty-second Congress   *CQ*, October 1961, no. 8, p. 18; *Hinton* 142; *Tienmin* 304.

19   The Great Safari 1962–65

The article by W. A. C. Adie, 'Chou En-lai on Safari', *CQ*, July 1964, no. 18, pp. 174–94, covers this period helpfully.

Sick leave   *Red Flag*, January 1977, and *SWB/FE*/5409. Malcolm MacDonald: *Inside China* (Heinemann, London, 1980) 57–9. (Zhou described the assassination of President Kennedy in 1963 as a 'despicable, shameful act': *New York Times*, 21 December 1963; also *CQ*, January 1964, no. 17, p. 270.) **Reuters interview**   (16 October 1963): *Strong* II 22–4. Overflying India: *The Hindu* (Madras), 5 December 1963.

Egypt   Nosebleed: *New York Herald Tribune*, 19 December 1963; *Hinton* 187. Zhou's remarks to **Nasser**   Mohamed Heykal, *Le Monde*, 10 January 1976.
Albania   *Strong* II 81.
Tunisia   Emmanuel Hevi, *An African Student in China* (Pall Mall, London, 1963) 49; *Daily Telegraph*, 31 January 1964; *Jewish Observer and Middle East Review* (London), 3 April 1964.
Ghana   *PD*, 11 January 1977, and *SWB/FE*/5412. General Gordon: in Jay and Linda Mathews, *One Billion: A China Chronicle* (Random House, New York, 1983) 11.

Somalia 'Revolutionary prospects': *Washington Post*, 4 February 1964; qualified: *PD*, 6 February 1964, see also *Christian Science Monitor* (Boston), 20 February 1964. 'We Afro-Asians': *Hsu* 200. Poem: *Guillermaz* 273.

Asia 'We, new' (speech in Rangoon, 14 February 1964): *NCNA*, 14 February 1964. Ceylon: *Guardian* (London), 28 February 1964; *The Times*, 29 February 1964; *NCNA*, 2 March 1964.

'No aggression' Vienna interview: *Kurier* (Vienna), 24 July 1964; and also *New York Times*, 7 August 1964 (Harold Hinton accepts identification of this unnamed 'high Communist official' as Zhou).

Neruda *CQ*, January 1967, no. 29, p. 135.

Nehru Zhou's reported remark to Ceylon parliamentary delegation in Beijing, October 1964: *The Times*, 12 October 1964. Malcolm MacDonald: op. cit. 72–3.

Illness Zhou made no known public appearance between 10 August and 21 September. Operation story: *New York Times*, 19 September 1964.

Call for nuclear conference *Beijing Review*, 23 October 1964. Reaction to **tests** *Enduring* 49; and Radio Beijing, 28 January 1977; also in *SWB/FE/*5425 (this source says that Zhou, after looking at these photographs at 1.30 a.m. on 4 November 1964 in Beijing, flew to Shanghai that morning to greet Sukarno and on to Moscow the next day!)

Kosygin and Mao K. S. Karol, *China, The Other Communism* (Heinemann, London, 1967) 350. (The Russian diplomats in Beijing who told this story to Karol were divided as to whether Mao had called Zhou Kosygin's 'friend' or 'agent'!)

Snow (interview of 22 October and 16 December): *Long* 224–37. **Liu** *My House* 479.

NPC speech (21–22 December 1964): *Guillermaz* 336; *CQ*, December 1977, no. 72, p. 693; *Wind* 224–5; and *Hsu* 216. Zhou also said in this speech, one of the most interesting in his career, 'It is imperative to revolutionize the leading Party and government organs at all levels.'

Karol (17 March 1965 interview): op. cit. 452.

Army training *Museum* 158–60. This is interesting because it is usually said that Zhou steered clear of military affairs in deference to Mao.

Indonesia New UN: *NCNA*, 25 January 1965. Sukarno: Justus van der Kroef, 'The Sino-Indonesian Rupture', *CQ*, January 1968, no. 33, pp. 20–21.

Japan 'No apologies': *Mortal* 162. 'East is east': *Far Eastern Economic Review*, 23 January 1976.

Second safari 'Favourable situation' (speech of 5 June 1965): *CQ*, July 1965, no. 23, p. 222. Ben Bella: Hevi, op. cit. 77. Heykal: *Le Monde*, 10 January 1976.

Malraux (interview of 2 August 1965): *Antimemoirs* (Hamilton, London, 1968) 367–8 and 365.

Stroke Nakajima Reio in *Chuo Korou* (Tokyo), March 1967.

20 Cultural Revolution 1966–67

This chapter and the next owe much to the first sustained attempt to interpret Zhou's role in the Cultural Revolution, Thomas W. Robinson's 'Zhou Enlai and the Cultural

Revolution in China' in Thomas W. Robinson (ed.), *The Cultural Revolution in China* (University of California Press, Berkeley, 1971), hereafter referred to as *Robinson*. See also his 'Chou En-lai's Political Style', *Asian Survey* (Berkeley), December 1970, vol. 10, no. 12, p. 1101.

Liu rumours A story of a 26 February 1966 plot given to a French journalist by Xie Fuzhi (Hsieh Fuchih) and Chen Boda – see *Chicago Daily News*, 19 May 1967.

'Weak-kneed' Michael Yahuda, 'Kremlinology and the Chinese Strategic Debate', *CQ*, January 1979, no. 49, p. 68.

Speech (of 30 April): *Tienmin* 337.

Speech (of 17 June 1966 in Bucharest): see *Tienmin* 338.

Speech (of 27 June 1966 in Albania): *Tienmin* 338–9.

Liu's teams See Charles Neuhauser, 'The Chinese Communist Party in the 1960s', *CQ*, October 1967, no. 32, p. 35.

Song's complaint (of 6 July 1966): see Soong Ching-ling in *Eastern Horizon* (Hong Kong), July 1981.

Night-soil man *PD*, 11 January 1977, and *SWB/FE*/5412. **'Never pour'** *Roots* 163.

'An umbrella' *PD*, 11 January 1977, and *SWB/FE*/5412; and *CR*, April 1977, pp. 23–4.

Han Suyin *My House* 432. Lost voice: Zhou's Red Guard speech of 25 September 1966, *Robinson* 305. **18 August** 1966 rally speech: in Jack Gray and Patrick Cavendish, *Chinese Communism in Crisis* (Pall Mall, London, 1968) 124. Ministries work (9 September 1966 speech): in *Karnow* 227. 'Not difficult' (speech of 13 September 1966): *CB*, no. 819. Speeches on **class origin** ibid. **'Comrades, students'** *SCMP*, no. 3785, and *CQ*, October 1966, no. 28, pp. 184–5.

'We were told' *My House* 468.

'I am talking' (speech of 25 September 1966): *Robinson* 297.

Tucking up *CR*, April 1977, p. 40. **Hotel** ibid. 25. 'No one left': *My House* 466.

Saving Hangzhou Cited in Lucian Pye, *Virginia Quarterly Review*, spring 1977, vol. 53, no. 2, p. 226.

'Millions believed' David and Nancy Milton, *The Wind Will Not Subside: Years in Revolutionary China 1964–1969* (Pantheon, New York, 1976) 108. 'Cleaning up muck' (speech of 1 October 1966): *Beijing Review*, 1966, no. 41; also *CQ*, January 1967, no. 29, p. 182. 'Red Guards cannot' (speech of 3 October 1966): *CB*, no. 819. Tibet: see *Karnow* 361.

Mao on rightists Jerome Ch'en, *Mao Papers* (OUP, London, 1970) 41–2. **On foot** (address of 24 October 1966): in *Karnow* 228. **Sun Yat-sen** ibid. 210. Jiang Qing (speech of 28 November 1966): *PD*, 4 December 1966. Arrest of Peng: see *SWB/FE*/6012.

Deng *Japan Times*, 29 December 1980.

'Burn alive' See foreign reports in *SWB/FE*/2361. Dog's head: *The Times*, 9 January 1967. **Kang** *Mainichi Shimbun* (Tokyo), 19 January 1967. Pathetic defence (of 19 January 1967): *Tienmin* 364.

Criticize line not man *Daily Telegraph*, 12 January 1967. Turns back (on 8 January

1967): *Tokyo Shimbun*, 11 January 1967. Rail minister: *Guardian* (London), 12 January 1967. Wages: see *Robinson* 201–2.

General Xiao *Japan Times*, 22 January 1967, and *Robinson* 226–7. New instructions (of 27 January 1967): *Tokyo Shimbun*, 4 February 1967. MacFarquhar: *New Statesman* (London), 6 January 1967. Harris: *The Times*, 2 March 1967. **Cadre classification** Jerome Ch'en, op. cit. 48–50. Posters on Zhou's **health** *CR*, April 1977, 24–5.

Russian Embassy *Robinson* 267. No power seizure in defence (speech of 18 February 1967): *Tienmin* 347. Extraordinary conference (of 13–16 February 1967): memoirs of Fu Chongbi, *PD*, 7 January 1979, and *SWB/FE/*6012. Mao wrote: *JPRS*, no. 49826. **Coal Minister** *PD*, 26 February 1967, and *SWB/FE/*6056; also *New York Times*, 25 February 1967.

Spring harvest (speech of 19 March 1967): *New York Times*, 22 March 1967, and *Tienmin* 339. 'Red Guards go back' (speech of 25 March 1967): *Japan Times*, 28 March 1967.**Guangdong** Bloodworth sees Zhou's goal as boosting Huang's prestige: *Bloodworth* 116, but see *Karnow* 316.

'Liu not Marxist' (7 April 1967 wallposter): *Japan Times*, 14 April 1967. Zhou as president: *New York Times*, 14 April 1967. 'Do not doubt Zhou' (instruction of 18 April 1967): *Mainichi Shimbun*, 26 April 1967.

21   Detained by Red Guards 1967–68

Wu Chuanpin K. S. Karol, *The Second Chinese Revolution* (Cape, London, 1975) 266; *Karnow* 441–2.

'I was responsible' *Hungweibao*, 18 October 1967, in *CQ*, October 1969, no. 40, p. 86. Whose **dictatorship** *Daily Telegraph*, 15 June 1967. **Siege** *My House* 473 and *SWB/FE/*6012. 'Hated gentleman': *SWB/FE/*2480. **Chen's rebuttal** *Asahi Shimbun*, 1 June 1967. Protection of cadres: *SWB/FE/*6012. Hong Kong speech of 24 June 1967: *SWB/FE/*2501; also *Karnow* 361.

'Mumbles agreement' Richard Harris in *The Times*, 7 July 1967. 'Ten questions': in Red Guard materials in *CB*, no. 844. Zhou on critics: *Tsu Kuo* (Beijing), May 1968, no. 49, cited in *Robinson* 225. Swiss account: *New York Herald Tribune*, 20 July 1967, and *Bangkok Post*, 28 June 1967 (the intermediary named was Fei Yimin of Hong Kong).

General Chen's offer *Hong Kong Star*, 27 July 1967. Chen Yi: *PD*, 7 January 1979. **Cambodia** Melvyn Gurtov, 'The Foreign Ministry and Foreign Affairs During the Cultural Revolution', *CQ*, October 1969, no. 40, pp. 88–9; also *CQ*, October 1967, no. 32, p. 224. British **burning** Helen Foster Snow in *Roots* 165; Jean Daubier, *A History of the Chinese Cultural Revolution* (Vintage, New York, 1974) 207–10 (he called the British chargé only an hour before he was to leave – *Topping* 266).

'You are ignorant' (speech of 25 August 1967): *Tienmin* 346–7.

Siege (of 26 August): Snow (*Long* 186) says Zhou was surrounded for 'more than two days and two nights by half a million . . . Red Guards'. Han Suyin (*My House*) says 'twenty-eight hours'. John Roots (*Roots* 115) says 'three days and two nights'. Fu Chongbi (*PD*, 7 January 1979) says 'eighteen hours'. Yet there could be no four better informed persons on this incident. Harrison Salisbury put it at forty-eight hours (*New York Times*, 11 January 1976). **Oxygen** *Youth 125.*

Chen Yi's confession Jack Chen, *Inside the Cultural Revolution* (Sheldon, London, 1975) 289. **'We need army'** (speech of 17 September 1967): *Karnow* 409–10, and see also 316. **Plundering** (speech of 20 September 1967): *CQ*, October 1967, no. 32, pp. 219–20. **Xie on Zhou** (speech of 9 October 1967): *Wen-ko T'ung-hsun, JPRS*, no. 43, p. 903. 'Decisive victory' (speech of 9 October 1967): in *Strong* II (23 October 1967); *SWB/FE/*2591 and *CQ*, January 1968, no. 33, p. 144.

'Less democracy' (speech of 8 November 1967): ibid., pp. 157–8. Railway (speech of 25 November 1967): ibid., p. 159.

'Very upset' (speech of 17 January 1968): *Karnow* 418. **Bodyguard**: *PD*, 7 January 1979, also *SWB/FE/*6012. **Chen Yi poster** Cited in Gurtov, *CQ*, October 1969, no. 40, pp. 94–5. Against revisions: *SCMP*, no. 4166. **Jiang's articles** *Witke* 59. Canton anniversary: *Tienmin* 351–2.

Traitors not deviators (speech of 27 March 1968): I am indebted to K. S. Karol (op. cit. 324–6) for this interpretation. Kuai: ibid. 331–2.

Guangxi Red Guard (talk of 25 July 1968 in Canton Red Guard pamphlet): *SCMP*, no. 4279.

Czech invasion (speech of 23 August 1968): *CQ*, October 1968, no. 36, p. 174.

Balance sheet (of 7 September 1968): *Strong* II (20 September 1968).

'Big tree' Fu Chongbi, *PD*, 7 January 1979. **Daughter** Fox Butterfield, *China Alive in the Bitter Sea* (Hodder, London, 1982) 355; she had married a Deputy Foreign Minister, Hsu Yihsin, according to *Bloodworth* 31 and 220.

Only the first Felix Greene, *Sunday Times*, 30 April 1972; also *Roots* 118.

Gains more *Long* 157–8.

22   Disciple in the White House 1969–76

Telephone *Wind* 355. Kosygin talks: *Topping* 356 and *Wind* 360.

Ninth Congress 'Let it pass' and devil: *My House* 489–90.

Anthony Grey *Hostage in Peking* (Michael Joseph, London, 1970) 312–13.

Zhou as 'mother' *Garside* 55.

Collapse *Arai* 47–8. Snow (interview of 18 August 1970): *Long* 10; (interview of 5 November 1970): *Long* 158 and 186.

Letter to Nixon *Kissinger* 701–2.

Zhou's plane *Tanjug*, 15 November 1976, and *SWB/FE/*5365.

Ping-pong *Kissinger* 709–10. **American correspondents** (interview of 21 June 1971): *Topping* 395–7. 'No sons': *Topping* 298–9. **Biologist** Professor Arthur W. Galston of Yale at 25 June 1971 US Senate Foreign Relations Committee hearing, *US Relations with the People's Republic of China* (US Government, Washington, 1972) 115. Franz **Michael** At 20 July 1971 US Senate Foreign Relations Committee hearing, op. cit. 325.

Kissinger 'First step': *Kissinger* 744. Zhou's 'ease of manner': *Kissinger* 792. 'Something I can use': Harrison Salisbury, *New York Times*, 11 January 1976. 'Mysterious land': *Kissinger* 746. Guessing numbers: *Kissinger* 750. **Lin** invite Brezhnev?: Stanley Karnow, *Washington Post*, 27 November 1971.

Lin's plot and death *Guillermaz* 462–3; Jack Chen, *Inside the Cultural Revolution* (Sheldon, London, 1975) 344; Yao Ming-le, *The Conspiracy and Murder of Mao's Heir* (Collins, London, 1983), gives an alternative version of these events, but we have no way of deciding between them. Strangling?: *My House* 567. 'The hour': *My House* 565. **Guangdong secession** *Whitson* 555.

Chen Yi funeral *My House* 545. **'All make mistakes'** Ross Terrill, *Mao: A Biography* (Harper & Row, New York, 1980) 367. **Invasions** *Topping* 372; *Wind* 352. **Kissinger again** *Kissinger* 777–84. **UN seat** John Service at 7 February 1972 US Senate Foreign Relations Committee hearing, op. cit. 24–5.

Third World *CQ*, December 1979, no. 80, p. 829; and *CQ*, December 1972, no. 52, p. 793. **Libyan bomb** Mohamed Heykal, *The Road to Ramadan* (Collins, London, 1975) 76–7.

Nixon visit *Nixon* 559–79. Trading indiscretions: *Kissinger* 1070–71. Pens: *Kissinger* 1071–2. Taiwan question: *Kissinger* 1089. 'No reason' for enmity: *CQ*, March 1972, no. 50, p. 397. Youth: *Newsweek*, 6 March 1972.

Cancer 'Transparent'. Rewi Alley in *My House* 586–7. Lawrence: BBC, 11 November 1972. **Smoking** (5 July 1927): Song Lianze (ed.), *Talks with Zhou Enlai* (New Navigation, Hong Kong, 1978) 17.

Science *Museum* 172. **Car accident** *CR*, April 1977, p. 42. Roxane: *Witke* 38. Poem (of Ts'ao Ts'ao): *Roots* 196. 'Long way to go': *Roots* 170.

Confucius The anti-Confucius campaign was in a superficially obvious sense directed against Zhou, but Merle Goldman argues the reverse, that it could have been Zhou attacking the Gang of Four: see *CQ*, September 1975, no. 63, p. 435.

Tenth Congress Jurgen Domes, *China After the Cultural Revolution* (Hurst, London, 1976) 179–87 and 249–52; John Starr, *CQ*, September 1976, no. 67, pp. 459–64; *CQ*, October 1973, no. 56, pp. 807–8; *Wind* 352 and 378–9; and A. Doak Barnett, *Uncertain Passage* (Brookings, Washington, 1974) 181.

Experts *My House* 591–2. Rittenberg: Warren Unna in *The Statesman* (Calcutta), 19 July 1978.

Europe *Frankfurter Allgemeine Zeitung*, 24 August 1973. **Watergate** C. L. Sulzberger, *New York Times* and *International Herald Tribune*, 27 October 1973.

Witke Mao's envy (March 1974 letter): *PD*, December 1976; *Mingbao* (Hong Kong), 28 October 1976 (the source is doubted by some but the sense of this particular passage is most plausible). Divorce: from private well-informed sources.

Nephew *My House* 593. **Classics** Radio Beijing, 5 January 1977, and *SWB/FE/*5409. Complete factories: Richard Baum (ed.), *China's Four Modernizations* (Westview, Boulder, 1980) 160–61. **Heart attack** *Toronto Globe and Mail*, 15 July 1974. Army Day: *Toronto Globe and Mail*, 1 August 1974. Mansfield: *Roots* 169.

Treatment reports Gowon: *The Times*, 17 September and 18 November 1974. **'Landlord element'** Robert Elegant, *International Herald Tribune*, 22 July 1974. Film: *Daily Telegraph*, 27 May 1974.

Wang tells tales *Issues and Studies* (Taipei), September 1977, p. 101 – again a suspect source but probably near the truth. Deng (to Ikeda): *Guardian*, 6 December 1974.

Changsha Hsu Pailing, *NCNA*, 12 January 1977, and *SWB/FE/*5417; also *CR*, April 1977, p. 42.

Fourth NPC January 1975. Zhou's report: *CQ*, June 1975, no. 62, pp. 350–55; and *CQ*, September 1976, no. 67, p. 466.
Operation *Stories* 159. Uraemia: Dr Chang Ching-chiang, *Agence France-Presse* (Taipei), 9 October 1980. **Kukrit** Ross Terrill, op. cit. 394.
Water Margin in *Mainichi Daily News* (Tokyo), 12 March 1976, and *CQ*, September 1976, no. 67, p. 474. Jiang telephones: *My House* 621–2.
Mao's poems *CQ*, June 1976, no. 66, pp. 410–11; *Arai* 258–60; *Enduring* 81.
Testament *Nishikawa* 258–62; Tass, 29 January 1976, from *Sankei Shimbun*, in *SWB/FE/*5126; and see *CQ*, September 1976, no. 67, pp. 487–8. There was a Chinese denial of any true will: *PD*, 5 May 1976, and *Japan Times*, 21 May 1976.
Mao at deathbed? *Japan Times*, 4 February 1976; *Garside* 12.

Notes to Epilogue

This draws upon the best eye-witness account of the period following Zhou's death, Roger Garside, *Coming Alive, China After Mao* (Deutsch, London, 1981); and also *My House* 626–7.
Funeral *CQ*, June 1976, no. 66, pp. 416–24.
Poems from *Garside*; Xiao Lau (trans. and ed.), *The Tienanmen Poems* (Foreign Languages Press, Beijing, 1979) 19 and 55; and David S. Zweig in *CQ*, March 1978, no. 73, p. 157.

Notes to A Summing-up

MacDonald *CQ*, July 1968, no. 35, p. 159.
'You make friends' *Bloodworth* 28.
Pye Lucian W. Pye, 'A Very Exceptional Communist', *Virginia Quarterly Review*, spring 1977, vol. 53, no. 2, p. 223.
Peyrefitte *Le Monde*, 10 January 1976.
Chen Boda *My House* 463–4.
Newspaper incident C. L. Sulzberger, *The Age of Mediocrity: Memories and Diaries 1963-1972* (Macmillan, New York, 1973) 8.
James MacDonald *CQ*, July 1968, no. 35, p. 158.
Not moderate See the case made by Warren Kuo, 'On Chou En-lai', *Issues and Studies* (Taipei), July 1972, vol. 8, no. 10, pp. 42–51.
Dalai Lama *My Land and People* (Weidenfeld & Nicolson, London, 1962) 106.

Index

Academy of Sciences, 244, 253–4, 282
Acheson, Dean, 194
Advanced Infantry School (USSR), 99
Afghanistan, 210, 212
Africa, 204, 216, 224, 279; Zhou's tours of, 229–31, 235
Afro-Asian Conference, second (proposed), 229, 230, 231, 236; *see also* Bandung conference
Aksai Chin, 222, 224, 232
Albania, 227, 229, 230, 240
Algeria, 230, 236
all-China Congress of Base Areas, 117
American Civil War, 280
American War of Independence, 280
Anderson, Jack, 155
Anhui Province, 149, 157–8
Anshunchang, 127
Antonioni, Michelangelo, 286
Arabs, 225
Associated Press, 152
Aswan Dam, 230
Attlee, Clement, 197
Atwood, William, 274
Auden, W. H., 147
Awakening, 48, 49
Awakening Society, 48, 51–2, 53, 60, 78
Ayub Khan, 236

Bai Chongxi, General, 87
Baltic Sea, 229
Bandung conference (1955), 17, 200–202, 203, 204, 212, 225, 229, 230

Baoan, 129, 132, 135
Barbusse, Henri, 58
BBC, 282
Beer, 55
Beethoven, Ludwig van, 286
Beidaihe, 233, 276
Beijing (Peking), 78, 146, 180; May Fourth Movement, 43, 45, 47, 49, 53; Northern Expedition, 83; Red Army enters, 175–6; Zhongnanhai, 181; Great Hall of the People, 184–5; Cultural Revolution, 239, 241; Red Guard rallies, 242–3, 244; foreign diplomats attacked in, 262; Zhou's death, 291–2
Beijing Hotel, 182, 183, 246, 289
Beijing University (Beida), 46, 239, 282
Belden, Jack, 307
Belgium, 65, 295
Ben Bella, Mohamed, 236
Beria, Lavrenti, 192
Berlin, 64, 65, 66, 91
Berne, 193, 195
Bertram, James, 143, 146, 147
Bhutto, President Zulfikar, 287
Billancourt, 55
Bloodworth, Dennis, 17, 167
Blyukher, General Vasili, 73
Bo Gu, 114, 119, 121, 122, 123
Bois de Boulogne, 64
Bolsheviks, *see* Soviet Union; Twenty-eight Bolsheviks
Borodin, Mikhail, 73, 75, 82, 89, 90
Bourguiba, President Habib ben Ali, 230

Boxer Rising, 22, 262
Braun, Otto, 114, 116–17, 118, 119, 121–3, 151
Brest-Litovsk treaty (1918), 284
Brezhnev, Leonid, 233
British–American Tobacco Company, 110
British army, 60
Bucharest, 240
Bukharin, Mikhail, 100–101, 165
Bulganin, Nikolai, 199
Burma, 158, 229, 238; relations with China, 189, 204; Zhou's visits to, 195, 231–2; Bandung conference, 200; Overseas Chinese, 210; border agreement with China, 223–4

Café Aurore, Paris, 56
Café Pascal, Paris, 58
Cai Chang, 58, 69
Cai Hesen, 58, 59, 79, 88
Cai Tingkai, General, 94
Cairo, 229–30, 236
Cambodia, 194, 195, 198, 203, 204, 209, 224, 262
Camp David, 225
Canton (Guangzhou), 71–3, 262, 264, 265
Canton Commune, 97
Carlson, Major Evans, 144, 148, 155
Catholic Church, 56
Central Bureau of Soviet Affairs, 113, 114
Central Committee, 167, 181, 298; and the Jiangxi Campaign, 115; withholds Zhou's report on wages, 215; and the Great Leap Forward, 221; agricultural policy, 226; and the Cultural Revolution, 241, 243, 245, 251
Central Executive Committee, 112, 113, 117
Central Revolutionary Military Council, 112, 117
Central Secretariat, 167
Ceylon, 200, 203, 212, 232
Chang Chun-ming, 309
Changsha, 48, 60, 89, 104, 106, 149, 287
Chapin, Dwight, 281
Chaplin, Charlie, 129, 183, 197
Charleroi, 65
Château Thierry, 55
Chen (Zhou's adoptive mother), 22, 23
Chen Boda, 258, 271; in the Cultural Revolution, 241, 247, 252, 255, 256, 265;

defends Zhou, 260; Mao purges, 273; on Zhou, 299
Chen Boer, 155
Chen Cheng, 145
Chen Duxiu, 48, 62, 65, 85, 86, 88, 89, 107–8, 296
Chen family, 22
Chen Nikia, 309, 316–17
Chen Qiongming, 75, 80
Chen Yi, 16, 69, 217, 276; in France, 54; Nanchang uprising, 93, 94; in civil war, 118; takes over Foreign Ministry, 216; Third World tours, 223–4, 229; in the Cultural Revolution, 250–51; Red Guards campaign against, 216, 259, 261–2, 263, 264–5; death, 277, 292
Chen Zaidao, General, 261
Chenpao, 270
Chi Benyü, 244–5
Chiang Ching-kuo, 101, 137
Chiang Kai-shek (Jiang Jieshi), 89, 109, 116, 122, 132, 156, 160, 245, 301; at Huangpu Military Academy, 73, 75; repression of peasants, 76; disputes with Communists, 80–81, 82; *Zongshan* gunboat incident, 81–2; Northern Expedition, 82–3; and the Shanghai revolution, 85–6, 88, 95, 99; Fifth 'Encirclement' Campaign, 117; and the Long March, 130; and the United Front, 130–33, 139, 140–42; captured by Northeastern Army, 134–8; war with Japan, 142, 144, 145, 149; New Life Movement, 147; and Zhou's accident, 151; relations with America, 155; relations with Zhou, 157; collapse of United Front, 157–8; Zhou on, 164; coalition negotiations, 168, 170, 172–3; Communists flee from, 173, 175; defeat, 176
Chinese Communist Party: formation of, 60–61; Zhou joins, 64; European branch, 64; alliance with Guomindang, 66, 68–9, 72–3; Soviet aid, 68–9; Zhou's role in, 71, 294, 296, 300; disputes with Guomindang, 80–81, 82; Northern Expedition, 82–3; Shanghai revolution, 83–7, 88; Fifth Congress (1927), 88, 296; Zhou becomes Secretary-General, 88; Nanchang uprising, 89–95, 97; Sixth Congress (1928), 99–101, 245; relations

with Soviet Communists, 104–5, 106, 107–9, 110; Shaoshan Report, 105; Central Bureau for Base Areas, 109; Mao's rise to power, 118, 122; United Front, 130–32, 138–42, 144, 152; captures Chiang Kai-shek, 134–8; war with Japan, 141–50; base in Chongqing, 153–8, 159; South China Bureau, 156; United Front collapses, 157–8, 162; Rectification Campaign, 159–60, 162–3, 165; Seventh Congress (1945), 166–7; coalition negotiations, 167–73; flees from Guomindang, 173–5; defeats Guomindang, 175–6; forms government, 176–8, 179–80; policy towards intellectuals, 206–7; Eighth Congress (1956), 208–9, 218; Hundred Flowers Movement, 213–14, 216, 301; Great Leap Forward, 216, 218, 219, 220–22; Cultural Revolution, 239–57, 258–69; Ninth Congress (1969), 271; Tenth Congress (1973), 283–4

Chinese People's Political Consultative Conference (CPPCC), 179–80

Chingdao, 278

Chirac, Jacques, 64n.

Chongqing, 153–8, 159, 160–61, 162, 166, 168, 187, 214

Chou, Eric, 186

Chu Ling-gin, 68

Churchill, Winston, 165, 194

Colombo, 54–5

Comintern, 46, 58, 81, 97, 101, 187; finances Zhou, 56; seeks alliance between Guomindang and Communist Party, 66; advisers in China, 72–3; *Theses on the China Problem*, 83; and the Nanchang uprising, 89–91, 296; Zhou and, 104, 105, 107; Zhou addresses, 151

Commission for Science and Technology, 264

Communist Manifesto, 48, 154

Confucianism, 283

Confucius, 32, 46, 72, 176, 249, 283, 285, 286

Cultural Revolution, 18, 69, 108, 160, 165, 216, 238–57, 268–9, 272, 284, 297; early signals, 235; aims of, 238–40; socialist re-education, 240, 242; Sixteen Points, 241–2, 243, 247, 248; attacks on Zhou, 183,

245–6; PLA enters, 252; Red Guards turn against Zhou, 258–67; Zhou tries to end, 267; Zhou justifies, 288

Czechoslovakia, 267

Da Gong Bao, 32

Dadu river, 126–7

Daily Express, 240

Dalai Lama, 209, 222, 300

Darwin, Charles, 25

Days at the Criminal Court, 51

Deng Xiaoping, 64, 238, 287, 293, 298, 301; in France, 54, 57; in Jiangxi, 115; economic reforms, 228; on Zhou in the Cultural Revolution, 249; in the Cultural Revolution, 251, 257; rejoins Politburo, 283; becomes Zhou's deputy, 288; and Zhou's death, 292

Deng Yingchao (Zhou's wife), 46, 52, 58, 67, 81, 98, 177, 184; May Fourth Movement, 45, 48, 49–50, 51, 77–8; marriage, 76–7, 78–9, 84–5; background, 77–9; Long March, 78, 120, 129, 130; miscarriage, 83; in Russia, 99; in Jiangxi, 112; war with Japan, 143, 146–7; in Yan'an, 163–4; coalition negotiations, 168; flees Guomindang, 173; on Zhou, 183; diabetes, 225; worries over Zhou's health, 254; and Zhou's death, 290, 291

Denson, John, 262, 271

Desai, Morarji, 224

Detention by the Police, 51

Dien Bien Phu, 193

Ding Ling, 109

Dixie Mission, 164, 166, 279

Donald, W. H., 136

Dong Biwu, 277

Dongguan School, 24, 25

Dostoyevsky, Fyodor, 71, 75

Dulles, John Foster, 194, 195, 196, 197, 200, 275, 280, 301

Durdin, Tillman, 147

East Asian Preparatory High School, Tokyo, 38

East Germany, 67

The East is Red, 184

East River, 90, 93

East Workers' University, Moscow, 66

Eastern Europe, 210, 211, 213

Eastern Expeditions, 75, 80, 90
Eden, Anthony, 194–5, 196, 200, 301
Egypt, 60, 202, 224–5, 229–30, 236
Eisenhower, Dwight D., 224, 225
Empire Conference, 57
'Encirclement' campaigns, 114, 116–18, 123, 127
Ethiopia, 231
Europe, 285
European labour movement, 55

Farouk, King of Egypt, 230
Fen, river, 144
Finance Ministry, 256
First Girls' Normal School, Tianjin, 48, 77
First World War, 38, 39, 55, 61
Fitch, George, 170
Five Principles of Peaceful Coexistence, 196
Five-Year Plans: First, 198, 207; Second, 208; Third, 244
Foreign Languages Institute, 241, 244, 258–9
Foreign Ministry, 157, 181, 189–90, 216, 259–60, 261–2, 264–5, 287
Formosa, see Taiwan
Four Modernizations, 288, 292, 293
France, 74; Zhou lives in, 51–3, 54–62, 64–70, 295; China seeks loan from, 59; 1954 Geneva conference, 193–5, 197; American War of Independence, 280; Pompidou visits China, 285
Fuji, Mount, 38
Fujian Province, 112, 134
Futian incident, 108, 113, 296
Fuzhou, 116

Galen, see Blyukher, General Vasili
Gandhi, Mahatma, 208
Gang of Four, 150; members, 277; loses prestige, 281; campaign against Zhou, 283, 286, 287, 289, 290, 292–3; and Zhou's death, 291
Ganzhou, 114
Gao Erwu, 24–5
Geneva, 204
Geneva conference on Indochina (1954), 17, 67, 193–5, 196–8, 199, 204
Germany, 57, 74, 288; Zhou visits, 64, 65, 67–8, 295; treaty of Brest-Litovsk, 284
Ghana, 230–31

Giscard d'Estaing, Valéry, 64n.
Gomulka, Wladyslaw, 211
Gordon, General Charles, 231
Göttingen, 67–8
Gowon, General, 287
Grand Canal, 19
Great Britain, 57, 74; Zhou visits, 55–7, 60; aid to Chinese warlords, 75; Korean war, 189; and the Sino-Indian border dispute, 222–3
Great Leap Forward (1958), 18, 216, 218, 219, 220–22, 226, 228, 297, 300
Great Wall, 174
Greece, 57
Green Gang, 98
Greene, Felix, 268
Grey, Anthony, 271
Gu Shunzhang, 85, 98, 101, 110–11
Guangchang, 118
Guangdong Province, 69, 71, 72, 90, 91, 93, 256, 277
Guangxi Province, 77, 265, 269
Guilin, 266–7
Guizhou Province, 121
Gulin, 141
Guo Morou, 144
Guomindang (National Party), 25, 33, 48, 60, 65, 74, 106, 109–10; alliance with Communist Party, 66, 68–9, 72–3; Soviet aid, 66, 72–3; Three People's Principles, 72; Eastern Expeditions, 75, 80, 90; Deng Yingchao joins, 78–9; disputes with Communists, 80–81, 82; Northern Expedition, 82–3; and the Shanghai revolution, 85–7, 88; Nanchang uprising, 89, 91, 92–5, 97; arrest of Communists, 110–11; defections from, 113; Fourth 'Encirclement' Campaign, 114, 116; defections to, 116; 19th Route Army, 116; Fifth 'Encirclement' Campaign, 117–18, 123; and the Long March, 121, 126, 127; United Front, 130–32, 138–42, 152; Chiang Kai-shek's capture, 135–7; Zhou refuses to join, 146; war with Japan, 147, 149, 165–6; spies on Zhou, 154, 155; United Front collapses, 157–8, 162; coalition negotiations, 167–73; Communists flee from, 173–5; Communists defeat, 175–6; security treaty with USA, 200; assassination attempt on

Zhou, 201; 1958 crisis, 218; African support for, 229; spreads rumours about Zhou, 261

Hailufeng, 96
Hammarskjöld, Dag, 17
Han Chinese, 215
Han Suyin, 104, 122, 159, 207, 225, 226, 242
Hangzhou, 98, 185, 246
Hanoi, 270
Harris, Richard, 253
He Long, General, 91, 92, 93, 95, 97
He Mengxiong, 107
Hebei Province, 173, 175, 217
Hemingway, Ernest, 155
Henan Province, 77
Heykal, Mohamed, 236
Hitler, Adolf, 151
Ho Chi Minh, 69, 71, 73, 193, 196, 270
Hong Kong, 54, 90, 183, 295; British fund unrest in Canton from, 75; Zhou takes refuge in, 95, 96–7; Guomindang exiles in, 179; Zhou claims China's right to, 260–61
Hsu Kai-yu, 308
Hu Hua, 313
Hua Guofeng, 64n., 293
Huai En, 313
Huaian, 19–21, 23–4, 26–7, 149, 183–4
Huaiyin (Qingjiang), 23
Huang, General, 256
Huang Aiyin, 60, 62–3
Huang Di, 141
Huang Jinghun, 109–10
Huangpu, 81–2, 83, 156
Huangpu Military Academy, 73–6, 79, 80, 86, 87, 91, 124, 252, 298, 301
L'Humanité, 56
Hunan Province, 89, 94
Hundred Flowers Movement, 206, 213–14, 216, 297, 301
Hungary, 210–11, 212, 213
Hurley, Ambassador Patrick J., 166

India, 203, 208, 245; Nehru visits China, 156, 200; and the Korean war, 189; Zhou visits, 195–6, 209–10, 212–13; Bandung conference, 200; Tibetan dispute, 209–10; border dispute with China, 209, 222–4, 230, 231, 232, 301; Chinese loans to, 226–7; and the Lin Biao affair; 278
Indochina, 193–5, 196–8, 278
Indonesia, 200, 203, 204, 208, 210, 235, 258, 260
Iraq, 231
Ireland, 60
Islam, 245
Islamabad, 275
Israel, 210

Japan, 57, 229; war with Russia, 26; Twenty-One Demands (1915), 33, 38; Zhou studies in, 37–44, 295; relations with China, 38–9; Versailles Treaty, 47; Manchurian campaign, 130–31, 132, 135; war with China, 141–50, 151–2, 165–6; surrenders, 167; relations with Communist China, 202–3; China seeks friendship with, 236; and the Vietnam war, 238; and the Lin Biao affair, 278
Japan-French Law School, 38
Jen Chohsuan, 309
Ji Pengfei, 280
Jiajin mountain, 127
Jialing river, 154
Jiang Qing (Mao's wife), 258, 261, 277; marries Mao, 130; and Zhou's accident, 150; in Moscow, 212; Red Guard rallies, 242; in the Cultural Revolution, 244–5, 247, 249, 252, 256, 260; denounces May 16th Group, 263; Lin Biao tries to discredit, 265; and Zhou's daughter's death, 268; and Nixon's visit to China, 281; interview with Roxane Witke, 282, 285; relations with Mao, 285; plots against Zhou, 286, 289; and Zhou's death, 299
Jiangsu Province, 19, 26, 98
Jiangxi Province, 90, 94, 104, 106, 108, 110, 112–19, 122, 149
Jinggangshan, 94, 103, 115, 289

Kádar, János, 211
Kaifeng, 170
Kang Nairu, 49, 154
Kang Sheng, 165, 250, 258, 260, 271
Kang Youwei, 25, 72
Karol, K. S., 235
Kashmir, 295
Kashmir Princess, 201

Kautsky, 48
Kawakami Hajime, Dr, 40, 44
Keatley, Robert, 274
Kennedy, John F., 17, 227
Kenya, 231
Khrushchev, Nikita S., 191, 192, 214, 224,
  230, 233, 257, 281, 302; 1954 Geneva
  conference, 193; Zhou asks for aid, 197;
  visits China, 199–200; de-Stalinization,
  210–11, 213; relations with Zhou, 211–
  12; tense relations with China, 217–18;
  industrial aid to China, 219; cancels aid
  for nuclear programme, 221; and the
  Sino-Indian border dispute, 223;
  withdraws technicians from China, 225–6,
  227; Camp David talks, 225; Mao
  lampoons, 290
Kim Il Sung, 189
Kishi Nobusuke, 203
Kissinger, Henry, 17, 273, 275–6, 278–9,
  280–81, 285
Kobe, 38
Korea, 38, 156, 188–90, 229
Korean war, 188–91, 193, 195, 204
Kosygin, Alexei, 233, 270, 272, 281, 302
Kotelawala, Sir John, 203
Kotnis, Dr, 150
Kowloon, 260
Kuai Dafu, 259, 265
Kung Chu, 115–16
Kyoto, 39–41
Kyoto University, 40

Labour Party (Britain), 197
Lafayette, Marquis de, 280
Lancashire, 46
Laos, 194, 195, 198, 204
Latin America, 224, 236
Lawrence, Anthony, 282
Lawrence, D. H., 143
Lebbe, Father Vincent, 55
Lenin, Vladimir Ilyich, 39, 188, 208, 226,
  227, 284, 301–2
Lenin University, 71
Leys, Simon, 307
Li Dazhao, 48, 53, 78
Li Fuchun, 54, 69
Li Fujing, 55
Li Lisan, 89, 96, 101, 104, 106, 141, 296; in
  France, 54, 57, 69; expelled from China,

59–60; Nanchang uprising, 90, 91, 93, 95,
  97; at Sixth Congress, 100; disputes with
  Zhou, 103–5; Red Army attacks
  Changsha, 106; disgrace, 106, 107, 108,
  110
Li Tien-min, 308
Li Xiannian, 246, 251, 287
Li Yuru, 52, 53
Liang Qichao, 24, 25, 72
Liao Chengzhi, 145, 250, 277
Liao Zhongkai, 73, 76
Libya, 279
Lichao, 117
Life magazine, 132, 193
Lille, 58
Lin Biao, 73, 176, 235, 256, 286; Nanchang
  uprising, 94; Long March, 124; war with
  Japan, 143; and the Hundred Flowers
  Movement, 213; and the Mao/Zhou split,
  218; and the Cultural Revolution,
  241, 244–5, 248, 252, 260, 264, 268, 269;
  and Liu's bid for power, 242; Zhou fuels
  Mao's suspicions of, 249; alliance with
  Zhou, 252–3; May 16th Group attacks,
  263; tries to discredit Jiang Qing, 265; as
  Mao's heir, 271; struggle for power, 271,
  272, 297; quarrel with Zhou, 273, 298;
  plans to assassinate Mao, 276–7, 278, 283;
  death, 276–7
Lincoln, Abraham, 280
Ling Yin Temple, Hangzhou, 185
Liping, 121
Liu Bocheng, 93
Liu Ning, 89, 93, 98, 146
Liu Shaoqi, 161, 163, 167, 253, 283; in the
  civil war, 110; rivalry with Zhou, 156, 164;
  and Mao's Rectification Campaign, 159–
  60, 178; flees Guomindang, 173, 175;
  Zhou on, 177; visits Russia, 192; reform
  programme, 204; struggle for power, 208–
  9, 233, 234, 237, 238–9, 242, 297; and the
  Hundred Flowers Movement, 213–14,
  216, 301; and the Great Leap Forward,
  216, 218; and the Mao/Zhou split, 219–
  20; economic reforms, 228; and the
  Cultural Revolution, 238–40, 251, 265,
  269; Zhou denounces, 256, 257; Red
  Guards look for evidence against, 259
Liu Wuchi, 309
Liuzhou, 265

Physical Culture Commission, 250
Pingxing Pass, 143
Poland, 211
Polevoy, Sergei, 46
Politburo, 167, 181, 206, 207, 214, 256, 271, 283, 291, 300
Pompidou, Georges, 285
Porthos, 54, 55
Pramoj, Kukrit, 289
Pu Shouchang, Dr, 186
Pu Yi, Emperor, 65
Pye, Lucian, 295

Qadafi, Colonel Mu'ammer al, 279
Qinghai, 126
Qinghua School, Beijing, 28
Qinghua University, 241
Qu Qiubai, 88, 97, 101, 104, 106, 107–8, 296
Quemoy crisis (1954), 200, 301

Rangoon, 199, 201, 226–7, 229
'Rebel Grand Army', 266
Rectification Campaign, 159–60, 162–3, 165, 178, 250, 297, 298
Red Army, 73, 165, 175; Fourth Army, 91, 103–4; creation of, 95, 98; Nanchang uprising, 95; Zhou builds up, 103–4, 106; Zhou and Mao disagree over, 113–15; First Front Army, 114; Jiangxi campaign, 114–19; Long March, 120–30; First Corps, 121; United Front, 141–2; war with Japan, 143–4; coalition negotiations, 168; defeats Guomindang, 175–6; Korean war, 191
Red Flag, 255
Red Guards: formation of, 239; Zhou and, 160, 240–41, 242–4, 246–8, 250–51, 300; excesses, 240, 248–50; rallies in Beijing, 242–3, 244; attack Zhou, 245, 258–67; Zhou tries to hold back, 255–6; besiege Soviet embassy, 255; detain Anthony Grey, 271; and foreigners in China, 284
Ren Bishi, 161
Renault, 56, 57, 59
Respect Work, 31–2
Respect Work and Enjoy Company Society, 31, 33
Reston, James, 196
Reuters, 229, 271
Revolutionary Military Council, 119, 121

Rittenberg, Sidney, 284
Romulo, Carlos P., 201–2
Roosevelt, Franklin D., 166, 301
Roots, John, 307–8
Roots, Bishop Logan Herbert, 90, 148, 295, 300
Rousseau, Jean Jacques, 25
Roy, M. N., 89, 92
Ruijin, 112, 118
Rumania, 239–40, 273

Saigon, 54–5
St Chamond, 57
Samson, Gerald, 152
Saturday Evening Post, 132
Sceaux, 66, 79
Schubert, Franz, 286
Scientific and Technical Commission for National Defence, 233
SEATO, 195, 198, 200, 201, 301
Second World War, 67, 151
Service, John Singer, 146, 165, 279
Shaanxi Province, 129, 131, 132, 139, 141
Shandong Province, 47, 278
Shanghai, 56, 96, 131, 171–2, 214, 277, 295, 297, 300, 301; foreigners in, 54; formation of Communist Party in, 60; revolution, 83–7, 88, 92, 95, 98, 99, 105, 110, 176; Northern Expedition, 83–4; Japanese capture, 141; Cultural Revolution, 245; Red Guards, 248; commune, 252
Shanghai Commercial Press, 85, 86
Shanghai Communiqué, 279
Shantou (Swatow), 76, 80, 82, 90, 94, 95, 96
Shanxi Province, 142, 143, 173, 174
Shaoshan Report, 105, 108
Shaoxing, 21, 149
Shenyang, 24–6, 38
Siberia, 39
Sichuan Province, 125, 126–9, 139, 297
Sihanouk, Prince Norodom, 203, 224, 262
Silesia, 57
Sima Qian, 32
Singapore, 54, 210
Sino-French Educational Association, 56
Sino-Soviet Treaty (1949), 187–8
Sixth Uncle, 171
Smedley, Agnes, 97, 143, 148
Smith, Adam, 33

Snow, Edgar, 35, 71, 73, 91, 97, 101, 113, 123, 132–3, 144, 146–7, 148, 150–51, 164, 226, 233–4, 269, 272, 285, 298
Snow, Helen Foster, 140
Social Problems Research, 40
Socialist Education Movement, 234, 239, 243, 249, 268, 300
Somalia, 231
Song Qingling (Madame Sun Yat-sen), 75, 81, 177, 240, 248
Soong May-ling, 136
Soong, T. V., 138
Soviet Union, 57, 208, 216, 295; Revolution, 39, 46, 54, 78; Sun Yat-sen seeks help from, 66; aid for Guomindang, 72, 74; and the *Zongshan* gunboat incident, 81–2; and the Northern Expedition, 83; and the Nanchang uprising, 89, 90–92, 95, 97; Zhou's visits to, 99–101, 104, 151; relations with Chinese Communists, 104–5, 107–9, 110; and the Japanese campaign in Manchuria, 135; pact with Hitler, 151; and civil war in China, 175; Zhou declares independence from, 179; Sino-Soviet treaty, 187–8; Korean war, 188–9, 190; Stalin's funeral, 192–3; 1954 Geneva Conference, 193–4; Khrushchev visits China, 199–200; Hungarian crisis, 210–11, 212, 213; tense relations with China, 217–18, 233; industrial aid to China, 219; detente with America, 225, 227, 233; withdraws technicians from China, 225–6, 227; Twenty-second Party Congress (1961), 227; Zhou tries to lead Third World away from, 229; and the Vietnam war, 238; Red Guards besiege embassy, 255; invades Czechoslovakia, 267; border dispute with China, 270; and the Lin Biao affair, 278; Brest-Litovsk treaty, 284; Zhou's dependence on, 296
Stalin, Joseph, 89, 94, 144, 227, 233, 301; and the Nanchang uprising, 92; Zhou's visit to Russia, 104; pact with Hitler, 151; and the civil war in China, 175; Sino-Soviet treaty, 187–8; aid to China, 191; funeral, 192–3; de-Stalinization, 210–11, 213, 218
Stalinism, 235
State Council, 180, 246, 252
State Department (USA), 177–8, 279, 280

Staufenbiel, Kunigund, 67
Stern, 67–8
Stilwell, General Joseph, 158
Stuart, Rev. John Leighton, 172, 178
Sudan, 231
Suez Canal, 54
Suez crisis (1956), 225, 230
Sukarno, Achmed, 204, 208, 235, 236
Sun Weishi (Zhou's adopted daughter), 130, 173, 268
Sun Yat-sen, 25, 33, 65, 71, 74, 93, 177, 208; seeks help from Russia, 66; Soviet aid, 72; Huangpu Military Academy, 73; Three Principles, 76, 140; death, 75; centenary, 248
Sun Yat-sen, Madame, *see* Song Qingling
Sun Yat-sen University, 101, 107
Syria, 224–5, 231

Tagore, Rabindranath, 212
Taiping rebellion, 23
Taiwan (Formosa), 138, 183, 186, 197, 198, 229, 275, 277; Guomindang retreats to, 176; and the Korean war, 188–9; Quemoy crisis, 200, 301; security treaty with USA, 200; claims seat in United Nations, 202; China/USA negotiations, 202, 203–4, 209, 272, 273; 1958 crisis, 218; Shanghai Communiqué, 279, 280–81
Taiwan Straits, 279, 292
Taiyuan, 143, 144
Takasaki Tatsunosuke, 44, 202–3
Tan Zhenlin, 249–50, 251, 255
Tanzania, 231, 236
Tao Zhu, 259n.
Thailand, 201, 202, 229, 289
Third World, 229–32, 279, 284
'Three-Anti Campaign', 191
Tianjin, 28, 45–9, 53, 56, 69, 77, 78, 99, 146–7, 187, 295
Tianjin Girl Students' Patriotic Association, 48
Tibet, 129, 195, 198, 209–10, 215, 222, 224, 247, 278
Time magazine, 190
The Times, 253, 261, 287
Tito, Marshal Josip, 71, 179, 230
Togliatti, 71
Tokyo, 38
Tolstoy, Lev, 46

Topping, Seymour, 274
Trans-Siberian railway, 71
Trevelyan, Sir Humphrey, 200
Trotsky, Leon, 89, 95
Trudeau, Pierre, 68
Truman, President Harry S., 188–9, 190
Tseng family, 21
Tsitsihar, 267
Tunisia, 230, 231
Turkey, 203
Twentieth Army, 92
Twenty-eight Bolsheviks, 105, 107, 108, 114, 122, 123, 163, 164

Uganda, 231
United Arab Republic, 224–5
United Front, 100–101, 113, 131, 138–42, 144, 152, 157–8, 162, 186, 300
United Nations: China's exclusion from, 179, 189, 198, 229; Korean war, 190; Taiwan claims seat, 202; Sukarno proposes rival to, 235; China admitted to, 279
United States of America, 74; Zhou wants friendly relations with, 155–6, 158, 164; relations with Zhou, 166, 301; and the coalition negotiations, 169–70, 172–3; backs Guomindang, 173, 175; and the new Communist government in China, 179–80, 187; Korean war, 188–90; 1954 Geneva Conference, 194–5, 196–7; SEATO, 195, 198; security treaty with Taiwan, 200; negotiations over Taiwan, 202, 203–4, 209, 272, 273; 1958 Taiwan crisis, 218; detente with Russia, 225, 227, 233; poor relations with China, 229; Vietnam war, 236; China resumes relations with, 272–6, 284, 285; Nixon's visit to China, 274, 276, 278, 279–82; and the Lin Biao affair, 278; Watergate crisis, 285; airmen shot down over China, 295
US Senate, 274–5
US Seventh Fleet, 188–9
USSR, see Soviet Union

Varovsky, SS, 72
Versailles Treaty (1919), 43, 47
Vienna Kurier, 232
Vietnam, 194, 229, 265–6, 273; 1954
Geneva conference, 193, 194, 196; Zhou visits, 209, 224
Vietnam war, 236, 238, 275
Visvabharati University, 212
Vladimirov, Peter 156
Vladivostok, 110, 112

Wall Street Journal, 274
Wan Donger (Zhou's mother), 20–22, 23
Wan Waithayakon, Prince, 202
Wang, Anna, 78
Wang Hongwen, 277, 283, 287, 289
Wang Jiaxiang, 125
Wang Jingwei, 85, 86, 87, 89
Wang Li, 244–5, 259, 261, 263
Wang Meng, 34
Wang Ming, 141, 159, 163, 164; Zhou supports, 105, 107–8, 296; criticism of, 109; in the civil war, 110, 112; rivalry with Mao, 112, 123, 297; visit to Moscow, 114; war with Japan, 144, 148; relations with Zhou, 156
Waseda, 38
Washington Conference (1921), 57
Water Margin, 289
Watergate crisis, 285
Wedemeyer, General Albert, 166
Wei Guolu, 125, 126, 127, 128
White, Theodore, 17, 153, 154, 156
Willkie, Wendell, 155
Witke, Roxane, 282, 285
Women's Patriotic Association, 77
Worker-Student Mutual Help Society, 58
Wu Chuanpin, 258
Wu Dager, 29, 37, 38, 39–41, 43–4, 57, 64, 139–40
Wuchan, 298
Wuhan, 85, 87, 88, 89, 90, 92, 95, 110, 145, 147–9, 261, 264
Wusuli river, 270

Xi'an incident, 134, 135–7, 139, 301
Xiang river, 121
Xiang Ying, 112, 149
Xiao Hua, General, 252
Xiao Jingguang, General, 117
Xibaipao, 175, 297
Xie Fuzhi, 263
Xinjiang, 224

Yan Fansun, 56
Yan'an, 111, 129, 132, 134, 135, 140, 141, 144, 146, 148–9, 159, 161, 162–5, 173, 279, 297
Yan'an Radio, 158
Yang Mei, 169
Yangzi delta, 28
Yangzi river, 19, 90, 110, 126, 149, 154, 278
Yao Dengshan, 258, 259, 260
Yao Wenyuan, 86, 277
Ye Jianying, Marshal, 76, 93, 124, 154, 287
Ye Ting, General, 91, 92, 94, 97, 149, 158, 169
Yellow River, 19, 170, 217, 278
Yemen, 231
Yiqian, 118
Yishi Gao, 55, 56–7, 60
YMCA, 45, 170
Young Marshal, *see* Zhang Xueliang
Youth, 61, 65
Youth Guards, 117
Youth League, 60, 61, 64, 65, 79, 100
Yu Qiuli, 251
Yuan Shikai, 32, 33, 35
Yunnan Province, 125, 126, 289

Zambia, 279
Zanzibar, 231
Zhabei, 85
Zhang Boling, Dr, 295; influence on Zhou, 29–30, 36; friendship with Zhou, 31, 36, 140, 154–5, 300; financial aid to Zhou, 45–6; in the Japanese war, 165; Communists put pressure on, 187
Zhang Chunqiao, 277, 286
Zhang Fakui, General, 91–2, 93, 94
Zhang Guotao, 96, 109, 110, 112, 142, 144; background, 89–90; Nanchang uprising, 91, 92–3, 94, 95, 97; Long March, 127–8, 297; defects to Guomindang, 145; and Zhou's diplomacy, 145
Zhang Linzhi, 256
Zhang Pengxian, 33–4
Zhang Xueliang (the Young Marshal), 131–2, 133, 134–9
Zhejiang Province, 21, 98, 149, 150, 159
Zheng Chunqiao, 293
Zhengzhou, 115, 170
Zhongshan gunboat incident (1926), 81–2, 301

Zhou Enchan, 23
Zhou Enlai
    private life: character, 16–18, 79, 149–50; love of acting, 30–31; poetry, 32, 33–4, 35, 37–8, 41–3, 49, 52, 62–3, 158; allegations of illegitimate child, 67–8; marriage, 76–7, 78–9, 285–6; adopts daughter, 130; diplomatic skill, 144–5, 153, 194, 294; injury to his arm, 150–51; prostate operation, 159; austerity, 181–2, 207; concerns for others, 182–3; attitude to his family, 183–4; women's rights, 184; ill-health, 228, 233; heart trouble, 254, 263; and his adopted daughter's death, 268; cancer, 282, 287; attitude to foreigners, 284–5; health deteriorates, 286–7, 288–90; death, 290, 291–3
    early life: 19–27, 294–5; at Nankai School, 28–36, 37; studies in Japan, 37–44; conversion to Marxism, 41–3, 48, 60–70; and the May Fourth Movement, 43–4, 45, 47–53; at Nankai University, 45–51; imprisonment, 50–51; life in France, 51–3, 54–62, 64–70; visits Germany, 64, 65, 67–8; returns to China, 69–70, 71; and the Huangpu Military Academy, 73–6; in Russia, 99–101, 104, 151
    civil war period: and the Eastern Expeditions, 75, 80; friendship with Mao Zedong, 76, 97–8; disputes between Communists and Guomindang, 80–81, 82; *Zhongshan* gunboat incident, 81–2; Northern Expedition, 82–3; Shanghai revolution, 83–7, 92, 99; becomes Secretary-General, 88; Nanchang uprising, 89–95, 97, 295–6; creation of Red Army, 95, 98; flees to Hong Kong, 95–7; relations with Mao, 103, 104, 156–7, 160–61, 163, 164–5; disputes with Li Lisan, 103–5; Shaoshan Report, 105, 108; disputes with Mao, 106, 107, 108, 117–19; relations with Soviet communists, 107–9, 110; orders executions, 109–10, 111–12; in Jiangxi, 112–19; Long March, 120–30, 297; Zunyi conference, 122–4, 296–7; supports Mao, 123–4; United Front, 130–32, 138–42; captures Chiang Kai-shek, 134–8; war against Japan, 142–3, 145–50, 151–2; refuses to join Guomindang, 145–6; in Chongqing, 153–

8, 159, 160–61; collapse of United Front, 157–8; relations with Chiang Kai-shek, 157; and Mao's Rectification Campaign, 159–60, 162–3, 165, 250; in Yan'an, 161, 162–5; relations with Liu Shaoqi, 164; coalition negotiations, 167–73; assassination attempt, 168; flees from Guomindang, 173–5; defeats Guomindang, 175–6

in government: forms government, 176–8, 179–80; as Premier, 180–87; 1954 National People's Congress, 198–9; assassination attempt, 201; on Party policy towards intellectuals, 206–7; and Mao's reform proposals, 207–8; Hundred Flowers Movement, 213–14, 216; loses post at Foreign Ministry, 216; manual labour, 216–17; and the Great Leap Forward, 216, 218, 220–22; split with Mao, 218, 219–20; Soviet industrial aid, 219; agricultural disasters, 225; loses Soviet technicians, 225–6, 227; breaks with Russian leaders, 227; relations with Mao, 227, 296–300; development of nuclear weapons, 233; economic problems, 233–4; and Liu's bid for power, 237, 238, 242; Cultural Revolution, 239–57, 268–9; Maoist plots against, 244–5, 250; Red Guards turn against, 258–67; arranges protection for government officials, 260; tries to end Cultural Revolution, 267; and Anthony Grey's detention, 271; quarrel with Lin Biao, 273; Tenth Party Congress, 283–4; Fourth National People's Congress, 287–8; Gang of Four campaigns against, 286, 287, 289, 290, 292–3; political will and testament, 290; achievements, 294–302; posthumous reputation, 301–2

foreign relations: 156; relations with Americans, 164, 166; declares independence from Russia, 179; formation of foreign policy, 179, 198; Sino-Soviet treaty, 187–8; Korean war, 188–91, 193; at Stalin's funeral, 192–3; Geneva conference, 193–5, 196–8; visits India and Burma, 195–6; Overseas Chinese problem, 199; Bandung conference, 200–2, 203, 204; relations with Nehru, 202, 209–10; and Tibet, 209–10; Taiwan negotiations, 209; visits to India, 209–10, 212–13; relations with Khrushchev, 211–12; Hungarian crisis, 211; tense relations with Russia, 217–18; border dispute with India, 222–4; Third World tour, 229–32, 235; influence in Indonesia, 235; woos Japanese, 236; border dispute with Russia, 270; resumes relations with America, 271–6, 284, 285; meetings with Kissinger, 275–6, 278–9, 285; and Nixon's visit to China, 279–82
Zhou Enshou, 23
Zhou Enzhu, 22, 23, 83, 102, 112, 171
Zhou Fohai, 74
Zhou Panlong, 21, 101, 149
Zhou Yigan, 21
Zhou Yigang, 24
Zhou Yinen (Zhou's father), 20–22, 23, 27, 155, 160, 246
Zhou Yiqian, 24
Zhu De, General, 96, 124, 165, 208, 298; joins Communist Party, 65; Nanchang uprising, 91, 93, 94; in the civil war, 112, 113, 114, 116, 118; Zunyi conference, 122, 123; Long March, 126; and the Hundred Flowers Movement, 213; and the Mao/Zhou split, 218; rehabilitation, 277
Zunyi conference (1935), 121–5, 128, 151, 296–7